# THE ARMIES
# OF ROMMEL

# THE ARMIES OF ROMMEL

George Forty

ARMS AND
ARMOUR

**Arms and Armour Press**
A Cassell Imprint
Wellington House, 125 Strand, London WC2R 0BB.

ISBN 1-85409-379-7

Maps by Anthony A. Evans.

Designed and edited by DAG Publications Ltd.
Designed by David Gibbons; edited by Michael Boxall;
printed and bound in Great Britain.

**Jacket illustrations:**
*Front:* Rommel, wearing his familiar tartan scarf and British
anti-gas goggles, studying a map of the Western Desert with, left
to right: Oberst Fritz Bayerlein (then Chief of Staff), Major von
Mellenthin (1a) and Generalleutnant Walther Nehring
(IWM MH 5594).
*Inset, top:* This portrait was painted by Willrich when Rommel
was a generallmajor (major general). It was probably painted
towards the end of his highly successful command of 7th Panzer
Division, as he is wearing the Knight's Cross, which he was
awarded on 26 May 1940. (Tank Museum)
*Back, left to right and top to bottom:* Rommel plans – a steely-
eyed Rommel planning his next moves, somewhere in North
Africa (IWM HU 5594); a serious-faced, greatcoated Rommel
during a visit to Berlin in 1941 (IWM RML 14); Rommel
accompanies the Italian 'Commando Supremo' in North Africa –
General Gariboldi (on right in forage cap) – at a parade
(IWM RML 33).

# Contents

# Introduction and Acknowledgements

This is my second book in Arms & Armour's series dealing with the armies of famous commanders. Last time I had the privilege of writing about one of my Second World War heroes – General George Smith Patton, Jr. This book deals with another one – Field Marshal Erwin Johannes Eugen Rommel. It has not been easy to write, principally because there are so many books about Rommel already in print that almost everything has been said before by someone else, although only a few of these deal with his entire life story. The 'pick of the crop' are those by David Fraser, David Irving, Desmond Young and Charles Douglas-Home, together of course with Sir Basil Liddell Hart's definitive editing of *The Rommel Papers* on which all books about Rommel naturally rely so heavily. All of these excellent books have, however, dealt more with the man himself, rather than with the troops under his command, which is the *raison d'être* for this series. So, as with the Patton book, I look upon this as being a 'nuts and bolts primer', to support the others and certainly not a vain attempt to replace any of them. Despite what I thought had been a carefully written introduction to the Patton book, in which I tried to make this point clear, I'm afraid that it was lost upon some reviewers; one, for example, found it a 'strange book', markedly different from what he had expected from its title, yet he closed his review by saying quite rightly that it should be considered as a 'technical resource' to be studied alongside other volumes referred to in the text for a rounded picture to be perceived. This is exactly what it was meant to be, but clearly I did not make this sufficiently clear in my introduction, which is why I am going to some length here to underline the point. Again, much of this book is devoted to facts and figures, to names and mini-biographies of those who served with or under Rommel, to organisations and staff tables, to descriptions of uniforms, weapons and equipment, to brief battle-records, etc. Naturally, the life story of Rommel is what holds it all together, but of necessity, this cannot be told in full detail as there is so much else to cram in. What I have tried to do is to gather all the varied material together in one volume, in the hope that it will answer the queries which inevitably spring to mind when one is reading a more erudite treatise about the life of the great commander himself.

Unashamedly I consider Rommel to have been one of the best field commanders of the Second World War on either side. Ruthless, impatient and single-minded he may have been, but brave, decent and honourable he undoubtedly was and this shines through all his doings, no matter who is

9

writing about him. Rommel's own philosophy, right up to the time when he suddenly realised the full impact of blind obedience to his Führer, is probably best explained in his own words, namely those with which he closes his book on the Great War, *Infanterie Greift An*, when, having told how the graves of the German soldiers who had followed the path of duty to the bitter end were to be found to the east, west and south, he goes on to adjure the reader – whom he assumes to be German – that these dead should be: '... a constant reminder to us who remain behind and to our future generations that we must not fail them when it comes to making sacrifices for Germany'. Rommel was always prepared to make the ultimate sacrifice for Germany on the battlefield. Sadly, for most of the war, he saw obedience to Hitler to be the same as obedience to the Fatherland – after all, had he not sworn to this effect along with every other German soldier? Too late he began to realise his mistake, but even then he would not take any direct action which he saw as being against the spirit of his oath. He paid for this mistake with his own life, having first made as certain as he was able that he would not fail those most precious to him who had to remain behind, while he followed his path of duty to the bitter end.

I have, as always, many people to thank for helping me with this book, in particular those who have allowed me to quote from their work; details of their kind assistance is reflected in the notes. In particular I must also thank the past curators and staff of the Panzermuseum at Münster who initially assisted me when I wrote *Afrika Korps at War* back in 1978, because I have used much of this background material again in this book. In addition, I must thank the present curator, Herr Heinz Winkler, who has once more kindly provided more detailed staff lists, biographical information, etc. Also my thanks go to those who have generously supplied photographs, in particular the Imperial War Museum and the Tank Museum, and to David Irving and Rolf Munninger. What a pity that it was impossible to include all the many vivid images of Rommel and his armies which I had collected, but I hope those that have been chosen will do them justice.

*Heia Safari!*
GEORGE FORTY
Bryantspuddle, April 1997

# 1
# Early Days (1891–1918)

## BEGINNING AS AN INFANTRYMAN

### A typical Swabian

Erwin Johannes Eugen Rommel was born in Heidenheim, Württemberg, some twenty miles north of Ulm, on 15 November 1891. Son of a school-teacher, who was also the son of a schoolteacher, Rommel inherited little from his strict, somewhat overbearing father, apart from an interest in and ability for mathematics and science. In general, he was an unremarkable, easy-going child, who took more after his mother Helene von Lutz, daughter of a local dignitary, Regierungs-präsident von Luz. Erwin Rommel had two brothers, Karl and Gerhard, and a sister, Helene, all of whom were much closer to their mother than to their father. As Erwin matured, however, he began to develop rapidly, proving himself to be both intelligent and hard-working. He also took a keen interest in numerous sporting activities such as skiing, skating, cycling and tennis, all of which would help him to build up the amazing physical toughness and unbounded energy that would be evident throughout his military career. In 1907 he broke his right ankle when jumping over a stream, but it set well and he later wrote that despite the most strenuous activities he never noticed any after effects. As he matured he began to show the inherent Swabian characteristics of stability, shrewdness and common-sense, which would remain with him throughout his lifetime, tempering at times the extraordinary speed of reaction, flair and panache which would become the hallmarks of his brilliant generalship.

The Army was in fact Rommel's second choice of profession, his first love being in the new field of aeronautics, having built a glider (which flew!) with a school friend in 1906, while studying aircraft design with a view to getting a job at the Friedrichshafen Zeppelin works. But his father advised against it and told him firmly that he should apply to join the army instead. Although the influence of the old Prussian nobility was at that time very strong within the German Army, the reforms that had followed the defeat of Napoleon, had led to a requirement for officers to be intelligent and well educated, rather than just 'well bred'. In March 1910, aged eighteen, Rommel, then a sixth-former, applied to join the Army of Württemberg. His sights were set on attending the Imperial Kriegschule at Danzig, but before being recommended for that august establishment, he had first to join up locally. Having a technical bent he applied for the artillery, then for the engineers, but both were full up, so he joined the 124th Württemberg Infantry Regiment, as a cadet, in July 1910. It was customary for a cadet

11

to prove himself a capable non-commissioned officer before being trained as an officer, and this proved no obstacle to the able, energetic and hard-working young Rommel. He was promoted to Corporal just three months after joining and Sergeant by the end of the year. In March 1911 he successfully completed his cadetship and entered the Kriegschule in the same month for an 8-months' course, which he passed satisfactorily. David Fraser, in his brilliant biography of Rommel, *Knight's Cross*, records that Rommel's final report showed him as being competent in all subjects tested including leadership, in which he was graded 'Good', and that: '... in January 1912 the monocled and dapper young Lieutenant Erwin Rommel rejoined the 124th Regiment in their barracks at Weingarten'.

Although he rejoined his Regiment complete in mind and body, anxious to show his abilities, young Rommel had left his heart behind in Danzig, having fallen in love with Lucie Maria Mollin, the dark-eyed, beautiful daughter of a West Prussian family, whom he had met at a formal ball held in the Kriegschule Officers' Mess. Despite the fact that she was a Catholic and he a Protestant, they became unoffically engaged, but would not marry until November 1916. She was, from that moment onwards, the one and only woman in his life – not only the love of his life, but also his best friend, favourite companion and trusted confidante to whom, when apart, he would write almost every day during their twenty-eight years of marriage.

## The Imperial German Army

The Württemberg Army was a part of the armies of Imperial Germany, known collectively as the German National Army. Although they were under Prussian control, certain elements retained some independence namely, Bavaria, Saxony and Württemberg. Of these only Bavaria and Saxony maintained their own officer corps, while Württemberg's officers had the same promotion prospects as those from Prussia. The armies of these three areas made up a sizeable 20 per cent of the total strength of the National Army, but in the majority of matters they were subservient to Prussian influence. The strength of the active army in peacetime (1912–13) was nearly 700,000 (34,870 officers and 663,578 NCOs and men), but this was a smaller percentage of the male population than the 1 per cent that was permitted by the Constitution, because the population of Germany had grown so rapidly from 41 million in 1871 to 65 million in 1910.[1] All able-bodied males between the ages of 17 and 45 were subject to conscription – three years with the colours (reduced to two years for all except mounted troops in 1893), followed by four years on the reserve, then a further five years with the Landwehr (third line troops used to back up the active army).

The 124th Regiment which young Erwin Rommel joined, was part of the 26th (Württemberg) Infantry Division, which together with the 27th Division made up the XIII (Württemberg) Army Corps Command, with its headquarters at Stuttgart. An Army Corps was the largest unit in the German Army, and had a total of 50 infantry divisions in peacetime (two Guard, six Bavarian and 42 Infantry). Each division generally comprised four brigades –

two infantry, one cavalry and one artillery, although there were some special groupings in a few divisions. The infantry brigades (51st and 52nd in 26th Division) both contained two infantry regiments, each comprising three 4-company battalions, making a total of twelve numbered companies, plus a separate Machine Gun Company (No 13). A battalion, commanded by a major, had four captains, eighteen lieutenants, an MO and his assistant, a paymaster and 1,054 other ranks. Attached to each battalion were a further 30 'train' soldiers with 58 horses, four ammunition wagons and four field kitchens, ten pack wagons (five large, five small) and a medical wagon. Companies totalled five officers, 259 other ranks, ten horses and four wagons. There were three platoons per company, each of four sections divided into two Gruppen (eight men), each commanded by a corporal (Gefreiter).

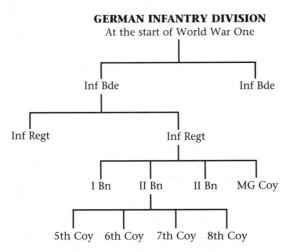

**GERMAN INFANTRY DIVISION**
At the start of World War One

Inf Bde      Inf Bde

Inf Regt      Inf Regt

I Bn   II Bn   II Bn   MG Coy

5th Coy   6th Coy   7th Coy   8th Coy

## The Great War Begins

For the next two years Rommel trained hard with his Regiment, but when the war clouds were gathering he found himself attached to the 4th Battery of the 49th Field Artillery Regiment, anxiously waiting for the order to return to his unit – 'I longed for my own regiment,' he later wrote, 'the King Wilhelm I, to be back with the men whose last two years of training I had supervised in the 7th Company, 124th Infantry (6th Württemberger).'[2] His fear of not getting back in time proved groundless and on 31 July 1914 he and his orderly, Private Hänle, packed their belongings and returned to Weingarten, their garrison city. On 1 August, they were donning their field grey uniforms, everyone happy and excited at the thought of going into action for the first time: '... the young faces radiated joy, animation and anticipation. Is there anything finer than marching against an enemy at the head of such soldiers?'[3]

Rommel's unit was part of the German Fifth Army (220,000 men) under command of the Imperial Crown Prince Wilhelm, which was responsible for the south Ardennes area, where they had to engage and hold the French forces, while further to the south the Sixth Army was to feint an attack, then withdraw in front of the enemy, hoping to entice them forward. At the same time the strong right wing to the north would sweep through Belgium and into the heart of France to complete the massive 'wheel' which was at the heart of the Schlieffen Plan.[4] Thus Fifth Army was the vital pivot around which this wheel would take place. But events did not go entirely according to plan; there were numerous changes, and in late August both the Fifth and Sixth Armies attacked, the former towards Verdun. In these early days Rommel experienced problems with his stomach (it would plague him throughout his military career), which he put down to the greasy food and freshly baked bread, but did not report sick because he did not wish to be thought of as a 'shirker'. After marching for some days, the 2nd Battalion had reached the vicinity of Longwy, to the north-east of both Verdun and the River Meuse. August 21st was a day of rest for most of the company, but Rommel and some other young platoon commanders were ordered out on a series of 5-man reconnaissance patrols to locate any enemy positions to their immediate front. None was found, but one can imagine the feelings of excitement tinged with fear, the adrenalin rush sustaining them at the time but quickly being replaced by the crushing fatigue which is the immediate reaction once the job is done and the pressure lifted.

However, there would be no rest for Rommel. Clearly his ability and energy had been noted long before the war began and, for the rest of that day and night, and on into the next day, he was sent on a series of liaison duties between his regiment and the flanking formations. Anyone who has carried out such duties knows the strain imposed, finding one's way across unknown terrain, usually in the dark, reaching a strange headquarters, then endeavouring to replicate the commander's words, remembering all the vital points, acting as the commander's 'mouthpiece' and bringing back a complete and accurate answer. All this Rommel had to do, not once but three times, his method of travel being by horse and on foot – no convenient LO's scout car or jeep in those days! By the end of the 21st, he had spent 24 hours continuously on the go without rest or food, and on returning to his platoon found that everyone was getting ready to move, rations had been issued, eaten and the mobile kitchens had departed. He managed a few gulps from his orderly's canteen and then he was off again – and this time he would soon be in the thick of the fighting.

## First Battle
Rommel's first action is graphically described in his book *Infantry Attacks!*, but always in a straightforward, matter-of-fact manner, without any mock heroics. It shows him to have been a brave and resourceful platoon commander, able to make up his mind quickly, seize the initiative and to bring overwhelming firepower to bear on the enemy when it was needed, while recognising the dangers and difficulties involved in novel techniques, such as house-to-house fighting. He had been sent with his platoon ahead of the rest of the battalion, advancing towards the village of Bleid, just over the French border into Belgium (see sketch map). It was 0500 hrs on 22 August, and there was thick ground fog which reduced visibility to less than 50 yards.

14

As his platoon advanced down the south-eastern side of Hill 325, through potato fields and vegetable gardens towards the village, they were engaged by enemy rifle fire and immediately went to ground. Looking through his binoculars Rommel could see no enemy, so he began to advance again. This happened on a number of occasions, but the platoon continued towards the outskirts of Bleid without sustaining any casualties. They were now some way ahead of the rest of the battalion, but this did not worry the young platoon commander. Reaching a group of farm buildings, Rommel, his platoon sergeant (Sergeant Ostertag) and two soldiers (he describes them as being 'range estimators') moved cautiously ahead of the rest of the platoon, reached the road into the village and, peering around the corner of a building, Rommel saw some 15–20 French soldiers standing in the middle of the road, talking and drinking coffee, completely relaxed and not realising that the Germans were so close. They did not see Rommel, who was now faced with making an important tactical decision – should he wait, take cover and call up the rest of the platoon, or should he try to make the most of the element of surprise and handle the situation with his three companions? As one might have expected, Rommel chose the latter course and, jumping out from behind the cover of the building, the four of them began to fire at the

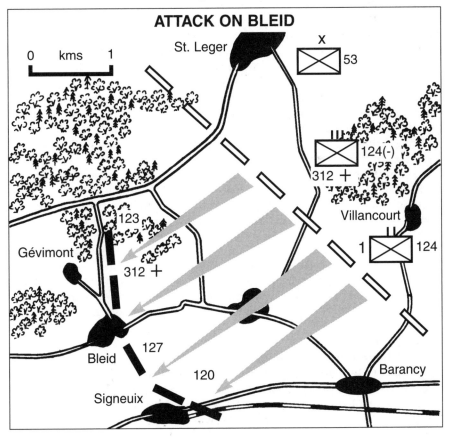

ATTACK ON BLEID

enemy. They killed or wounded a number of the surprised Frenchmen, but the rest took cover and began to return fire. During this engagement Rommel shot his first enemy soldier – 'my rifle cracked; the enemy's head fell forward on the step'.

There followed a brief period of reorganisation, while Rommel prepared his platoon for house-to-house fighting, for example: finding suitable timber beams to use as battering-rams, collecting bundles of straw which could be set alight to smoke out stubborn enemy from rooms and cellars. Making full use of fire and movement, the platoon began systematically to clear the village house by house, but sustained numerous casualties in the process. Bleid was now ablaze and Rommel sensibly moved his men out and tried to establish contact with the rest of his battalion. The fighting continued for the remainder of that day, with Rommel and his men constantly in the thick of it, so that by the time night came all were nearly dead from fatigue. Breaking off the battle, the regiment congregated west of Bleid around the village of Ruette, having lost some 25 per cent of its officers (including two of Rommel's best friends) and 15 per cent of its men dead and wounded. However, they had got the better of the enemy all along the line and so had achieved their first victory. They could find nowhere to sleep under cover, nor any straw to lie on, so had to make do with the damp, cold ground, which prevented everyone from getting any proper sleep, while Rommel's stomach was also playing up. Dawn was once again accompanied by thick, cloying fog, making contact difficult to maintain.

Rommel's observations from these early hours of battle are, as one would expect of such a competent soldier, sensible, down-to- earth remarks about the need to practise compass marching at night or in bad visibility, of being capable of developing maximum firepower quickly, of using short-range weapons (hand-grenades and machine-pistols) in house-to-house fighting, of maintaining basic camouflage and concealment at all times. The fighting continued as the Germans pursued the French in a south-westerly, then westerly direction. Towards the end of the month they were subjected to their first really heavy artillery barrage which they found very wearing, although casualties were surprisingly light. Rommel was in the thick of it constantly, often cut off, reported dead on at least one occasion. His considerable ability was recognised in early September when he was appointed Battalion Adjutant. Not only did this involve him in working closely with his CO, but also in carrying out numerous recce and liaison duties, as well as taking command of tricky situations whenever they occurred. The inevitable results were that he was badly wounded in hand-to-hand fighting[5] and received his first decoration – the Iron Cross, Second Class.

## Company Commander

Despite the fact that his wound was slow to heal, Rommel was soon itching to get back to his battalion and by Christmas he had managed to get himself discharged from hospital. He did not like serving in a replacement battalion, so returned to his unit in January 1915, to find himself appointed to command the 9th Company. The regiment was now serving in the western part of the Argonne. The battlefield situation had completely changed, the fluid fighting of 1914 having given way to the stalemate of trench warfare along the entire Western Front, from the Swiss border to the sea. Intricate trench systems, barbed wire, land mines, poison gas, the machine-gun and the artillery shell, would not only slow warfare to a crawl, but would also inflict horrendous casualties on both sides. Rommel was not overly impressed with what he found on his arrival at his new company positions and quickly set about improving their defences which in his opinion were too weak and vulnerable to enemy shellfire. With his customary energy and efficiency he swiftly put his 'two hundred bearded warriors' as he describes them, to work, improving the 440-yard-long company sector until it was up to scratch. 'For a 23-year-old officer there was no finer job than that of company commander,' he was to write later. 'Winning the men's confidence requires much of a commander. He must exercise care and caution, look after his men, live under the same hardships and – above all – apply self discipline. But once he has their confidence, his men will follow him through hell and high water.'[6] Rommel would stick to these principles throughout his army career; no matter at what level of command he might find himself, he would always think of his men, always share the hardships, always make himself do everything – and more – than he required of others. Is there any wonder why such a commander would be revered and respected by friend and foe alike?

'Static Warfare' was undoubtedly a misnomer because the days were full of action. Morale was high – everyone still expecting the 'Big Push' when spring arrived. Meanwhile, in order to pin down the maximum number of enemy in the Argonne area, a series of small, diversionary attacks were ordered for the end of January, in which Rommel's regiment took part. During one such attack, in which he had been invited by the neighbouring battalion commander to 'join in the fun', he had the unenviable task of having to deal with one of his platoon commanders who had lost his nerve and would not move forward when ordered. Rommel quickly sized up the situation, realised that all would be lost unless the company moved forward without further delay and informed his platoon commander that he could either obey his orders or be shot on the spot. Fortunately the man chose to obey and the enemy obstacles were safely negotiated, but this put Rommel's company way out 'on a limb', well ahead of both his own battalion positions and those of the neighbouring battalion who had invited him to take part in the battle, hotly engaged by overwhelming enemy forces. He was now faced with three possible courses of action: he could remain in his exposed position, use up all his ammunition and then surrender – that was the safest way, but obviously a non-starter as far as he was concerned; secondly, he could withdraw through the enemy obstacle line once again, which was bound to cause considerable casualties, as the enemy fire was now intense; thirdly, he could attack – the last thing the enemy would expect – then withdraw, it was to be hoped unscathed, while the disorganised enemy was trying to discover what was happening. As one might expect, Rommel unhesitatingly chose to attack – no wonder his soldiers used to say: 'Where Rommel is, there is the front!' Using his reserve platoon,

17

he swiftly cleared the French from the positions they had just re-occupied, then doubled his men back through the wire in single file, reaching his battalion in their new position, with only five men wounded, all of whom he brought back with him.

The fact that Rommel had acted entirely on his own initiative, neither asking his own battalion commander's permission to get involved in someone else's operation and then fighting his own private battle – which fortunately he won – does not appear to have worried him one iota. He had taken risks which he felt were entirely necessary, seized the tactical advantage and acted on his own judgement, supremely confident of his own abilities to win through. Having weighed up the situation and decided that the surprise he would achieve by doing the unexpected, entirely justified his actions, he calmly went ahead and did what he wanted, relying on his unerring ability to choose to do the right thing. He does not say what his battalion or regimental commander thought of the situation, merely remarking that it was a pity they hadn't been able to exploit his success! However, as independent tactical judgement had always been an accepted principle in German military training, instead of receiving a rebuke, he was awarded the Iron Cross, First Class – the first such award in his regiment. This is the stuff of which legends are made and Rommel was now a famous regimental character. But although he was far too sensible a young man to become swollen-headed by such adulation, he was quickly brought down to earth by the vagaries of the army system. A newly arrived lieutenant, without battle experience but senior to Rommel, was appointed to take over his company, and he had to become a platoon commander once again. Rommel could have taken the easy way out when his CO offered to transfer him to another company, but he refused, preferring to stay with his men.

Rommel remained in the trenches in the Argonne for a further five months, taking his first leave of the war in August 1915 and finding on his return, that he had been given command of the 4th Company. Later he was switched to the 2nd, spending some time with them in the Crown Prince Fort, a shellproof shelter in a blocking position, some 160 yards behind the front line. While there he was promoted to first lieutenant (Oberleutnant) and told that he was being transferred to the newly forming Württemberg Mountain Battalion, which had just been activated near Munsingen under the command of a Major Sprosser. Rommel was sad to leave the gallant soldiers of the 124th with whom he served for so long and also, strangely enough, '... the blood-soaked, hotly contested soil of the Argonne'. But he must have been excited to know that he would be getting command of a company in this new, élite unit and even commented that he found the new mountain uniform which was eventually issued: '... most becoming'!

## SERVICE WITH THE MOUNTAIN BATTALION

Rommel had now joined the Königliche Württemberg Gebirgsbataillon, which consisted of six rifle companies and six mountain machine-gun platoons. Before the war the only German troops to be trained in mountain warfare had been the light infantry (Jäger) battalions, plus the 82nd Infantry Brigade. However, after experiencing the winter conditions on the Vosges Front during 1914–15, it was decided to form more specially trained and equipped units to operate in snowy, mountainous areas. First to be formed were the Bavarian Schneeschuh Bataillon and the Württemberg Schneeschuh Kompanie. They were grouped together and later expanded to form Jäger Regiment 3, which was part of the Alpenkorps. Then came the formation of Rommel's new unit, the Württembergisches Gebirgs und Schneeschuh Bataillon. The additional machine-gun platoons certainly boosted the firepower of this élite unit which, initially anyway, must have lacked artillery support, there being only a limited number of true mountain guns in service prior to the outbreak of war and most of these were employed in the German colonies. However, greater involvement in mountain warfare resulted in the development of suitable light artillery pieces (see later).

**Uniform and Personal Equipment**
Mountain units wore a grey-green uniform with green facings and twisted cord on the shoulders, similar to that worn by foresters. The 'stand and fall' collar of the tunic bore the letter 'S' on each side. A mountaineering cap similar to the Austrian cap was worn, with two cockades in front and an edelweiss (a small, white Alpine flower) badge on the side. Mountain ankle boots and puttees were also worn, and a special mountaineering rucksack replaced the normal calfskin pack. It contained spare clothing, washing and shaving gear, an additional 60 rounds of rifle ammunition, and personal effects.[7] Belts and attachments were of blackened leather. From the stout leather belt all manner of items were hung including: a brown canvas bread bag, a water-bottle, an entrenching tool in a leather carrying case, a bayonet in its scabbard, two sets of three cartridge pouches worn one on each side of the belt buckle (each could hold 15 rounds, so a rifleman carried 90 rounds on his belt, plus 60 in his pack – 150 rounds in total). From mid-1915 onwards the gas mask, carried in a metal canister, became an additional indispensable item, and hand-grenades were often clipped to belts, or carried in bags around the neck. On top of the pack were fastened aluminium mess tins (also blackened), rolled greatcoat and groundsheet. The total weight of an infantryman's equipment was some 55–60 pounds, to which has to be added the specialist skiing items. Rommel and his men were well laden!

**Weapons and Equipment**
  **Basic weapons.** As in other armies, the basic weapon of the soldier was the rifle. Officers and senior NCOs carried swords and pistols, but the former swiftly went out of fashion except for parades (one is reminded of Bruce Bairnsfather's splendid cartoon of what a young British officer thought he would do with his sword – to proudly lead his men 'Over the Top' – and what he actually used it for in the trenches – as a toasting-fork!).

As we have seen already, Rommel, like many junior officers, often used a rifle when in action. Machine-gunners could not carry rifles, so were normally armed with pistols. The standard rifle calibre was 7.9mm, and pistols were usually 9mm.

**Rifles and Carbines.** The main rifle was the Gewehr 98, which had entered service in 1898. It weighed 9 pounds 3 ounces, had an overall length of 3 feet 10.8 inches and its magazine (housed in the stock) held five rounds. It could be fitted with a 25-round magazine (Ansteckmagazin), but this was difficult to handle and not often used. Sighting was via a 'barleycorn' foresight and a 'bed' backsight which was graduated for 200 metres and then every 50m from 300m to 2,000m. Three sets of telescope sights were issued to each company for use by snipers, and later in the war detachable luminous sights were produced for night work. A trained soldier could fire between 10 and 15 aimed shots per minute. The Gewehr 98 had a barrel length of 30 inches, but there were also two shorter models. The Gewehr 98 was normally fitted with a long, narrow-bladed bayonet, designated Seitengewehr 98, although there were a number of shorter models, all of which were capable of being fitted to the standard rifle. Some German bayonets had what was called a 'saw back', which consisted of a double row of teeth on the back edge. They were originally issued to artillerymen and pioneers for use as a saw – and were most effective – but they received considerable bad press, thanks to Allied propaganda.

**Pistols.** The most common pistol was the 9mm Luger Pistole 08, which weighed 1.8 pounds and had an 8-round magazine in the grip. It was also possible to fit a 32-round magazine to the base of the grip. Another widely used pistol was the Model 1898 Mauser, normally 7.63mm but some were manufactured to accept 9mm ammunition. Both pistols had a wooden holster which could be attached as a stock, making it possible to fire the pistol from the shoulder with considerable accuracy. Other small arms issued towards the end of the war included Bergmann submachine guns (MP 18/1), but they were never issued on a wide scale. Hand-grenades were normally either the Stielhandgranate – known by the British as the 'stick grenade' or 'jam-pot', or the much smaller Eirhandgranate 'egg' grenade. There were also rifle grenades, fired from cup dischargers, smoke and gas grenades (not widely used) and portable flares.

**Machine-Guns.** The German High Command was the first to appreciate the tremendous firepower of the machine-gun and, having decided as early as the 1890s that the Maxim was the best design, serious trials took place. As a result, the Maschinengewehr 08, was accepted by the Army in October 1908 and went into quantity production. So at a time when most European armies (including the British) were still debating the value of the new weapon, the German Army already had them in service. When the Great War began, 12,500 were in use, with some 200 being delivered monthly, rising to 300 by 1917 and to a peak figure of 14,400 in the autumn of 1917. The 7.9mm calibre MG08 was a reliable and solidly constructed weapon, with a total weight of about 62 kilograms (including two spare barrels and a sledge mounting). Alternative mountings included a stretcher, carried by two men, and a tripod. Produced by the government factory at Spandau and by Deutsche Waffen und Munitionsfabriken, the water-cooled weapon had a cyclic rate of fire of 300rpm (which could be boosted to 450rpm), cartridges being fed from a 250-round fabric belt. There was also a lightened version, the MG 08/15, which used the same Maxim standard recoil-operated mechanism, with a pistol grip, a butt, a bipod and other minor changes which reduced the weight to only 18 kilograms. It had a cyclic rate of fire of 450rpm and was fed from fabric ammunition belts holding 50, 100 or 250 rounds.

## Mountain artillery

The prerequisite of a gun or howitzer designed for mountain warfare is the need for it to be capable of being dismantled into its principal components and carried by mule or man-pack in the most difficult conditions of terrain and weather. Lightness is therefore essential, but this must be balanced against the gun's performance, which depends upon the weight and effectiveness of its shells, having a reasonable range and the ability to fire at high elevation so that it can engage the enemy over the crests of ridges and mountain peaks. As already mentioned, at the start of the war, the German Army had only a few true mountain guns (Gebirgs Kanone 05), but once mountain warfare got into its stride, on the Italian Front for example, the situation was quickly rectified. The Mountain Gun produced by Krupp was the 7.5cm GebK L/14Kp, which had a weight in action of 491 kilograms and could be broken down into seven mule loads. Its shell weight was 5.3 kilograms, its muzzle velocity 280m/sec and its maximum range 4,700 metres. The Austrian firm of Skoda also produced their excellent 7.5cm GebK15, and both firms produced a smaller number of 10.5cm pieces which had a shell weight of some 14.4 kilograms and a maximum range of 4,900 metres.

## Into Battle Once More

Rommel was given command of the 3rd Company, which comprised 200 young veterans who had been drawn from all branches of the service and they were allocated just a few short weeks to train in order to become an efficient mountain unit. Then, towards the end of November, after a final inspection by Major Sprosser (whom Rommel describes as being a 'martinet') they were transferred to Aarlberg for ski training. This was a happy time for Rommel and his men. Despite training hard from dawn to dusk, they enjoyed plenty of off-duty 'bonding' in the improvised day room, of the St Christopher Hospice near the Aarlberg Pass, listening to mountain tunes played by their company band – and no doubt all joining in the songs! They were helped by the excellent Austrian rations which included cigarettes and wine, so Christmas was celebrated in style – a far cry from the mud and blood of the Argonne. Then, a few days after Christmas they boarded a troop train, heading not for the Italian front as they had hoped, but westwards, to occupy a southern sector of the Western Front. There, on a stormy New Year's Eve, they relieved a Bavarian unit on a 10,000-yard-long sector of the South Hilsen Ridge. The front was far too long for them to hold continuously so they developed and improved a series of strong-points, each of which was a miniature fort with its own all-round defence plus ample stocks of ammunition, food and water. Rommel used his battle experience to the full, ensuring that every dugout had two exits and strong overhead cover. The French lines were further away than in the Argonne, the nearest being a few hundred yards. Raids into enemy positions were the order of the day and Rommel proved adept at such operations, taking pris-oners and returning safely. He managed another short leave in October 1916, going back to Danzig to marry his beloved Lucie Maria. Then, at the end of October, the Gebirgsbataillon was on the move again, this time far to the east to the Romanian Front. Arriving after a difficult journey, they were attached to a cavalry brigade, with orders to move forward into the mountains as quickly as possible. There had been bitter fighting in the area a few days previously when, following an abortive attack on the Vulcan and Skurduk Passes, the 11th Bavarian Division had been repulsed and were now badly scattered. Climbing up narrow footpaths for hours, carrying all their equipment – including four days' uncooked rations – the battalion moved slowly forward. They met a few Bavarian stragglers and heard all about their close-quarter battles in the fog, with an enemy described as being: '... wild and dangerous adversaries'. But the Mountain Battalion were a tough lot, well trained and hardy. Despite the terrible conditions they struggled on towards their allotted positions, first soaked to the skin by freezing rain, then with their clothes and packs frozen solid once they reached the snow line. Conditions deteriorated; a blizzard enveloped the mountains and visi-bility was soon down to a few yards. It did not improve and without shelter or hot food, many of the men soon began to suffer high fever and vomit-ing. Both Rommel and the next-door company commander made represen-tation to the sector commander that they should be withdrawn, but although the MO evacuated some 40 men, they were threatened with court-martial if the gave up one foot of ground. Next day the situation was even worse; 90 per cent of the men were now suffering from frostbite. Rommel went to see the sector commander to explain the situation and on his return found that his fellow company commander had decided to move off the ridge come what may. Fortunately, the weather cleared, they were relieved by fresh troops (equipped with pack-animals) and were given a chance to recover, so that in three days they were back in good shape. They then moved forward to new positions, tangled with the Romanians, who were dug in 'across the way', but nevertheless Rommel had time to admire the view, the fog in the plain below breaking like ocean waves: '... against the sunlit peaks of the Transylvanian Alps. A wonderful sight!'

The Gebirgsbataillon soon proved itself to be a tough and able fight-ing unit, and Rommel continually showed his bravery and ability during the months that followed. For example, in January 1917, in the area of Gagesti, in bitter weather, he and his men infiltrated enemy positions by night, then opened fire and took a large number of prisoners. In May 1917 they moved back to France, to the Hilsen area in which they had been located before moving to Romania. Rommel, who was now commanding a force comprising a third of the battalion (two rifle and one machine-gun companies), took over a sector on the Hilsen Ridge, but they were returned to Romania in August 1917. Rommel and his men (now he had three rifle and two machine-gun companies) were soon embroiled in a fierce battle for Mount Cosna. Rommel was responsible for the attack and made certain that nothing was left to chance, personally deploying the machine-gunners after ensuring that they had a covered approach to their fire positions, then going in with the assaulting companies despite being wounded in the arm and losing a lot of blood. The machine-guns produced devastating fire, making up for the lack of supporting artillery, and the attack was successful. They took their initial objectives and the following day found Rommel, now in command of six rifle and two machine-gun companies, successfully continuing the assault, then holding the positions against heavy enemy pressure during which the battalion held on despite heavy casualties. In total the ski troops had suffered some 500 casualties in killed and wounded during the two-weeks' battle.

### Pour le Mérite

Following the Mount Cosna battle Rommel was able to get a few weeks' leave, going to the Baltic with Lucie (whose name he shortened to 'Lu' in his letters) to rest and recuperate, which he undoubtedly needed after such a strenuous campaign. He returned to the battalion in October 1917, by which time they had moved from Romania to Austrian Carinthia on the Italian Front. It would be here that Rommel would be awarded the highest German decoration, the *Pour le Mérite*,[8] for capturing Monte Majur, the key Italian position, during the twelfth battle of Isonzo (also known as the Battle of Caporetto), which would result in a major Italian defeat and rout.

Briefly, what happened was that Rommel, who had been given command of three rifle companies and one machine-gun company, known as the 'Rommel Detachment', was ordered to follow up the first phase of the action, then once the River Isonzo had been crossed and the first Italian line breached, they would take over as advance guard. The attack began in pouring rain on 24 October, after a 1,000-gun preparatory barrage, and the first phase was completely successful. Soon Rommel's force, now in the lead, reached steeply wooded slopes, leading to the second Italian line. Instead of making the obvious approach, Rommel took his men up a steep gully on the left, then found an unguarded path into the Italian positions, overcoming any Italian outposts he found on the way. By evening they had reached the third enemy line and could see the main Italian positions several hundred feet higher up on the Monte Majur ridge. Rommel was then ordered by the battalion commander of the Bavarian unit on his immediate left, to come under his command as support for an assault on the ridge the following morning. Rommel initially refused, stating that his orders came only from Major Sprosser, who was senior to this particular battalion commander. Nevertheless the order stood, namely that he should follow-up the Bavarian assault and then occupy the ground they took. Rommel was clearly most unhappy, and while his men were resting that night, he worked out his own plan.

Major Sprosser and the rest of the battalion arrived at 0500 hours and agreed to Rommel's plan, which was to move west, well clear of the Bavarians and attack a different section of the ridge. Just before dawn Rommel, now commanding two rifle companies and one machine-gun company, set off, while Sprosser reached 'an understanding' with the Bavarian commander! Infiltrating through the Italian positions, the 'Rommel Detachment' first captured an artillery battery, then pushed on, after leaving part of their force (roughly one company) in the gun position. Later when this company was counter-attacked by an Italian battalion, he returned, took the enemy in the rear and forced them to surrender, taking more than 1,000 prisoners which he sent back under guard. The rest of the Gebirgsbataillon arrived and were led forward by Rommel some two miles in single file and succeeded not only in capturing a supply column, some 2,000 Bersaglieri troops and 50 officers, but also in cutting the main enemy supply route. Next Rommel boldly went on to the main Italian positions, which he entered with just a handful of riflemen, calling upon the enemy to surrender – 43 officers and more than 1,500 soldiers complied! Finally, Rommel and his remaining men scaled Monte Majur from the rear, captured the dominating ridge and took the Italians defending it prisoner. In more than three days of constant fighting Rommel's force had taken more than 150 officers and 9,000 soldiers prisoner, capturing 81 guns into the bargain. Shortly afterwards, with just six men, Rommel swam the Piave by night, then walked into the village of Longarone and took the surrender of the entire garrison!

This was to be his last action and for it and his other exploits he was awarded the *Pour le Mérite* as was his battalion commander, the redoubtable Major Sprosser. In addition, a Gebirgsbataillon officer named Schorner was awarded the same decoration, allegedly for having captured Monte Majur, an honour which Rommel clearly considered belonged to the 'Rommel Detachment' alone. Rommel would thereafter be attached to a higher headquarters as an assistant staff officer, following '... with heavy heart' the battles in which the mountain battalion took part during the rest of the war. In closing his book *Infantry Attack!*, Rommel was clearly already thinking of battles yet to come, when he says that the last resting-places of the German soldiers who had followed the path of duty to the bitter end should be: '... a constant reminder to us, who remain behind and to our future generations that we must not fail them when it becomes a question of making sacrifices for Germany'. Could he have ever guessed how complex it would be for him to make his own personal sacrifice for the Fatherland?

**Notes to Chapter 1**
1. Figures quoted in Nash, *Imperial German Army Handbook.*
2. Rommel, *Infantry Attacks!*
3. Ibid.
4. The Schlieffen Plan was the German operational plan in the event of war with France, prepared by General Count von Schlieffen in 1905, while he was CGS (Chief of the General Staff). It assumed that Germany would

have to fight the French and the Russians simultaneously and initially would have to concentrate on the French as being the more dangerous of the two. He predicted that the French would advance via the Belfort Gap towards Alsace Lorraine and should be encouraged to do so, first by a feint attack there, followed by a German withdrawal. Then a major German assault would be launched via the Low Countries and northern France in a wide arc, the right wing passing just west of Paris, in a massive wheel, which would then continue eastwards forcing the French back towards the Moselle, where they could be smashed against the 'anvil' of the Lorraine fortresses and the Swiss frontier.

5. Rommel, armed with a rifle and bayonet, had found himself in a close-quarter fight with five enemy soldiers. He managed to shoot two, missed another and then found that his magazine was empty. Resorting to the bayonet – he was an extremely adept bayonet fighter – he charged the remaining enemy, but was hit by a rifle bullet in the left leg, which tore a hole the size of a fist in his thigh, knocking him to the ground. Desperately trying to staunch the blood with his right hand, he managed to roll behind an oak tree, expecting at any moment: '... a bullet or a bayonet thrust'. He lay there for some time before the enemy retreated and he was rescued by two of his men, taken back to the battalion aid post and finally evacuated to a base hospital at Stenay.

6. Rommel, *Infantry Attacks!*

7. In the *German Army Handbook*, compiled by British Intelligence and issued on a need to know basis, the individual soldier's personal kit is listed as: 1 pair slacks, 1 forage cap, 2 shirts, 1 pair socks, 2 handkerchiefs, 1 rice bag, 1 'housewife' (sewing and mending kit), 1 pair drawers, 1 pair lace shoes, 1 set boot brushes, 1 grease tin, 1 copper tin and 1 salt bag.

8. The Order of the *Pour le Mérite* was the highest German award for individual gallantry in action. It comprised a Maltese cross in blue enamel (hence its nickname 'The Blue Max'), edged with gold and with four golden eagles between the arms of the cross. On the upper arm was the letter 'F' in gold surmounted by a golden crown; on the other three arms were the words '*Pour le Mérite*'.

# 2
# Between the Wars
# (1919–1939)

## PEACETIME SOLDIERING

### A New Beginning

At the end of the Great War Rommel had ended up as a highly decorated substantive Captain (Hauptmann), aged 27, serving on the staff of LXIV Corps on the Western Front – a job which had not appealed to him because he was far more interested in active soldiering than dealing with reams of tedious paperwork which was an inevitable feature of a staff officer's duties. Shortly after the Armistice he returned to regimental duty with his old regiment, the 124th Württemberg Infantry, in the same barracks in Weingarten where he had joined them just eight years previously. After spending a few months there, in the summer of 1919 he was sent to command No 32 Internal Security (IS) Company at Friedrichshafen. This was his first experience of commanding personnel who did not want to be soldiers or to obey commands, being mainly insubordinate naval ratings with distinct Communist leanings. Despite their initial attitude – they refused to drill, booed Rommel because he wore his *Pour le Mérite* and generally misbehaved themselves on and off parade – it did not take Rommel long to sort them out and in a few weeks his company was well on the way to being a properly motivated military unit, some of his soldiers even being invited to join the local police (including Rommel himself!), for which they would be paid a valuable bonus. But when Rommel explained that he would prefer to return to his regiment, most of the men asked to go back with him, being willing to forego the police bonus to do so. The IS duties with which Rommel's company were concerned, were mainly in Münsterland and Westphalia, dealing with various disaffected elements of the civilian population of the beaten and humiliated Fatherland. One operation for example, necessitated dealing with a group of revolutionaries who were storming the Gmund town hall, Rommel dealt with them quickly and efficiently, using fire hoses in place of machine-guns!

Among the greatest humiliations placed on Germany were the strict conditions imposed by the Treaty of Versailles, which came into effect from 31 March 1920. These, for example, limited the size of the army to just 100,000 men, including 4,000 officers, which was sufficient for just seven divisions of infantry and three of cavalry – a far cry from the two million plus Imperial Army of 1918! The new Reichsheer, which was the ground element of the Reichswehr, was to be constituted only of volunteers, universal compulsory military service being abolished. In order to prevent the build-up of a reserve it was ruled that officers should serve for 25 years, NCOs and privates for twelve years. It was further stated that the army was to be devoted exclusively to the maintenance of order within the borders of Germany – all the overseas territories having been confiscated. Germany was also banned from possessing tanks, heavy artillery or poison gas and armoured cars could only be used for police work. The Great General Staff was abolished, and staff colleges and military academies were closed, although arms schools were allowed to remain open. The army was also forbidden to have a field command echelon higher than that of corps. Similar restrictions were placed on the size and armament of the navy, submarines, for example, being totally banned, and all types of military aircraft were banned and the Flying Corps abolished. All production or importation of arms was prohibited, as was the sending of military missions abroad

## Infantry Division Establishment

The Treaty of Versailles had even laid down the permitted establishment of an infantry division:

| Unit | Max no per div | Max strength allowed | | |
| --- | --- | --- | --- | --- |
| | | Officers | NCOs/men | Total |
| HQ | 1 | 25 | 70 | 95 |
| HQ div infantry | 1 | 4 | 30 | 34 |
| HQ div artillery | 1 | 4 | 30 | 34 |
| infantry regt | 3 | 210 | 6,900 | 7,110 |
| trench mortar coy | 3 | 18 | 450 | 468 |
| div cav sqn | 1 | 6 | 150 | 156 |
| fd art regt | 1 | 85 | 1,300 | 1,385 |
| pioneer bn | 1 | 12 | 400 | 412 |
| signals det | 1 | 12 | 300 | 312 |
| div med sect | 1 | 20 | 400 | 420 |
| parks & convoys | | 14 | 800 | 814 |
| TOTAL | | 410 | 10,830 | 11,240 |

(Compare with the total 1918 establishment for an infantry division of 11,643, plus a field recruit depot of 100 per each of the 9 infantry battalions, so the total was 12,543).

The size of the entire officer corps of the Reichsheer, including all staffs whatever their composition, was limited to just 4,000. The regular officers in the German Imperial Army alone had numbered more than ten times that figure and, although 25 per cent of them had been killed during the Great War, there was no lack of volunteers for Germany's tiny new army. The architect of the building of the new Reichswehr, and its first commander, was the far-sighted Colonel General (Generaloberst) Hans von Seeckt, who was determined from the outset that every member of his new army would be not only a leader but also an instructor, in readiness for the day when they would be able to expand once more. So someone of Rommel's calibre and ability was clearly a prime candidate. In January 1921 he was appointed to command a company (three platoons, each of an HQ and four sections of two Gruppen (sub-sections) each consisting of a lance-corporal and eight men) with a total strength of five officers and 259 men, of the Reichsheer Infanterie Regiment 13, based on Stuttgart – his old Württemberg regiment having sadly disappeared in the re-organisation. For the next nine years he spent a fairly uneventful time with his regiment, taking over the machine-gun company in 1924, attending a series of courses on subjects such as driving and maintenance, gas, etc., all of which improved his military skill without advancing his career. However, reports during this period not only spoke of him as a 'quiet, sterling character, always tactful and modest in his manner', but also said that he had shown himself in war to be an exemplary combat commander who additionally showed: '... good results training and drilling his company'. This report went on to suggest that Rommel might make a good military instructor and closed with the words: 'There is more to this officer than meets the eye.'[1]

In addition to military pursuits, Rommel qualified as a ski instructor, tried to interest Lucie in skiing and other outdoor activities, and at the same time ensured that his men took part in as much sport as possible. The Rommels must have enjoyed this relatively tranquil period of their life, taking trips abroad – for example to Italy to have a look at his old battlefields – and celebrating the birth of their only child, Manfred, who was born in December 1928. The following year Rommel became an instructor at the Infantry School in Dresden. He proved to be a natural instructor, much respected by his contemporaries and hero-worshipped by the cadets. During his four years at the school, he started to put together his book *Infanterie Greift An* (*Infantry Attacks!*), which was finally published in 1937, after he had spent more time improving it during a tour as an instructor at Potsdam. In essence it was, as the title suggests, a book about the infantry actions in which he had taken part, full of anecdotes and sketches which brought the Great War battlefield vividly to life. After each, however, Rommel draws a number of succinct and valuable conclusions, which show his innate grasp of what was really important on the battlefield. It was to prove an instant best-seller.

## Command

In October 1933, Rommel was promoted to Lieutenant Colonel (Oberstleutnant) and given command of 3rd Jäger Battalion, 17th Infantry Regiment, then stationed at Goslar in the delightful Harz Mountains. The Jäger (Rifle) battalions wore a distinctive grey-green uniform and shako, and, as befitted such 'hunters', Rommel insisted that all his officers learn to hunt and shoot, until they became adept at stalking and killing. These were probably two of the happiest years of his life, moulding his battalion into a first-class fighting force, always at home in the mountains despite the weather and the condition of the terrain. Soon after his arrival, some of the battalion officers had tried to 'best' him by inviting their new CO to climb a local mountain and then to ski down it. Rommel immediately took up the challenge and proved himself better than all of them by climbing up and skiing down no fewer than three times in rapid succession – they refused his invitation for a fourth attempt! The battalion already had a long and valiant history, stretching back to the King's German Legion of the Napoleonic era; now they had a commanding officer who was described by his regimental commander as being: 'head and shoulders above the average battalion commander in every respect'.

### Enter Adolf Hitler

In 1933 Adolf Hitler was appointed Chancellor under President Paul von Hindenburg. It had been in 1919, that an obscure but highly decorated infantry corporal, holding both the Iron Cross Second and First Class for bravery during the Great War, began his rise in politics. As a low grade army political officer, he had been sent to investigate the right wing German Workers' Party. In July 1921 Hitler had become its leader and changed its title to the National Socialist German Workers' Party (Nationalsozialistische Deutsche Arbeiterpartei – the NSDAP – or Nazi for short). The Party was now far more radical, violently opposed to Communism and the constrictions of the Treaty of Versailles, and most of its members, in particular Hitler and his 'partner' Ernst Röhm, were not afraid to use violence to achieve their aims. In 1923 France and Belgium had sent troops to occupy the Ruhr in an effort to get Germany to keep up with its reparation payments. The situation was not helped by the 'galloping' inflation which had reached ludicrous proportions – in November 1923, for example, the exchange rate for a single US dollar was 130,000,000,000 Marks! The Nazis tried to take full advantage of the situation, but their Putsch failed and Hitler was sent to gaol. During his nine months behind bars, he wrote *Mein Kampf* in which he set out all his radical views, including both his anti-Communist and anti-Semitic feelings and his belief that the German people deserved more Lebensraum (living space) even if they had to fight to achieve it.

In 1929, the NSDAP joined publicly with the Stabhelm, a Party of nationalistic veterans, and the right wing German National People's Party, led by an industrialist named Hugenberg. This gave them the financial support they had been lacking and, in the elections of 1930, the Nazis were the second largest political Party. Three years later, in January 1933, Hitler was appointed Chancellor. The burning of the Reichstag the following month, was used as an excuse to blame the Communists for trying to destabilise the government, so that many of them could be removed, then to seize power and finally, to outlaw all other political Parties. When Hindenburg died a year later, Hitler declared himself Reichsführer as well as Chancellor and the 'New Order' was born, under the rallying cry of 'One People, One Nation, One Leader! (*Ein Volk, Ein Reich, Ein Führer!*).

While these political manoeuvrings were taking place, the German armament industry was, first covertly, then quite openly, defying the Treaty of Versailles. The withdrawal of the Inter-Allied Control Commission inspectors, who left Germany in 1927, removed the only outside 'eyes' that had been able to scrutinise events closely. From now on, re-armament gathered pace and new weapons rolled off the assembly lines. For example, such weapons as the famous 8.8cm AA/anti-tank gun (the '88'), which was to wreak havoc among Allied armour during the Second World War, had been fully developed by 1933. At the same time, the German armed forces began to expand, doubling by 1934, then trebling by 1935, while tanks and first line aircraft were added in ever increasing numbers. Although Rommel must have realised that all this was happening (and probably approved whole-heartedly with it), he was not immediately affected. Then, quite by chance, he was to meet Adolf Hitler in September 1934, when his battalion provided a guard of honour for the Führer who, as head of state, was visiting Goslar for a civilian thanksgiving ceremony. Both Desmond Young and Charles Douglas-Home, in their biographies of Rommel, comment on the ceremony, saying that it had been intended that the SS would provide a single rank of their men who would take up position directly in front of Rommel's troops, to ensure Hitler's safety. Rommel is reputed to have said bluntly, that if that were the case his battalion would not turn out. He was then asked to go to see Himmler and Goebbels who were in Goslar, organising the event. Over luncheon at a local hotel he explained that such a proposal would be an insult to the men of his mountain battalion, stressing that they were perfectly capable of safeguarding Hitler. Fortunately both Heinrich Himmler and Joseph Goebbels took a liking to Rommel and they agreed, so the incident passed off without any recriminations on either side. 'With Hitler, Rommel's first meeting was purely formal. He saluted; he was introduced; he shook hands; his *Pour le Mérite* was observed; he was congratulated on the turnout of his battalion.'[2]

## IN THE SERVICE OF THE FÜHRER

### Expansion
A month before their first meeting Rommel, together with every other member of the German armed forces, had been required to swear a new personal oath of loyalty to the Führer, who had appointed himself Supreme Commander of the Armed Forces:

> 'I swear by God this sacred oath: I will render unconditional obedience to Adolf Hitler, the Führer of the Reich, supreme commander of the armed forces, and that I shall at all times be prepared, as a brave soldier, to give my life for this oath.'[3]

On 15 October 1935 Rommel was posted as an instructor to the War Academy (Kriegschule) at Potsdam. Once again he proved to be just as brilliant and admired as he had been at Dresden. And he had plenty of new officers to teach! Hitler's expansion of the armed forces was now well under way, conscription having been brought back in March 1935; in 1937 he formally abrogated the provisions of the hated Treaty of Versailles. By the end of 1937 there were more than 550,000 men under arms, and tank building, in line with all other armament production, was increasing on a massive scale.

For example, Hitler had placed an order with Krupp for 100 new light tanks to be delivered by March 1934, with 650 more to follow a year later. Although Rommel was yet to become involved in the new theories of 'Lightning War' (*Blitzkrieg*) as expounded by such armoured gurus as Heinz Guderian, the Führer had already been 'bitten by the tank bug'. After watching one of Guderian's demonstrations of an armoured force consisting of light tanks, armoured cars, motorcycles and anti-tank guns, he is said to have exclaimed excitedly: 'That is what I need! That is what I'm going to have!'

Rommel's next meeting with Hitler was to be during the late summer of 1936, when he was attached to the Führer's escort party for the Nuremberg rally. He was in charge of security arrangements and earned Hitler's praise for the way he dealt with matters. For example, just before one of Hitler's car journeys, he instructed Rommel to make certain that no more than six other cars accompanied him. Finding a seething mass of politicians, generals, SS gauleiters and other hangers-on, all with their cars and all expecting to be allowed to join the bandwagon, Rommel merely permitted the first six cars to proceed, then personally stopped the rest and when they complained told them icily, that he had stationed two tanks a little further down the road to block it so they would be sensible to follow his instructions! On his return Hitler sent for him and congratulated him on his handling of the situation. In addition, Rommel's reputation was enhanced at this time by the publication in 1937, of his book *Infanterie Greift An (Infantry Attacks!)*, which no doubt Hitler read. It is clear also that there was an immediate rapport between the two men. Both could be described as 'self-made', both disliked the class-ridden élitism of the old German aristocracy which in the past had stifled the careers of many of those with humbler ancestry. Furthermore, for someone as intensely patriotic as Rommel, with no ambition outside the army, the fact that Hitler had chosen to expand and modernise everything would have outweighed any misgivings he might have had over the brutality and boorishness of the swaggering storm troopers of the SA.

**Liaison Officer to the Hitler Youth**
While still at Potsdam, in February 1937 Rommel was appointed as the War Ministry's Liaison Officer to the Hitler Youth (Hitler Jugend – HJ), the male branch of the German Youth movement, which, together with the League of German Girls (Bund Deutscher Mädel), had been set up in 1933 and was now an enormous organisation embracing well over 60 per cent of German youth – the HJ alone numbered nearly 5½ million boys. It was under the direction of Youth Leader (Reichsjugendführer) Baldur von Schirach, a charismatic 29-year-old, with whom Rommel soon clashed. They had very different views about the education and training of the boys, which Rommel wished to formalise by employing young, bachelor army lieutenants, while Schirach was keen to keep them under the SA. At this time Schirach had more clout than Rommel, who was eventually sent back to Potsdam in 1938 and was, as Desmond Young comments: '... rather pointedly not given the golden badge of the Hitler Jugend'. What a difference to the HJ Rommel might have made had he stayed, or for that matter to the SA whom, it had

also been proposed that the army should take over, with Rommel being given the job of 'smartening them up'! No doubt, however, Rommel was only too pleased not to have had such an unenviable task.

### Führerbegleitbataillon

Just before completing his 3-year tour of duty at Potsdam, Rommel found himself on another temporary assignment on behalf of his Führer, when, in October 1938, he was appointed to command the escort battalion of Hitler's field headquarters for the occupation of the Sudetenland. The Germans' drive for *Lebensraum* had begun in March 1936 when they had re-occupied the de-militarised Rhineland in direct contravention of the Treaty of Versailles. After two more years of building up his forces, Hitler struck again in March 1938, annexing Austria and officially integrating it into Germany under the Anschluss (Connection) on 13 March. This was followed in October 1938 by the 'peaceful' occupation of the Sudetenland, the first stage in the complete annexation of Czechoslovakia, which inevitably followed on from the 'peace at any price' diplomacy of British, French and other European politicians. Rommel had been hand-picked for the job, which once again brought him to the personal notice of Adolf Hitler and his senior personal staff. Hitler had decided to tour the cities of the once-disputed border territory, in the Führersonderzug (special railway train), which he would use again during the invasion of Poland. The Führerbegleitbataillon (FBB) (distinguished by their vehicle flash which was a solid yellow steel helmet emblem) would guard the train at halts, providing perimeter security. In such circumstances, it was an interesting job and one which clearly Rommel must have realised would inevitably bring him both promotion and prestige.

The tour was soon over and, on 10 November 1938, Rommel was promoted to Colonel (Oberst) and appointed to command the Kriegschule at Wiener Neustadt. The appointment would last until August 1939 and provide the Rommel family with their last period of settled home life before war came. Not that he was left in peace for very long, being called for twice during March 1939 to command the Führer's mobile headquarters; the first time on 15 March, during the occupation of Prague, and again on the 23rd at Memel, when Hitler sailed into the Baltic port to supervise its 'voluntary' return to the Reich by Lithuania.

### Major-General and Headquarters Commandant

Hitler assembled all his Army Group commanders and their Chiefs of Staff at Obersalzberg on 21 August 1939, to break the news to them that they were about to invade Poland. Hitler did not know if this would spark off a second world war, but went on to explain the various situations that would apply if Britain and France did, as they had warned, go to war in support of Poland. One small but important factor which had to be considered, was where the Führer should be located in order to exert his control over the battle in the east, should that prove necessary, or to be able to move swiftly westwards should the Allies launch an attack from that direction. Clearly a mobile headquarters was needed, so it was decided that the special train would be used again. Shortly after the conference Rommel was called to Berlin where he learnt that he had been selected once again to be Hitler's Headquarters Commandant. There was also a very pleasant surprise awaiting him in that he was not only to be promoted to Major-General (Generalmajor), but this promotion was to be back-dated to 1 June.

Late on 25 August, Rommel's escort battalion started to make its way to Bad Polzin, in Pomerania, not far from the Polish frontier, where the German forces were now massing for their surprise attack. 'Fall Weiss', as the assault on Poland was called, involved two army groups, amounting to more than 1½ million men. In the build-up to their assault the Germans had made most effective use of the existing road and rail systems to move the troops into their concentration areas. Most of them went by rail, but the new autobahns had also played their part in getting both men and equipment unobtrusively to their forward positions. Strict radio silence was observed in the concentration areas, but ordinary garrison traffic was maintained to put Polish military intelligence off the scent. To move all the troops plus the huge quantities of equipment, ammunition and supplies which they would need to fight a modern *Blitzkrieg*-type war, was a far greater task than anything the Germans had ever attempted before. And to do it clandestinely was an amazing feat. 'Fall Weiss' achieved complete tactical surprise, the Polish reservists were still being called to their units when the first panzers rolled over the frontier. The Führer's train left Berlin at 2100 hours on Sunday 3 September 1939, three days after the invasion had started, with the following on board: Hitler, the OKW[4] leadership (Keitel and his adjutants, plus Jodl and one of his junior staff officers), Colonel Schmundt (the Wehrmacht's Chief Adjutant to the Führer), three junior adjutants to represent each of the services, General Bodenschatz (LO from the C-in-C Luftwaffe), Obergruppenführer Wolfe (LO from the C-in-C SS), Obergruppenführer Bruckner (SA adjutant to the Führer), Martin Bormann (Chief of the Party Chancellery), Dr Dietrich (Chief Press Officer of the Reich), Ambassador Hawell (Foreign Office representative), the Kriminalkommando (professional detectives of the security service – the Reichssicherheitdienst – for the protection of high Nazi officials, its Dienstelle 1 was assigned to guard the Führer). They arrived at Bad Polzin at 0156 hours on 4 September. About a quarter of an hour later, the Ministers' train (Ministerzug) arrived carrying von Ribbentrop and Himmler. Both trains remained in the station overnight under Rommel's protection.

### Hitler's train

Although no documents exist which give the exact components of the Sonderzug during the Polish operation, Mr D. Rabier, in an article in *After the Battle* magazine No. 19, 1977, explains that in the early years of the war, the train (which had been given the name 'Amerika' by Hitler) normally consisted of:

Two locomotives in tandem.
Flakwagen (armoured railway wagon, with anti-aircraft platforms at each end).

Baggage car.

Führerwagen (for Hitler's personal use, complete with drawing-room and bath).

Befelswagen (command car, used for conferences with map tables and a separate compartment for a small communications centre).

Begleitkommandowagen (for the escort).

Dining-car.

Two guest cars.

Badewagen (bathroom).

Another dining-car.

Two sleeping-cars (for enlisted men).

Presswagen (for the press).

A second baggage-car.

A second Flakwagen.

On 5 September the train moved on to Plietnitz, south of Neustettin, while Hitler toured Fourth Army's area in the north by car. A few hours later the train moved again to a small station some 15 kilometres south of Plietnitz, where it could be more easily guarded. Further moves followed on the 5th, 8th, 13th and 18th, ending up at Goddentow-Lanz, near Lauenburg in the extreme north-east of Pomerania, about 65 kilometres north-west of Danzig.[5] Then, on the 19th the Führer's HQ moved to the Kasio Hotel in Zoppot, a few kilometres from Danzig. Hitler continued to visit the battle area until 25 September, when it was clear that all organised Polish resistance had ended. Next morning the train left for Berlin where it arrived at 1705 hours. During these tours of the battle area Rommel had the greatest difficulty in getting Hitler to keep out of danger, confirming his opinion of the Führer's personal courage. 'I had great trouble with him,' Rommel told Lucie. 'He wants always to be right up with the forward troops. He seemed to enjoy being under fire.'[6] Rommel would revise this opinion some years later, but in 1939 his admiration for Hitler knew no bounds and they often chatted together in an easy, friendly way. Rommel shared his lunch table and much else, receiving an inscribed copy of *Mein Kampf* ('To General Rommel with pleasant memories') when he ceased to command the Hauptquartier.

### Organisation of the Escort Battalion

The total strength of Rommel's escort battalion was sixteen officers and 367 NCOs and men (the normal early wartime infantry battalion establishment was fourteen officers and 846 NCOs and men). However, their weaponry included four 37mm anti-tank guns and twelve 20mm anti-aircraft guns, plus a full range of small arms. Personnel were drawn from the Berlin Wachregiment (Guard regiment), the AA components came from Luftwaffe Regiment General Göring. Rommel organised his men into three groups:

Group 1: train guard and outer perimeter security.

Group 2: reserve, against emergencies.

Group 3: 'Front Group', namely those who would accompany the Führer and his entourage on their daily visits to the battlefront. Hitler travelled in a 6-wheeled Mercedes-Benz, its licence plates and other insignia covered. There were normally two groups within the convoy:

| *Group 1* | *Group 2* |
|---|---|
| Hitler's car | two cars for Ministers |
| two cars for escort | Himmler's car |
| one car for aides | Dr Dietrich's car |
| | spare car for visitors |
| | reserve car |
| | baggage car |
| | field-kitchen car |
| | petrol bowser |

Rommel invariably accompanied the Führer in his car. On a few occasions Hitler also used a light aircraft and again Rommel went with him.

### Uniform

The basic uniform of the escort battalion was exactly the same as for normal German infantry, which is fully explained in the next chapter and, apart from their always immaculate turnout, the only different item worn was their special cuff title (*Armelstreifen*). Such cuff titles were worn by certain élite or special units of the German Army, or sometimes awarded as a battle honour. Rommel's escort battalion wore the FÜHRERHAUPTQUARTIER cuff title on the left cuff. It was a black band 4cm wide with gold edging and gothic lettering in gold. In early 1941 a new version with silver lettering was introduced.

### Special Weapons

**3.7cm Pak 35/36 L/45.** The 37mm Rheinmetall-Borsig anti-tank gun was normally found in panzerjäger companies. It had been developed between 1933 and 1936 and had seen action with the Condor Legion[7] during the Spanish Civil War. In its day it was a first-class weapon, but was becoming outdated by 1941, when more than 15,000 had been produced. It had a weight in action of 328 kilograms. With a muzzle velocity of 762m/s, its 0.68kg AP round could penetrate 38mm of armour at 30° at 400 yards. After 1940, its performance was improved by using the tungsten-cored AP 40 round.

**2cm Flak 30.** Developed by Rheinmetall-Borsig from the Solothurn SS-100, it was introduced into service in 1935. It was a good AA weapon, but had a low rate of fire (120rpm) and was prone to jamming. The basic mount was triangular and it was transported in the field on a light 2-wheeled carriage (in the special train's Flakwagen it was used on its mounting for on the spot AA defence). Weight in action was 450kg, muzzle velocity (HE tracer) 900m/s, with a maximum effective ceiling of 2,200 metres. The normal Flak 30 crew consisted of a detachment commander and five men: No 1 gun layer (bearing and elevation); No 2 range setter; No 3 loader; No 4 ammunition number; No 5 range taker.

## Notes to Chapter 2

1. Irving, *Trail of the Fox.*
2. Young, *Rommel.*
3. Snyder, *Encyclopedia.*
4. The OKW was the Supreme Command of the Armed Forces (Oberkommando der Wehrmacht). Its Chief was Field Marshal Wilhelm Keitel, whose fawning attitude to the Führer had already earned him the nickname Lakeitel – a punning reference to the German word for footman or lackey.
5. The car journeys after Plietniz were: 5 Sept north-west across the Gross Born troop training area to the south-west of Neustettin; 8 Sept south to Ilnau, north-east of Oppeln in Silesia; 13 Sept further south of Oppeln to Gogolin; 18 Sept north to Goddentow-Lanz, near Lauenburg in Pomerania, some 65km north-west of Danzig. During his stay here Hitler (accompanied by Rommel) drove to Danzig and made a radio broadcast.
6. Young, *op. cit.*
7. The ground element of the 'volunteer' German Condor Legion contained both light tanks (PzKpfw I) and no fewer than thirty anti-tank gun companies.

# 3
# The Ghost Division
# (1939–1940)

## A FIELD COMMAND (SEPTEMBER 1939 – JUNE 1940)

Rommel returned to Berlin on 26 September ahead of the train, to arrange Hitler's arrival reception and to sort out new quarters for his battalion at the Chancellery. The Führer and the rest of his staff arrived at 5 p.m. at the Stettiner Station where Rommel and the Führerhauptquartier provided the guard of honour as always. Two days later, the complete battalion was paraded to receive new Colours from their Führer. The Poles capitulated on the 27th and a few days afterwards Rommel flew to Warsaw to prepare for Hitler's 'Victory Parade', which was to take place on 5 October. He was appalled by the chaos and squalor he found in the ruined capital, where many houses and shops had been destroyed by the Luftwaffe and some 40,000 people, mainly civilians, had been killed or wounded. He was a member of Hitler's entourage during the 2-hour parade and then returned to Berlin. But he was not to stay there for long. During their conversations Rommel had already hinted to Hitler that he would like be appointed to an operational command, which at his rank meant becoming a divisional commander. The obvious choice would seem to have been a mountain division, but Rommel favoured a panzer (tank) division. Clearly he had seen how successful the new *Blitzkrieg* (lightning war) had been in Poland, and had recognised that two of the most important elements in the new tactics had been the panzer divisions, together with their ever-present close air support, from the Luftwaffe's 'on call' Stuka dive-bombers. Besides, there would be little for a specialised mountain division to do on the Western Front. So, despite the fact that he was an infantry officer who knew next to nothing about armoured fighting vehicles, Rommel decided to 'hitch his star to a tank'. The army personnel branch disagreed, but Hitler overruled them and in doing so began the next chapter in the career of a leader whom friend and foe alike would soon acknowledge as being one of the best armoured generals of the war.

On 6 February 1940 Rommel was ordered to proceed to Bad Godesberg to take command of 7th Panzer Division (7th Pz Div). This was one of the newer panzer divisions, which had initially been raised in 1938 at Gera, an industrial city on the River Weisse Elster in Thuringia, in east-central Germany. The Thuringians were not noted for their fighting ability, but their new commander would soon change all that. The 7th Pz Div had begun life as the 2nd Light Division (2 leichte), one of four light motorised divisions, raised by mechanising the cavalry in a completely separate programme from the formation of the first five panzer divisions. They were small, motorised formations, containing approximately one battalion of 90 light tanks, plus a number of motorised infantry (Schützen) battalions/regiments. Supporting units such as artillery, engineer and reconnaissance, etc., were all similar to those found in panzer divisions.[1] In 1938 they had passed under control of Guderian's Inspectorate of Mobile Troops and all had taken part in the invasion of Poland. The initial units of 2nd Light Division had included 66th Panzer Battalion and 6th and 7th Mechanised Cavalry Regiments. At Gera the division had been commanded and trained by Lieutenant-General (later General of Panzer Troops) Georg Stumme, who was still commanding in Poland and from whom Rommel took over. Stumme was rated as being one of the best German panzer commanders, idolised by his soldiers, who were always his first concern. He was to meet Rommel again in North Africa.

**Getting Back Into Trim**

After the Polish campaign the four light divisions were re-organised as the 6th, 7th, 8th and 9th Panzer Divisions, each having its tank strength raised by the addition of a panzer regiment of three battalions, all that is except 9th Pz Div which received only a 2-battalion regiment. For 'Fall Gelb', Hitler's attack in the west, the newly formed 7th Pz Div would be part of General Hermann Hoth's XV Army Corps, but that exciting adventure was still some months away and first Rommel had to get himself fighting fit and get to know his new command. The former was easy for someone with Rommel's iron will and he began jogging every morning, sweating off the weeks of good living at Hitler's headquarters. At the same time he began to make his mark with the units of his division. Not only did he embark upon a whirlwind tour of his new command, but he also put them through an intensive training programme, featuring plenty of live gunnery firing. Firepower is one of the three most important characteristics of the tank (the other two being protection and mobility), so continual firing practice was essential to keep the tank crews up to the mark. These were followed by movement exercises, road discipline training and of course, all arms tactical field exercises, with the commanders of every type of unit, learning how to work together smoothly, for example, by communicating with one another on the radio quickly and efficiently. Rommel hated inefficiency of any kind and, although he was normally a fair and just man, he dealt ruthlessly with anyone he did not consider was up to the mark. For example, he sacked one of his battalion commanders only three weeks after taking command of the division, making sure that the unfortunate officer was out of his unit and on his way within two hours! 'Word of this rapid firing will soon get around,' he wrote, 'and some of the others will pull their socks up.'[2]

## ORGANISATION OF SEVENTH PANZER DIVISION *c.*1940

The 7th Panzer Division had been formed from 2 leichte on 18 October 1939. When Rommel took it over, his division had as its basic elements: a panzer regiment, a motorised infantry brigade of two motorised rifle regiments and an artillery regiment, together with battalion-sized reconnaissance, anti-tank, engineer, signals and motorcycle units, plus normal supply and administrative units as found in every division. The divisional order of battle, as at 10 May 1940, was:

## a. Tanks

Panzer Regiment 25, which had been assigned to the Division on 18 October 1939, comprised three tank battalions (Panzerabteilungen) – I/25, II/25 and 66. The oldest was Pz Bn 66, which had been raised on 10 October 1938 and was assigned to the Regiment on 1 November 1939. I/25 had been raised with the HQ on 1 November 1938, but II/25 was not formed until 1 April 1940 (formerly I/23 independent battalion). The Regiment had a total of 225 tanks: thirty-four PzKpfw I, sixty-eight PzKpfw II, ninety-one PzKpfw 38(t), eight Pz Bef (Wg) 38(t) (these were the Command (*Befels*) version) and twenty-four PzKpfw IV, as at 10 May 1940. On 2 June, while the Division was at rest (see later), two more Pz I, twenty Pz 38(t) and one Pz IV arrived, to make up for battle casualties. Although some sources say that the Regiment had some PzKpfw III, this was never actually the case. The crews of some PzKpfw 38(t) often referred to their Czech-built tank as 'III', which is probably how the mistake occurred. Even Desmond Young in his epic biography of Rommel falls into this trap and quotes the Division's tank losses as including twenty-six Mark III instead of 38(t) (see later). The Regiment was commanded by another *Pour le Mérite* winner, Colonel (Oberst) Karl Rothenburg. At 44 (five years younger than Rommel), he was a tough, highly experienced panzer commander, considered to be one of the best tank officers in the army. His battalion commanders were: I/25 Major Schmidt; II/25 Lieutenant-Colonel Ilgen; 66 Major Sieckenius. His Adjutant was Lieutenant Student.

The PzKpfw 38(t), was Czech-built – hence the (t) = 'tchechoslowakisch' – the Germans having 'obtained' these tanks, plus a quantity of the slightly older PzKpfw 35(t), when Czechoslovakia was overrun. This unexpected windfall had made it possible to equip the four leichte divisions so rapidly. The Czech factories then continued to build 38(t) for the Germans, more than 1,400 entering German service in total. Their 3.7cm Skoda gun was considerably more powerful than the 2cm of the PzKpfw II. The 38(t) were undoubtedly better than either the PzKpfw I or II, but the best of the panzers of the period were, the heavier, better armed PzKpfw III and IV which had only recently become available in any quantity. By May 1940 there were 329 Mark III and 280 Mark IV in service and they would play a vital role against the Allies in France, who had more tanks on balance than did the Germans, but whose tactics of 'penny packeting' (spreading them out in small numbers across the whole front in the infantry support role) proved disastrous.[3]

**Additional armour.** Rommel had extra tanks placed under his command on two separate occasions, the first being for the crossing of the River Meuse when Pz Regt 31 (commanded by Colonel Werner), belonging to 5th Pz Div,

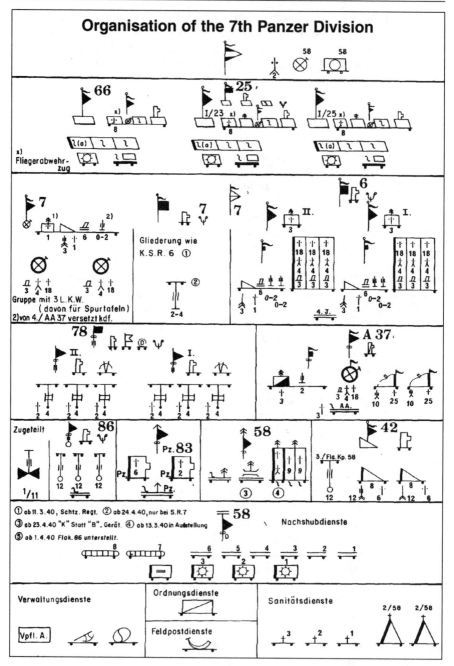

## Organisation of the 7th Panzer Division

was attached because Rommel's division was making faster progress. Then, after the enforced 2-day halt (24–26 May) caused by Hitler's personal 'Halt Order' (see later), 5th Panzer Brigade, commanded by General Haarde, for the attack on Lille. This brigade was also part of 5 Pz Div, which, having

40

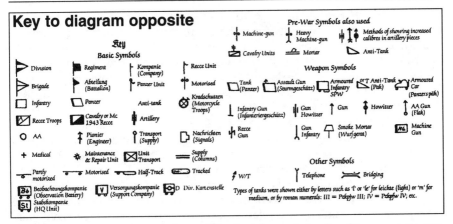

been formed before the war began, had a panzer brigade of two panzer regiments (each of two battalions), rather than a single 3-battalion panzer regiment. At the start of the campaign it had considerably more tanks than Rommel (324 as against 225 in Pz Regt 25). Its tanks included some PzKpfw III (both gun and command), which again may have led to the mix-up on tank types in 7th Pz Div, which I have already mentioned.

## Tanks in 7th Panzer Division

|  | *PzKpfw I* *Ausf b* | *IPzKpfw II* *Ausf D & E* | *PzKpfw 38(t)* *Ausf A* | *PzKpfw IV* *Ausf B* |
|---|---|---|---|---|
| Wt (tons) | 6 | 10 | 9.4 | 18.8 |
| Crew | 2 | 3 | 4 (in German service) | 5 |
| Dimensions (metres) |  |  |  |  |
| Length | 4.42 | 4.64 | 4.61 | 5.92 |
| Height | 1.72 | 2.02 | 2.4 | 2.68 |
| Width | 2.06 | 2.30 | 2.12 | 2.83 |
| Armament | 2 x MG13 1 x MG34 | 1 x 2cm 2 x MG34 | 1 x 3.7cm 1 x MG34 | 1 x 7.5cm 1 x MG34 |
| Armour (mm) |  |  |  |  |
| max | 13 | 30 | 25 | 30 |
| min | 6 | 5 | 8 | 5 |
| Max speed (km/hr) | 40 | 55 | 40 | 40 |
| Range (km) | 140 | 200 | 250 | 200 |

## b. Motorised Infantry

**Schützen Brigade 7.** Commanded by Colonel (Oberst) Friedrich Furst, it had been raised on 27 October 1939 from 7th Cavalry Brigade. It comprised:

(i). Schützen Regiments 6 and 7. Each consisted of two battalions of motorised infantry. Later the Schützen (Rifle) regiments of the motorised infantry divisions would become known as panzer grenadiers. Those in the light divisions were originally from the strong cavalry branch which, before 1935, had formed three of the ten Reichsheer divisions. The infantry rode in Krupp 'Proz-KW' 6x4 trucks (no half-tracks were yet available), so they could move quickly on roads and tracks but not across country, but were protected from bad weather and could carry extra loads of ammunition, entrenching tools, engineer stores and rations. The two regimental commanders were Colonel von Unger and Colonel von Bismarck; their adjutants were Lieutenant Hoffmann and Captain Littau; their battalion commanders: I/6 Major von Paris and II/6 Lieutenant-Colonel Junck; I/7 Major Cramer and II/7 Major Bachmann respectively.

(ii). Kradschützen Bataillon 7. This was the motorcycle infantry battalion, which provided a cross-country infantry element before the arrival of the half-track. By using motorcycles with side-cars, they were able to cooperate with tanks, and were very useful for reconnaissance, being speedy, easy to conceal and able to negotiate all but the very worst terrain. The Germans manufactured many good motorcycles so replacements were no problem. The battalion was commanded by Major von Steinkeller and had been raised on 1 November 1939 from I/7th Reconnaissance Battalion.

(iii). sIG Kompanie 705. Attached to 7 Schützen Bde was a heavy gun company of six self-propelled 15cm heavy infantry howitzers, mounted on PzKpfw I chassis. The howitzer was mounted complete with its wheels, on top of a turretless chassis of a PzKpfw I, giving a weight in action of 8,500kg. It had 75° of elevation and 25° of traverse only, and carried 25 rounds of ammunition, which had a range of 4,700 metres.

**Additional infantry.** Just before they began the drive on Cherbourg on 17 June, the division was reinforced by another motorised infantry brigade known as Brigade Senger, commanded by General Fridolin von Senger und Etterlin.

## c. Artillery

**Artillerie Regiment 78.** Most important of the supporting arms was the artillery. Although they were supplemented by the Luftwaffe's close air support, this in no way reduced the value of quick, accurate fire support which the field artillery regiment provided, with its two battalions, each of three 4-gun batteries of le FH18 10.5cm field howitzers. The Regiment had been raised on 10 November 1938, with only two battalions (I/78 and II/78) and started 'Fall Gelb' with just these two. But from 5 June 1940, II/45 Bn was attached from GHQ troops and would, in February 1941, become III/78. In France this battalion had two batteries of 15cm field howitzers and one battery of 10cm guns. The Artillerie Regiment was commanded by Colonel Frolich, with Lieutenant Monhausen as his adjutant. The three battalions were commanded by: I/78 Lieutenant-Colonel Dr Kessler; II/78 Major Crasemann; II/45 Major von Kronhelm. The 10.5cm field howitzer le FH18 had been first produced in 1935, weighed 1,985kg in action and fired a 14.8kg shell to some 10,675 metres. Maximum elevation was 40° and traverse 56°.

### d. Reconnaissance

**Aufklärungsabteilung 7.** The armoured reconnaissance battalion, which contained some 50 heavy and light armoured cars, mechanised infantrymen and motorcycle troops, had been raised on 1 November 1939 from II/7 Reconnaissance Battalion. It was initially commanded by Major Erdmann who was killed on 28 May 1940, his place being taken by Captain von Luck. The 4.8ton SdKfz 222, 3-man leichter Panzerspähwagen, had entered service in 1936 and was armed with a 2cm gun and a coaxially mounted MG34. There was also a radio version – the SdKfz 223(Fu) – which was fitted with a large frame aerial. The powerful 8-wheel schwerer Panzerspähwagen SdKfz 231 and 232(Fu) had a crew of five, and weighed 8.3 tons combat loaded.

### e. Engineers

**Pionier Bataillon 58.** The Engineer battalion was raised on 10 November 1938. With 950 combat engineers, it was initially commanded by Major Brinkau who was killed on 13 May 1940, being replaced by Major von Mertens. In addition to the engineers, there was a total of thirteen PzKpfw I and Pzkpfw II, including one of the latter modified to carry a mobile bridge. On 26 May, when 7th Panzer Division resumed its advance, the division also had 635th Engineer Regiment under command.

### f. Anti-Tank

**Panzerjägerabteilung 42.** There were thirty-six 37mm anti-tank guns in the battalion, divided into three batteries of twelve guns each. The battalion was commanded by Colonel Mickl. Raised on 10 November 1938, until March 1940 this unit had been known as Panzer Abwehrabteilung 42.

### g. Anti-Tank/Anti-Aircraft

**FlaKabteilung 3/59.** Major Schrader commanded the battalion of truck-mounted/towed FlaK guns (20mm or 88mm) which had three 12-gun batteries. They were actually GHQ troops, but permanently attached to the Division.

### h. Signals

**Nachrichten Bataillon 83 (transm).** Good radio communications are the lifeblood of all armoured formations, so the 600-strong battalion, raised on 1 August 1939, was a most important unit. Its commander was Major Muller. Its vehicles included both the light and heavy armoured car/radio vehicles (Funkwagen (Fu)) such as the SdKfz 223(Fu) 4 rad and the SdKfz 263 (Fu) 8-rad, which had a fixed turret but no armament other than a single MG, thus allowing for more radio equipment and an extra radio operator.

### i. Supply

Versorgungstruppen. The Supply troops, numbered '58', were:
58th Motorised Divisional Supply Battalion
    1–7/58th Motorised Transport Columns
    8–10/58th Motorised Fuel Transport Columns
    1–3/58th Motorised Motor Maintenance Columns

58th Motorised Supply Company
58th Motorised Divisional Rations Administration Detachment
58th Motorised Butchery Platoon
58th Motorised Bakery Company

## j. Administrative Units
These included:
58th Motorised Military Police Detachment
    1–2/58th Motorised Medical Companies
    1–3/58th Motorised Ambulance Companies
58th Motorcycle Messenger Platoon – attached to Div HQ
58th Motorised Divisional Mapping Detachment – ditto

## Attached Luftwaffe Units
On 10 May 1940 the following Luftwaffe units were attached to 7th Pz Div:
I/23rd Flak Battalion
86th Light Flak Battalion
1(H)/11th Reconnaissance Squadron

## Divisional Headquarters Staff
Although the strength, composition, transport, equipment, etc., of the various German divisions that fought in the Second World War varied considerably, the divisional staffs were organised in a very similar way. They were normally divided into three groups: Tactical (Führungsabteilung), Personnel (Adjutantur) and Supply (Quartiermeister). Only the most senior posts (designated by the Roman figure I) had to be held by General Staff officers (i.e., Ia, Ib or Ic).

    **a. The Tactical group** included the Chief of Operations (Ia) who also acted as Chief of Staff, and the Chief Intelligence Officer (Ic) together with their respective staffs. The latter was directly subordinate to the former, as were the various other combat oriented Ia staffs, including artillery and air liaison. The artillery commander (ArtilleriefAührer or Arfu) was most important, being responsible for recommending the allocation of artillery units from corps or army troops. This Tactical HQ was sometimes known as the Divisional Command Post (CP). Early on in the assault on France, Rommel had perfected his own method of tight combat control, by making maximum use of both wireless and personal contact. This enabled him to stay at the front, remaining 'where the action was', being able to impose his personality on all aspects of the battle, including giving his orders personally to his regimental commanders. This was vital because the encoding for wireless transmissions would have taken far too long, especially if situation reports had had to be sent back to divisional HQ for the HQ staff to work out their contents, brief the commander, then encode and issue his orders. Instead Rommel stayed at the 'sharp end', but he also endeavoured (not always successfully!) to maintain continuous wireless contact with his divisional operational staff, which remained in the rear, and a detailed exchange of views normally took place early each morning and each afternoon between Rommel and his Ia when he was at his HQ. Rommel commented that this method of command: '... proved extremely effective'. In essence it meant that he dealt on the spot with the running of the battle, while his staff dealt with longer-term matters – and presumably helped to keep swanning VIPs 'off his back'! As will be explained, Rommel's Ia was not entirely happy about the arrangement.

    **b. The Personnel group** was headed by the IIa, the Chief Personnel Officer. Under him were the IIb (Second Personnel Officer), the III (Chief Judge Advocate), the IVd (Chaplain) and various sections required for the functioning of the headquarters, such as transport/motor pool, security, etc. IIa handled officers' affairs, while IIb dealt with the other ranks, but routed all requests for replacements via IIa, who additionally looked after III, IVd and the MT officer.

    **c. The Supply group** was normally separated from the CP and was commanded by the Ib (Divisional Quartermaster or Chief Supply Officer). It contained the Chief Administrative Officer (IVa), the Chief Medical Officer (IVb), the Chief Veterinary Officer (IVc) and the Motor Transport Officer (V), all of whom were in charge of their own sections.

    In addition to these three main groups, divisions had special staffs assigned on a temporary or permanent basis. These might include: Commander Divisional Supply Troops (subordinate to Ib); the Senior Military Police Officer; the Commander of flame-thrower projector troops (cf. Chemical Warfare section in the US Army); the Gas Protection Officer and the National Socialist Guidance Officer.

**Personalities.** In 7th Pz Div, in addition to Major-General (Generalmajor) Erwin Rommel as commander, the following were some of the most important members of the headquarters:
(i). Tactical Group
    General Staff Officer Ia Major Otto Heidkämper.
    Intelligence Officer Ic Major Ziegler.
    (Rommel's Gefechtsstaffel was a part of this group – see below).
(ii). Personnel Group
    General Staff Officer IIa Captain von Metzsch
    Chief Judge Advocate Dr Schulz
(iii). Supply Group
    Senior Medical Officer Colonel Dr Baumeister
    Commissariat Officer (QM) Intendant-Rat Fiebig
    **Otto Heidkämper,** Rommel's Ia, was a highly competent young staff major, with considerable moral courage. He found Rommel's method of command extremely difficult for himself and the rest of the staff and was brave enough to say so in a memo to his commander, on 13 June, which infuriated Rommel! He was initially so cross that he wrote to Lucie that he was having: '... a lot of trouble with my Ia at the moment', going on to list all the 'shortcomings' which Heidkämper had complained about – such as Rommel's always being far too near the front line and so in con-

stant danger of being killed or wounded which would leave the division leaderless; of introducing his own 'lines of thrust' despite the fact that they seldom conformed with anyone else's; and, against all orders from above, signing his main routes with the sign 'DG 7', which enabled follow-up units and supply columns to find their way quickly. Rommel justified everything to his corps commander and made peace with Heidkämper with whom he actually normally got on very well. However, Rommel comments: 'it was necessary to assert my authority'. No one would ever be able to stop him from commanding in his own inimitable way, whatever the risks to life and limb!

**Major Ziegler,** the Intelligence Officer, would later accompany Rommel to North Africa, again as his IO, as would his gallant Adjutant, Major Schräpler (again as Adjutant).

### Personal staff

**Gefechtsstaffel.** Rommel often refers to this (lit: 'Action Staff' or 'Fighting Echelon'), which was his own small, personal headquarters group – additional to the CP – consisting of his staff car, his Adjutant, his aide(s), together with communications troops (including an 8-wheeled armoured signals vehicle and some dispatch riders), plus a small protection team (with an armoured car). This group invariably accompanied him into action, most of the time moving from cover to cover just behind the leading troops. Rommel seems to have travelled with his Adjutant a great deal of the time except for a short period when Schräpler was wounded during the crossing of the Leffe weir, though he soon returned. Schräpler would write to Frau Rommel from time to time (he respecfully uses: 'meine gnädigste Frau' in his letters). Poor Schräpler would lose his life in the desert when he was accidentally run over by Rommel's command vehicle in December 1941. Another officer mentioned by name in *The Rommel Papers* is Captain Stollbreuck, Rommel's escort officer.

**ADCs.** His aide-de-camp, 30-year-old Lieutenant Joachim Most, whom Rommel described as being: 'a brave man, a magnificent soldier', was killed at his side near Wailly during the Arras counter-attack, on 21 May. He lies buried in the German military cemetery at Bourdon, posthumously promoted to Captain. Rommel mentions two other aides: Lieutenant Luft and Lieutenant Hausberg. The former may have been Rommel's personal signals officer, used as an aide after Most was killed and when he was not in charge of Rommel's armoured radio vehicle. The other, Lieutenant Hausberg, had served with Rommel at Hitler's HQ and was posted to 7th Pz Div towards the end of the campaign in France, arriving on 17 June, while the division was on its way to Cherbourg. 'I immediately installed him as ADC,' wrote Rommel in his diary.

**NCOs.** Two NCO members of the Gefechtsstaffel mentioned frequently were: his Signals Corporal (Gefreiter) Heidenreich (promoted from private after rescuing someone from drowning while crossing the Meuse) and Lance-Corporal König, Rommel's driver. Rommel clearly admired their bravery and competent basic soldierly abilities, commenting after one action that they ' ... particularly distinguished themselves by their cool courage ...'

**Batman.** Rommel also had a batman, Lance-Corporal Herbert Günther who, as his soldier-servant, cleaned and polished his boots, belt, etc., kept his uniforms clean, tidy and properly pressed and generally looked after his basic needs. As with other senior commanders, Rommel took his batman with him whenever he changed jobs, so Günther went with him to North Africa and then back to Europe. He had an abiding admiration for Rommel, speaking of him as being the best of masters, who never lost his temper and always appreciated his efforts. Günther often wrote to Lucie, especially when Rommel was too busy even to write to his beloved wife. He shared all the same hardships as Rommel, even being injured in the desert during an air raid on Rommel's HQ.

**Nazis.** In addition to his normal military staff, Rommel had two important Nazis attached to his headquarters: Lieutenant Karl August Hanke, adjutant and personal assistant to Propaganda Minister Goebbels from 1933 to 1941, and Karl Holz, chief editor of *Der Stürmer*, a violently anti-Semitic newspaper. Both would later become Gauleiters (District Leaders), the former for Lower Silesia, the latter for Franconia. Hanke had been sent to be Rommel's second aide-de-camp, and although prone to high-handed behaviour which made him very unpopular with many of the officers in the division, he eventually proved a remarkably efficient and brave soldier.[4] Initially, Rommel had put him into a PzKpfw IV to learn about tank soldiering and, as we shall see later, Hanke must have learnt his lessons well, because he fought a successful tank action in one against some French tanks in Avesnes on 17 May.

**Other means of transportation.** When he wanted to be right up 'at the sharp end' Rommel would get into a tank: 'I placed myself in a Panzer III which was to follow close behind him' (presumably this is a mistranslation for a PzKpfw 38(t) as already explained, while 'him' was Colonel Rothenburg, commander of Pz Regt 25). On other occasions he would ride on or in Rothenburg's own tank. Nor was Rommel averse to taking personal command of one of his units if he felt it necessary: 'I now took personal command of the 2nd Battalion of 7th Rifle Regiment and for some time directed operations myself.'[5] In addition of course, as an ex-infantry officer, he was, unlike many armoured soldiers, perfectly at home on his feet, so when the need arose, he would dismount and go forward on foot.

## THE GERMAN SOLDIER, MAY 1940

### Basic Dress and Equipment

The Schütze (infantry private) of the Schützen Brigade, like all other German soldiers, wore the M1936 service uniform both in barracks and in the field. It comprised a thigh-length field-grey tunic, straight field grey trousers (flared riding-breeches for the cavalry), which were stuffed into the tops of black leather, nail-studded jackboots. The tunic had a dark green high collar (on each side of which were patches of dark green cloth bearing the traditional Prussian double collar bars (Litzen) ). There were five large metal 'dimple-finish' buttons down the front, one on each of the four patch pockets, and one on each shoulder close to the collar, on which to fix the shoulder-straps. Above the right breast pocket was the national emblem of the straight spread-winged eagle, clutching in its talons a circular wreath containing a swastika, in white thread on a dark green background. Trousers had side pockets and a hip pocket. A leather belt and leather equipment was worn, the belt buckle being of dull white metal like the buttons. The belt plate bore the German eagle and swastika motif, with the words 'GOTT MIT UNS' (God is with us) surrounding them. The shoulder-straps were of dark green cloth, piped in different branch of service colours (Waffenfarbe), the main colours being: white for infantry, pink for armour, golden yellow for cavalry, bright red for artillery, grass green for armoured infantry, black for engineers, copper brown for recce units, lemon yellow for signals, light green for Jäger and mountain troops.

Normal head-dress in battle was the M1935 'coal-scuttle' steel helmet, but the side-cap (Feldmütze) in field-grey was often worn. It had a roundel (red, white and black) on the front of the turned-up portion, and on the front of the crown was a smaller version of the breast eagle. The double-breasted 12-button (two rows of six) greatcoat was of field-grey cloth with a dark green falling collar.

The basic personal equipment comprised the belt, a set of black leather 'Y' straps, triple ammunition pouches, entrenching tool, bayonet (84/98) in its black steel scabbard, canvas bread bag, canteen, gasmask in its fluted metal cylinder, tent square (Zeltbahn) and the canvas pack which contained washing gear, rifle cleaning kit, spare clothing, tinned rations, tent pegs and rope for the tent square. The large M1939 pack, which contained the remainder of the soldier's clothing, equipment and personal items, was not often worn in action. Two more vital items which everyone carried were the service book and identity discs. In the former, the soldier's record of service was recorded (it also contained his photograph, signature, army number, etc.). Around every soldier's neck was a two-piece aluminium, oval identification disc, bearing his name and the number of his field post or replacement troop. When a soldier died, one half was broken off and given to the burial officer to pass on. Squad leaders also carried binoculars, message bag, torch, compass and a whistle.

**Officers' dress.** Officers wore a similar, but much better cut, field-grey tunic of finer material, with more elaborate Litzen on the dark green collar. Most officers wore flared riding-breeches although sometimes straight trousers were worn (cf. other ranks). In addition to the steel helmet and side-cap, officers wore the service cap (Schirmmütze), which had a black peak, dark green band and field-grey crown.

**Tank crew uniforms.** Perhaps the most striking uniform worn in 7th Pz Div was the distinctive black uniform of the armoured troops – Sonderbekleidung der Deutschen Panzertruppen – which consisted of a protective headgear (the Schutzmütze – a padded inner head protector and a flamboyant outer beret), a short double-breasted jacket and long straight trousers, all in black cloth. Officers initially wore a black Sam Browne-style belt, other ranks wore the normal black leather belt.

**Personal Weapons**
The soldier's rifle was the 7.92mm Karabiner 98k and, at the start of the war, all members of a 10-man rifle squad (Schützengruppe), including the squad leader, carried one. The 'k' stood for *kurz* (short) and it was first put into general production in 1935, many thousands being produced thereafter. It was a good, accurate rifle, but its main disadvantage was the 5-round capacity magazine. There must also have been some machine pistols in service, like the 9mm Maschinenpistole 38, the forebear of the MP40 which was destined to become one of the most renowned of all German submachine-guns. It was in production from 1938 until replaced by the MP40 in 1940. It had a 32-round magazine and was known to the Allies as the 'Schmeisser', despite the fact that Hugo Schmeisser had nothing to do with its design. Stick Grenade 24 and Hand Grenade 39 were also two basic infantry weapons, as were the Pistole (Walther P38 or Luger P08) and the Flare Pistole (Leuchtpistole) 38. The squad's light machine-gun was the 7.92mm Maschinengewehr MG34, with its 50-round belt, which could be linked to form a 250-round belt. It used the same ammunition as the rifle. It had a rate of fire of 800–900rpm and could be used on a built-in bipod or a large tripod, capable of being turned into an AA mount (not much liked, so the gunner usually used someone else's shoulder). The MG34 was also used on tanks and other AFVs. It was a good, reliable, much liked LMG and continued to be used, even when superseded by the MG 42. Gas operated, its sight range extended from 200 to 2,000 metres. Its only major drawback was that it got hot quickly and asbestos gloves were needed to change barrels. The anti-tank rifle (Panzerbusche) 39, fired a special 7.92mm round, which could penetrate 25mm of armour plate at 300 metres. It was virtually obsolete before the war began.

## *BLITZKRIEG* TACTICS

Before launching into the campaign itself, perhaps a few words on the theory of the new 'Lightning War' (*Blitzkrieg*) would be useful, as they will help to show how the German attacking force which comprised only 2.4 million men, with a total of 2,574 tanks, 7,710 field and anti-tank guns, was able to defeat so quickly and effectively, the combined Allied forces of 3.65 million, who fielded more than 3,000 tanks plus some 15,000 field and anti-tank guns.

Simply stated, *Blitzkrieg* was a tactical system which General Heinz Guderian had perfected to pierce the enemy's front, and then to encircle and destroy all or part of his forces. Its major elements were surprise, speed of manoeuvre, shock action from both ground and air, with the retention of the initiative by the attacking force. It required that all commanders use their

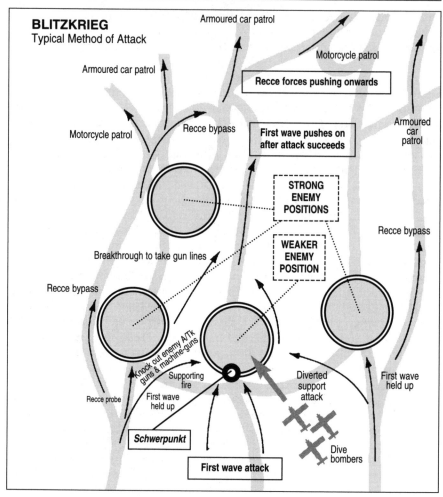

**BLITZKRIEG**
Typical Method of Attack

Armoured car patrol

Motorcycle patrol

Armoured car patrol

Motorcycle patrol

Recce bypass

Recce forces pushing onwards

First wave pushes on after attack succeeds

Armoured car patrol

STRONG ENEMY POSITIONS

WEAKER ENEMY POSITION

Recce bypass

Breakthrough to take gun lines

Recce bypass

Knock out enemy A/TK guns & machine-guns

Supporting fire

Diverted support attack

First wave held up

Recce probe

First wave held up

*Schwerpunkt*

Dive bombers

First wave attack

initiative to the full and that all troops involved be highly trained. Imagine that the panzer division – a force of all arms with close air support – is advancing with reconnaissance elements out in front, whose task is to locate the main enemy positions. These recce elements will consist of armoured cars on the main roads and motorcycle patrols on side roads and tracks. They will probably have an artillery forward observation officer with them, who can call quickly (over the radio) for fire support if and when needed. Having located the enemy and reported back, the recce forces will try to bypass the main enemy positions and keep going, so as to maintain the momentum of the advance. They will of course be in constant radio communication with the force commander, who will regulate their speed of movement and decide whether the whole force should bypass or engage the enemy positions discovered. The commander will be well forward, travelling just behind the vanguard. If and when he decides to attack, he will probably give his orders over the radio and the requisite striking force will then concentrate as quickly as possible – immediately off the line of march (*Aufmarsch*) – to a narrow sector of the enemy front. The centre of gravity of the attack, the Schwerpunkt, will be where the commander considers is the best place to assault, and not where the enemy is strongest. The attack will be put in with overwhelming force, making use of all available firepower, including dive-bombing from the air – in the words of Guderian: '*Klopfen nicht kleckern!*' (Thump them hard - don't pat them!). The main aim of the attack is to penetrate the enemy line and, once this is successful, a follow-up force will pass through and press on with the advance, avoiding the main enemy positions. These tactics were known as 'space and gap tactics' (*Flächen und Lückentaktiken*), the aim being to get armoured forces around behind the main enemy positions so as to be able to take control of their lines of communication.

Meanwhile, behind the leading armoured groups are additional forces, probably based on motorised infantry, whose task it is to mop up any pockets of enemy left, and generally tidy up and make safe the tattered ends of the enemy line – *aufrollen* as it was called – so as to maintain the breakthrough. The spearhead will continue to exploit, pressing forwards with the aim of encircling as many of the enemy forces as possible. The faster and deeper they penetrate the enemy rear areas, the larger would be these envelopments. The dictum was to reinforce success and abandon failure, switching forces from any dead ends to other parts of the battlefield where they could be of more use. Such manoeuvres required excellent teamwork, good command and control, careful timing and, above all, good continuous voice communications. In addition to speed and strength of the attack, the element of surprise was also essential to success, so there could be no massive build-up or long-drawn-out manoeuvring, giving the enemy time to prepare. Instead, an overwhelmingly powerful attack force would hit the enemy without prior warning, smashing through them on a relatively narrow front.

The other essential ingredient of a successful *Blitzkrieg* attack was a continuous supply of fuel, ammunition, rations and other necessaries. Fuel was of prime importance if the momentum of the attack was to be maintained. A panzer division used about 2,000 gallons a mile on cross-country movement, less of course if they stuck to the roads. Each division had its own main supply route (*Rollbahn*) and the supply columns needed very careful handling so as to get to the right place at the right time. Panzer troops would also to some extent 'live off the land', filling up their tanks at the civilian garages they happened to pass. In the campaigns in France each panzer division carried sufficient fuel for about 200 kilometres (125 miles) and thereafter resupply was difficult. They also had sufficient rations for nine days within divisional resources so the bulk of the resupply vehicles could be used to bring up ammunition and fuel. Success therefore lay partly in the tactical combination of a force of all arms – of which tanks were the most important ingredient – with aircraft in close support, attacking without warning from an unexpected direction, and partly from the exploitation of the breakthrough thus achieved. This exploitation had to be carried out as quickly as possible, with the armoured forces racing ahead of the main army, acting independently and driving deep into the enemy's rear areas.

## PLANNING THE ASSAULT IN THE WEST

### 'Fall Gelb'

The basis of the assault on the west was a plan known as 'Fall Gelb' (Case Yellow). This had been drawn up by the Army Command (Oberkommando des Heeres (OKH) ) to achieve Hitler's objectives and was, in many ways, initially very similar to the Schlieffen Plan of 1914.[6] The aim was to reach the Channel coast by attacking through Belgium and Luxembourg, with the exposed southern flank strongly protected. In Phase 1, a pincer movement with Liège as its fulcrum, would engulf Brussels and central Belgium. The main force, consisting of Army Group B (37 divisions) would remain to the north, while Army Group A (27 divisions) would cover the southern flank. In Phase 2, the attack would continue west, towards Ghent and Bruges, then on to the Channel coast. Holland would be occupied by a small force of some three divisions. There would be no assault on the Maginot Line.

This plan was not well received either by Hitler or his senior generals. The Führer said that he would much rather see the main effort concentrated south of Liège in order to achieve the breakthrough to the west. Various meetings followed and in late October 1939 a revised plan was produced. Apart from a limited operation in the Maastricht area, no incursion of Holland was planned. The main thrust was to be made to the north and south of Liège by Army Group B (now increased to 42 divisions), while Army Group A (23 divisions) would attack through the Ardennes, cross the Meuse and then carry on to Rheims and Amiens, thus protecting the flank of Army Group B. Simultaneously, Army group C (20 divisions) would tie down the Maginot Line. With a reserve of 10 divisions, the total needed was 95 divisions.

Again, neither Hitler nor the generals liked the new plan. For example, the failure to invade Holland would allow the Allies to use Dutch airbases while prohibiting their use to the Luftwaffe. Even when this was modified, there still remained objections; in particular, the plan was too limited in its strategic aims. The Commander of Army Group A (General von Rundstedt) and his Chief of Staff (General von Manstein) led the criticism and were strongly supported by a number of panzer commanders, including Guderian. They devised a far more daring plan, in which the main attack would be made through the Ardennes, precisely where the French were confident that no major assault could be made. All the Allied planning was based upon this assumption, so what better place for a surprise attack by a heavily armoured group? After dealing with the scant opposition (as the area was not heavily defended) the panzers would cross the Meuse and head for the Channel coast, below the mouth of the Somme, thus completely cutting off all British and French forces which had been drawn into Belgium to meet the conventional attack which the Allies would be expecting. The OKH, however, who were now busy with the detailed planning for the revised second plan, did not take kindly to this audacious idea.

However, fate was about to play a part in the proceedings. First of all, there was a major breach of security. Two Luftwaffe officers, one of whom (Major Reinberger) had top secret papers relating to 'Fall Gelb' in his briefcase, were flying in bad weather close to the Belgian border, when they had to make a forced landing near Mechelen, not realising that they had strayed into neutral territory. They were placed under arrest, and, in desperation, Reinberger tried to burn the papers, but was only partly successful. The Belgian authorities lost no time in passing the details to the Allied High Command. The Germans were naturally extremely worried by this gaffe, yet in fact it would work to their advantage, because it confirmed the Allies' belief that the main attack would be in the north. The next 'wild card' was the onset of winter which necessitated postponing the assault. This gave time for the revised plan to be tested by the OKH in a series of map exercises, which revealed a number of serious flaws. It also allowed them time to think about Army Group A's 'reckless plan' and the more they examined it the better they liked it. Also at this time Colonel Schmundt, Hitler's chief adjutant, had a long talk with von Manstein (the architect of the plan) at Army Group A, and on his return to Berlin immediately briefed the Führer who showed a keen interest in the new plan. On 17 February 1940 von Manstein, accompanied by some of the newly appointed corps commanders, was given the opportunity of presenting the Army Group A plan to Hitler, who promptly called von Halder and von Brauchitsch to the Chancellery for an emergency meeting the following day. Hitler proceeded to outline the new plan as though it were his idea and was pleasantly surprised to find the generals most receptive! Agreement on all the main points was rapidly reached and, in a mood of fresh confidence, everyone settled down to detailed planning.

**The Final Plan**
The assault had three distinct but connected operations:
  a. The airborne assault and subsequent overrunning of Holland, in order to protect the northern flank of the German armies advancing into Belgium, Luxembourg and France.
  b. The air and land attacks on Belgium with the aim of drawing the Allied armies forward to the Dyle Line[7] positions, and away from the planned German main thrust.
  c. The advance through the Ardennes and Luxembourg by strong armoured forces (Army Group A) to seize bridgeheads across the Meuse in the Sedan area. The main drive for the River Meuse would be led by von Kleist's Panzer Group which spearheaded List's Twelfth Army, with Guderian's corps of three panzer divisions and Reinhardt's corps of two panzer divisions thrusting towards Sedan and Montherme respectively.

**7th Panzer Division's Position in the Assault**
The 5th Panzer Division (Hartlieb) and Rommel's 7th Panzer Division made up XV Panzer Corps (Hoth), which was part of von Kluge's Fourth Army (fourteen divisions in total). They were the most northerly army of von

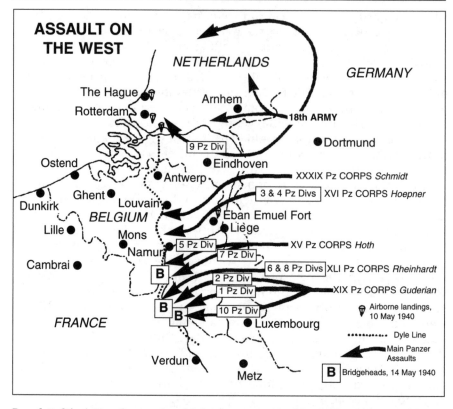

**ASSAULT ON THE WEST**

NETHERLANDS

GERMANY

The Hague

Arnhem

Rotterdam

18th ARMY

9 Pz Div

Dortmund

Ostend

Eindhoven

Antwerp

XXXIX Pz CORPS *Schmidt*

3 & 4 Pz Divs | XVI Pz CORPS *Hoepner*

Ghent

Louvain

Dunkirk

**BELGIUM**

Eban Emuel Fort

Lille

Liège

Mons

5 Pz Div

XV Pz CORPS *Hoth*

Namur

7 Pz Div

Cambrai

6 & 8 Pz Divs | XLI Pz CORPS *Rheinhardt*

**B**

2 Pz Div

1 Pz Div

XIX Pz CORPS *Guderian*

**B** **B**

10 Pz Div

Airborne landings, 10 May 1940

*FRANCE*

Luxembourg

•••••••••• Dyle Line

Main Panzer Assaults

Verdun

Metz

**B** Bridgeheads, 14 May 1940

Rundstedt's Army Group A, which also contained both Twelfth Army (List) and Sixteenth Army (Busch). Hoth's panzer corps was to drive through the northern part of the Ardennes, covering the right flank, aiming to cross the Meuse between Givet and Namur. General Hermann Hoth had already commanded XV Corps in the assault on Poland, being awarded the Knight's Cross of the Iron Cross for his skill and bravery in that campaign.

**Centre Lines.** Each panzer division was allocated a centre line (CL), boundaries and objectives for the various phases of the assault. The 7th Pz Div's CL ran from their concentration area in the Eifel, across the Belgian frontier to St-Vith and Vielsalm, crossing the River Ourthe at Hotton. From Hotton it ran via Marche and Ciney to the River Meuse at Dinant and on in a westerly direction into France, to Arras, via Philippeville, Avesnes and Le Cateau.

## THE CAMPAIGN: PHASE 1
## ACROSS THE MEUSE (9–14 MAY 1940)

### The Assault Begins

During the afternoon of Thursday, 9 May 1940, the signal 'Fall Gelb, 10.5.40, 5.35 Uhr' was sent out to all units involved. They then had to

await the confirmatory code-word 'Danzig'; 'Augsburg' would have signalled a postponement. 'Danzig' was received eventually, but not until
2220 hours (German time). The 7th Panzer Division crossed the frontier at
0530 hours on 10 May, to the east of St-Vith. When they reached St-Vith
they found that three of the four bridges in the town had already been
captured by 'undercover' troops. Now it was a question of moving the vast
mass of wheeled and tracked vehicles, on through the densely wooded
area, along twisting, narrow roads, with defiles, steep hills and many natural and artificial obstacles. The roads and forest tracks had been barri-
caded by Belgian Army troops of the *Chasseurs Ardennais*, and deep craters
had been blown in many of the main roads. But as they were mostly left
undefended, there were few places that held up the panzers for long –
Rommel comments that some could be bypassed by moving across country or on side-roads, but where this was impossible his pioneers quickly set
to work to clear them. There was some opposition from both the *Chasseurs
Ardennais* and French mechanised forces, but this was quickly overrun and
by the middle of Day 2 they had reached Hotton and crossed the River
Ourthe. Twenty-four hours later they were west of Ciney and Leignon and
by the afternoon of 12 May 7th Pz Div's leading elements had reached the
Meuse. As Rommel's division was making faster progress than 5th Pz Div
on their immediate right, the corps commander, General Hoth, decided to
attach Colonel Werner's Panzer Regiment 31 – which was some way ahead
of the rest of that division – to 7th Pz Div.[8] Rommel had hoped to
'bounce' a crossing over the Meuse, but the French blew the bridges before
this could be effected. For example, at Dinant the bridge was blown at
1620 hours just as Rothenburg's leading tanks arrived. The railway bridge
at Houx was blown earlier, at 1445 hours, and the road bridge at Yvoir
went at 1630 hours, just as Werner's leading elements reached there. However, between the two panzer regiments, men of Major von Steinkeller's
motorcycle battalion had reached the village of Houx, where there was an
island in the river. Stealthily they made their way to the island via a weir,
found it unoccupied and pushed on across to the west bank via a closed
lock gate. Rommel now had men across the river and had soon reinforced
them with several rifle platoons from Schützen Brigade 7. Once the enemy
realised what had happened they began to shell the position heavily, so
further reinforcement or evacuation of casualties was impossible.

Rommel himself, accompanied by Captain Schräpler, reached
Dinant at about 0400 hours on the 13th. He had already deployed his
artillery into good covering positions, with artillery forward observation officers (FOOs) down with the leading troops at the potential crossing sites. He
found that further attempts to cross in rubber boats were being thwarted by
heavy enemy fire, and anti-tank guns had started knocking out his tanks on
the eastern bank. He ordered some houses set on fire to try to mask the crossing attempts with smoke, but soon appreciated that a crossing at Dinant
would be impossible for the moment. Returning to his headquarters, he
found both Hoth and the Army Commander (von Kluge) there, gave them
an up-to-date briefing, discussed the situation with his Ia, Major Heidkämper,

then drove back to the river and continued northwards. His command vehicle was engaged both by enemy and friendly fire (he was bombed!) and eventually he had to make his way forward on foot. Schräpler was wounded in the arm on their way to the Leffe weir, where Rommel had ordered some tanks and guns to meet him. The footbridge had been barred by the enemy, so they moved further north to the crossing point, where he: 'took personal command of 2nd Bn, Rifle Regt 7' and, ordering the tanks to keep up continuous fire across the river, started to get men across in rubber boats – himself and his aide, Lieutenant Most, crossing in one of the first boats. Undoubtedly Rommel's presence and positive action changed the entire situation, and despite strong enemy pressure they were able to maintain and improve their bridgehead.

Rommel then recrossed the river and drove north to the Schützen Regt 6 area, where some anti-tank guns had been ferried across to strengthen the bridgehead and bridge-building had started under heavy enemy fire. It was here that Rommel is reputed to have jumped into the river to help the sappers – he had called for a bridge of 16 tons capacity so that he could get all the tanks across. Rommel's 8-wheeled armoured signal vehicle crossed with the leading tanks, but Rommel did not remain in one place for long, he

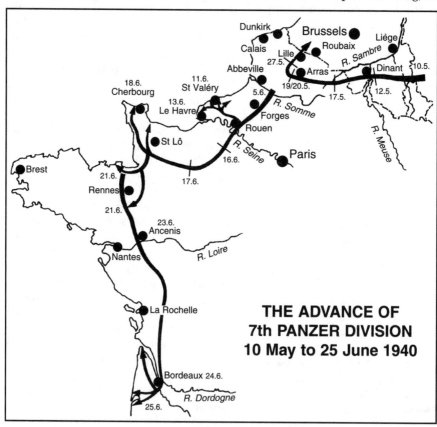

**THE ADVANCE OF
7th PANZER DIVISION
10 May to 25 June 1940**

spent the rest of the night ferrying tanks across while the bridge was being completed and generally organising everything and everyone. But the river was 120 yards wide and the ferrying was slow; by dawn there were only fifteen tanks on the west bank. In the early hours French counter-attacks began but were repulsed, and the bridge was completed by dawn. Rommel then received a message that Colonel von Bismarck's Schützen Regiment 7 was surrounded at Onhaye, three miles west of Dinant, and immediately decided to go to his assistance with all available armour. It was in the Onhaye area, during the ensuing battle, that Rommel, who had got into one of Rothenburg's tanks, was wounded in the face by a shell splinter, when the tank was hit twice and slithered down a steep slope whilst taking evasive action. The fighting continued with casualties on both sides – at one time Rommel thought that Rothenburg's tank had 'brewed up', and Rommel's armoured signals vehicle (commanded by Lieutenant Most) which had taken cover in a nearby wood, was hit in the engine and immobilised. Slowly the Germans gained the upper hand and by evening had secured their bridgehead and were preparing for the drive westwards the following day.

Rommel's successful bridgehead across the Meuse was the first of three German crossings, the other two being achieved by Rheinhardt's corps (just a narrow foothold which they had to fight to maintain) and by Guderian's corps (only one really susbstantial foothold, with a bridge completed by first light on the 14th). The result of this German pressure was to persuade the French Ninth Army commander, General Corap, to make the fatal decision to withdraw completely from the river line to his next main defence line. This led to a 60-mile gap being created in the Allied front, a situation which the panzers were quick to seize upon in their subsequent drive westwards. This defensive line, as far as the area opposite 7th Pz Div was concerned, ran along the line of the railway to the east of Philippeville, fifteen miles west of the Meuse.

## THE CAMPAIGN: PHASE 2
## BREAKTHROUGH FROM THE MEUSE (15–19 MAY 1940)

'My intention for 15 May', Rommel wrote later, 'was to thrust straight through in one stride to our objective, with 25th Panzer Regiment in the lead and with artillery and, if possible, dive-bomber support.' These were typical *Blitzkrieg* tactics, with the infantry following up the tank attack in their vehicles, but dismounting to fight. Rommel was anxious about his flanks because he was some way ahead of the flanking divisions, so he decided to curtain them off with artillery fire. His objective was the district around Cerfontaine, which was some eight miles on from Philippeville. Cerfontaine is a few miles from the Belgian–French border, behind which was part of the Maginot Line extension – only a shallow belt of pillboxes and anti-tank obstacles, but Rommel did not know how weak it was. He had decided to advance with the leading elements of Pz Regt 25 so that he could direct the attack in detail, but before leaving the divisional CP he agreed on various methods of simplifying radio transmissions, to cut down time and make encoding easier. First he agreed the main thrust line (running from the church at Rosée a few miles west of Onhaye, to the church at Froidchapelle four miles west of Cerfontaine) with his Ia (Heidkämper) and his Arfu (Frolich), which was then marked on all maps, with numbered targets all the way along it. If fire were needed anywhere, Rommel could merely call for it over the radio, referring to the target number – everyone was happy and the system worked well. At 0900 hours on the 15th, Rommel met a Luftwaffe ground liaison officer (GLO), who told him that Stukas had been allocated to support his division and, as Rothenburg's panzers had already begun to move forward, Rommel asked for them to go into action immediately in front of the advancing armour.

The Junkers Ju–87 dive-bomber was a deceptively clumsy-looking aircraft, with a crew of two men, who, after training at the Dive-Bomber School, could guarantee to get at least 50 per cent of their bombs within a 25m radius of the target. They would normally fly in threes in 'Vee' formation at about 15,000 feet and at about 150mph. Major attacks might be supported by an entire Gruppe of 30 bombers, protected by fighters. As they approached the target the fighters split, some going down to 3,000 feet so as to be able to protect the Stukas as they pulled out of their dive. Before beginning his dive the pilot switched on his reflector sight, trimmed his aircraft, set the pull-out altitude on his contact altimeter (an automatic device which would ensure a proper pull-out even if the pilot blacked out), closed the radiator flaps, throttled back the engine and opened the ventilation air supply to the windscreen to prevent it misting up when the aircraft entered the moist lower air. Finally the pilot switched on the 'Screamer' (a morale-shattering siren) and opened the dive brakes. Undoubtedly the dive-bombers were most effective in the early campaigns, but suffered heavy casualties in the Battle of Britain and had to be withdrawn, being used thereafter only where the Germans had total air superiority.

Rommel left the CP with his Gefechtsstaffel, to join Pz Regt 25, near Onhaye, getting into Rothenburg's tank on arrival and instructing Lieutenant Most to follow on as usual from bound to bound, with the vehicles (including the armoured car and the signals vehicle). They moved off and the first enemy contact came at Flavion, with a short engagement with some French heavy tanks – Char B1 bis of 1re DCR – which should have been able to deal effectively with the panzers, being far more heavily armoured (max 60mm) and mounting both a 75mm howitzer and a 47mm gun. Brushing the enemy aside the panzers pressed on, engaging in a favourite Rommel tactic (also favoured by General George S. Patton, Jr) of firing on the move at likely targets as the column moved through the woods to Philippeville. This 'prophylactic' fire caused the enemy to 'tumble out of the woods' as Rommel puts it, all thoroughly unnerved after being repeatedly dive-bombed. Everything worked perfectly and the Germans were soon on their objective. Enemy soldiers had started to surrender in large numbers, even considerable numbers of tanks – fifteen in one group alone, mostly undamaged. Rommel endeavoured to keep his units free from having to look after masses of prisoners, simply ordering them to give up their arms and then to march eastwards along the divisional centre line. At one stage he returned eastwards with one of Rothenburg's tank companies to re-establish contact with the following-up infantry and had some difficulty in extracting them from the hordes of enemy troops trying to surrender. A few French soldiers escaped to the south, and at one stage Rommel drove south to Neuville to cut off the French retreat in that direction. But in the main the enemy troops were totally bewildered by the speed and shock action of his advance, and only too happy to surrender – some of the officers from Philippeville being far more worried about keeping their batmen and saving their kit than actually fighting!

## STUKA ATTACK

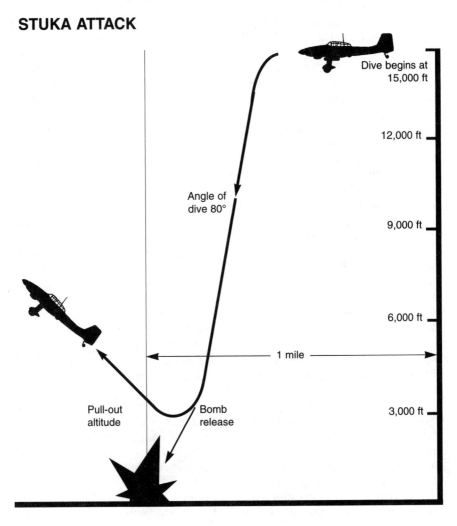

Dive begins at 15,000 ft

12,000 ft

Angle of dive 80°

9,000 ft

6,000 ft

1 mile

Pull-out altitude

Bomb release

3,000 ft

The 7th Panzer Division pressed on westwards from Philippeville, averaging an amazing 40kmph, brushing aside the enemy who, everywhere, appeared to be completely mesmerised by their speed of advance. Near Senzeille (four miles west of Philippeville) for example, they met a complete unit of French motorcycle troops who were so stunned to see them that they promptly drove their motorcycles into the ditch and surrendered *en masse*. The chaos reflected the complete breakdown of the French command system, based as it was on linear defence and thus unable to deal with the Schwerpunkt of 'lightning war'.

On the 16th Rommel was eager to move on as quickly as possible and tackle the Maginot Line defences, but was told to stay at his CP to meet the Army Commander (von Kluge) later that morning. Hoth finally gave him permission to advance at about 0930 hours, but when von Kluge arrived he seemed surprised about the delay – so even the German command structure did have its communications problems! Nevertheless, once Rommel had explained his plan all was approved by Kluge and the race was on once more. Rommel's intention was first to cross the frontier at Sivry, reconnoitre the Maginot Line positions on a wide front, while massing his artillery around Sivry. Panzer Regt 25 would then advance on the fortifications in extended line, under heavy artillery covering fire, then hammer the enemy positions with direct tank gunfire. Finally the Schützen Brigade, with tank support, would assault and take the fortifications. Only when this had been achieved would they continue the breakthrough to Avesnes, twelve miles west of Sivry. For Rommel, this has to be a fairly careful, methodical assault, unlike the speed and élan with which he had swept the division across the Meuse. But he wanted to be sure that his attack would succeed and clearly did not know how hard it would be to tackle the supposedly impregnable Maginot Line. In fact, the Line proper ended at Longuyon and these later westwards extensions were by no means as strong, having been hastily and imperfectly constructed the previous winter. For the attack Rommel, as always, was at the front, riding in Rothenburg's command tank. His second aide, the ambitious Nazi, Lieutenant Hanke, was following in a PzKpfw IV. Having crossed the border, they were heading for Clairfayts when they heard from their recce elements in front that the road was mined, so they were forced to detour. 'Suddenly', writes Rommel, 'we saw the angular lines of a French fortification about 100 yards ahead.' They had reached the Maginot Line. Nearby were a number of fully armed French soldiers who made as if they wished to surrender, but when firing began in an another area, got back into their bunkers and started shooting. Rommel, who had an excellent view of the battle, describes graphically how, under covering fire from tanks and artillery, his infantry and engineers pushed forward into the fortified area. Men of the panzer engineer company crawled up to the concrete pill-boxes and threw 6lb demolition charges in through the firing slits. Eventually, as evening approached, the pill-boxes were captured and a way through to the west was cleared.

It was a moonlit night and Rommel ordered the advance to continue with all speed towards Avesnes. His 'prophylactic fire' stratagem was to be continued and would prove its effectiveness time and time again, the tanks simply bursting through any organised resistance with all guns blazing, then moving on as quickly as possible, leaving the bewildered and disorganised enemy wondering what had hit them! Rommel had tried to get permission from corps to advance to Landrecies, some eleven miles west of Avesnes, but communications were poor and he could not get through, so he decided on his own initiative to let the panzer regiment have its head and to follow it up with the rest of the division as quickly as possible. This time the aim would be to capture the crossing over the Sambre at Landrecies. Dawn was breaking as they finally smashed their way through at Avesnes, where some determined French tanks had been holding them up. In fact, it was Lieutenant Hanke in his PzKpfw IV who eventually won the day. The leading battalion then moved off, with Rommel at its head, followed by the rest of Rothenburg's regiment, with the motorcycle battalion close behind. No resupply had been possible during the night, so they had to be sparing with ammunition stocks – so no prophylactic fire this time. The roads were clogged with refugees and enemy troops, guns and vehicles of all types. Rommel comments that his troops' shouts of: '*A droite!*' did not always have the desired effect. When they eventually reached Landrecies they found a vast crush of men and vehicles in the narrow streets, but no resistance. The German tanks rolled safely over the bridge to the western bank, where they found a French barracks full of troops. As the column of tanks rumbled past its gates, Hanke drove on to the parade ground and ordered the troops to be fallen in and then to march eastwards. Rommel pressed on towards Le Cateau, eight miles west of Landrecies, reaching the hills outside the town at 0615 hours on the 17th, having driven nearly fifty miles since the previous morning. They were now well in front of the other panzer divisions on their flanks.

Rommel – none too pleased to discover that all he had at the front, overlooking Le Cateau, was a small part of the panzer regiment and the motorcycle battalion, the rest being held up behind them by the chaos on the roads – realised that his division was too strung out to take on any determined enemy resistance. So he set off eastwards, to try to link up with the rest of the column. He had a hair-raising trip, finding several stranded vehicles, driving at high speed through Landrecies after being told that there was danger there from enemy tanks/anti-tank guns, losing his escort tank through mechanical breakdown, endlessly trying to clear the route and to get the bewildered French troops moving eastwards. If there was a German vehicle with them, they were happy to march as prisoners, but when left to their own devices they merely bivouacked at the roadside and waited to be told what to do next. Eventually Rommel reached Avesnes, where his divisional HQ staff began to arrive at about 1600 hours, followed by unit after unit during the night and early the next morning. The number of prisoners also increased (an estimate of those taken by the division during the 2-days' breakthrough of the Maginot Line being more than 10,000 men with 100 tanks, 30 armoured cars and 27 guns, this figure being qualified by the statement that the division: '... had no time to collect large numbers of prisoners or equipment'!), One artillery battalion alone captured 48 French tanks, just as they were about to launch an attack on the rear of 25 Pz Regt. After arranging the layout of his division between Sivry and Le Cateau, Rommel took just 1½ hours' rest. Then, shortly before midnight, orders were received to continue the attack towards Cambrai on the 18th.

Before the advance could continue however, a more pressing matter had to be addressed. At about 0700 hours, Rothenburg's adjutant arrived at the CP and reported that a large enemy force was now located in Pommereuille Wood, midway between Landrecies and Le Cateau. He had managed to get through in an armoured car, and the regiment was holding its position, but was now cut off and in urgent need of fuel and ammunition. Rommel immediately dispatched the remaining tank battalion, with the re-supply vehicles; 37 Armoured Reconnaissance Battalion would follow on behind. By the time he (accompanied by both Most and Hanke) caught up with the panzer battalion they were heavily involved with the enemy tanks, which were superior in both firepower and armament. Flanking manoeuvres initially met with little success until Rommel personally took the tank battalion on a wide southern sweep through the woods via Ors, some four miles south-west of Landrecies and, after more heavy fighting, managed to link up with Rothenburg. The resupply vehicles did not follow them around the Ors route, so were held up for several more hours, which meant that the panzer regiment was still incapable of movement, lacking both fuel and ammunition. Eventually, as soon as the situation had improved, Rommel ordered the regiment to form up for their attack on Cambrai (fifteen miles further on from Le Cateau), to commence at 1500 hours.

## THE CAMPAIGN: PHASE 3
## SUCCESS AT CAMBRAI, REVERSES AT ARRAS (19–21 MAY 1940)

Rommel now gave orders for the panzer battalion he had brought up to continue on to Cambrai, while 1st Battalion of Schützen Regiment 6, commanded by Major von Paris, which had been reinforced with tanks and two troops of AA guns, was ordered to secure the roads leading from Cambrai to the north and north-east as quickly as possible. 'Bataillon Paris', as it was called, advanced on a broad front and in depth, across the fields to the north-west of Cambrai, all the vehicles throwing up great clouds of dust, while the tanks and guns fired intermittently at the town. The result was that the enemy thought they were facing a massive tank attack – the soft-skinned troop carriers throwing up so much dust that the enemy thought they were all AFVs and consequently offered no resistance! Cambrai was taken easily and the bulk of the division was able to rest and re-organise while Rommel planned the next phase, which was to advance on the evening of the 19th, his objective being the high ground south-east of Arras. While he was discussing the plan with his staff, General Hoth arrived and ordered a halt to proceedings, on the grounds that the troops were now too exhausted to continue. Rommel did not agree – and said so! He argued that most of his forces had been 'resting' for the past twenty hours, so were perfectly able to continue, and a moonlight night attack would lessen the risk of casualties. Hoth gave in and, at 0140 hours on the 20th the attack began, Rommel, as always, accompanying the leading tanks. By 0600 hours they had reached Beaurains, some 2½ miles south of Arras, but things were not all going according to plan. The infantry had not followed up the tanks, and at about 0300 hours Rommel – impatient as always – had gone back in his armoured car to see what was holding them up. To his chagrin he discovered that the French had infiltrated his lines of advance and for a while the whole plan was in jeopardy, until the arrival of an infantry regiment plus some artillery, which took up position just south of Arras. There were rumours of some enemy divisions, both British and French, concentrating in the Arras area, but having dealt with the enemy infiltration, Rommel pressed on.

On the 21st, Rommel had planned to advance around the town towards the north-west, leading with his tanks as always, with his infantry behind in depth. But despite the fact that his left flank was covered by the SS 'Death's Head' (Totenkopf) Division and 5 Pz Div was advancing to the east of Arras, he decided to cover his exposed flank with artillery and put his armoured reconnaissance battalion between the tanks and infantry, to maintain communications and keep the routes open. Subsequent events would prove this action eminently sensible. As always, Rommel and his Gefechtsstaffel, were accompanying the tanks, but he once again became exasperated with the apparently slow movement of the follow-up infantry, so returned in his armoured car to find out what was holding them up. He located some of his Schützen battalions and proceeded to lead them northwards to link up with the armour, which had now reached Wailly to the south-west of Arras. There they came under fire from enemy tanks which were advancing from Berneville and Bac du Nord (in the north-west, across the railway line). There was some confusion as the infantry went to ground, while Rommel desperately sought to establish a screen of anti-tank guns, which eventually halted the enemy attack. The tanks were the heavily armoured British Matilda Mks I and II and a fierce battle ensued before they could be stopped, most of the German anti-tank guns being unable to penetrate their thick armour. The gun which finally did the damage was the 88mm, soon to become a legend in its own right and the scourge of Allied tank commanders. But although they destroyed seven Matildas, Panzer Regiment 25 lost at least six PzKpfw 38(t) and three PzKpfw IV, plus some PzKpfw I and II, the total estimate being about 30 tanks of all types. According to a note in *The Rommel Papers*, the official history of the division gives the casualties as 89 killed, 116 wounded and 173 missing – four times those suffered in the breakthrough into France, so it was a nasty shock to Rommel, quite his worst experience to date. To make matters worse, the dead included his brave ADC, Joachim Most, who was killed at his side, promoted posthumously to captain and now buried in the German military cemetery at Bourdon.

The enemy which had given 7th Pz Div this 'bloody nose' were a mixed force of British tanks and infantry, comprising 4th and 7th Battalions of the Royal Tank Regiment (1st Army Tank Brigade) and 6th, 8th and 9th Battalions of the Durham Light Infantry (151 Infantry Brigade), together with some artillery, anti-tank guns and machine-guns. All were battle-weary, the tanks, for example, having driven some 120 miles on their tracks over the past five days, losing about 25 per cent of their strength from breakdowns. The counter-attack was a hastily planned affair, the force advancing in two columns, each roughly consisting of a tank battalion and an infantry battalion, plus supporting arms, about three miles apart. Their mission was to advance from Arras southwards, to cut off Rommel's pene-tration. They suffered from a complete lack of air support, had little artillery support, no infantry/tank radio communications, they had never operated together before meeting in the concentration area and worst of all, had left in such a hurry that proper orders had never been passed down to individ-ual tank commanders. Despite all this, the counter-attack was, at the start, amazingly successful, not just because of the tank casualties inflicted, but because news of the counter-attack caused both Rommel and his higher headquarters enormously to overestimate the strength of the enemy, which sent shock-waves all the way back to Hitler. Some historians are in fact cer-tain that it was this that prompted the Führer to give his famous halt order in front of Dunkirk. Von Rundstedt later wrote: 'A critical moment came just as my forces reached the Channel. It was caused by a British counter-stroke southwards from Arras on 21 May. For a short time it was feared that the panzer divisions would be cut off before the infantry divisions could come up to support them. None of the French counter-attacks carried the threat of this one.'[9]

## THE CAMPAIGN: PHASE 4
## STOPS AND STARTS ON THE WAY TO LILLE (22 MAY–2 JUNE 1940)

Seventh Panzer Division's advance on the 22nd was somewhat slower than before the Arras battle, but at about 1415 hours, they crossed the River Sharpe and captured Mont-St-Eloi only to have it snatched back by the French 4th Dragoon Regiment. Fifth Panzer Division finally took back the small town on the 23rd, while Rommel pushed on to Hersin, then reached Cuinchy on the la Bassée Canal at dawn on the 24th. It was at this time that Hitler's order not to cross the Aa Canal line was received, so 7th Pz Div halted at Cuinchy, where Rommel continued a letter he had started to Lucie on the 23rd: 'Dearest Lu, With a few hours sleep behind me, it's time for a line to you. I'm fine in every way. My division has had blazing success. Dinant, Philippeville, breakthrough the Maginot Line and advance in one night 40 miles through France to Le Cateau, then Cambrai, Arras, always far in front of everybody else. Now the hunt is up against 60 encircled British, French and Belgian divisions. Don't worry about me. As I see it the war in France may be over in a fortnight.' He added more to his letter on the 24th, saying that they were now in front of Béthune, then added a final postscript on the 26th in which he mentions the enforced halt, commenting that a day or two without action had done everyone a lot of good. He also listed the division's casualties to date as being 60 officers and 1,500 men killed and wounded (about 12 per cent of the total divisional strength). He mentions Schräpler's return, Most's death, closing on a more optimistic note that the likelihood of any further hard fighting was remote – but perhaps this was as much to calm Lucie's fears as anything else. On the afternoon of 26 May, Lieutenant Hanke, on behalf of the Führer and acting on his personal orders, decorated Rommel with the Knight's Cross of the Iron Cross.[10]

The advance was resumed on the evening of the 26th, Schützen Regt 7 pushing troops across the canal and widening the bridgehead near Cuinchy until elements of both battalions had crossed to the northern bank. Rommel crossed early next day, dodging sniper fire in the process. The engineers had built pontoons and were constructing an 8-ton bridge, but Rommel ordered a 16-ton bridge to be built by 635th Engineer Battalion, which had just been placed under his command. He also personally directed fire from 20mm AA guns, then a PzKpfw IV, at the troublesome snipers, destroying all the houses from 300–600 yards west of the bridgehead and sweeping all the scrub with fire. Once this had been done, he gave fresh orders to the PzKpfw IV to engage opportunity targets, including enemy tanks, while he moved supporting weapons, including 88mm guns and tanks across. At this time, Pz Bde 5, belonging to the neighbouring 5th Pz Div, was also placed under his command. Rommel was impressed by the large numbers of 'spick and span' tanks they possessed, commenting that they had a far larger tank strength than his division! Rommel personally briefed the brigade commander, General Haarde, but once the attack towards the outskirts of Lille began he appears to have had great difficulty in maintaining radio communications with him. Because of the staggering results which 7th Pz Div achieved, one is inclined to think that every facet of the operation, such as radio communications between their AFVs especially the tanks, were far better than those of the Allies, when this was patently not the case. Radio communications were poor on numerous occasions, hence Rommel's need to be right up in the battle area, so that he could physically impose his will on the proceedings. However, the lack of fully cross-country vehicles in his Gefechtsstaffel constantly made his job difficult.

Despite these problems Rommel pressed on with his breakout from the bridgehead, with Pz Regt 25 smashing its way through the enemy in the neighbourhood of Lorgies. Then the rest of the division, plus Pz Bde 5, was able to debouch and advance on a broader front. Rommel himself was soon speeding forward, joining up with Rothenburg's command vehicle on the road to Lille, from where they moved swiftly towards Lomme, on the outskirts of the city, isolating the French garrison and thwarting all their attempts to break out. Rommel did not go in with Pz Regt 25's final assault, preferring to hold himself available so as to be able to reinforce or resupply the panzer regiment should it again be cut off as at Le Cateau. He brought up the rest of his troops and put them into flanking positions, effectively sealing off the western exits from the city. Fierce fighting continued as the French forces (nearly half their First Army) desperately tried to break out.

There were casualties on both sides, including Major Erdmann, CO of the 37th Reconnaissance Battalion, who was killed in a friendly fire accident, the shells coming from a 150mm artillery battery of a neighbouring division. By the 29th the worst of the fighting was over and on 31 May Lille was surrendered. The 7th Pz Div was at rest from the 29th until 2 June, when Adolf Hitler visited the front and chose not only personally to congratulate Rommel, but also to allow him to accompany his Führer for the entire day – the only divisional commander to do so. This was partly due to the fact that Rommel had sent him a full report of his division's exploits, but also because of the genuine regard felt by both men for each other. 'We were all very worried about you,' Hitler had remarked during his visit, referring to the thrusting exploits of the Gespensterdivision (Ghost Division), as 7th Panzer had been named by commentators both friendly and hostile, '... a formation so elusive, so hard to pin down whether by an enemy or on staff maps, so unpredictable'.[11]

## THE CAMPAIGN: PHASE 4 (continued)
## THE SOMME AND ON TO THE SEINE (3–10 JUNE 1940)

On the 3rd, Seventh Panzer Division made all the necessary preparations to begin advancing again, this time towards the Somme. They started on the 4th, Rommel writing to his wife that the six days' rest had done everyone a lot of good and enabled them to get their equipment more or less back into good shape. There had also been some major regrouping of German forces, brought about by the fact that the evacuation of most of the British forces from Dunkirk between 28 May and 4 June,[12] had seen a virtual end to the fighting north of the main German penetration. Hoth's corps was now part of von Bock's Army Group B which was deployed along the Somme on the right of the German forces, 7th Pz Div being the extreme right-hand division. The intended crossing area was between Longpré and Hangest, where the ground was both flat and marshy. Two railway lines crossed both the canalised river and the main Longpré–Hangest road in the area, snaking between the two along raised embankments on the water meadows. Had the French blown all or some of the bridges as they had done on both flanks, the Germans would never have got across. However, they did not do so before Rommel's troops arrived, who were then able to prevent demolition being attempted by putting down continuous artillery and machine-gun fire. The Division then 'bounced' a crossing over all four railway bridges in the early hours of 5 June – a remarkable feat. The combat engineers swiftly converted them to take road vehicles and, as one might have expected, the first to cross was Rommel's armoured command vehicle! Hangest took some hours to clear because the Senegalese infantry who were holding it fought bravely, but it was eventually taken by the motorcycle battalion at about noon. This allowed the armour to debouch and advance at speed across the flat going towards Quesnoy-sur-Airaines. This time Rommel rode at the rear of the tank column in his command vehicle and managed to maintain good radio communications with everyone, including Heidkämper. On reaching Quesnoy, they found the village defended by more Senegalese infantry, who again fought stubbornly, especially within the walls of the château. However, some sustained direct fire from the guns of the PzKpfw IVs, soon penetrated their defences.

Having got around the village, they found themselves faced by a wide plain, covered with fields of tall-standing corn. The panzers swept on, wiping out any enemy who stood and fought, or forcing others to withdraw. Most of the time they were under bombardment by enemy artillery, and the French colonial infantry division fought bravely, so the advance was a slow one. As they approached Montagne-le-Fayel, some eight miles west of the Somme, a corps order was received forbidding any forward movement past Montagne because of fears of being dive-bombed by their own Stukas. Rommel ordered everyone to halt and dig in. There were strong enemy forces in front, especially on the right flank, including some enemy tanks, but the 88mm anti-tank guns and the panzers soon disposed of these threats.

The advance resumed at 1000 hours on 6 June, Rommel having given orders for a Flächenmarsch ('area march'), a manoeuvre for crossing open country which the division had practised prior to the assault on France. The division formed up in a rectangle some 2,000 yards broad and with a depth of about 21,000 yards, with orders to avoid possible enemy strongpoints – such as villages, woods, etc., and to keep away from main roads. Panzer battalions would be at the front and on the flanks, the wheeled vehicles would be inside the rectangle. Tank guns would be traversed accordingly and 'prophylactic fire' on the move, would be aimed at suspected enemy positions. Despite some inevitable dispersal, all elements of the division were thus reasonably close together and could rapidly swing into an attack in any direction. Using this method of advance Rommel moved his division some twenty miles during 6 and 7 June, so that by 1730 hours on the 7th the entire division was in the area of Menerval, about forty-five miles west of the Somme, and his reconnaissance elements had reached the River Andrelle and cut the Paris–Dieppe road near Saumont. Rommel celebrated Lucie's birthday (6 June), writing on the 7th that it had been: '... a thoroughly successful day. We laid about us properly ... We're all very, very well. Slept like a top.' Along the Andelle they were held up by a scratch force comprised of some British lines of communications troops, with no artillery and only a few anti-tank guns, but supported by about 90 tanks of the British 1st Armoured Division, which had been refitting to the rear. They did not prove to be much of an obstacle to Rommel's forces who crossed the Andelle at Sigy on 8 June via a ford, then found an unblown bridge close by at Normanville. Rommel was now poised to take on Rouen, but was given new orders by Hoth and it was 5th Pz Div who took the city on the 10th, while 7th Pz Div was ordered to turn away from the Seine and to advance northwards instead, towards St-Valéry and Le Havre to cut off British and French forces, who were making for these ports. Rommel went off 'hell for leather' around the north of Rouen, reaching Barentin at 0730 hours on the 10th, giving orders over the radio for the rest of the division to join up with him. It was all somewhat chaotic, with reports of strong enemy formations being received from higher command, which never actually materialised. Clearly the Allied troops were making a desperate bid to reach the ports and the Germans were determined to prevent them.

## THE CAMPAIGN: PHASE 5
## ST-VALERY-EN-CAUX AND AFTER (10–15 JUNE 1940)

Rommel's orders to his reconnaissance battalion were simple: to make for Yvetot, some twelve miles to the north, then reconnoitre towards the coast as rapidly as possible. As the division advanced on this new axis, enemy forces were moving parallel with the same intention. But they were anxious to escape, not to stand and fight, so despite the constant sightings and reports of considerable enemy forces Rommel just kept pressing on all out for the sea, at an average speed of 25–40mph. Rommel and his signal section reached the coast at les Petites Dalles, ten miles east of Fécamp, the sight of the sea thrilling everyone. They got out of the vehicles, and walked down to the beach to the water's edge – several dispatch riders went in up to their knees, while Rothenburg drove his command tank through the beach wall and down to the water. As soon as he had sufficient strength, Rommel decided to push on to Fécamp, then to turn back east in order to take possession of the port of St-Valéry as quickly as possible. It was by now 2300 hours, quite dark, fairly chaotic on the roads with traffic jams and refugees. Rommel was just behind three of his tanks, when they were engaged by an enemy anti-tank gun which damaged the track of the leading tank, bringing it to a halt, while the other two drove up the embankment at the side of the road. This left Rommel's command vehicle in the direct line of fire at a range of only some 150 yards! As none of the tanks opened return fire, Rommel got out and ran over to the embankment to the nearest tank (a PzKpfw II), where he found the commander of the leading tank. After telling him exactly what he thought of him for not opening fire and for leaving his tank, Rommel ordered the PzKpfw II to engage with both its 20mm and machine-gun. The resulting 'fireworks' caused the enemy to cease firing. But the road was still blocked by the knocked-out tank and only the command vehicle could manage the embankment, so the rest (staff car, armoured cars and dispatch riders) all had to go back to spend the night with the motorcycle battalion, while Rommel drove off alone with the panzer company.

The division left Veulettes about 1200 hours and advanced along the coast to St-Valéry. Rommel took his Gefechtsstaffel and accompanied Panzer Regiment 25. But as soon as they got on to the hills only a mile or so from Veulettes, they came under heavy artillery fire. They were able to get some tanks forward, but resistance was strong. Nevertheless, by the afternoon, the panzer regiment had managed to get tanks on to the high ground overlooking the port, thus preventing troops from embarking. Rommel sent an envoy under a flag of truce to invite the garrison to surrender, but this was refused. Heavy fire was maintained on St-Valéry all that night, and next day, after more heavy fighting, some of the tanks managed to penetrate the town, with Rommel, first in his command vehicle and then on foot, accompanying them. The town hall and many other buildings were on fire as Rommel and the leading tanks, managed to reach the harbour and persuade the enemy to surrender. General Ihler, who had commanded the French IX Corps, was taken prisoner on the east side of the town and came to see Rommel, explaining that he was only surrendering because he had no ammunition left. He told them that there were five divisions involved, including one British. Subsequently no less than twelve generals were brought in as prisoners, including Major-General Victor Fortune, GOC 51st Highland Division and his entire staff. Although it was difficult to estimate the full extent of the prisoners taken, the estimate was some 46,000, which included at least 8,000 British.

There followed another short period of rest for the Ghost Division, from the 13th to the 16th, during which time they moved down behind the leading German troops, south of Rouen. The Germans were preparing to exploit to the Loire, but had also to clear the Cherbourg peninsula, because it was there that the remaining British forces, including reinforcements from UK and whatever French divisions were still in one piece, would supposedly make a last-ditch stand. This odd plan, dreamed up by the British War Cabinet, was to be put into effect by General Alan Brooke, ex-commander of II Corps, who had been evacuated from Dunkirk, then sent back to Cherbourg, arriving there on the 13th. Fortunately the French vetoed the plan as being 'absurd', despite the fact that unconditional surrender appeared the only alternative. Brooke reckoned that he needed at least fifteen divisions to hold 'Fortress Brittany', but was told he had to make do with what he had (i.e., elements of 52nd Infantry Division, which had already begun to land at Cherbourg, together with the promise of a Canadian division to follow). The eminently sensible General Brooke fortunately had other ideas and managed to speak by telephone to both the CIGS and Winston Churchill, and more importantly, to convince them that the idea was crazy. What was needed was a speedy evacuation from Cherbourg and St-Nazaire. Brooke left St-Nazaire on 18 June, and the last British ship departed from Cherbourg at 1600 hours the same day – by which time German artillery was already bombarding the port.

## THE CAMPAIGN: PHASE 6
## THE END AT CHERBOURG, THEN ON TO BORDEAUX (17–25 JUNE 1940)

Air reconnaissance reported the presence of warships and transports at Cherbourg, and 7th Pz Div was sent off at high speed south-westwards from the Seine on the 17th, having been reinforced by Brigade Senger – a motorised brigade commanded by General Fridolin von Senger und Etterlin – to capture the port and prevent any embarkation taking place. They advanced in two columns, neither of which met any serious opposition, Rommel being with the left-hand column. They covered 150 miles during the first day and night, pressing on all the time, ordering the masses of French troops including artillery and anti-tank guns, which they passed en route to lay down their arms and surrender. Most were very disconcerted but did as they were bid. At one point they overtook convoys of brand-new American-built vehicles, then, near Montreuil at about 1730 hours, they stopped for an hour's rest, a meal and most importantly, to refuel. Cherbourg was still more than 130 miles away, and although the right-hand column had met some enemy resistance just before the halt, Rommel decided to push on through the night, sticking to the main road via Flers, Coutances and Barneville, in a single column. They reached Barneville without any major incidents, then pushed on towards Cherbourg. Approaching the port, they came under shell and machine-gun fire from troops of the covering forces which the French had deployed to protect the port while the evacuation was in progress. This enemy fire continued despite the fact that many other French troops in the area had white flags and were trying to surrender. Rommel sent an ultimatum to the port that unless they surrendered by 0800 hours on the 18th, he would attack. The covering force withdrew and the German forces were able to advance again, until they came under fire from some of the forts which ringed the port. It was decided to wait until the 19th before launching any major assault, as this would give time for everyone to catch up, so that Rommel would have all the necessary armour, artillery and infantry, to launch a properly co-ordinated attack.

The following morning Rommel, who had spent the night in the unaccustomed luxury of the Château de Sotteville (the ex-residence of the port commandant), went out to join his forward troops, who had infiltrated into the western outskirts of Cherbourg, and personally assisted in directing fire on to any forts that were still firing. However, hostilities were not going to last for long. Rommel managed to get a message to the French commander saying that, unless they surrendered by 1245 hours, the attack would recommence. When no reply was received, he began an artillery barrage and dive-bombing attacks, which started fires in the dock area. At the same time Brigade Senger moved into the port from the east. Hostilities ceased in the late afternoon, a formal surrender document being signed at 1700 hours in the Préfecture Maritime. Rommel then drove with his Ia through the port, visiting first the British area and the maritime station. He commented on the hundreds of almost brand-new lorries left behind by the British, found that the seaplane base had not been touched by the bombardment and later, at Fort Querqueville, discovered an aerodrome with fourteen undamaged aircraft standing in spacious hangars.

With the final surrender of Cherbourg, the fighting ended for Rommel and his 'Ghost' Division. They were ordered south, reaching Rennes on the 21st, then moving on to Bordeaux, so that, when the Armistice came into effect on 25 June the division was in the Bordeaux–Rochefort area. Rommel wrote home on the 25th: 'At last the armistice is in force. We're now less than 200 miles from the Spanish frontier.' In an earlier letter he had described the war as '... gradually turning into a lightning tour of France' – and what a successful 'tour' it had been for these 'tourists'!

**Die Rechnung.** After six weeks of fighting 7th Pz Div had captured nearly 98,000 prisoners, 277 field guns, 64 anti-tank guns, 458 tanks and armoured cars, more than 4,000 lorries, 1,500+ cars, 300+ buses, 300+ motorcycles and 1,500+ horse-drawn vehicles. The prisoners included the admiral of the French Navy (North) and four other admirals, a corps commander, plus four divisional commanders and their staff. On the debit side 682 of the division's officers and men had been killed, 1,646 wounded and 296 were missing. Tank losses amounted to just 42 totally destroyed, which could be broken down by Mark as follows: three PzKpfw I; five PzKpfw II; twenty-six PzKpfw 38(t);[13] eight PzKpfw IV. Rommel had enhanced his reputation with both the army and the civilian population, although perhaps his methods of ignoring regulations when it suited him had not endeared him to the General Staff. His soldiers adored him and thoroughly approved of his method of 'sharp end' command – commanding 'from the saddle' is how he put it. Although he was happy to accept the publicity and adulation, he was also quick to ensure that the bravery and ability of those under him was properly recognised, both Rothenburg and Bismarck being awarded the Knight's Cross on his recommendation. Rommel's star was undoubtedly in the ascendancy and he would soon be chosen for even greater things by his approving and friendly Führer.

**Notes to Chapters 3**
1. The initial internal organisation of the four light divisions which fought in Poland did vary. For example, the 1st had a motorised infantry brigade of one regiment and a motorcycle battalion; the 2nd and 4th each had two motorised infantry regiments and the 3rd a motorised infantry regiment and a motorcycle battalion. Each had an organic tank battalion and the 1st had an organic tank regiment. The 1st had a recce battalion, while the rest had recce regiments. The divisional artillery comprised two light battalions of towed howitzers. Engineer, signal and other normal attachments were similar to those of the infantry and panzer divisions, but all were motorised. The strength of a light division was approximately 11,000 officers and men. (Figures taken from *The German Campaign in Poland (1939)* by Major Robert M. Kennedy, US Army pamphlet No 20255)
2. Irving, *Trail of the Fox.*
3. The Allied Order of Battle for the Western Front showed more than 3,000 Allied tanks, mainly French but with nearly 400 British and a few Belgian, while the Germans fielded only 2,574, mainly the lighter PzKpfw I and II.
4. In *The Rommel Papers*, Liddell Hart quotes a note from Manfred Rommel in which he says that Rommel finally had to remove Hanke from the Mess after he had boasted that he even had the power to remove Rommel from his command! Rommel later sent a long report to Hitler's adjutant.
5. Hart, *Rommel Papers.*
6. See Chapter 1, Note 4.

7. The Dyle Line was the Allied defensive position in Belgium which was to be occupied and held by the Allies if the Germans attacked.
8. The Headquarters of Pz Regt 31 and its battalion HQs, all contained PzKpfw III and PzKpfw III Befel, which also undoubtedly accounts for some of the misinformation that there were PzKpfw III in 7 Pz Div.
9. Quoted in Liddell Hart, *The Tanks*, vol. 2.
10. Major Schräpler wrote to Lucie, proudly telling her about the presentation, apologising for typing his letter, but explaining how his wound did not allow him to write legibly. He expressed to Frau Rommel the feelings of every soldier in the division, that they were honoured to serve under Rommel and were certain that no one deserved the award more than he did.
11. Fraser, *Knight's Cross*. This gave rise to a new unofficial divisional sign being adopted by 7th Pz Div, which featured a ghost instead of the original circle with a north–south diameter. After France this was again changed to a 'Y' or an inverted 'Y' with three dots to its right.
12. More than 338,000 men were rescued by some 860 Allied vessels (nearly 700 British), leaving just 51st Highland Division, which had been operating under French command on the Saar front, together with some elements of the British 1st Armoured Division.
13. It is this figure which is incorrectly shown as being PzKpfw III.

# 4
# North Africa
## Operation Sunflower (Sonnenblume) and the Afrikakorps (February 1941 – July 1941)

'IT'S ONE WAY OF GETTING MY RHEUMATISM TREATMENT'

### Problems in Europe
The euphoria which had followed the outstanding victory over the Allies in France and the Low Countries slowly evaporated, as Great Britain did not, as had been fondly expected, sue for peace. Then the aerial assault, which came to be known as 'The Battle of Britain' and was a necessary precursor of the proposed invasion of Great Britain, code-named Operation 'Sealion' (Seelöwe), ended with the British as the clear winners. This led to the invasion being first delayed, then quietly cancelled, when Hitler decided to crush Russia instead and turned his attention eastwards. Now, as the year ended, there were problems in the occupied countries, which led to all German troops being put on the alert. Rommel, much to his annoyance, had to break off his Christmas leave and drive quickly back to Bordeaux, where the division was now stationed. But it all proved to be a 'storm in a teacup' and the 'Ghost' Division filled in the time thereafter, in typical Rommel style, with weeks of intensive training, despite the snow and ice of a hard winter. Their commander had decided to make up his lost leave in early February, but was again thwarted, this time by a summons to report to Hitler's Headquarters.

There he was briefed first by Field Marshal von Brauchitsch, then by the Führer himself. He was to take command of a force comprising one tank (panzer) division and one light (leichte) division, which was being sent to Libya to assist the Italians. Rommel was able to let his wife know where he was going by telling her in a letter: '... It's one way of getting my rheumatism treatment' – he had long suffered from rheumatism and some time ago had been advised to take a cure in Egypt, so she would realise immediately that was to be his destination. He also told her that the new job was: '... very big and important'. Naturally he was sad to be leaving 7th Panzer Division and no doubt his soldiers were disappointed to see him go – they would send him messages in later years assuring him that despite his absence, the 'Rommel spirit' was still alive in the Gespensterdivision. Erwin Rommel was promoted to Lieutenant-General (Generalleutnant) in January 1941 and the following month was appointed Commander-in-Chief of German Troops in Libya. Rommel had been personally selected for the job by Hitler, who was later to explain that he had chosen him because he knew how to inspire troops and that would be essential for a force which had to fight in such arduous conditions. The original choice as commander of the German force was to have been Major-General Freiherr Hans von Funck, who had been sent to North Africa in early

January, but his reports were so negative that Hitler decided to replace him. The code-name given to the operation was 'Sonnenblume' (Sunflower).

## Problems in North Africa

The problems that had led to the decision to send German troops to North Africa had culminated in the disastrous defeat of the Italian forces there by General Sir Richard O'Connor's victorious XIII Corps, which was comprised of Australian, British and Indian troops. For the loss of 500 killed, 1,373 wounded and 55 missing, his tiny force had destroyed the entire Italian Tenth Army of four corps, capturing 130,000 prisoners, 400 tanks and about 1,300 guns. With this victory the whole of Cyrenaica lay in British hands, and the road to Tripoli was wide open. O'Connor was anxious to press on and was already sending armoured car patrols out towards Agedabia and El Agheila. No resistance was met, but a few stragglers were captured along the coast road towards Sirte. On 7 February O'Connor sent a personal message by radio to General Sir Archibald Wavell, GOC-in-C Middle East, giving him full details of the completeness of the victory, feeling confident that he would be given the green light to press on, it being clear that there was no other organised army between Cyrenaica and Tripoli. He then sent his BG Ops, Brigadier 'Chink' Dorman Smith, back to Cairo; he arrived there on 11 February and was scheduled to see Wavell the following day. When he got to the head-quarters, he was amazed to find that all the maps of the desert, which had adorned the walls of the C-in-C's office, had been replaced by maps of Greece. Wavell had already tried to persuade Churchill to allow O'Connor to go for Tripoli, sending a signal on 10 February which began: 'Extent of Italian defeat at Benghazi makes it seem possible that Tripoli might yield to a small force if dispatched without undue delay.' The Prime Minister's reply had clearly quashed any ideas of further advances in North Africa, because he intended to go to the assistance of Greece, and was going to send an expeditionary force there, denuding Wavell's forces in North Africa to do so. Clearly he had no idea that the Germans intended to send troops to North Africa, although whether such knowledge would have changed his mind is uncertain.

Churchill later explained that he did not go to the aid of Greece just to save the Greeks, or so as not to lose face with the Americans, but he also wanted to form a Balkan Front in order to delay the German invasion of Russia, and to be fair, he succeeded in this aim for at least six weeks. This is evidenced by a statement made by General Alfred Jodl, Chief of the Operations Staff of the German High Command (OKW), after the war, to Field Marshal Smuts, when he said that in his opinion Germany had lost the war because she had been obliged to divert divisions to meet the British landing in Greece. 'This meant she lost six weeks. She lost time – and with time she lost Moscow, Stalingrad and the war.'[1] Whatever the reasons, troop reductions were ordered and O'Connor's victorious little army was soon to be a shadow of its former self.

## 'Could you obtain some magnificent German tanks?'

As early as June 1940, Air Marshal Italo Balbo, the Governor of Libya, had asked Marshal Pietro Badoglio, Chief of the Italian Supreme General Staff

74

(Capo di Stato Maggiore Generale), to get some German assistance. 'Now that the French campaign is going to end,' he wrote on 20 June, 'could you obtain from the Germans about fifty of their magnificent tanks, plus the same number of their armoured cars for Libya?' He was killed a few days later, so the request was never followed up.[2] Whether or not Hitler or his High Command ever got to hear about the request is unclear. They were driven to the decision to send armoured forces to help their Allies simply because they were worried that the inept Italians were going to lose their entire hold on North Africa in the same way as they had begun to lose it in East Africa. Operation 'Sunflower' was therefore put into action. After a few days of briefing and getting his kit together (Rommel writes that his head is: '... swimming with all the many things there are to be done'), he flew to Rome on 11 February, where he saw the Italian Chief of Staff, General Guzzoni, then to Sicily to meet the Luftwaffe Commander for the Central Mediterranean, General Geissler. Next morning Rommel flew on to North Africa, landing at Castel Benito airfield, fifteen miles south of Tripoli. The first German combat troops would land at Tripoli harbour just two days later. From their speedy arrival one might assume that the Germans had always intended to send troops to North Africa, but that was not the case. General Siegfried Westphal, who served as Rommel's Chief of Staff, gave a lecture to the Anglo–German Association in April 1959, in which he dealt with the subject of German preparedness and said: 'I remember a small incident in 1938. I was at that time in the Operations Section of the General Staff in Berlin. One of my tasks was to justify the demands of the operational staff in the training, organisation and technical fields, etc., to the other departments and offices of the High Command. I had therefore to be a kind of "pike in a carp pond" as my section chief, the late Field Marshal von Manstein, put it. One day an officer of the section who had to arrange for the provision of maps which would be necessary in case of war, came to me: he suggested that the existing supply of maps of the West, East and South-East, should be augmented by sets for both Scandinavia and North Africa. One never knew what might happen. The absence of maps of Palestine had already proved to be a great disadvantage in the previous war, and so on. Well, I rejected this suggestion immediately, on my own initiative and met with the full approval of my superiors. None of us ever dreamed of the possibility of ever having to wage war in the desert. It must be remembered that Germany then no longer had any possessions outside Europe, and for this reason we were not accustomed to think in all-round terms. I met that officer again three years later when I went to Libya and he was in charge of our transport in Italy. He soon reminded me of that conversation of ours. Not without triumph in his voice, he pointed out that he had been right. The German troops now had to make do with makeshift maps, the markings on which differed often by several kilometres from the real position. I had opportunity enough in the coming months to satisfy myself that this was correct. And whenever – as often happened – the bad maps were cursed, I always had rather a bad conscience!'

This anecdote may serve to show that there had been no preparations of any sort in the German Army before the Second World War for a possible campaign outside Europe. As a matter of fact, as we shall see later, German troops landed in North Africa at the beginning of 1941 almost completely unprepared for their new task. All this should prove that it was almost a complete surprise to the German military command to have to send troops to North Africa. It had no time to make thorough preparations for this type of operations. Consequently only the most necessary organisational and sanitary measures could be taken. It was equally impossible to accustom the troops gradually to the great heat and to change their training to prepare them for fighting in country providing no cover. The plans for the lines of supply also had to be made at very short notice. Moreover, initially troops as well as heavy equipment were all transported by sea. When, however, shipping losses piled up, all transport of personnel was carried out by air only. All measures therefore had to be more or less *ad hoc*; experience could mostly only be gathered on the spot.[3]

## Preparations for North Africa

**Fit to fight.** Once it had been decided to send troops to North Africa, urgent, detailed planning began. First of all, the troops chosen to form the initial force had to be medically examined to make certain they were fit to serve in the desert. In view of the hurry to send the first troops these initial tests were nothing special and were based upon the standard form of medical examination and called: The Armed Forces Medical Certificate of Fitness for Tropical Service (Wehrmachtarztliches Zeugnis uber Tropendienstfähigkeit). Also of course, they had to be inoculated against cholera and typhus. But after the spring of 1941 they were further required to pass the 'Fitness for Tropical Service Certificate', although this was not always possible because of shortages of medical facilities.

**Western Desert peculiarities.** Next they had to equipped with tropical uniforms and equipment, and their vehicles had to be camouflaged with sand-coloured paint. Training programmes had to be adapted to include relevant subjects such as operating in wide open spaces, field hygiene, water discipline, etc. A suitable ration scale had to be worked out, which was not based upon the same foods that formed staple elements of normal European theatre diet – for example, white bread and potatoes were replaced with Zweiback (twice-baked) black bread in a carton and legumes such as peas and beans, dried of course. Rice was also issued, but the basic food for many was bread – German Kommisbrot or Italian Maisbrot, together with something to spread on it. As butter would go rancid quickly in the heat, olive oil and tinned sardines were substituted. The Italians were pressed into providing a range of foodstuffs – such as cheese, cooking oil, coffee beans and marmalade, plus tins of preserved meat. These were stamped 'AM', standing for 'Administrazione militare' (cf. the British 'WD' for War Department). It was christened 'Alter Mann' (Old Man), supposedly by Rommel himself, although the troops also called it 'Alter Mausel' (Old Mule) or 'Asinus Mussolini' (Mussolini's backside)! The

German rations were both solid and sustaining, but not particularly appetising, so naturally the soldiers always craved something different. It was a great delight, therefore, to capture an enemy supply dump, for example, when Tobruk was finally taken, so that they could feast on bully beef, hard tack biscuits, jam and even white bread and tinned fruit. On the 'other side of the hill', the British enthused about the German rations and cursed their own. Occasionally fresh meat was obtained, for example in the shape of a live pig to fatten up for a special occasion, or perhaps a goat, but these were few and far between. Rommel never showed much interest in food, being quite content to set off for a day in the desert with just a small packet of sandwiches, or a tin of sardines and a chunk of bread. He always drank sparingly; he carried a small flask of cold lemon tea, but often brought it back untouched. He also did not like hot tea or coffee when brewed with brackish desert water. Desmond Young tells of one occasion which typifies Rommel's eating habits. One day he invited an Italian general to lunch with him in the open. 'It was rather awkward,' he remarked afterwards. 'I had only three slices of bread and they were all stale. Never mind, they eat too much!'

**Pay – Overseas Allowance.** All German troops who served in North Africa received additional pay in the form of a local overseas allowance which amounted to 3 Reichsmarks a day for Officers and NCOs and 2 RM for soldiers.

**The Jerrycan.** One of the most invaluable items of the desert war was the well-made, robust, 20-litre (4½-gallon) 'Jerrycan' – as the British called them. They were much preferred by the British to their own flimsily constructed 4-gallon petrol tins, which continually leaked and led to a loss of some 30 per cent of all fuel – a scandalous waste, but one which the British seemed incapable of curing. Everyone on both sides who could, of course, equipped themselves with Jerrycans, which were used for water as well as for petrol, oil and lubricants – properly marked so that everyone knew from the outside what to expect!

### Journey to Africa

The trip necessitated an overland journey to Italy and then travel by sea or air across the Mediterranean, protection being provided mainly by the Luftwaffe and the Italian Navy, against air and sea attacks by the British. Although the naval and air bases on the island of Malta were a continuing source of frustration which was never neutralised, convoy protection, provided mainly by the Italian Navy, was both generous and effective. It has been estimated that of the 206,402 men transported to Africa, 189,162 (more than 90 per cent) arrived safely, and the tonnage of stores and vehicles moved was as follows:

| Item | Tonnage dispatched | Tonnage arrived |
| --- | --- | --- |
| Arms and ammunition | 171,060 | 149,462 |
| Trucks and AFVs | 275,310 | 243,633 |
| Fuel | 599,338 | 476,703 |

There were, however, problems on the dockside in Naples from where many convoys left. For example, while loading Panzer Regiment 5 of 5 leichte Division, the transport ship *Leverkusen* caught fire, resulting in the loss of ten PzKpfw III and three PzKpfw IV. The rest of the regiment was loaded safely and arrived in Tripoli from 8 to 10 March 1941. The tanks of Pz Regt 8 also followed without incident. But Rommel was initially so short of tanks that he had to order his workshops to produce large numbers of dummies (see photograph), which were made of wood and blankets and mounted on Volkswagen vehicles. The first combat vehicles to arrive did so on 14 February 1941, being 3 Reconnaissance Battalion and 39 Anti-Tank Battalion, both belonging to 5 leichte Division.

**Tropical uniform.** Full details of the DAK uniforms will be covered later, but here is a brief description of what one reinforcement officer thought about the items which were issued initially: 'We drew our tropical clothing. I could hardly believe what wonderful things German soldiers got for war. I received as my most important bit of furniture a huge rubber sealed tropical chest. The contents were really precious – a tropical helmet, a tent, a mosquito net with carrying case, a face veil, a sleeping-bag, a pair of desert boots, a pair of tropical shoes, long trousers, short trousers, breeches, coat, blouse, string vests, a body belt of lamb's wool (here a little shake of the head) goggles and much, much more. Nobody thought about what would happen to these wonderful things in the future, to which were added a wonderful rucksack, blankets, and the usual officers' accoutrements like binoculars, map case, pistol and ammunition pouch, etc. There are obviously no sharpshooters in Africa as we hadn't been given a steel helmet. Therefore we thought that the red-lined caps must be able to give us great protection.'

## Basic Organisations

Although the composition of tank and infantry divisions and units altered with the battle circumstances, it is relevant to look now at the general composition of the main types of German division in 1941–2, so as to have a fair idea of what they contained. Probably more than on any other front, *ad hoc* groups were formed in the desert campaigns to meet special situations, these Kampfgruppen being known normally by the name of the commander (e.g., Kampfgruppe Audorff or Gruppe Bach). It is a tribute to the flexibility of the German organisational structure that this was possible with the minimum of fuss and that they worked so well in battle.

## Rommel's First Headquarters

Aufklärungsstab Rommel. Before the official establishing of the Deutsches Afrikakorps (DAK), the headquarters staff of the German Army in Africa was known as Aufklärungsstab Rommel, and his official title was Commander in Chief of German Troops in Libya (Befelshaber der Deutschen Truppen in Libyen). This HQ only lasted from 6 to 19 February 1941 and comprised Rommel plus the following:

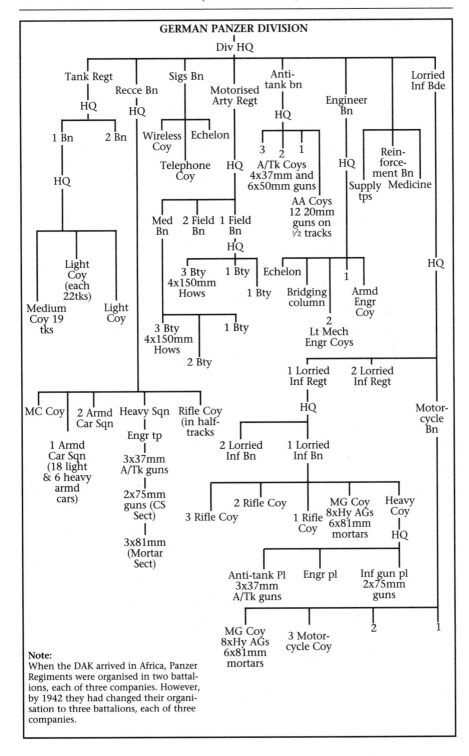

**GERMAN PANZER DIVISION**

Note:
When the DAK arrived in Africa, Panzer Regiments were organised in two battalions, each of three companies. However, by 1942 they had changed their organisation to three battalions, each of three companies.

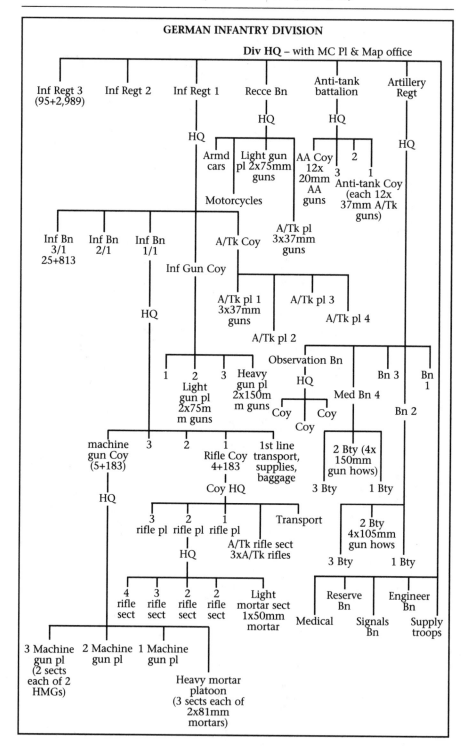

GERMAN INFANTRY DIVISION

Div HQ – with MC Pl & Map office

Ia (Chief of Staff) Lieutenant-Colonel von dem Borne
Ic (Intelligence) Captain von Plehwe
Luftwaffe Liaison Officer Major Grunow
Engineer Officer Lieutenant-Colonel Hundt
HQ Commandant Lieutenant-Colonel Behrendt.


## THE DEUTSCHES AFRIKAKORPS (DAK): ORDER OF BATTLE

The order of battle (orbat) of the DAK, showing the senior members over the years of its existence, is given below. However, details of the complete initial staff list of the HQ DAK is shown on page 90. Of course the DAK Orbat also altered over the period of its life, but the orbat shown gives a good indication of its early composition, before 5 leichte Division became 21st Panzer Division.

### Corps Commanders
19 Feb–15 Aug 1941: Lieutenant-General Erwin Rommel (promoted to General of Panzer Troops (Gen d.Pz.Tr.) on 1 July 41). Went on to command the Panzergruppe (see later) on 15 Aug 41.
15 Aug–8 Mar 1942: Lieutenant-General Ludwig Crüwell.
9 Mar–31 Aug 1942: Lieutenant-General Walther K. Nehring (promoted to Gen d.Pz.Tr. on 23 June 1942 at Tobruk). The COS, Colonel Bayerlein, took over temporarily when Nehring was wounded on 31 August.
31 Aug–17 Sept 1942: Major-General Gustav von Värst.
17 Sept–4 Nov 1942: Gen d.Pz.Tr. Wilhelm Ritter von Thoma, who was captured on 4 November; Colonel Bayerlein took temporary command until 19 November.
19 Nov 1942–16 Jan 1943: Gen d.Pz.Tr. Gustav Fehn, who was wounded on 16 January.
16 Jan–17 Feb 1943: Major-Gen Kurt Freiherr von Liebenstein, who was wounded on 17 February.
17 Feb–5 Mar 1943: Major-General Heinz Ziegler took over temporarily.
5–12 Mar 1943: Gen d.Pz.Tr. Hans Cramer.

### Corps Headquarters staff (Stab des Korps) The senior officers over the years were:
Chief of Staff: Lieutenant-Colonel von dem Borne; Colonel Fritz
Bayerlein; Colonel H. W. Nolte
Ia: Major Ehlert; Major Wustefeld; Major Westphal; Major Trevert
Ib: Major Otto
(Chief Supply Officer): Major Willers; Major Walter Schmidt;
Lieutenant-Colonel Dr Muller (DAK Transport Officer)
Ic: Captain Graf Baudissin (captured); Major G. F. W. von Mellenthin; Captain Laubinger; Captain Liebl
IIa: Major Schräpler; Colonel Schulte-Heuthaus
IVb Senior Medical Officer; Dr Barnewitz.

**5 Light (leichte) Division** (later re-organised as 21st Panzer Division)
The division, some 9,300 men strong, was initially mainly made up of men and equipment from 3rd Pz Div and many of its vehicles still carried the 3rd Panzer symbol (an inverted 'Y' with two strokes alongside its right top). On 1 October 1941 it was retitled 21st Panzer Division, the vehicle symbol being a square-shaped capital letter 'B' (see drawings). Initially it had received Pz Regt 5 from 3rd Pz Div, which only comprised approximately 120 tanks, only half of which were PzKpfw III and IV. Its reconnaissance element (Recce Bn 3) contained armoured cars, VW 'dune buggies' (Kubelwagen) and motorcycle troops; its two anti-tank battalions (Panzerjäger) were armed with 37mm and 50mm anti-tank guns. Its most effective anti-tank weapons were undoubtedly the deadly dual-purpose 88mm AA guns of its AA battalion. The Divisional order of battle on arrival was:

Divisional Headquarters
HQ zbV (zu besonderer Verwendung – for special employment)
Panzer Regiment 5
Anti-Tank Battalions 33* and 39 (motorised (mot))
Machine-Gun Bns 2* and 8 (mot)
I.Bn/Artillery Regt 75 (mot)
AA Bns 605** and 606***(mot)
Reconnaissance Staff 2 (Army)/14 Panzer**
Recce Bn 3 (mot)
Telephone Company/Signals Bn 'Libya'
One Company/Engineer Bn 39* (mot)
Special Supply Staff 668 (mot)
Supply Bns (mot) 532, 533**, 3./39 (mot) and one Bn unnumbered
Water Columns 797, 801, 803, 822 (mot) and one Column unnumbered
Water Purification Columns 800 and 804 (mot)
Heavy Water Columns 641** and 645** (mot)
Tyre Sections 13*** and 210*** (mot)
MT Workshops 122 and 129 (mot)
1./Medical Company 83 (mot)
4./Base Hospital 572 (mot)
Ambulance Platoons 631 and 633 (mot)
Bakery Coy 531 (mot)
Field Police Troop 309 (mot)
Field Post Office 735 (mot)

All the above units were re-assigned to 21st Pz Div except * to 15th Pz Div, ** to Panzerarmeeafrika, *** to DAK.

**Tank strength.** On arrival Pz Regt 5, having lost ten PzKpfw III and three PzKpfw IV while loading, contained: twenty-five PzKpfw I Ausf A; forty-five PzKpfw II; sixty-one PzKpfw III; seventeen PzKpfw IV; three kl Pz Bef Weg and four gr Pz Bef Weg ( the 'kleine' being based on PzKpfw I, the 'grosse' on PzKpfw III Ausf D). Total tank strength = 155.

NB. To complete the organisational structure of 5 leichte/21 Pz Div, the revised orbat for 21st Pz Div (wef 1 Oct 41) is shown on page 92 of this chapter.

### 15TH PANZER DIVISION

This contained Pz Regt 8, Motor Rifle Brigade 15, and 33 Pz Artillery Regt, together with battalion-sized supporting units, mainly numbered '33'. Its vehicle sign was a triangle with a vertical stroke through its centre (see drawings). Its full orbat was:

## Divisional Headquarters

Map-store 33 (mot)
Dispatch Rider (DR) Section
Panzer Regiment 8
Motor Rifle (Schützen) Brigade 15
  (mot)
  Infantry Regiments 115 and 200
  (mot)
  Machine-Gun Battalion 8 (mot)
  Motorcycle Battalion 15
Artillery Regiment 33 (mot)
Reconnaissance Regiment 33
  (mot)
Anti-Tank Battalion 33 (mot)
  Signals Battalion 33 (mot)
Engineer Battalion 33 (mot)
Field Replacement Battalion 33

Supply Battalion 33 (mot)
  Supply Columns (1 to 11) 33
  Tank Replacement Column 33
  (mot)
  Water Filtration Column 581
  (mot)
  Workshop Company 33 (mot)
  Supply Company 33 (mot)
Ambulance Company 33 (mot)
Field Hospital 33 (mot)
Bakery Company 33 (mot)
Butchery Company 33 (mot)
Divisional Rations Detachment 33
  (mot)
Military Police Platoon 33 (mot)
Field Post Office 33 (mot)

**Tank strength.** On arrival, Pz Regt 8 comprised: forty-five PzKpfw II; seventy-one PzKpfw III (5cm KwK L/42 guns); twenty PzKpfw IV; ten Pz Bef Weg. Total tank strength = 146.

## Luftwaffe

I./AA Regiment 18 (mot)

I./AA Regiment 33 (mot)

## Corps Troops

Reconnaissance Company 580
  Oasis Battalion zbV 300
  (specialised water unit)
Anti-tank Battalion 605 (mot)
Anti-Aircraft (AA) Battalion 606
  (mot)
Signals Battalion 475 (mot)
  Light Signals Column
  Radio Train 10
  Tank Radio Column
  Radio Column

  Cable Column
Supply Battalion 572 (mot)
  Heavy Motor Vehicle Columns
  (1 to 6)
  Heavy Motor Vehicle Column
  for workshop supplies
  Motor Vehicle Workshop
  Ammunition Supply Company
  588
Water Supply Battalion (mot) 580
  Water Supply Company 659

Water Distillation Company 655
Heavy Water Supply Columns
641, 645 and 651
Filtration Column 877
Military Geological units 8 and
12 (mot)
Field Replacement Battalions 598
and 599

Bakery Company 554 (mot)
Corps Resupply Point (mot)
Military Police Troop 498 (mot)
Field Post Office (mot)
Corps Map Store 576 (mot)
Luftwaffe
I./AA Regiment (mot) 18
I./AA Regiment (mot) 33

CORPS COMMANDERS (IN ADDITION TO ROMMEL)

**Lieutenant-General Ludwig Crüwell.** When Rommel's command was raised to the status of a Panzergruppe, his place as Corps Commander was taken by the able and effective General Crüwell, who had commanded the neighbouring 2nd Motorised Division to 7th Pz Div in France. Born in Dortmund on 20 March 1892, he joined the army in 1911 and served as a Lieutenant in the Great War, ending the war as regimental adjutant of his regiment (9th Dragoons). Post-war he served in the Reichswehrministerium, then in 1922 he was promoted to Rittmeister (Captain in the Cavalry) and after completing staff training took up a staff appointment with 2nd Cavalry Division in Breslau. Promoted Colonel in 1936, two years later he became the CO of Panzer Regt 6 on 1 February 1938 and was promoted to Major-General in December 1939. Brave and skilful, on 1 September 1941 he was awarded the Oakleaves to the Knight's Cross he had won while commanding 11th Pz Div in Russia, and was promoted to Gen d. Pz.Tr. in December 1941. It was Crüwell who was the prime mover in the initial German successes during the 'Crusader' operations when he managed to get his forces deep into General Cunningham's rear areas without detection and then to link up with the Italian Ariete and Trieste Armoured Divisions. He had a number of hair-raising escapes; for example, his command vehicle was surrounded by British light tanks in November 1941, but German 2cm Flak gunfire chased them away before he could be captured. He celebrated his 50th birthday at Umm er Rzem Oasis near Derna and was later shot down in his Storch light aircraft over Got el Ualebon, on 29 May 1942, while commanding the Italian front and leading the attack on the Gazala Line. He landed behind enemy lines, was taken prisoner, and was not released until the end of 1947. He died in Dortmund on 25 September 1958.

**Lieutenant-General Walther K. Nehring.** Another fine senior commander, Nehring was born in Stettin on 15 August 1892, joined the army in 1911 as an officer candidate and by 1915 was a Lieutenant in 152nd Infantry Regiment. He served in various posts during the Great War, winning the Iron Cross 2nd and 1st Class. He was accepted for the Reichswehr after the war and soon joined the 'father' of the panzer forces Heinz Guderian, playing an important part in the formation and development of the new arm. In July 1934 he became CO of Panzer Regt 5 and by the time the war began was Chief of Staff XIX Army Corps. In October 1940 he was given command of 18th Panzer Division, commanding them in Russia and winning his Knight's Cross there in July 1941. He took over command of the DAK on 9 March 1942, was promoted to Gen d. Pz. Tr. on 22 June at Tobruk, having borne the main brunt of the battles waged against his DAK armour. He almost got shot by two lost, half-starved British soldiers (Lieutenant Bailey and Sergeant Norton) during a bathing expedition to the sea the same day, but managed to bluff his way through a nasty encounter with them! He was wounded in the arm while negotiating a minefield on 31 August 1942 during an air attack on his headquarters, and had to be taken to a dressing-station. Subsequently he returned to operations and in November 1942 assumed command of all German forces in Tunisia. Later *Stab* Nehring changed its title to XC Korps, and was then absorbed into Panzerarmeeoberkommando 5 (Pz AOK 5), which was formed to strengthen the German command structure in Tunisia. Kesselring wrote later in his memoirs that Nehring: 'faced a task of immense difficulty, but one of extraordinary fascination for a young general. His appointment was regarded as an instance of my unbounded optimism.' He remained in command until 9 December 1942 when he handed over to General von Arnim. A brilliant improviser and a brave soldier, Walther Nehring was awarded both the Oakleaves and Swords to his Knight's Cross. After leaving North Africa, he became Deputy Commander of Fourth Panzer Army, then Commander of XXIV Korps and finally in March 1945, Commander First Panzer Army, which he led to 'safety in the West' away from the Russians. Taken prisoner by the Americans, he was released in May 1948. He died in Düsseldorf on 20 April 1983.

**Major-General Gustav von Värst.** See under 15th Pz Div.

**Gen d.Pz.Tr. Wilhelm Ritter von Thoma.** One of the most experienced panzer officers in the Panzerwaffe, von Thoma had commanded the tank element of the Condor Legion, sent by Hitler to assist Franco's Nationalists during the Spanish Civil War. He then commanded a panzer brigade in 2nd Pz Div in Poland, was later sent to North Africa in October 1940 on a 'fact-finding' mission for the Führer, which directly resulted in the formation and dispatch of the DAK. He was captured by the British, after Hitler's 'Victory or Death' signal sent to the DAK during the British El Alamein offensive in October 1942. David Irving in *The Trail of the Fox* tells how von Thoma, having decided to desert, put on all his medals, denounced Hitler's 'Stand Fast' order as lunacy, and drove off into the middle of the battle in his tank. Colonel Fritz Bayerlein had driven after him but could not reach his commander, helplessly watching as von Thoma standing 'gaunt and erect' near a burning tank while British tanks converged on him. He later dined with Montgomery, who treated him 'most chivalrously'. Irving also says that a British intelligence summary captured later, indicates that von Thoma had given away Rommel's plans and dispositions in further talks with Monty. This account is at variance with Basil Liddell Hart's *The Other Side of the Hill*, in which he says that von Thoma told him, during a post-war interview, that he had been racing in a tank from one critical point to another during the battle, his tank being hit several times, and in the end was trapped when it caught fire and he had to bale out. He showed him his cap which had several holes in it, explaining that they were symbols of lucky escapes from the 24 tank fights he had been in during the war in Poland, France, Russia and Africa (he also said he had been in 192 tank actions in Spain). Von Thoma also stated that he had not been asked for information while dining with Monty, quite the reverse, the British general having told him accurately the state of the German forces, their dispositions and supplies! He concluded by saying that although Montgomery had been very cautious in handling the battle, despite his immensely superior strength, he was the only field marshal in the war who had won all his battles!

This latter account was verified to me recently by an ex-member of the 10th Royal Hussars (10H) who was serving with the regiment at El Alamein when they captured von Thoma. Sgt Ron Huggins, who now works as a volunteer in the Tank Museum Library, told me about the incident which involved their Internal Communications Section (the old nomenclature for the Reconnaissance Troop) then under the command of Capt Grant Singer. He and his driver, Tpr Lindsay, had a narrow escape when they were engaged by the tank von Thoma was travelling in during his recce – a PzKpfw III. Their Daimler Scout Car was holed by a 50mm solid shot which passed between them without injuring either man. They managed to get back unscathed to their own tanks, where Capt Singer pointed out the position of the enemy AFV to B Squadron Commander, who immediately opened fire. 10H had just been issued with the new American-built M4 medium Sherman tanks and it was not long before they hit the panzer with their 75mm guns and set it on fire. 'Von Thoma was the only one to bale out – the rest of the crew being killed – and he stood there waving a white cloth. Capt Singer was sent to take him prisoner. As the scout car approached, Capt Singer could see the man was a German officer of high rank. The two officers then saluted each other and the German said in perfect English: "General Ritter Von Thoma". Von Thoma clambered onto the back of the scout car and was driven directly to Montgomery's HQ, where he gave his binoculars to Tpr Lindsay and, when Capt Singer was killed the very next day, von Thoma wrote a personal letter to Capt Singer's mother expressing his condolences. This letter is now on display in the regimental museum.'

**Gen d. Pz. Tr. Gustav Fehn.** Rommel put Fehn in temporary charge only a few days after he had arrived in North Africa; he was subsequently wounded, on 15 January 1943. Born in Nüremberg in 1892, he served in the Great War and was promoted to Major-General in August 1940. Before arriving in North Africa he had commanded XXXX Pz Korps and after leaving North Africa, he went on to command XXVI Pz Korps, XXI Armee Korps and finally, XV Mountain Corps. He was killed by Yugoslav partisans in June 1945. He had been awarded a Knight's Cross whilst commanding Rifle Regiment 33 in 1940, and the German Cross in Gold in July 1942.

**Major-General Kurt Freiherr von Liebenstein.** Born in Jebenhausen on 28 February 1899, he joined the army as an officer candidate in 1916 and served with the 26th Dragoon Regiment during the Great War, winning both Iron Crosses. Post-war he was accepted into the Reichswehr, then into the Wehrmacht and served as the ADC to the German Military Attaché in Paris. At the start of the war he joined the Army General Staff, being appointed Ia of 10th Pz Div in February 1940, then in 1941, he was Guderian's Chief of Staff at the time of the invasion of Russia and subsequently commanded 164 leichte Div from December 1942 and brought them to North Africa. He was injured in a car accident on 17 February 1943 while commanding both DAK and Kampfgruppe DAK and was taken prisoner on 12 May 1943. He was the holder of the Knight's Cross and the German Cross in Gold. In 1956 he became a Major-General in the Bundeswehr.

**Gen d. Pz. Tr. Hans Cramer.** Born in Minden on 13 July 1896, he joined the army in September 1914 and was promoted Lieutenant at the end of the year. He won both Iron Crosses with 15th Infantry Regiment and was wounded during the Great War. He then served in the Reichwehr's 18th Infantry Regt, before commanding a squadron of 13th Cavalry Regt at Hanover. Later he commanded the Cavalry Instruction and Training Battalion, then in early 1939 he was promoted Lieutenant-Colonel and commanded the armoured reconnaissance instruction battalion. He commanded Pz Regt 8 in 15th Pz Div at the start of the war, bringing them to North Africa where he served with distinction. He took Sidi Aziz on 16 May 1941, then Capuzzo and Halfaya Pass, being awarded his Knight's Cross for these exploits. He was badly wounded at Sollum but served as Chief of Staff of the General Mobile Forces while recovering from his wounds. On 5 March 1942 he was awarded the German Cross in Gold. On 1 October 1942 he was appointed to command the Mobile Forces and promoted to Major-General the following month. After service in Russia, he was named to command the DAK on 1 March 1943, being promoted Gen d. Pz. Tr. on 1 May. He was destined to be the last commander of DAK and it was he who signed the final message from the Korps when it surrendered on 12 May 1943. He died in Hausberge in 1968.

DIVISIONAL COMMANDERS

**5 leichte.** 20 February–22 July 1941: Major-General Johannes Streich. He was born on 16 April 1891 in Augustenburg in East Prussia. He joined the army in 1911 and fought throughout the Great War, reaching the rank of Lieutenant, commanding a company and winning both Iron Crosses. Post-war he served in the Reichswehr in an MT company, then in 1930 played a part in the development of the Pzkpfw I to IV as a technical adviser in the Army Ordnance Office. In 1937, he took command of Pz Regt 15 and was promoted to Colonel in April 1938. Described by some historians as being 'slightly built, spry and mild mannered', he fell foul of Rommel both in France when he was commanding Pz Regt 15 and then in North Africa, during the attack on Tobruk, by challenging his judgement. He was relieved of his command. When he left Rommel told him: 'You were far too concerned with the well-being of your troops,' to which Streich is reported to have replied: 'I can imagine no greater words of praise for a divisional commander.'[4] He had been awarded the Knight's Cross for his bravery in France – his regiment smashed through the blocking position at La Bassée, taking more than 20,000 prisoners and reaching the Atlantic coast. He was promoted to Major-General and given command of 5 leichte before coming to North Africa where they disembarked in February–March 1941.

23 July–1 October 1941: Major-General Johann von Ravenstein. Lean, aristocratic and good looking. Born in 1889, in Strehlen, Silesia, he joined the army in 1909, being commissioned as a Lieutenant in the 7th Grenadier Regiment. He served in the Great War, was wounded several times during his four years on the Western Front and was, like Rommel, awarded the *Pour le Mérite* (25 June 1918) for bravery during the Battle of the Marne. After the war he left the army but rejoined in 1934 as CO II Bn of 60th Inf Regt – it later became 4th Cavalry Rifle Regt, which he took into action in France in 1940. He was recommended for his Knight's Cross on 3 June 1940 and promoted Major-General in May 1941 to command 21st Pz Div and took them to North Africa. He was captured by the New Zealanders on 29 November 1941, while on his way to a conference at DAK HQ during the 'Crusader' battles (see later). Ravenstein mistakenly drove straight into the positions of 21st NZ Battalion on Point 175. He tried to hide his identity – he had determined that he was going to call himself 'Colonel Schmidt', but was taken to meet General Freyberg and, on being introduced, clicked his heels, bowed and blurted out 'von Ravenstein General' before he could stop himself! He died in Duisburg in March 1962

On 1 October 1941, 5 leichte was re-organised and strengthened to become 21st Panzer Division, which first saw action in mid-November 1941. It fought on throughout the campaigns finally surrendering on 13 May 1943.

**21st Panzer.** 1 Oct–29 Nov 1941: Major-General Johann von Ravenstein (see above). Lieutenant-Colonel Gustav-Georg Knabe took temporary command 29–30 November.

30 Nov 1941– 30 Jan 1942: Lieutenant-General Karl Böttcher, who had been Rommel's artillery commander. Born in Thorn in 1889, he served in the Great War. He was promoted to Major-General in March 1940. He was awarded the Knight's Cross in December 1941. and died at Bad Wimpfen in February 1975.

30 Jan–31 Aug 1942: Major-General Georg von Bismarck, born in Neumark in 1891, served during the Great War. He had commanded 7th Rifle Regiment in the Ghost Division in France and been awarded a Knight's Cross on 30 September 1940. He was wounded on 17 July, Colonel Alfred Bruer taking over temporarily until he returned. But on 31 August von Bismarck was killed by enemy mortar fire near El Alamein.

31 Aug–18 Sept 1942: Colonel Carl-Hans Lungershausen.

18 Sept–21 Dec 1942: Major-General Heinz von Randow, cavalryman and holder of the German Cross in Gold, who was killed near Tripoli on 21 December, just a few days after being promoted to Lieutenant-General. Colonel Hans-

Geog Hildebrandt took over temporarily, only to be replaced by Colonel von Hülsen when Hildebrandt went on sick leave on 25 April 1943. Heinrich Hermann von Hülsen was later promoted to Major-General on 1 May and was captured by the British on surrendering with his division on 13 May 1943.

**15th Panzer.** 22 Mar–10 Apr 1941: Major-General Heinrich von Prittwitz und Gaffron, holder of the Knight's Cross. He was killed by a direct hit from an anti-tank gun, the first German general to be killed in the Africa campaign. Rommel had put him in command of the leading German troops attacking Tobruk (in preference to Streich) far too soon after he had arrived. He was then bullied by Rommel into rushing to the front in a borrowed car, overshot friendly positions and was killed together with his driver.[5]
15 Apr–25 July 1941: Oberst (promoted to Major-General in the field) Hans-Karl Freiherr von Esebeck. Born in Potsdam in 1892, he served during the Great War and was promoted Colonel in June 1938. He was wounded in the face by a shell splinter in front of Tobruk and evacuated to Europe. He was refused permission to return to North Africa, commanded a division in Russia, was arrested in 1944 for his part in the conspiracy to assassinate Hitler and spent the rest of the war in a concentration camp. He had won the Knight's Cross in July 1940 and the German Cross in Gold in August 1942. He died in Dortmund in January 1955.
25 July–6 Dec 1941: Major-General Walther Neumann-Silkow. He was seriously wounded on 6 December 1941 when a shell burst beside his command vehicle. He was evacuated to Benghazi hospital where he died two days later. He had won the Knight's Cross while commanding 8 Schützen Bde in France (date of award 5 August 1940).
6–8 Dec 1941: Oberst Erwin Menny in temporary command.
9 Dec 1941–26 May 1942: Lieutenant-General Gustav von Värst. A fine and talented commander, he was wounded on 26 May 1942. He went on to command DAK from 31 August to 17 September 1942 and, as Gen d. Pz. Tr., Pz AOK 5 from 9 March to 9 May 1943, when he was taken prisoner. He was a holder of the Knight's Cross which he won in France while commanding 2 Schützen Bde (date of award 3 July 1940).
26 May–8 July 1942: Oberst Eduard Crasemann in temporary command.
8 July–31 Aug 1942: General von Värst returned to command, but was then sent to take over temporary command of DAK when General Nehring was wounded on 31 Aug 42.
1–17 Sept 1942: Major-General Heinz von Randow, who was then transferred to command 21st Pz Div when von Värst returned. He was killed in December 1942 during the withdrawal, when still commanding 21st Pz Div.
17 Sept–11 Nov 1942: General von Värst's third period of command which ended when he went on sick-leave.
11 Nov–12 Dec 1942: Oberst Eduard Crasemann in temporary command, against General von Värst's return.
12 Dec 1942–13 May 1943: Oberst Willibald Borowietz. He was promoted to Major-General on 1 January, and Lieutenant-General on 1 May 1943. Taken prisoner, he died in US captivity.

## INITIAL STAFF LIST OF THE DAK

| | | |
|---|---|---|
| Befehlshaber | Commander | Generalleutnant E. Rommel |
| Chef des generalstabes | Chief of Staff | Obersleutnant von dem Borne |

**Führungsabteilung Ia** — **Command Division Ia**

| | | |
|---|---|---|
| Ia = Generalstabsoffizier für Führung und Ausbildung | Ia = First general Staff Officer for Leadership & Training | Major i. G. W. Stefeld |
| 01 = Führungsgehilfe beim Stab Ia | Principal Staff Assistant of Staff Ia | Hauptmann Heuduck |
| 05 = Führungsgehilfe beim Stab Ia | ditto | Oberleutnant von Hosslein |
| 06 = Führungsgehilfe beim Stab Ia | ditto | Oberleutnant d. R. Dr Wagner |
| Ia/Mess. = Offizier für Vermessung und Kartenwesen | Officer for Survey and Mapping | Hauptman (Ing.) Hintze |
| Ia/Verk. = Offizier für Verkehrswesen | Officer for Transportation | Major Tootz |
| Ia/Pi. = Offizier für Pionierwesen | Officer for Engineer Employments | Hauptmann Götzelmann |
| Ia/Gabo = Offizier für Gasabwehr | Officer for Gas Defence | Hauptmann d. R. Tschirner |

| | | |
|---|---|---|
| **Abteilung Ic** = 3. General stabsoffizier für Feindnach-richten | **Division Ic** = Third General Staff Officer for Enemy Information | Hauptmann i. G. Röstel |
| 03 = Führungsgehilfe beim Stab Ic | Principal Staff Assistant and Staff Ic | Oberleutnant d. R. Behrend |
| 04 = Führungsgehilfe beim Stab Ic | ditto | Leutnant d. R. Siegfried |
| Ic/Prop. = Offizier für Feindpropaganda | Officer for Enemy Propaganda | Leutnant d. R. Behrend |
| Dolm = Dolmetscher | Interpreter | Sonderführer Freiherr v. Neurath |
| ditto | ditto | Oberleutnant d. R. Will |
| ditto | ditto | Sonderführer Dr Franz |
| ditto | ditto | Dr Hagemann |
| Nach. Führer = Nachrichten-Führer | Leader of Intelligence Collection | Major Reimer |
| Stoluft = Stabsoffizier-Luftwaffe (Verbindungsoffz. zur Luftwaffe) | Staff Officer-Air Force | Major Heymer (Air Liaison Officer) |

| | | |
|---|---|---|
| **Ober-Quartiermeister-abteilung** | **First Quartermaster Division** | |
| Leitung/Ib = 2. Generalstabs-offizier für Nachschub Versorgung | Direction/Ib = Second General Staff Officer for Supplies | Major i. G. Schleusener |

| | | |
|---|---|---|
| t. Qu. 1 = Generalstabs-ffizier für Nachschub (Nachschubführer) | General Staff Officer for Supplies (Supply Officer) | Major i. G. Otto |
| = Führungsgehilfe Qu. M. Abt. | Principal Staff Assistant of Quartermaster Division | Oberleutant d. R. Kloppmann |
| = Führungsgehilfe Qu. M. Abt. | ditto | Oberleutnant d. R. Lichtwald |
| = Führungsgehilfe Qu. M. Abt. | ditto | Leutnant d. R. Ziemke |
| nition (Munitionsver-orgung) | Officer for Ammunition Supply | Hauptmann (W) Strohbehn |
| ffen und Geräteversor-ung | Officer for Weapons and Equipment Supply | Oberleutnant (W) Palme |
| teilung Heeres-Motor-sierung (Kraftfahrwesen) | Army Motorisation Division (motor vehicles) | Major (E) Kohmen |
| tarbeiter | Technical Adviser | Technischer Oberinspektor Neugebauer |
| t. V Korpsingenieur (Kraftfahrberabeiter) | Division V Corps Engineer (Motor Vehicle Action Officer) | Major (Ing.) Hofweber |
| Mitarbeiter | Technical Adviser | Technischer Oberinspektor Rubner |
| t IVa Intendant für Verpflegung, Bekleidung und Besoldungswesen | Division IVa Commissariat Officer, for Food, Clothing and Pay Service | Korps-intendant Intendantur-Rat Dr Alves |
| tarbeiter | Assistant | Stabszahlmeister Rohmer |
| tarbeiter | ditto | Oberzahlmeister Fröhlich |
| tarbeiter | ditto | Zahlmeister Schneider |
| t. IVb Korpsarzt/Sanität-versorgung | Division IVb Corps Surgeon Medical Support | Korpsarzt Oberstarzt Dr Stahm |
| jutant | Personal Staff Officer | Stabsarzt Dr Lehmann |
| otheker | Pharmacist | Stabsapotheker Dr Daudert |
| meenachrichtenschule | **Army Signal School** | |
| hrer | Leader | Major Luebsike |
| jutant | Personal Staff Officer | Oberleutnant d. R. Stahl |
| fz. z. V. (Offizier zur sonderen Verwendung) | Officer for Special Duties | Hauptmann d. R. Freiherr von Wechmar |
| jutantur (IIa) | **'A' Branch (11a)** | |
| ter | Director | Major Schräpler |
| teilung IIa = für Offiziers-ngelegenheiten | 11a – For matters concerning officers | 1. Adjutant Major Schräpler |
| teilung IIb = für Unter-offiziers-und Nannschafts-ngelegenheiten | 11b – for matters concerning NCOs & men | 2. Adjutant Major Schulze Brocksien |
| uptbüro | **Main Office** | |
| ter | Director | Sekretär Weihrauch |
| sistant | Assistant | Herr Krämer |

*Continued overleaf*

91

| Gerichts-Abteilung III | Courts Martial Dept | |
|---|---|---|
| Kriegsgericht/Richter | Senior Judge | Oberkriegsgerichtsrat Stark |
| Kriegsgericht/Richter | Judge | Feldkriegsgerichtsrat Dr Schönberg |
| Urkundsbeamter | Documents Official | Intendantur-Inspektor Himmler |
| | | |
| Hauptquartier (H. Qu.) | HQ Defence Unit | |
| Kommandant | Commandant | Major Zimmerman |
| Führer der Feg./Feld-gendarmeerie-Staffel | Head of Military Field Police | Leutnant d. R. Saumer |

### 21ST PANZER DIVISION ORDER OF BATTLE (WEF 1 OCTOBER 1941)

Divisional staff of whom the
  senior posts were:
Ia: Major von Heuduck; Major
Freiherr von Süsskind und
  Schwendi;
  Colonel Stempel
  Ib: Captain Böhles
  Ic: Lieutenant Rickert
  IIa: Captain Garke
  SMO: Dr Franz-Josef Pott
Units
  Map-store 200 (mot)
  Map Printing Troop
  DR section
  Pz Regt 5
  Anti-tank Bn 39 (mot)
  Inf Regt 104 (mot) (including
  MG Bn 8 as its III battalion)
  Arty Regt 155 (mot)
  Recce Bn 3 (mot)
  Sigs Bn 200 (mot) (including a
    tank sigs coy, a tank radio coy
    and a light sigs column)

Engr Bn 200 (mot)
Reinforcement Bn 200 (mot)
Supply Bn 200 (mot) including:
  Light Supply Columns (1 to 11)
  200 (mot)
  Tank Spare Parts Column 200
    (mot)
  Water Purification Column 200
    (mot)
  Heavy Fuel Supply Column 200
    (mot)
  Workshop Coy 200 (mot)
  MT Repair Coy 200 (mot)
  Supply Coy 200 (mot)
  Medical Coy 200 (mot)
  Field Hospital 200 (mot)
  Ambulance Platoon 200 (mot)
  Bakery Coy 200 (mot)
  Butchery Coy 200 (mot)
  Div Supply Section 200 (mot)
  Military Police Troop 200 (mot)
  Field Post Office 200 (mot)

## DAK HEADQUARTERS PERSONALITIES

**Lieutenant-Colonel von dem Borne.** First COS of DAK, who had been Rommel's 1a in the Aufklärungsstab Rommel. Heinz Werner Schmidt describes him in *With Rommel in the Desert* as being a powerfully built, slightly corpulent man, with a full face, intelligent eyes and a good sense of humour. David Irving calls him 'calm and circumspect', but he does not appear to have risen high in rank after his DAK service.

**Colonel Fritz Bayerlein**, on the other hand, who took over from von dem Borne in October 1941, was to become one of Rommel's best-known commanders. Born in Würzburg on 14 January 1899, he had fought as a private in the Great War. He then left the army but rejoined in 1921. He fought first in the campaigns against Poland as a staff officer in 10th Panzer Division, then in February 1940 became Ia of XIX Pz Korps from which Panzergruppe 2 was later created and fought in the Russian campaign. In October 1941 he was transferred to North Africa and became Ia of DAK. He was awarded the Knight's Cross on 26 December 1941, followed by the Oakleaves in July 1943 and the Swords in July 1944.[6] He became COS of Panzergruppe Afrika/Panzerarmee Afrika/1 italiensche Armee, but was posted back to Europe before the end of the Tunisian campaign, so escaped capture. After a brief period on the officer reserve, he served from October 1943 as commander of 10th Pz Div on the Eastern Front, taking part in the desperate breakout battles there. He ended his wartime career in the rank of Lieutenant-General, first as commander of the crack *Panzer Lehr* Division, in NW Europe, fighting in Normandy and the Ardennes offensive, then finally as commander of LIII Army Corps in the final battles in the West which continued right up to the last days of the war. He adored Rommel, who in turn took an instant liking to him – they also shared a mutual dislike for General Streich of 5 leichte which must have helped! Bayerlein also was highly regarded by his soldiers, Rommel remarking in a letter to Lucie on 14 January 1943, that it was Bayerlein's birthday and that he was being 'serenaded', going on to say that '...The Afrika Korps has a particularly high regard for him and has much to thank him for'. After the war Bayerlein wrote a book about the fighting in North Africa entitled: *Krieg ohne Hass* (*War Without Hatred*).

**Major Siegfried Westphal.** Perhaps the most able of the DAK operations officers was the aristocratic, brilliant and highly intelligent Siegfried Westphal, who would rise to the rank of General of Cavalry. Born on 18 March 1902 in Leipzig, he graduated from the famous Berlin Lichterfelde Cadet School on 10 November 1918 and joined the 12th Grenadier Regiment. Post-war he was accepted by the Reichsheer, becoming a Lieutenant in the 11th Cavalry. By 10 November 1928 he was commanding a squadron in the 13th Cavalry Regiment. Assigned to the War College in 1932, he was transferred to the operations section of the General Staff in 1935. This was to be his forte and although he commanded another cavalry squadron for some months, he returned to the staff to become Ia of 58th Infantry Division on 26 August 1939. Soon afterwards he was Ia of XXVI Army Corps and took part in the invasion of France and the Low Countries, serving afterwards on the cease-fire commission as a Major. On 15 June 1941 he was assigned to DAK as Ia. He would remain as Rommel's 'right-hand man' for the next eighteen months. Described by some as the 'conscience of Panzerarmee Afrika', he was twice recommended for the Knight's Cross by Rommel, but only awarded it once (see below). He subsequently served as Chief of Staff of the deutsche-italienische Panzerarmee Afrika, and commanded 164 leichte Afrika Division temporarily from 6 to 30 December 1942. Wounded in late May 1942, the following year he became Head of the Operations Staff to Field Marshal Kesselring, C-in-C

South in Italy, then was Head of the German Operational Section with the Italian High Command. Finally, in 1944, he moved on to become von Rundstedt's COS in the West. Taken prisoner, he spent 2½ years in captivity after the war and gave evidence at the Nuremberg trials on behalf of the German General Staff. He was the holder of the Knight's Cross, which he won in November 1942, when Ia of the deutsche–italienische Pz Armee, and the German Cross in Gold which he was awarded on 19 December 1941. The perfect staff officer, his code of honour was that General Staff Officers were entirely anonymous, acting always in the name of the commander – and naturally in their best interests.

**Major Otto.** Rommel described the DAK Quartermaster as being 'a first-class man, who organised supplies along the coast by small ships, thus considerably easing the pressure on our lorry columns' – high praise indeed from the 'Desert Fox'.

### ROMMEL'S PERSONAL STAFF
**Adjutant, batman and ADCs.** Rommel brought some of his 7th Pz Div staff with him from France, including his loyal Adjutant Major Hans Joachim Schräpler, and his equally loyal batman Corporal Herbert Günther, who not only looked after his clothes in the desert as he had done in France, but also now cooked his simple meals. Major Schräpler, who had been seriously wounded in France (see Chapter 3), was often used to command *ad hoc* operations (e.g., during the siege of Tobruk he led a break-in party which penetrated the defences). Sadly he was run down and killed in an accident involving one of Rommel's captured armoured command vehicles in December 1941. A third member of the ex-7th Pz Div personnel was Captain Hermann Aldinger, a reserve officer who had served in the same battalion as Rommel in the Great War and was also his old friend and confidant. He had been with him in France and would remain beside him for the rest of the Field Marshal's short life.

Given conditions in the desert, batman Günther must have had his work cut out to keep his officer looking clean and tidy. There were occasions when this was impossible, as some of the photographs of Rommel show, but if it were important for the 'Desert Fox' to look immaculate, Günther obliged. When he arrived, Rommel was wearing his normal continental uniform, but he had been fitted for a number of tropical uniforms, made of a fine light khaki cotton twill, worn with breeches and black leather riding-boots. He wore breeches on many occasions, trousers on others, sometimes shorts, and even a pith helmet or a cloth field cap, although his normal head-dress was his General's peaked cap (Schirmmütze). Rommel preferred to wear shirts with button-down collars to make the wearing of his *Pour le Mérite* and Knight's Cross easier (see later for full description of this shirt). He also found his long, dark olive-green leather overcoat a blessing in the bitter cold of the desert nights. Two items which were unique to Rommel were his tartan-style scarf and the British anti-gas goggles (see later) which became his trademark.

Rommel also took on Lieutenant (later Captain) Heinz Werner Schmidt as his operational aide. As well as accompanying Rommel on the battlefield, Schmidt dealt with much of the General's 'fan mail' in the evenings, sending out postcard photographs from a large carton full of them, the photograph having been taken by Hitler's official photographer, Hoffman of Munich; Rommel always personally signed each card. Schmidt remained with Rommel until November 1942, when he asked for a transfer to a combat unit. Rommel was sympathetic ('Quite right, Schmidt, as a lieutenant I should have done exactly the same ...' And he added with an unusual twinkle: 'A staff officer's life does not appeal to me either.') This was as far as their familiarity went. Schmidt records that it was months before Rommel called him anything other than by his rank. His successor was Lieutenant Graf von Schweppenburg, a disabled young war veteran, but he only stayed with Rommel for three months.

Rommel was as hard on his staff as he was on himself. In his book *Afrika Korps*, the late A. J. Barker talks of Rommel as being known by his own men as an: 'ambitious and ruthless driver, a hard man who placed more reliance on the whip than the carrot'. Certainly those closest to him on the battlefield tended to become battle casualties!

**Nazis.** As in 7th Pz Div, Rommel was allotted an aide who was a confirmed Nazi, namely a tough and ambitious member of the SS, the 36-year-old Lieutenant (later Captain) Alfred Ingemar Berndt. He was attached from Goebbels' Propaganda Ministry to look after DAK public relations, especially for Rommel. He did a splendid job, keeping Rommel and his DAK in the public eye, as well as maintaining the Rommel Diary and learning into the bargain to become a brave and resourceful soldier, despite his somewhat murky background. Rommel used him as a go-between with Hitler and he accompanied Rommel when he received his Field Marshal's baton from the Führer. When Rommel was ill in August 1942, Berndt looked after him, procuring a good cook, installing a small kitchen and arranging for fresh fruit and vegetables to be flown in daily (naturally without Rommel knowing or he would have refused them). He wrote of this to Frau Rommel, also saying that they fished, shot pigeons, obtained chickens and eggs in order to keep up Rommel's strength. Berndt accompanied Rommel when he left Africa for good.

**Private Medical Adviser.** Professor Dr Horster of Würzburg, one of the best-known stomach specialists in Germany, treated Rommel in North Africa, finding that he had chronic stomach and intestinal catarrh, nasal diphtheria and considerable circulation problems. Rommel talked about the excellent care he received from the 'good Doctor Horster'. It was he who suggested a final rest cure for Rommel and left Africa with him.

**Private Secretary.** Clerical Corporal (later Sergeant (Feldwebel)) Albert Böttcher was an extremely important member of Rommel's staff, being his private secretary. Böttcher accompanied him everywhere in Cyrenaica, filling numerous shorthand pads with his letters, etc., which were fortunately preserved in *The Rommel Papers*. On at least one occasion Rommel sent Böttcher home to see Lucie, bringing with him a selection of gifts for her coming birthday. After the war, David Irving tried to trace him but discovered that he had committed suicide, having had a drink problem.

**Interpreter.** An important personal staff member at this time was Rommel's personal interpreter, Lieutenant Wilfried Armbruster, described by David Irving as being a 'bright young lieutenant with an Italian mother and a talent for mimicry'. On one occasion he and Rommel each shot a gazelle from moving staff cars, which made a splendid Christmas dinner in 1942!

**War Correspondent.** Another member of the 'PR Team' was Lutz Koch, Rommel's personal war correspondent, who broadcast many stirring eye-witness descriptions of battles – such as the fall of Tobruk, after which Rommel was promoted to Field Marshal.

**Vehicles and Vehicle Crews.** As in France, Rommel had his own small number of highly mobile vehicles, forming his *Gefechtsstaffel*, including armoured cars, staff cars, Volkswagens and captured British armoured command vehicles. Three of these last named, British AEC 4x4 Mark I ACVs, had been taken at the same time as two British generals (O'Connor and Neame) were captured. Rommel kept two of the ACVs, nicknamed them Mammuten (Mammoths) and gave them personal names 'Max' and 'Moritz' after two characters in a children's story by Wilhelm Busch. The driver of Rommel's Sdkfz 250/3 armoured car which he used for cross-country travel, was initially a Corporal Eggert. He was killed by a ground-strafing aircraft ten miles west of Bardia in mid-April 1941 when it attacked the headquarters column. Another fatality of the strafing was his dispatch rider, Private Kanthak. The driver of Rommel's Mammut was also wounded because the armoured shield over the driver's windscreen, was not in place and as a result, Rommel took over and drove the vehicle himself all night (he wrote to Lucie about the incident, saying that the road was terrible and as he wanted to get back to the main HQ that night, they turned off into the desert, navigating by the stars. But it clouded over, so they had to wait until morning to complete their journey.)

What was different from the Ghost Division Gefechtsstaffel were the 14–15 motorised radio stations, which followed behind the small command staff to maintain communications between Rommel and his main HQ. Personal orders from Rommel were always transmitted using a special call sign which took precedence over all other radio traffic.

**Kampfstaffel.** This was a small army unit with the task of protecting the Corps/Army HQ, which assumed considerable importance in the open desert spaces.

**Above:** Erwin and Lucie Rommel, photographed after he was awarded his *Pour le Mérit* on 18 December 1917. (David Irving)

**Above right:** A radio vehicle in operation during Reichswehr manoeuvres in the late 1920s. (Tank Museum)

**Below:** Major-General Erwin Rommel, Head-quarters Commandant of the Führerhaupt-quartiere, seen here with Adolf Hitler and Martin Bormann (with goggles), at Maslowie airfield, Poland, 10 September 1939. (*After the Battle*)

**Top:** All German soldiers were made to swear an oath of allegiance to Adolf Hitler as Führer of the Reich and Supreme Commander of the armed forces. (IWM - HU 18034)

**Above:** The Führer with Rommel on the Polish front. (Tank Museum)

**Left:** The crew of this PzKpfw IV belonging to 7 Pz Div are standing in front of their tank, wearing a selection of uniforms. The tank commander, for example, is not wearing his black panzer uniform, and only two of the crew are wearing the padded Schutzmütze tank beret. (Tank Museum)

**Right:** The 15cm sIG 33 gun, mounted on the PzKpfw I chassis, was a most effective infantry support gun. In 7 Pz Div they were in s IG Kompanie 705 attached to 7 Schützen Brigade. (Author's collection)

**Below:** Men of Rommel's division crossing water obstacles in rubber boats. Note that all are carrying their respirators in the well-known cylindrical metal containers. (Tank Museum)

**Above:** PzKpfw IIs of Pz Regt 25 crossing a bridge built by 7 Pz Div's engineers across the Canal de la Bassée. Note the muzzle covers on the 20mm cannon and MG 34 (to keep the dust out). The tank commander wears the Iron Cross 2nd Class, plus a panzer assault badge. (Tank Museum)

**Below:** The main mortar used to provide direct fire support for the infantry was the 8cm GrW34; the crew are seen here loading the 3.5kg shell. The mortar had a maximum range of 2,400m. (Tank Museum)

**Below:** The two standard hand-grenades – the HE Stick grenade (Stielgranate 24) and HE egg grenade (Eirgranate 39). (IWM - MH 345)

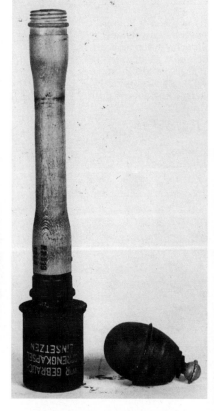

**Above:** The main anti-tank gun of Panzer-jägerabteilung 42 was the 37mm, of which there were three batteries each of twelve guns. (Tank Museum)

**Below:** An interesting display of infantry small arms comprising two standard rifles (Karabiner 98K), an MG 34 machine-gun, plus ammunition belts. Note also the gasmask and two tin gasmask containers. (IWM - E 3091)

**Above:** The men who conquered France so swiftly were tank crewmen like this tired and grubby tank driver, of Pz Regt 25, which had driven across France in a remarkably short time, taking nearly 98,000 prisoners for the loss of just 42 tanks totally destroyed. (Tank Museum)

**Left:** A close-up of a German Other Ranks wartime field-grey tunic Model 1936, with field-grey collar. Note the shoulder, collar and chest insignia, also the medals, etc., of this *unteroffizier* – probably dark green shoulder straps with silver NCO *tress* (lace) and white *Waffenfarbe* outer piping; silver *tresse* around collar with light-grey collar bars (*litzen*); breast eagle, Iron Cross, etc. (IWM - HU 23340)

**Above:** Excellent picture of a rifle section of a motorised infantry unit moving through a village street during May 1940. Note, for example, the stick grenades thrust into their belts, and gas-capes in containers on their chests. (IWM - MH 12845)

**Below:** Motorcyle troops, wearing their rubberised protective coats (Schutzmantel). They are clearly on traffic duty; note the position of the gasmask container, worn around the neck. (IWM - HU 233332)

**Above:** A rear view of Rommel's eight-wheeled Panzerfunkwagen Sd Kfz 263. The plate on the rear, WH-143179, shows that it belonged to Wehrkreis XIV (i.e., 14th Military District). (Tank Museum)

**Left:** Rommel standing on the main coastal road – the Via Balbia. He is wearing his normal uniform, although he did occasionally wear shorts instead of breeches and boots. He is also wearing a pair of the British anti-gas goggles which he 'acquired' from his opponents. They became one of his 'trademarks'. (IWM - HU 5623)

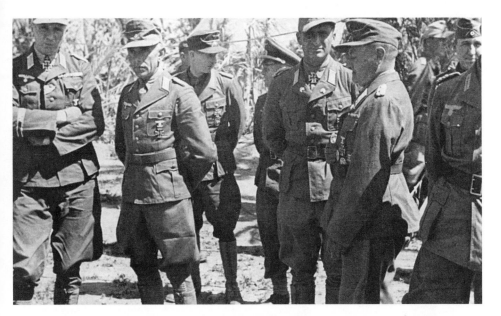

**Above:** An excellent photograph of a group of officers in tropical uniforms – all looking immaculate! It was taken on 20 March 1942 at Umm er Rzem oasis. Left to right: Colonel Menny, Colonel Bruer, Major von Heuduck, Major-General von Bismarck (in peaked cap), Captain Kümmel, Colonel Muller, Colonel Pfeiffer and Colonel Ewert. (Panzermuseum)

**Below:** A cheerful group of panzer grenadiers from 15 Pz Div, wearing battle-stained uniforms. Note the basic rifleman's webbing straps and belts. There is also a selection of breast badges: the Gefreiter (corporal), for example, is wearing an Infantry Assault combat badge, plus his Iron Cross 2nd Class in its normal place. (IWM - NA 1815)

**Top:** The Italians always formed a major portion of Rommel's fighting troops. Here Rommel talks with a number of Italian officers at the Casa Cantoniera Umm er Rzem (an Italian guard station on the Via Balbia). The photograph shows a number of different Italian temperate and tropical uniforms as well as a captured British ambulance to the rear. (Rolf Münninger)

**Left:** Three captured Italian generals (left to right: Brigadier Massina, Major-General Brunetti and Brigadier Bignani of the Trento Division). They wear an interesting mix of temperate and tropical style officers' uniforms. (IWM - E 19149)

**Left:** Even in the desert, Italian tank crews often still wore their special leather crash-helmets, black leather coats and ammunition bandoliers. (Author's collection)

**Above:** The DAK on the march in January 1942. The panzers are followed by a mix of lorries and half-tracks. (IWM - MH 5828)

**Below:** This Feldpost Volkswagen is dwarfed by an SdKfz 251/7 half-track, which is being used as the prime mover for an 8.8cm AA/anti-tank gun. (IWM - MH 5830)

**Top left:** The most feared weapon on the desert battlefield was the 8.8cm AA/anti-tank gun, which could easily defeat any tank armour plate at considerable ranges. (Tank Museum)

**Centre left:** This SdKfz 251/7 half-track is towing a heavy 15cm 5 FH 18 howitzer. (IWM - MH 5869)

**Bottom left:** The VW Kübelwagen was used for a wide variety of tasks, especially because it was found to be greatly superior to motorcycles on most surfaces – except for shifting sands. (IWM - HU 5616)

**Above:** The 105mm howitzer (10.5cm le FH 18) was the standard light field howitzer, which was fitted with a muzzle brake when used with more powerful propellant loads. (IWM - MH 5568)

**Below:** PzKpfw III Ausf E/F/Gs were armed with a 3.7cm main gun, but later upgunned to the 5cm, giving the tank better firepower than the British armour (e.g., 2pdr on Matilda Mk 2) which opposed them in the early days. (Tank Museum)

**Above:** 2cm Flak 38 dual-purpose light AA/anti-tank guns, lorry-mounted for speedy manoeuvre in the anti-tank role. (Author's collection).

**Left:** Digging-in. This infantryman is digging a foxhole with his entrenching tool (kleiner Spaten) which was carried in its cover on the left hip. (IWM - MH 5834)

**Top right:** Laying and lifting mines was an important and unending task for the engineers. Rommel made great use of his 'Devil's Gardens' at El Alamein. Here a German pioneer removes a British anti-tank mine. (IWM - MH 5863)

**Bottom right:** Small numbers of Tiger Es were sent to North Africa towards the end of 1942 and took part in various battles in Tunisia. This Tiger was taken off the battlefield near Medjez-el-Bab virtually undamaged. The Tiger with its 88mm gun was superior to most other tanks on the battlefield. (Tank Museum)

**Above:** Bersaglieri of the 5th Regiment in action during the Axis withdrawal in 1942. Their feathered helmets made them instantly recognisable. (Stato Maggiore dell'Escercito)

**Below:** Italian armoured cars on patrol in a village in North Africa. The Fiat-Ansaldo AB 41 was probably the best Italian armoured car of the war. (Tank Museum)

**Radio Intercept.** A most important unit which arrived in late April 1941 was the third company of Intelligence Unit 56 – later to be known as 621 Radio Intercept Company, commanded by Lieutenant Alfred Seebohm. Until it was captured in 1942 and Seebohm was killed, this unit provided Rommel with invaluable tactical information on enemy plans and strengths. Seebohm had painstakingly compiled irreplaceable code-books and enemy orders of battle – the capture of this information must have been an eye-opener to the British to discover how slack their radio security was!

SENIOR OFFICER CASUALTY RATE
The problems of commanding troops in a 'fluid' campaign in an area such as North Africa, where the front line was often so changeable, where map reading and route finding were exceptionally difficult, exacerbated by the poor maps (see Siegfried Westphal's remarks earlier in this chapter) and such natural problems as sandstorms and mirages, meant that one could never be 100 per cent certain that even senior officers would be as safe as in other theatres. Add to this the method of command which Rommel advocated for all his commanders – of which he was a shining example – that they should lead from the front, and it was obvious that many would become battle casualties. Here is a list (not exhaustive) of divisional commanders and above, who were killed, wounded, missing, captured or surrendered.

**Killed – seven:** Major-General Heinrich von Prittwitz und Gaffron on 10 April 1941; Major-General Walter Neumann-Silkow died in Derna Hospital on 9 December 1941; Major-General Max Sümmermann on 10 December 1941; Major-General Georg von Bismarck in an air attack on 31 August 1942; General of Cavalry Georg Stumme died of a heart attack on 24 October 1942; Major-General Heinz von Randow on 21 December 1942; Lieutenant-General Wolfgang Fischer on 1 February 1943.

**Wounded – nine (in addition to Rommel):** Lieutenant-General Heinrich Kircheim in April 1941; Major-General Neumann-Silkow on 6 December 1941 (died of wounds two days later); Major-General Richard Veith on 28 April 1942; Lieutenant-General Gustav von Värst on 26 May 1942; Major-General Georg von Bismarck on 17 July 1942; Gen d. Pz. Tr. Walther K. Nehring and Major-General Kleeman both on 31 August 1942 in the same air attack that killed Gen von Bismarck (Kleeman was wounded again on 2 September 1942 when his car hit a mine near the Alam Halfa ridge); Gen d. Pz. Tr. Gustav Fehn on 16 January 1943; Gen d. Pz. Tr. Kurt Freiherr von Lebenstein on 17 February 1943.

**Missing – one:** Lieutenant-General Kurt Thomas on 1 April 1943.

**Captured – seven:** Major-General Hans-Karl Freiherr von Esebeck on 25 July 1941; Major-General Johann von Ravenstein on 29 November 1941; Lieutenant-General Theodor Graf von Sponeck on 12 May 1942; Lieutenant General Willibald Borowietz on 13 May 1942; Lieutenant-General Ludwig Crüwell on 29 October 1942; Gen d. Pz. Tr. Wilhelm Ritter von Thoma on 4 November 1942; Major-General Fritz Freiherr von Broich on 12 May 1943.

**Surrendered (at the end of the campaign) – five:** Colonel-General Jurgen von Arnim; Major-General Heinrich-Hermann von Hulsen; Lieutenant-General Gotthard Franz; Generale di Armata Giovanni Messe; Major-General Karl Bülowius.

In addition of course, a number of commanders, including eventually Rommel himself, had to leave the theatre on medical grounds, and a small number of others – such as Major-General Johannes Streich – were sacked.

## A SOLDIER OF THE DEUTSCHES AFRIKAKORPS

**Dress**
I have already mentioned some of the wide range of items which had caught the imagination of one German officer before he was posted to North Africa. Before presenting a full list of personal uniform and equipment, it is worthwhile noting that just as in the British and Commonwealth forces, mixtures of dress which might not have been tolerated in other theatres of war were permitted in the Western Desert by both armies – and even the great 'Desert Fox' himself wore such items – multi-coloured tartan scarf and British goggles, the latter becoming one of his trademarks. Captain Heinz Werner Schmidt recalled how Rommel had first found the goggles, among the debris from captured vehicles at Mechili airport. He took an immediate fancy to them and said: 'Booty – permissible I take it even for a general!' From then on they became the distinguishing mark of the 'Desert Fox'. They were in fact quite flimsy anti-gas goggles, so Rommel must have 'acquired' a fairly large supply. At times, when the extended lines of re-supply were broken by enemy action on land or sea, the DAK had to depend upon scrounging from their Italian allies, or scavenging from the enemy, that is to say, using captured enemy stores which would then be 'adapted' to resemble their German equivalent.

**Tropical Uniforms.** The specially designed, olive-green tropical uniform, comprising a jacket, shirt, trousers or shorts, head-dress, etc., was the result of a lot of hard work by the Tropical Institute of the University of Hamburg, who were given the task of designing it in 1940. Once approved, the clothing was produced by manufacturers in Berlin and Silesia. They managed to complete their task in time for the first two divisions to be properly equipped before they departed, although there was some variation in shades of colour in the initial uniforms, which was speedily rectified. Most importantly, the 'customer' on the whole definitely approved of the smart and comfortable uniform. They could wear it when on leave in Germany during the summer period (1 May to 30 September) and it was approved for wear in other semi-tropical regions, such as Crete, Italy and the Crimea. The jacket was basically of the same design as the standard single-breasted army field jacket. It was usually worn open at the neck, but it could be fastened right up to the throat. Made of lightweight cotton, it had five buttons in front, four pockets (two breast, two side, all pleated), all with olive-coloured 'pebbled' buttons. A tropical eagle was worn above the right breast pocket – the eagle being in light blue embroidery on a copper brown background (some officers wore normal-style bullion eagles instead). There were four varieties of nether garments: long, straight trousers; field trousers, worn tucked into boots; riding-breeches, worn with riding-boots or lace-up tropical boots; shorts, worn with long socks, shoes or boots. But the wearing of shorts was only permitted between 0800 and 1700 hours, as an anti-malarial mosquito precaution. Long socks (sometimes rolled down) were invariably worn with shorts, together with regulation shoes or boots. I have not come across any examples of the suede desert boots (known colloquially as 'brothel creepers') favoured by some British officers, ever being worn in the DAK, but the canvas and leather, lace-up tropical boot was widely worn, as was the ankle boot. Long socks or tropical boots were essential wear to prevent desert sores, which were slow to heal. The tropical shirt was of olive-green cotton drill. It had two pleated breast pockets with buttons, four buttons down the front and two buttons per cuff. The shirt had detachable shoulder-straps and could be worn with an olive-coloured tie – but only with the blouse, otherwise it was always worn open-necked.[7]

**Head-dress.** A variety was worn, but the only truly 'tropical' items were: the peaked field cap (Feldmütze mit grossem Schirm), a 'fore and aft' cap without a peak – both these two were of olive-green drill; the tropical/pith helmet, made of cork and canvas, later issues being covered with wool. Bulky and cumbersome to carry, especially if a steel helmet had to be carried as well, they were not widely worn except in rear areas. The steel helmet was the normal M35 model, sand-coloured (with or without real sand being applied to the wet paint) and sometimes worn with cloth helmet cover.

**Special items.** A number of special items of clothing appeared from time to time, such as: a very smart white tropical uniform (worn with white shirt and black tie); a tropical greatcoat (identical to normal but in olive-green); fine grain leather greatcoats (high-ranking officers only); a protective coat for motorcyclists (Schützmantel); olive or tan scarves, sweaters and gloves (also in grey).

**Luftwaffe personnel.** As explained later in this chapter, Luftwaffe personnel operated with DAK throughout the campaigns. Initially they wore standard army tropical uniform, with only the red felt-backed collar tabs of the Luftwaffe's European jacket as a distinguishing symbol. But from late 1941 they were mostly issued with the Luftwaffe's own version of the army uniform.

### Equipment
Because of the damage which heat and lack of humidity cause to leather, most of the leather items of personal equipment were replaced by olive-coloured webbing. Waistbelts, ammunition pouches, etc., of web material were issued, although many soldiers (especially officers) continued to wear leather, and 'Y' straps and 'D' rings continued to be of leather. Olive-coloured canvas breadbags – used to contain a variety of items as well as rations (e.g., washing gear, eating utensils) – were widely used, and the most important life-saving item was the 2-pint felt-covered aluminium/enamelled steel canteen complete with cup (Feldflasche und Trinkbecher). Olive-coloured canvas rucksacks with webbing or leather fittings were issued to hold personal items, spare clothing, etc., and the similarly coloured canvas pack (Tornister) was the same as the normal European issue. Other important items which did not vary from normal issue were: mess kit (Kochgeschirr), entrenching tool, gas mask and canister (possibly sand-coloured), rolled shelter quarter. Various models of sand/dust goggles, some with clear, others with amber, lenses were issued to all members of mechanised units, although drivers and motorcyclists received a heavier version. Some troops, including the 'Desert Fox' preferred captured British anti-gas goggles as has already been mentioned.

### Insignia
The only major difference between the tropical rank insignia and normal was the colour of the background material, which matched the tropical uniforms, although it was not uncommon to see European-style chevrons and shoulder-straps, etc., being used on tropical uniforms.

**Cuff Titles.** One of the main distinguishing items was of course the 'AFRIKAKORPS' cuff title, worn on the right sleeve, some 15cm from the bottom of the sleeve. There were various cuff titles, the first official one being authorised on 18 July 1941 for members of DAK fighting in North Africa. On 15 January 1943, the 'AFRIKA' cuff title was introduced as a campaign decoration for all three branches of the Wehrmacht. The criteria for this award were: six months' service on African soil, or wounded in combat in the North Africa theatre, or contracting an illness there which meant evacuation but only after at least three months before contracting the illness.

### Personal Weapons
The majority of personal weapons as used in France 1940 (see Chapter 3) were employed in North Africa, all having proved themselves in battle. But an exception was probably the Machine Pistol 40 (MP 40) which had been in short supply in 1940 – just three or four per company – but was

now in mass production at a number of centres, with sub-assemblies being made by sub-contractors. It was a perfect example of quick and cheap production (cf. the British Sten Gun) and was such a good weapon that it soon became much prized by friend and foe alike. It was ideal for close-quarters fighting and was issued in great numbers (more than 48,000 were manufactured during the war). The 9mm MP 40 weighed just under 9 pounds, had a magazine capacity of 32 rounds and a cyclic rate of fire of 500rpm.

## VEHICLES AND HEAVY WEAPONS

### Tanks

Until the arrival of such lend-lease vehicles as the American M3 Medium (Grant/Lee) and M4 Medium (Sherman), Allied armour was hopelessly outgunned by the more heavily armed panzers, known as 'Specials'. Examples of such AFVs were the improved PzKpfw III Ausf H onwards, which mounted the KwK L/42 5cm gun in place of the shorter range 3.7cm. Even a proportion of the German armour which first arrived in North Africa was armed with these more powerful guns. In addition, the PzKpfw IV which initially mounted the useful medium support 7.5cm KwK L/24 gun, was re-armed at Ausf F2 stage, with the long-barrelled 7.5cm KwK L/43 gun. This really was 'Special'! Add to this formidable array, the arrival of the dreaded PzKpfw VI Tiger with its 88mm gun in December 1942, to join the continuing presence of the same calibre 8.8cm Flak/anti-tank gun probably the most effective and most feared anti-tank gun of the war – and one can well appreciate the problems faced by Allied armour. As the tables below show, these weapons, despite their relatively small numbers, presented continual problems for the British, especially when employed with the battlefield brilliance of a master tactician such as the 'Desert Fox'.

### Other AFVs

The Western Desert was the perfect arena for recce vehicles and it was the leading armoured cars of the Mechanised Reconnaissance Battalion 3 (Aufklärungsabteilung 3 (mot) ) of 5 leichte Division which made first contact with an advanced recce unit of British 2nd Armoured Division, near Mersa el Brega at 0950 hours on 31 March 1941. AA3 contained both light and heavy armoured cars (see table below), but it was undoubtedly the large, 8-wheelers which made the most profound impression, with their thick armour and powerful weapons – for example, the same 7.5cm gun as mounted on PzKpfw IV. In addition to armoured cars, the recce battalion also possessed integrated mechanised infantry with their own mortars and medium machine-guns, plus close-support artillery, engineers, etc. The mechanised infantry especially, made use of the other invaluable German AFV, the half-track, which again gave them a battlefield superiority over their opponents. As the other table shows, there was an enormous range of half-tracks, both light and heavy, varying from the remarkable little tracked motorcycle (Kettenkrad) to the SdKfz 250 (leichter Schützenpanzerwagen) series to the SdKfz 251 (mittlerer Schützenpanzerwagen) the standard medium half-track which was used to carry or tow a wide variety of weapon systems as well as being the 'maid of all work' as a recce vehicle or troop carrier (APC) and on to heavier, more specialised half-tracks.

## Examples of German armoured cars

| | | |
|---|---|---|
| SdKfz 221, 222 and 223 | | SdKfz 231, 232, 234 |
| light armd car (leichter Panzerspähwagen) | | heavy armd car (schwerer Panzerspähwagen) |

(Details below are of the SdKfz 222 and the SdKfz 232)

| | | |
|---|---|---|
| Weight (tons) | 4.8 | 8.3 |
| Crew | 3 | 4 |
| Dimensions (metres): | | |
| Length | 4.8 | 5.8 |
| Height | 2 | 2.4 |
| Width | 1.9 | 2.2 |
| Armament | 1x2cm KwK 30 | 1x2cm KwK 30 (233 had a 7.5cm StuK37 L/24) |
| Armour (mm): | | |
| max | 8.0 | 15.0 |
| min | 5.0 | 5.0 |
| Max speed (km/hr) | 85 | 85 |
| Range (kms) | 300 | 300 |

## Examples of German half-tracks

| | SdKfz 250 | SdKfz 251 |
|---|---|---|
| Weight (tons) | 5.4 | 7.8 |
| Crew | 2 plus | 2 plus |
| Dimensions (metres): | | |
| Length | 4.6 | 5.8 |
| Height | 1.7 | 1.8 |
| Width | 2.0 | 2.1 |

Armament: various MGs, mortars, anti-tank guns, 7.5cm guns

| | | |
|---|---|---|
| Armour (mm): | | |
| max | 15.0 | 14.5 |
| min | 6.0 | 6.0 |
| Max speed (km/hr) | 60 | 53 |
| Range (kms) | 300 | 300 |

## Artillery

In keeping with the rest of the German Army, DAK had a wide range of artillery guns of all types, its anti-tank guns, for example, ranging from the small but effective 2.8cm sPzB 41 tapered-bore weapon and the more

# The Penetrative Capabilities of German Tank and Anti-tank-Guns

| Vehicle | Aspect | 300 | 500 | 600 | 700 | 800 | 900 | 1000–1100 | 1200 | 1400 | 1500–1600 | 1700–1800 | 2000–2100 | 2500–2600 | Over 3000 |
|---|---|---|---|---|---|---|---|---|---|---|---|---|---|---|---|
| STUART | Side | | | | | | 37mm A/Tk | | | | | | | Mk IV Special | Mk VI Tiger, 76.2mm, 75mm, 88mm A/Tks |
| STUART | Front | | 37mm A/Tk | | | | | | Mk IV | | Mk III, IV & III Special & 50mm A/Tk | | | Mk IV Special | Mk VI Tiger, 76.2mm, 75mm, 88mm A/Tks |
| GRANT | Side | Mk IV | 37mm A/Tk | | | Mk III | | | Mk IV | | Mk III, IV & III Special & 50mm A/Tk | | | Mk IV Special | Mk VI Tiger, 76.2mm, 75mm, 88mm A/Tks |
| GRANT | Front | | | | | | | Mk III Special 50mm A/TK | | | | | | 76.2mm, 75mm A/Tk; Mk IV Special | Mk VI Tiger, 88mm A/Tks |
| SHERMAN | Side | Mk IV | 37mm A/Tk | | | Mk III | | | Mk IV | | Mk III, IV & III Special & 50mm A/Tk | | | Mk IV Special | Mk VI Tiger, 75mm, 88mm A/Tks |
| SHERMAN | Front | | | | | | | Mk III Special 50mm A/TK | | | | | | 76.2mm, 75mm A/Tk; Mk IV Special | Mk VI Tiger, 88mm A/Tks |
| CRUSADER II & III | Side | | | | | | 37mm A/Tk | | Mk III | | Mk III, IV & III Special | | | Mk IV Special | Mk VI Tiger, 76.2mm, 75mm, 88mm A/Tks |
| CRUSADER II & III | Front | 37mm A/Tk | | Mk IV | | | | Mk III Special 50mm A/TK | Mk III | | Mk III Special 50mm A/TK | | | Mk IV Special | Mk VI Tiger, 76.2mm, 75mm, 88mm A/Tks |
| VALENTINE I–IV | Side | 37mm A/Tk | | | | | | | Mk III | | Mk IV Special 75mm A/TK | | | Mk IV Special | Mk VI Tiger, 76.2mm, 75mm, 88mm A/Tks |
| VALENTINE I–IV | Front | | | | | | | | | 76.2mm | | Mk IV Special 75mm A/TK | | | Mk VI Tiger, 88mm A/Tks |
| VALENTINE I–IV | Side | 37mm A/Tk | | | | | | | Mk III | | | | Mk IV Special 75mm A/TK | | Mk VI Tiger, 76.2mm, 75mm, 88mm A/Tks |
| VALENTINE I–IV | Front | | | | | | | | | | | | | | Mk VI Tiger, 88mm A/Tks |
| CHURCHILL | Side | 37mm A/Tk | | Mk IV | 76.2mm | | | Mk IV Special 75mm A/TK | | | | | | | Mk VI Tiger, 76.2mm, 75mm, 88mm A/Tks |
| CHURCHILL | Front | | | | | | | | | | | | Mk VI Tiger, 88mm A/Tks | | |

**The Penetrative Capabilities of Allied Tank and Anti-tank Guns**

Yards (horizontal axis): 0, 100, 200, 300, 400, 500, 600, 700, 800, 900, 1000, 1100, 1200, 1300, 1400, 1500, 1600, 1700, 1800, 1900, 2000, 2100, 2200, 2300, 2400, 2500, 2600, 2700, 2800, 2900, Over 3000

| Armour / Facing | Penetrating weapons (by approximate range in yards) |
|---|---|
| **Pz KpFw III — Side** | ≈200: 2 pdr, Crusader II, Valentine I & IV · ≈1600: 2 pdr, Crusader II, Valentine I & IV · ≈2300–2400: Stuart & Grant 37mm · ≈2500: Crusader II, Valentine IV & 2 pdr · ≈2600: Crusader III, Churchill IV, Valentine IX · ≈2700: 6 pdr II · Over 3000: Sherman 37mm HV, Crusader III, Churchill IV, Valentine IX, 25 pdr, 6 pdr II, III & IV |
| **Pz KpFw III — Front** | ≈400: 2 pdr, Crusader II, Valentine I & IV · ≈500: Grant & Stuart 37mm · ≈800: 6 pdr, Crusader II, Churchill IV, Valentine IX · ≈1000: 2 pdr, Crusader II, Valentine I · ≈1300: 25 pdr · ≈2000: Sherman |
| **Pz KpFw III SPECIAL — Side** | ≈300: Crusader II, Valentine I & IV, 2 pdr · ≈900: Crusader III, Valentine IV, 2 pdr · ≈800: Crusader III, Churchill IV, Valentine IX, 6 pdr · ≈1600: Crusader II, Valentine IV, 2 pdr · ≈2300: Stuart & Grant 37mm · ≈2400: Crusader II, Valentine IV & 2 pdr · ≈2600: Crusader III, Churchill IV, Valentine IX & 6 pdr II · Over 3000: Crusader III, Churchill IV, Valentine IX, 25 pdr, 6 pdr II & IV |
| **Pz KpFw III SPECIAL — Front** | ≈1500: 6 pdr II, Crusader III, Churchill IV, Valentine IX, Sherman · ≈1300: 25 pdr |
| **Pz KpFw IV & SPECIAL — Side** | ≈300: Crusader II, Valentine I & IV, 2 pdr · ≈1000: Crusader III, Valentine I & IV, 2 pdr · ≈800: Crusader III, Churchill IV, Valentine IX, 6 pdr · ≈1000: Stuart & Grant 37mm · ≈2000: Crusader III, Churchill IV, Valentine IX, Grant & 6 pdr II · ≈2400: Crusader II, Valentine IV & 2 pdr · ≈2600: Crusader III, Churchill IV, Valentine IX, 6 pdr II · Over 3000: Crusader III, Churchill IV, Valentine IX, 25 pdr, 6 pdr II & IV |
| **Pz KpFw IV & SPECIAL — Front** | ≈600: Stuart & Grant 37mm · ≈1000: Valentine I & IV, Crusader II, 2 pdr · ≈1300: 25 pdr · ≈2000: Sherman · ≈2600: Sherman & 25 pdr |
| **Pz KpFw VI TIGER — Side** | ≈200: 2 pdr, Crusader II, Valentine I & IV · ≈600: Stuart & Grant 37mm · ≈1000: Crusader III, Churchill IV, Valentine IX, Serman, 6 pdr II · ≈1400: 25 pdr · ≈2100: Tanks using 6 pdr V guns, 6 pdr IV |
| **Pz KpFw VI TIGER — Turret & Upper Sides** | ≈400–500: Crusader III Churchill IV Valentine IX, 6 pdr II & III, 25 pdr · ≈700: Tanks using 6 pdr V guns, 6 pdr IV · ≈1200: 17 pdr at certain ranges |
| **Pz KpFw VI TIGER — Front** | — |

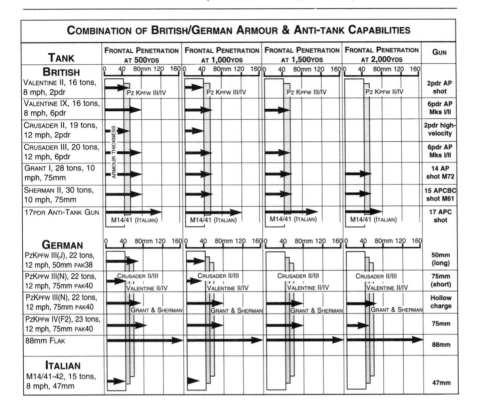

| COMBINATION OF BRITISH/GERMAN ARMOUR & ANTI-TANK CAPABILITIES | | | | | |
|---|---|---|---|---|---|
| **TANK** | FRONTAL PENETRATION AT 500YDS | FRONTAL PENETRATION AT 1,000YDS | FRONTAL PENETRATION AT 1,500YDS | FRONTAL PENETRATION AT 2,000YDS | GUN |
| **BRITISH** | 0  40  80mm 120  160 | 0  40  80mm 120  160 | 0  40  80mm 120  160 | 0  40  80mm 120  160 | |
| VALENTINE II, 16 tons, 8 mph, 2pdr | Pz KPFW III/IV | Pz KPFW III/IV | Pz KPFW III/IV | Pz KPFW II/IV | 2pdr AP shot |
| VALENTINE IX, 16 tons, 8 mph, 6pdr | | | | | 6pdr AP Mks I/II |
| CRUSADER II, 19 tons, 12 mph, 2pdr | | | | | 2pdr high-velocity |
| CRUSADER III, 20 tons, 12 mph, 6pdr | | | | | 6pdr AP Mks I/II |
| GRANT I, 28 tons, 10 mph, 75mm | | | | | 14 AP shot M72 |
| SHERMAN II, 30 tons, 10 mph, 75mm | | | | | 15 APCBC shot M61 |
| 17PDR ANTI-TANK GUN | M14/41 (ITALIAN) | M14/41 (ITALIAN) | M14/41 (ITALIAN) | M14/41 (ITALIAN) | 17 APC shot |
| **GERMAN** | 0  40  80mm 120  160 | 0  40  80mm 120  160 | 0  40  80mm 120  160 | 0  40  80mm 120  160 | |
| PzKPFW III(J), 22 tons, 12 mph, 50mm PAK38 | | | | | 50mm (long) |
| PzKPFW III(N), 22 tons, 12 mph, 75mm PAK40 | CRUSADER II/III / VALENTINE II/IV | CRUSADER II/III / VALENTINE II/IV | CRUSADER II/III / VALENTINE II/IV | CRUSADER II/III / VALENTINE II/IV | 75mm (short) |
| PzKPFW III(N), 22 tons, 12 mph, 75mm PAK40 | GRANT & SHERMAN | GRANT & SHERMAN | GRANT & SHERMAN | GRANT & SHERMAN | Hollow charge |
| PzKPFW IV(F2), 23 tons, 12 mph, 75mm PAK40 | | | | | 75mm |
| 88mm FLAK | | | | | 88mm |
| **ITALIAN** | | | | | |
| M14/41-42, 15 tons, 8 mph, 47mm | | | | | 47mm |

widely-used 3.7cm PaK 35/36 L/45 up to the highly lethal 8.8cm, via 4.7cm, 5cm and 7.5cm weapons. But the 8.8cm PaK 43 did not enter service until post-North Africa, so the '88' which was met there was the 8.8cm FlaK 18, 36, 37 or 41,[8] all of which were used in the ground role. The '88' could penetrate some 80mm of armour at 1,500 metres. In addition to having the support of field and heavy artillery,[9] both wheeled and tracked, the infantry had their own 7.5cm light and 150mm heavy infantry guns:

| | *7.5cm le.IG 18* | *15cm s.IG 33* |
|---|---|---|
| Calibre | 75mm | 150mm |
| Range (metres) | 1,000–2,500m | 1,500–3,000m |
| Crew | 6 | 7 |

The former was light and handy, the latter too heavy and cumbersome for the infantry, despite being very effective and reliable.

There were normally three batteries in an artillery regiment, two of them equipped with twelve 10.5cm howitzers each, the third having a mix of 10cm or 10.5cm guns and 15cm howitzers – see details below. But a wide range of artillery was used, including many captured Russian, French, etc., pieces.

## Examples of German towed artillery

| Type | 10.5cm le.FH 18 | 10cm K 18 | 15cm s.FH 18 |
|---|---|---|---|
| Calibre | 105mm | 105mm | 149mm |
| Max range (metres) | 10,675 | 19,075 | 13,325 |
| Muzzle velocity | 470m/s | 835m/s | 520m/s |
| Shell wt (kg) (HE) | 14.8 | 15.4 | 43.5 |

## Examples of German self-propelled artillery

| | 4.7cm PaK(t) (Sf) auf PzKpfw anti-tank gun (Panzerjäger) | 15cm s.IG auf PzKpfw II heavy tracked infantry gun |
|---|---|---|
| Calibre | 47mm | 150mm |
| Weight (tons) | 6.4 | 11.2 |
| Crew | 3 | 4 |
| Performance | Could penetrate 47mm armour at 1,000m | Max range 4,700m |
| Rounds carried | 74 AP, 40 HEAP | 30 |

Various elements of DAK's artillery were often grouped together for certain operations, but from early 1941 all the miscellaneous artillery units of the Panzerarmee were consolidated into Artillerie Kommando 104, with Major-General Böttcher in command (until he became commander of 21st Pz Div on 29 November 41) when Colonel Mickl took over. The units concerned were:

Staff Artillery (Arty) Regt 221
Staff Heavy Arty Bn 408
  2.u.3. Bty/408
  Arty Bn 364
  5./Arty Regt 115
Staff II./Arty Regt 115
  4./Arty Regt 115
  4./Army Coast Arty Bty 149
  2. Bty/408

6/Arty Regt 115
  Arty Bty 362
Staff Heavy Arty Bn 528
  2. and 3. Bty/528
Arty Bty 533
Arty Bty 902
(Source, Bender and Law)

## Mines

These were used extensively as were booby-traps, especially during the long withdrawal after Alamein. Non-ferrous mines were still not in quantity supply, so the main anti-vehicle mines were Tellermines (Tellerminen). Although there were a number of different patterns, they mainly consisted of a flat cylinder of metal with a sprung lid, designed to be set off by pressure from above. Effective and universally hated were the anti-personnel shrapnel burst 'S' mines (Schützenminen), which could be set off by pressure, tripwire or electrically detonated.

## SPECIALISED UNITS

**The Brandenburgers.** There were a small number of these Commando-type units in North Africa, the first of which arrived in June 1941. They included: 'Sonderverband 288', which was an independent motorised battlegroup which fought with 90 leichte Afrika-Division and, from 31 October 1942, became known as 'Panzergrenadier Regt (mot) Afrika' and 'Tropical Company Brandenburg', formed by a Lieutenant Von Könen from South-West Africa. This comprised Germans who had lived abroad and spoke foreign languages well. Its first personnel arrived in North Africa in October 1941.

Although Rommel did not entirely approve of Commando-type operations, he did allow them, especially after the British had carried out similar operations (e.g., the attempt on his life: see page 137). Von Könen and his gallant band did not surrender with the DAK, but having acquired some fishing boats and rubber dinghies managed to escape, crossing the Mediterranean and landing safely in southern Italy.

**Secret Field Police.** In September 1941 a unit of the Geheime Feldpolizei was set up, charged with the prevention of sabotage, espionage, black-market activities and so on. They often wore civilian clothing.

**Paratroops.** See page 158 for full details of the Ramcke Parachute Brigade, which was transferred from Greece in the summer of 1942.

**German Red Cross.** About 100 German nurses served in North Africa during all phases of the campaign, some being killed and wounded. Most of the nurses were with the Army Nursing Branch, but about 25–30 served with the Luftwaffe.

### Supporting arms and services
These operated normally as elsewhere, but adapted well to the desert conditions, having to face all the natural problems which beset them as well as the enemy, of which the almost constant presence of windblown sand contributed many difficulties, affecting delicate instruments, radios, vehicle engines and weapons.


## TACTICS

### The DAK in Battle
A British report on DAK tactics, made after the Sidi Rezegh battles of November–December 1941, summarised the major characteristics:

**Offensive Action.** Before launching an attack, they would spend the earlier part of the day on detailed reconnaissance of the target area, using armoured cars, tanks and small infantry detachments. The main aim was to lure the defence into disclosing gun positions, etc., by engaging these 'baits'. OPs would be watching carefully and any guns that did open fire would be pinpointed and subsequently neutralised with heavy fire, once the attack began. Next, tanks and anti-tank guns, plus motorised infantry support, would be brought up to within 2,000 yards of the objective. By now it was usually midday and replenishment would take place behind an anti-tank gun screen. The attack would be launched at about 1500 hours, tanks coming forward, supported by very accurate tank (usually from the heavier PzKpfw IVs) and artillery fire on to British artillery and anti-tank gun positions.

This fire would cause a great deal of dust in the area of the objective, tending to confuse the defenders, and the attack would generally be made from out of the setting sun, in order to make it more difficult for the British artillery. Any movement of defence support weapons towards the objective was immediately engaged by artillery. Groups of German tanks would then advance simultaneously from several different points, in strong, compact formations, their aim being to neutralise the whole area. Tanks then engaged British artillery and tanks, and while this 'duel' was in progress, the DAK would bring up their anti-tank guns and place them between the tank positions, in effective and inconspicuous locations. Where possible they would be sited among derelict vehicles to make them more difficult to spot, and undoubtedly their fire caused many casualties.

The next phase of the attack took place when one of the tank formations had penetrated the objective area. Immediately, motorised infantry would advance to within a few hundred yards of their final objectives before debussing, followed by anti-tank guns and automatics. Rapid consolidation followed with strong all-round anti-tank defence. By this time it was usually growing dark which helped to cover this critical period of consolidation, so there was rarely an opportunity to counter-attack, once they had gained the objective. Their success in this form of attack was undoubtedly due to the preponderance of anti-tank guns and the fact that the PzKpfw III and IV outgunned, outranged and had better vision devices than the opposing cruisers. However, this type of attack was costly in both manpower and *matériel*.

**Defence and Withdrawal.** The DAK displayed the same ability to co-ordinate all arms together in defence and withdrawal as they did in the attack. Falling back steadily, from one prepared position to another, they did not allow themselves to get involved in a running fight. They would offer maximum resistance, but only for as long as the position could be held without risk of defeat, but they were susceptible to any strong threat against their communications. Their overall policy was, sensibly, to save men and *matériel* and sacrifice ground. Having chosen a piece of ground suitable for defence against tanks or mobile infantry assault, they would put out their reconnaissance forces a good deal closer to their anti-tank screen than would the British. The basis of their defence was their field artillery and anti-tank guns – the latter being well forward as a secure screen, in which and behind which were the infantry and field guns. Within this defensive box there were two forms of mobile reserve – first, an anti-tank gun reserve to stiffen up any part of the screen; second, tanks ready for immediate counter-attack roles. On occasions, reserve tanks came outside the anti-tank gun screen with the definite aim of luring British tanks on to the screen. Tanks were generally most active in the afternoons.

Withdrawal was from one defensive position to another in two phases. During Phase 1, all administrative vehicles and a proportion of the unarmoured transport would be withdrawn. In Phase 2, tanks moved forward in a covering screen behind which the remainder could disengage and mount. Vehicles formed into close compact columns and moved off at high speed with the rearguard of tanks protecting them. Ideally the first phase took place in the dark or under cover of the midday haze. The second phase was nearly always done in the fading light or under cover of early darkness. While acting as the rearguard, tanks were extremely offensive and, with their superior range, very effective. On at least one occasion they charged British guns in order to give their unarmoured vehicles space in which to disengage.

**Air and Ground co-operation.** Despite the large degree of Allied air superiority the Germans were, on a few important occasions, able to achieve a high degree of direct air support for the ground troops, both by bombing and ground strafing. They operated very close to their own troops both in offensive and defensive operations and this led, on occasions, to air attacks on their own forces.

**General conclusions from these observations.** This report was compiled on behalf of Major-General 'Strafer' Gott,[10] while he was commanding British 7th Armoured Division, and he ended it by making these conclusions:

a. In every phase of battle the DAK co-ordinated their anti-tank guns, field artillery, infantry and tanks, working as all-arms teams.

b. Moves were characterised by speed and compactness. Movement of vehicles was guarded by an outer screen of tanks and an inner screen of anti-tank guns.

c. Their columns were difficult targets for light tank forces to attack, but were vulnerable to air attack or to the harassing fire of 'Jock Columns' (these usually consisted of two troops of 25pdrs – their main hitting power – one or two motor companies of mobile infantry, anti-tank and AA artillery, a sapper detachment and, for protection, armoured cars and tanks).[11] To overcome their vulnerability, frequent long night marches were undertaken.

d. Offensive methods were extremely costly and relied little on manoeuvre. Their method of withdrawal was unlikely to check for very long a determined pursuit that continually threatened their flanks.

## DIVISIONAL SIGNS AND SYMBOLS ON VEHICLES

Generally all vehicles, including AFVs, were painted sand-coloured before being shipped to North Africa, although this was not done at the beginning so as to conceal their destination for as long as possible. In fact, in some areas, the basic dark grey paint was just as good as yellow, while the spraying of sand on to oiled surfaces provided an excellent *ad hoc* camouflage colour.

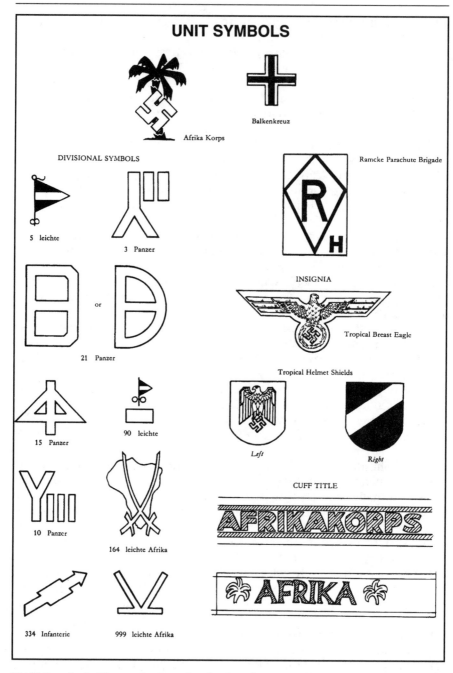

**UNIT SYMBOLS**

Afrika Korps

Balkenkreuz

DIVISIONAL SYMBOLS

5 leichte

3 Panzer

21 Panzer

or

15 Panzer

90 leichte

10 Panzer

164 leichte Afrika

334 Infanterie

999 leichte Afrika

Ramcke Parachute Brigade

INSIGNIA

Tropical Breast Eagle

Tropical Helmet Shields

Left

Right

CUFF TITLE

**DAK Symbol.** The majority of vehicles that served in DAK units had the Afrikakorps symbol emblazoned on them. As the drawings show, this was a palm tree, with a large swastika on its trunk, generally stencilled on using white paint. Its location on vehicles varied considerably.

**Balkenkreuz.** As in other theatres, the German cross appeared on all vehicles, as did the appropriate Divisional Sign, usually in white or black. Other standard markings such as tank identification numbers and vehicle registration plates were used in the normal way.


## LUFTWAFFE AND KRIEGSMARINE SUPPORT

### Support from air and sea
Although Rommel did not directly command German or Italian air and sea forces during his campaigns in North Africa, they clearly played a most important part in his operations, as did the RAF and the Royal Navy; the supply line was vital to both sides.

**The Luftwaffe.** When the DAK arrived in North Africa the situation in the air was no different from that on the ground. Despite numerical inferiority the RAF had retained the initiative everywhere, and made a considerable contribution to the ground campaign against the Italians. But in the first weeks of 1941 the Luftwaffe's Fliegerkorps X with a strong bomber element arrived in Sicily and soon made their presence felt. On 10 January a convoy of four fast merchantmen was attacked south of Malta. The escorting battleship *Warspite* was hit, and the aircraft carrier *Illustrious* was hit by six bombs, but managed to get to Malta with great difficulty. Next day the cruiser *Southampton* was sunk and the cruiser *Gloucester* was hit by a bomb that failed to detonate. The rest of the escort vessels reached Malta safely although badly damaged, and the four merchantmen also arrived at their destination. Allied shipping together with the British stronghold of Malta would now begin to receive continual air bombardment by Axis aircraft. A Luftwaffe detachment was stationed just outside Benghazi at Benina, some 200 miles behind the land front, and began nuisance mine-laying along the coast in ports such as Sollum. The next stage was for the Luftwaffe to take a hand in the ground war. Dive-bombers were soon operating from around Tripoli, their escort fighters deploying from forward landing strips. Their strength grew apace until by late spring 1941, there were nearly 175 Luftwaffe aircraft operating in North Africa – some 90 Messerschmitts (including both 109s and 110s) and a bomber force of 84 Ju–87s. The units concerned were:

**Bf–109** – I Gruppe/Jagdgeschwader (JG) 27 and 7 Gruppe/Jagdge-schwader 26 (a Geschwader was an operational unit of three Gruppen (approximately 93 aircraft in total))
**Bf–110** – III Gruppe/Zerstorergeschwader (ZG) 26
**Ju–87** – II Gruppe/Sturzkampfgeschwader (SG) 2.
**Night-fighters** from both I Gruppe/Nachtjagdgeschwader 3 and II Gruppe/Nachtjagdgeschwader 2 were also operational, protecting port and other installations against RAF bombers. Other Luftwaffe units which supported DAK were II/JG 27 and elements of JG 2, JG 26, JG 53 and JG 77; ZG

I, SG I, SG II and KG 26 (KG = Kampfgeschwader, i.e., bomber formation). General von Waldau was Fliegerführer Afrika.

**Flak units, paratroops and other ground troops.** The major role played by Luftwaffe Flak units also merits mention. Details of such units have been included in all the various orbats in this book, and the exceptional performance of the dreaded 8.8cm FlaK AA gun, in its anti-tank role, rightly gets continual praise, as do the tough paratroopers of Ramcke's parachute brigade (fully covered elsewhere). The disposition and tasks of Flak units on field operations was naturally left to the Army, although they did maintain their own channels of administrative control, over such items as dress, equipment and reinforcement or replacement of personnel. A third Luftwaffe formation also appeared later in the campaign, namely the Division Hermann Göring, commanded by Major-General Josef Schmid, which is fully covered in Chapter 7, because this unit only took part in the Tunisian campaign.

### Senior Commanders
Fliegerführer Afrika, then Commander Fliegerkorps Tunis: Major-General
    Hans Seidemann
Commander Fliegerkorps II: Major-General Bruno Lörzer
Commander Fliegerkorps X: Lieutenant-General Otto Hoffman von
    Waldau
Fliegerführer 2: Colonel Benno Kosch
Fliegerführer 3: Colonel Walter Hagen
Commander 19 Flak Division: Major-General Gotthard Frantz (from
    January 1943)
Commander 20 Flak Division: Major-General Georg Neuffer

Later in the campaigns, the RAF achieved almost total air superiority, although on occasions the Luftwaffe could still wrest it back over a small area, to cover a specific operation. But the British Desert Air Force became a dominating factor in the campaigns, for example, by the excellence of their air reconnaissance.

**The Kriegsmarine.** Although the German Navy had no major warships based in any North African port, they did assist the Italians in convoy protection and also had smaller vessels operating in coastal security roles. Main naval bases were at Bizerta and Tripoli, and Benghazi and Tobruk were both used once they had been captured. The role of the Italian Navy in convoy protection has also been mentioned.

## THE CAMPAIGN

### To and Fro in North Africa
War in the desert areas of North Africa was unlike anything that the victorious Panzerwaffe had experienced before. The Bedouin say that the desert is

a fortress to him who knows it and a grave to him who does not, so it was truly remarkable how quickly the men of the DAK – and their British and Commonwealth opponents – adapted to the strange conditions. The entire area was sparsely populated apart from a strip along the Mediterranean coast through Egypt and on to Libya, where most of the population was located in small ports like Benghazi, Tobruk, Bardia and Derna, which would soon gain an importance out of all proportion to their size. Inland in many places there was a steep escarpment, several hundreds of feet high, with few vehicular tracks up it, one of the most important being the winding path through Halfaya Pass, a few miles south-east of Sollum. Beyond the escarpment lay the desert – sand, stones and rock, with only a few good tracks linking the occasional oasis or *bir* (well), the only sources of fresh water. Accurate means of navigation was essential to all travellers for their continued survival, and because the maps were on the whole poor and the ground relatively featureless, a good compass (prismatic and/or sun) was a vital item of equipment. The climate ranged from scorching heat by day to extreme cold by night, and the hot dry wind, known as the Khamsin, coming from the south, could whip up great clouds of dust and sand, which penetrated every crack and crevice, every eye, ear and nostril in a matter of seconds. Once one has experienced such conditions it is easy to see why the Bedouin say that after five days of the Khamsin even murder can be excused!

In such conditions regular lines of supply are essential, as living off the land is impossible and the type of fluid warfare which such open, uninhabited regions fosters, prohibit the establishing of large static dumps in isolated or unguarded locations. So the various campaigns were to a great degree dictated by the length and viability of the supply lines. As soon as the 'elastic' became too far stretched and resupply became virtually impossible, it was necessary to fall back, allowing the initiative to pass to the enemy. As the map clearly shows, this was the pattern of events for the better part of two years, up to October 1942. Thereafter, the side with the initiative, namely the British, had such overwhelming superiority as to negate this principle, although resupply still dictated the speed of progress and remained very difficult for both sides.

## THE CAMPAIGN: PHASE 1
## ARRIVAL AND FIRST OFFENSIVE, FEBRUARY–APRIL 1941

### Arrival
Rommel, accompanied by his reconnaissance staff (Erkundsstab Rommel), including his Chief of Staff Lieutenant-Colonel von dem Borne, plus Hitler's Chief Adjutant, Colonel (later Major-General) Rudolf Schmundt, had left Sicily by air on 12 February 1941, landing at Castel Benito airfield, near Tripoli, at about midday. After reporting to the Italian commander, General Italo Gariboldi, for an up-to-date briefing he put the Italian general 'in the picture', outlining how he intended to defend Tripolitania. Gariboldi showed little enthusiasm for Rommel's aggressive intentions, having been

very discouraged by the recent overwhelming Italian defeat at the hands of the British. Then Rommel took to the air again, accompanied by Schmundt, to carry out his first aerial reconnaissance in North Africa, something he would do a great deal in the early days while getting to know his new battlefield. During this recce Rommel noticed that the leading ships of the first convoy were arriving in Tripoli harbour, carrying mainly rear services and supply units. They were accompanied by most of the rest of his small HQ staff, plus various 5 leichte units including an 88mm FlaK battery, Supply Columns 800 and 804, the divisional rations unit, four companies of 572 Field Hospital, Tyre Repair Company 13 (mot) and Reconnaissance Staff 681.[12] As soon as Rommel touched down he drove to the docks where he gathered all the new arrivals together on the dockside for a brief parade – probably designed to put some backbone into the Italians, many of whom appeared to be interested solely in getting back home to Italy as quickly as possible! Rommel was anxious to make his force appear stronger than it actually was and immediately ordered workshops just south of Tripoli to start constructing a large number of dummy tanks – made mainly of wood and blankets, and mounted on little Volkswagen staff cars – to deceive British air reconnaissance.

The first combat troops of DAK to arrive in Tripoli were Major Baron von Wechmar's Reconnaissance Battalion (Aufklärungsabteilung 3 (mot)) and Major Jansa's Anti-Tank Battalion (Panzerjägerabteilung 39 (mot)), both of 5 leichte Division, who arrived by sea on 14 February. The 6,000-ton transport was swiftly unloaded, work continuing throughout the night by torchlight despite the potential danger from enemy aircraft, and creating a record for the port of Tripoli! Next morning the troops drew their tropical kit, then assembled in the main square in front of Government House, radiating, as Rommel put it: '... a complete assurance of victory'. As with other new arrivals, Rommel inspected them and, after a short march past, they paraded through the port with their vehicles, then pushed on down the coast, first to Misrata, then on to Sirte, still behind the Italian front-line positions, to be held in mobile reserve.

Rommel flew down to Sirte to inspect the Italian troops there. They amounted to approximately one infantry regiment – the only fighting force immediately available to oppose the British, the remainder being some 200 miles to the west. But Rommel, although naturally anxious about this situation, was favourably impressed by the Italians and their commanders (Colonel Grati and Major Santa Maria). Nevertheless he immediately persuaded the Italians to dispatch a division to Sirte as quickly as possible. On the 16th, the German recce units made their first moves against the enemy, working with Major Santa Maria's troops. Rommel also formally took over the front that day, sending the commander of 5 leichte (Major-General Streich) to take command on his behalf, while Colonel Schmundt returned to pass on Rommel's first situation report to Hitler. He wired back on the 19th that the Führer was very pleased with Rommel's initiative, that 15th Panzer Division would soon be on its way and that Hitler had even chosen the name for Rommel's new corps – Deutsches Afrikakorps.[13] Schmundt also assured Rommel that a 'historical distortion of his services would not take place again' – a veiled reference to the way in which through bad staff work two other officers had been wrongly credited with feats of bravery against the Italians during the Great War, which should rightly have been credited to Rommel, resulting in both receiving the *Pour le Mérite* ahead of him!

**First Action**
On 24 February, a small force of armoured cars and motorcyclists contacted a patrol of the King's Dragoon Guards, supported by some Australian anti-tank guns. The skirmish ended with the Germans taking one officer and two soldiers prisoner and destroying a number of vehicles (two scout cars, a lorry and a car), with no loss to the Germans – 'a good omen' commented Rommel, also telling Lucie that his lads were already at the Front and that as far as he was concerned the enemy could come whenever they liked. Clearly Rommel must have been growing suspicious at the lack of activity on the part of the British, who had, without his knowledge, been decimated by the withdrawal of troops to send to Greece, while the experienced 7th Armoured Division had been replaced by part of the newly arrived 2nd Armoured Division, so that it could rest and refit back in Egypt. General O'Connor, the victor over the Italians, had also gone back to Egypt and his place had been taken by the newly arrived General Sir Philip Neame, who completely lacked any knowledge of mechanised desert warfare. General Streich advanced up to the defile at Mugtaa on 4 March and laid a minefield there to close it, while the British withdrew eastwards.

Next to arrive in Tripoli was Panzer Regiment 5, who completed their disembarkation on 8–10 March. As already explained, they had lost some tanks to a fire at Naples while loading. Nevertheless the twenty-five PzKpfw I Ausf A, forty-five Pz Kpfw II, sixty-one PzKpfw III, seventeen PzKpfw IV, three Kl Pz Bef Wg and four Gr Pz Bef Wg (total 155) made an impressive sight as they paraded through Tripoli then drove eastward along the coast road. Rommel moved his HQ up to Sirte on 13 March by road and had himself taken off for Sirte in an Italian light recce plane, known locally as a 'Ghibili'. But they ran into a real 'Ghibili' (a violent sandstorm) and the pilot had sensibly turned back, much to Rommel's annoyance. He made the journey by car in the full force of the sandstorm, appreciating for the first time the effects of such terrible conditions, which included in addition to almost impossible visibility, clouds of red dust, unbearable heat and high winds – 'Silently I breathed my apologies to the pilot.' wrote Rommel, adding that a Luftwaffe pilot had crashed that same day as a result of the sandstorm. Two days later, at the request of the Italian High Command, he sent a mixed German and Italian force, under Lieutenant-Colonel Graf von Schwerin southwards towards Murzuk to protect that flank against Free French activity and to gain practical experience of long desert marches. It also provided an excellent opportunity to test their equipment in these new conditions. Shortly afterwards, the entire Italian Brescia Infantry Division arrived in the line at Mugtaa, freeing 5 leichte Division for 'mobile employment'.

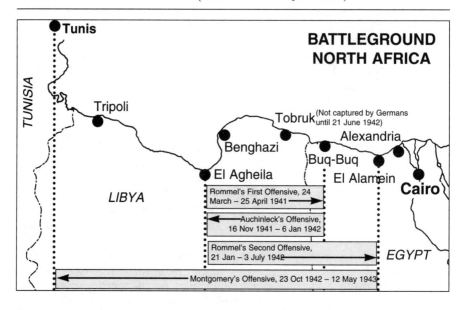

On 19 March Rommel flew to Hitler's HQ to discuss the situation and get fresh instructions. It was a visit which he did not like much, despite the fact that he received the Oakleaves to his Knight's Cross from his Führer. The main problem was that the Army C-in-C, Field Marshal von Brauchitsch, poured cold water on Rommel's hopes of being able to make a major impact against the British in North Africa. He was told that there was no intention of striking a significant blow against the enemy in the foreseeable future. His force was merely a Sperrverband (an armoured blocking force), intended merely to bolster the morale of the Italians in Tripolitania. There would be no further reinforcements once the agreed complement of DAK units had arrived and, while Rommel could attack as soon as 15th Panzer Division was complete – i.e., at the end of May – he should only go as far as Benghazi, concentrating on making sure that Tripolitania was secure rather than trying to inflict a major defeat on the enemy. In fact Rommel had already ordered 5 leichte to be ready to attack El Agheila towards the end of March and clearly had ideas for further immediate conquests even before the arrival of 15th Pz Div. The Reconnaissance Battalion (AA3) took El Agheila on 24 March with ease, the British withdrawing to Mersa el Brega without a fight. Rommel decided to press on to Mersa el Brega, which was an ideal position from which to defend against a possible British attack as well as being a good 'jumping-off' place for any assault on Cyrenaica.

When 5 leichte did advance on Mersa el Brega early on 31 March, there was a fierce engagement, initially with British reconnaissance forces at Maaten Bescer, then in the afternoon on the main position, where the British garrison included the tanks of C Squadron, 5 RTR. Their cruisers engaged the tanks of Panzer Regiment 5, plus some supporting Italian M 13/40s, and held the German attack. Rommel was now in his element, right up in the thick of the fighting with his ADC Aldinger and his Chief of Staff, von dem Borne. They reconnoitred a route north of the coast road to out-flank the British position and, when this proved successful, MG Battalion 8, put in a 'dashing attack' through the rolling sandhills, pushing the British back and capturing the Mersa el Brega defile. The British had to withdraw so hurriedly that they left behind some 30 lorries and 50 Bren gun carriers, while the tank v. tank engagements between Pz Regt 5 and 5 RTR resulted in six British Mk IVA cruisers being knocked out, and the Germans losing two Mk IIIs and a Mk IV.

Having received confirmation from both air and ground recce that the British had withdrawn farther and faster than anticipated, Rommel decided to press on to try to take Agedabia, disregarding his orders not to attempt such a manoeuvre until the end of May. On 2 April, 5 leichte began moving forward astride the Via Balbia and that afternoon, not only took Agedabia but also pushed on rapidly to the Zuetina area. Rommel's plan was now to divide his forces into three prongs: the left-hand prong (Brescia Division led by AA 3) would advance along the coast towards Benghazi; the right-hand prong (part of 5 leichte plus the recce battalion of Ariete Division) would strike across Cyrenaica via Ben Gania and Bir Tengeder, then turn northwards towards El Mechili and Derna, to cut off the British escape route. Between these two, an armour heavy force (Pz Regt 5 plus various units of 5 leichte and Ariete ) would make for Msus and El Mechili. Rommel, who was constantly up at the front relentlessly driving his men on, must have been very surprised by the lack of aggression shown by the enemy. This was undoubtedly the result of the very negative orders which had been given to Neame by C-in-C Middle East, General Wavell, that he should, if pressed, give up Benghazi and retreat eastwards so as to keep his forces intact. As the German pressure developed the British forces disintegrated and what should have been an organised withdrawal degenerated into what can only be described as an undignified rout. Wavell was perhaps unduly influenced by the fact that he thought he knew what Rommel's orders were, thanks to the fact that the British had cracked the secrets of the German Enigma code-machine. But he could not read the mind of the 'Desert Fox'!

This phase of the operation began on 2 April, Rommel moving his headquarters forward to Agedabia the following day. It is clear from his diary that he made full use of his ADCs, for example, sending Berndt forward that morning some 20 miles northwards to check on reports of a large enemy tank concentration on the Benghazi road. Berndt found them to be abandoned Italian tanks from the previous British victory. Rommel was then off again with Aldinger, heading into the desert, along a route which the Italians had said was impassable, but he made it and was soon up with the leading troops of the right-hand column, impressed by the good deployment of the Italian recce battalion which was attached to that force. Returning to his HQ he found that 5 leichte commander was saying that he needed a 4-day halt to replenish fuel and ammunition. One can imagine Rommel's reaction! He ordered them to unload all their lorries and to send them back immediately to the divisional dump at Arco dei Fileni,[14] taking with them spare crews (found from tank crews) for a 'round the clock' refuelling trip.

Rommel waved aside Streich's protests that it would ground his division by retorting that this was the way to save bloodshed and to conquer Cyrenaica – another black mark against the unfortunate Streich who would be sacked a few months later.

Having taken Agedabia, the left-hand column swept on to Benghazi (4 April), then to Barce (5 April) and Derna (7 April). In the centre, the tank column took the petrol dumps at Msus and Mechili (6 April) before reaching the coastal plain at Gazala (7 April), some 40 miles west of Tobruk. The right-hand column carried out its wide right-flanking movement through the desert – an operation which the British had never expected the newly arrived Germans, who lacked knowledge of both the terrain and conditions, would ever have attempted. The night of 6 April also saw DAK capture their most important prisoners, namely, Generals O'Connor and Neame. The former, who was undoubtedly the most experienced and able 'desert campaigner' on the British side, was the only one who might have seen through Rommel's plan, because he had done something very similar to the Italians only a few months previously. He had been sent up to the Front by Wavell to advise the inexperienced Neame. That evening they had been travelling back to XIII Corps headquarters at Tmimi after reconnoitring in the Marturba area. In the dark, their driver overshot the turning and drove on towards Derna, with the two generals fast asleep in the back of the car. As they had no proper escort, they were easily captured by a 5 leichte motorcycle patrol after a brief exchange of fire. A third British general, Gambier-Parry, commander of 2nd Armoured Division, had also been captured with his entire headquarters at Mechili.

Rommel's whirlwind advance had not only thrown his enemies into confusion, but had also caused some disquiet among the German and Italian High Commands, both Keitel and Gariboldi sending signals that he had exceeded his orders and should go no further. Rommel, however, craftily used the German signal to bluff Gariboldi into thinking that he had been given complete freedom of action, so the advance continued, all the columns moving forwards, with Rommel constantly urging them, often from his Fieseler Storch (Stork) light recce aircraft – he became a regular sight over the battlefield, regularly flying well ahead of his leading troops, allowing them no respite. 'If you don't move on at once, I shall come down. Rommel', threatened the tiny notes which fluttered down from his low-flying Storch, on to the heads of any unfortunate armoured car commander whose progress the 'Desert Fox' reckoned was far too slow!

By 11 April, the British had been swept out of the whole of Cyrenaica, apart from a small beleaguered force in Tobruk, where two Australian brigades, plus the remnant of 3rd Armoured Brigade, were holed up, grimly determined to fight off all comers. The leading DAK troops arrived there on 10/11 April, but an improvised attack was defeated. 5 leichte made a properly co-ordinated assault on 14 April, but, although they made initial breaches in the defences, they were eventually beaten off. Apart from holding this stronghold, which was to survive a lengthy siege, it had been for the British, an ignominious defeat as the Germans closed up to the frontier and prepared to cross. On 25 April, they struck at Halfaya Pass, and on the 26th pushed the British back to a line from Buq Buq on the coast to Sofafi. Rommel tried another major assault on Tobruk on 30 April, but although some ground was taken in the western sector, the attack had to be called off after four days of heavy fighting. The importance of Tobruk cannot be over-emphasised; it was not just a thorn in Rommel's flesh, although it was only a small port of some 4,000-plus inhabitants. In fact, apart from Benghazi, it was the only safe, accessible port for more than 1,000 miles, between Sfax in Tunisia and Alexandria, so its capture would have greatly shortened Rommel's lines of supply. In addition of course, its continued defiance had a tremendous morale-boosting effect on the Allies, who were, at that time, short of victories on every Front.

Despite this setback, Rommel was cock-a-hoop. In just over half a month he had recaptured all the territory the British had won from the Italians. At first his letters home had been ecstatic, containing such phrases as: 'we've been attacking since the 31st with dazzling success .... You will understand that I can't sleep with happiness'; 'To-day will be another decisive day. Our main force is on its way after a 220-mile march over the sand and rock of the desert'; 'It's wonderful to have pulled this off against the British' and 'The lads stuck it magnificently and came through the battle, both with the enemy and nature, very well.' But for the time being that was the end of the type of rapid, audacious tactical moves that would come to symbolise the 'Desert Fox' and his remarkable intuitive feel for desert warfare. For the time being it was 'hard pounding' against the stubborn defenders of Tobruk at the end of an all too long supply line. Rommel, who appreciated the need to capture the port, was clearly angry at the lack of success which 5 leichte was having – another, somewhat unfair black mark against Streich, showing Rommel's bad side – his difficult moods, intolerance and refusal to admit he was ever wrong. But the men of the DAK were now, just like the soldiers of the Ghost Division, totally under the spell of his magnetic personality. They knew that he was undergoing the same conditions as they were, eating the same food, pushing himself to the limits even harder than he pushed them. They knew that he loved every one of his 'Afrikaners' as he called them, and they in turn would willingly do anything or go anywhere for him. And, more surprisingly, Rommel's burgeoning reputation was having an effect on the enemy as well, who were sadly short of heroes.

## THE CAMPAIGN: PHASE 2
## 'BREVITY' AND 'BATTLEAXE', MAY–JUNE 1941

There were by now some 164,000 German and Italian troops in North Africa, with more than 15,000 vehicles, not to mention more than 5,000 horses and mules, all of which needed regular supplies – one estimate was at least 30 shiploads a month (about 70–80,000 tons) which would exceed the capacity of the port of Tripoli, and the forward troops alone needed some 1,500 tons daily. So the major ports in Axis hands, Tripoli and Benghazi, had to be improved, especially as far as AA protection was concerned. 'Rommel makes preposterous demands', comments Halder in his diary. 'His wishes can be satisfied only in so far as preparations for Barbarossa (the assault on the USSR) permit.' Later he is even more scathing: 'By overstepping his orders, Rommel has brought about a situation for which our present supply capabilities are insufficient.' He sent his deputy, Lieutenant-General Paulus, out to make an on the spot report and he passed on the instructions from the OKH, that Rommel should consider the holding of Cyrenaica as being his primary concern, even if he did not take Tobruk, as they had rightly appreciated that the British would attack again soon, in an endeavour to relieve the garrison there. Paulus, a staff officer through and through, was clearly disturbed by Rommel's wilfulness and his penchant for acting on his own initiative and then endeavouring to justify his actions – provided they were successful! The continued attacks on Tobruk were causing considerable casualties, yet achieving nothing and eventually Rommel had to accept that all he could do was to try to tighten the siege and eventually be able to force them into submission.

**Operation 'Brevity'.** The Axis forces were now in positions on or over the Egyptian frontier, their main garrisons being at Sollum, Halfaya Pass, Musadi, Fort Capuzzo (including Points 206 and 208) and Sidi Omar, with a local reserve at Bardia, in total some 6,000 men. Their purpose was as Rommel put it: '... to deny certain operations to the enemy', while his mobile forces would provide '... adequate opposition to any enemy offensive concentration against our Tobruk front, and at the same time to beat off an attack by the British motorised forces located east of Sollum'. But they had only just begun to put out wire and lay minefields, so their defensive positions were still rudimentary. 'Our dispositions at the middle of May were far from fulfilling these requirements,' he wrote. 'The Sollum front was not yet fully manned ... fortification of Halfaya Pass or of the Sollum Pass had hardly begun.' Rommel gave orders for another defence line to be constructed at Gazala, on the lines of the Tobruk defences, which he admitted had '... shown themselves so admirably suited to meet modern methods of attack'. On the 'other side of the hill', Wavell, who was being constantly pressed by Churchill to retake Cyrenaica and relieve Tobruk, on hearing that the Convoy Tiger[15] was on its way, launched an attack (Operation 'Brevity') on 15 May, to recapture Halfaya Pass. It was aimed at three points – the pass itself, Fort Capuzzo and Sollum, the first being captured quickly, the second seized but only after heavy fighting. Rommel thinking that this was the beginning of a major British assault, brought up reinforcements, retook Capuzzo and then, on 27 May, recaptured the Halfaya Pass, the British withdrawing in some confusion, leaving considerable amounts of booty. Rommel now re-garrisoned the pass, placing in command a remarkable soldier, Captain (ex-pastor) Wilhelm Bach, who would later win glory defending it against all comers.

**Operation 'Battleaxe'.** Despite the failure of 'Brevity' Wavell was not discouraged; Convoy Tiger had arrived. One ship, containing nearly 60 tanks and ten aircraft had been sunk by a mine, but the rest had escaped the U-boats and brought their precious cargo safely to Egypt. 'The Tiger now only needs to grow claws,' signalled Wavell to Churchill on 25 May and three days later he was confirming to the Prime Minister that he was ready to attack. On the German side, they too had received reinforcements, namely 15th Panzer Division, which had been shipped in three convoys, arriving on 24 April, 2 and 6 May. Its main tank strength was contained in Pz Regt 8, which had forty-five PzKpfw II, seventy-one PzKpfw III, twenty PzKpfw IV and ten PzKpfw Befel (total 146). The Halfaya Pass garrison now comprised some 500 German and 400 Italian troops, with considerable anti-tank and artillery weapons, including five 88mm and a battery of French-made 155mm guns. Rommel ensured that the '88s' were well dug-in so that as little as possible of the gun could be seen above ground. He had plenty of Italian infantry at his disposal so was again able to deploy significant garrisons at Fort Capuzzo, Points 206 and 208, Sollum and Musaid, with a local reserve at Bardia. He had also deployed a fair number of anti-tank guns on the Hafid Ridge as well as at Halfaya Pass. Although Enigma provided the British with much information about the German/Italian deployment, Rommel's own radio intercept had been listening to the British radio nets and was able to keep him equally well informed. The British intention for 'Battleaxe' was to break through the Axis defences on the Egyptian–Libyan border, drive on Tobruk and exploit to Derna and Mechili. A major frontal attack would be made on Halfaya Pass using the newly arrived heavy Matilda Mk II tanks plus part of 4th Indian Infantry Division, while 7th Armoured Division and the remaining units of 4th Ind Inf Div swept around on the desert flank, with 7th Armoured Brigade aiming at the Hafid Ridge (Point 208) and 4th Armoured Brigade plus the 4th Ind Div units going for Fort Capuzzo and Point 206; then, in a second phase, moving on to Sollum on the coast. Rommel was well prepared for all these eventualities and had moved up his newly-arrived tanks as well as those of 5 leichte.

The heavy fighting which followed ended in a victory for the defence. Bach's garrison at Halfaya Pass did magnificently, on the first day (15 June) alone knocking out eleven Matilda Mk IIs. Both Point 206 and Fort Capuzzo were captured on the 15th by 4th Armd Bde, and 7th Armd Bde initially gained a foothold on Hafid Ridge. After his static defensive positions had blunted the full power of the British attacks, Rommel moved 5 leichte in a wide right hook towards Sidi Omar where it was soon locked in combat with 7th Armd Bde in a violent tank battle, which continued on 16 June, by which time 7th Armd had lost most of its tanks through enemy action or mechanical failure. Meanwhile 4th Armd Bde, which was being withdrawn to conform with 7th Armd Bde, was in heavy combat with Pz Regt 8 of 15th Panzer Division. 'This operation had obviously taken the British completely by surprise,' wrote Rommel, going on to explain how they had intercepted a message from GOC 7th Armd Div asking for the C-in-C of the desert force to come to his headquarters, presumably to take control. Rommel decided to try to close the net around the British forces and ordered both 5 leichte and 15th Pz Divs to press on towards Halfaya Pass on 17 June; they reached there soon after 1600 hours. They found that the bulk of the British armour had already made its escape between the head of the German column and the pass. But they had lost more than 220 tanks (although only 87 were complete write-offs which were destroyed or taken, the rest were repairable). The British for their part, claimed 100 German tanks knocked out, but Rommel put his losses at 25.

Rommel was once again triumphant: 'I've been three days on the road', he wrote on the 23rd, 'going round the battlefield. The joy of the Afrika troops over this latest victory is tremendous. The British thought they could overwhelm us with their 400 tanks. We couldn't put that amount of armour against them, but our grouping and the stubborn resistance of German and Italian troops who were surrounded for days together, enabled us to make the decisive operation with all the forces we still had mobile. Now the enemy can come, he'll get an even bigger beating.'

### Notes to Chapter 4

1. Quoted by John Baynes in his biography of Gen O'Connor, *The Forgotten Victor*.
2. Balbo was shot down by his own AA gunners as he came into land at Tobruk on 28 June, whether by accident is not entirely clear. Some have it that he was deliberately murdered on the orders of Mussolini. He had been greatly respected by the RAF, who dropped a wreath and a note of condolences.
3. Forty, *Afrika Korps*, vol. 1.
4. Irving, *Trail of the Fox*.
5. In *Trail of the Fox*, Irving comments on the bad blood between Rommel and General Streich. Hearing of Prittwitz's death, Streich, driving a British staff car, chased after Rommel who was in his armoured command truck, to tell him the news. Rommel saw him approaching and, just in case, ordered a 20mm gun in his escort party to be ready to fire should the car contain enemy. He was furious when Streich jumped from the car, red-faced and shouting about Prittwitz's death. 'How dare you drive after me in a British car,' Rommel remonstrated. 'I was about to have the gun open fire on you.' 'In that case,' retorted the angry Streich, 'you would have managed to kill both your panzer division commanders in one day Herr General!'
6. The Knight's Cross (Ritterkreuz), the Third Reich's highest award for outstanding service and bravery, was the natural successor to the *Pour le Mérite* and was instituted on 1 September 1939. It was worn around the neck, and three additional honours could be added to the Cross for further meritorious service/bravery: Oakleaves (*Eichenlaub*); Swords (*Schwerter*); Diamonds (*Brillanten*). Only 159 Swords and 27 Diamonds were ever awarded.
7. The exceptions to this rule were holders of the Knight's Cross, who wore

it closed so that their Ritterkreuz was properly displayed.

8. The first 8.8cm FlaK 41 were not issued generally to troops until 1943, but pre-production examples were sent to North Africa and saw service there, although they were beset with problems.

9. The Germans did not use the 'medium' artillery classification, but designated their artillery as either light or heavy. Guns were Kanone, gun/howitzers were Haubitze and mortars Mörser.

10. Lieutenant-General W. H. E. Gott, CB, DSO, MC, late KRRC, went on to command XIII Corps and, in August 1942, was chosen to command Eighth Army. On his way back to Cairo a few days later, his aircraft was attacked by a German fighter and shot down. Gott survived the crash, but was killed by machine-gun fire while attempting to free personnel from the wreckage.

11. These tiny *ad hoc* 'battle groups' were the brainchild of Major-General J. C. (Jock) Campbell, VC, DSO, MC, late RHA, who also commanded 7th Armd Div. He was killed in February 1942 when his staff car overturned near Halfaya Pass.

12. Law and Luther, *Rommel*.

13. Rommel's HQ became known as Stab Deutsches Afrikakorps on 21 Feb 1941.

14. Known by the British as 'Marble Arch', this was a large white triumphal arch built by Mussolini on the frontier between Tripolitania and Cyrenaica.

15. One of the most significant convoys to reach North Africa in this period. Sent by Churchill in May 1941, it was a 'fast convoy' and brought both additional armour and aircraft – nearly 400 tanks (half cruisers and half the more heavily armoured Matilda Mk II), together with 50 Hurricanes.

# 5
# Panzergruppe Afrika/
# Panzerarmee Afrika
## (August 1941 – August 1942)

### PANZERGRUPPE AFRIKA (AUGUST–DECEMBER 1941)

The outcome of the two British operations 'Brevity' and 'Battleaxe' was that Wavell lost his job and was moved to India. Rommel had always admired Wavell – 'The only British general who showed a touch of genius was Wavell' – he wrote later. It is also said that he carried a copy of Wavell's essays on generalship (translated into German) with him during the North Africa campaign. Wavell was replaced by General Sir Claude Auchinleck, and General Sir Alan Cunningham, who had done so well in East Africa, became GOC Eighth Army.

Rommel on the other hand was promoted to General der Panzer Truppen on 1 July (he was still only 49) and on 15 August saw his command raised to the status of Panzergruppe. In addition to the DAK[1] – now under command of General Ludwig Crüwell – Rommel had another German division, Afrika Division z.b.V. (zu besonderer Verwendung, i.e., for special employment), which comprised certain units that were already serving in Africa, plus others which had been brought in more recently by air. The division was under command of Major-General Max Sümmermann, who would be killed a few months later. Rommel also had command over some Italian divisions, thanks to the good sense of the Italian Army 'Comando Supremo', Ugo Cavallero, who always insisted that there should be only one commander for all the German and Italian front-line units and had said that it should be Rommel. This was at variance with the opinion of the supposed Supreme Commander, North African Command, Generale Ettore Bastico, who had replaced the affable, 'pliable' if pessimistic Gariboldi, with whom Rommel had developed an excellent working relationship. 'Bombastico', as he was known, was quite the reverse! Rommel found him difficult and autocratic. He also refused to give Rommel full control over the only really mobile part of the Italian forces in Libya, namely XX Corps, a special independent 'manoeuvre' corps (Corpo d'Armata di Manovra), which was made up of the Ariete and Trieste Divisions and the Raggruppamento Esplorante reconnaissance group (RECAM), commanded by the equally difficult Generale Gastone Gambara – on more than one occasion Rommel is said to have referred to them as: 'a couple of shits'! Thus Gambara reported direct to Bastico, while Rommel had full control over the other four Italian divisions, namely: Pavia, Bologna, Savona and Brescia which made up XXI Corps. None of this was conducive to a happy relationship and Rommel did little to soothe injured Italian pride as the South African official war history of the period aptly explains: 'Rommel had arrived in Africa six months earlier in charge of an enlarged light division placed at the disposal of the local Italian HQ to stiffen up their anti-tank defence. He was now safely established as the commander of a large army, with powers which, by alternately ignoring his Italian chief and treating him with studied insolence, he made into a virtually independent jurisdiction.'[2] Rommel did, however, respect some Italian officers; for example, he had a very high regard for Generale Enea Navarrini, the XXI Corps commander (David Irving describes Navarrini as being Rommel's 'trusty friend'), and he commented more than once that Italian soldiers fought bravely and could give a good account of themselves when they were well-officered. He also said that there were some splendid Italian officers who made tremendous efforts to sustain their men's morale, but he had little time for most of them, especially Gambara, who was replaced by Generale Barbassetti in April 1942, after saying that all he wanted was to live until the day when he could lead an Italian army against the Germans – 'What a fool!' commented the Desert Fox!

## Outline Organisation of Axis forces – August 1941

SUPREME COMMANDER NORTH AFRICAN COMMAND
(MARSHAL ETTORE BASTICO)

Panzergruppe Afrika*
(Gen d. Pz. Tr. Erwin Rommel)
DAK (General Ludwig Crüwell)
  15th Pz Div
  21st Pz Div
  Afrika Inf Div z.b.V.**
  55 Savona Inf Div
XXI Italian Corps
(Generale Enea Navarrini)
  17 Pavia Inf Div
  25 Bologna Inf Div
  27 Brescia Inf Div
  102 Trento Mot Inf Div (motorised in name only)

Italian XX Armd Corps
(Generale Gastone Gambara)
  132 Ariete Armd Div
  101 Trieste Mot Div
  RECAM

*Panzerarmee Afrika would evolve from the Gruppe on 30 January 1942, being also known as deutsche–italienische Panzerarmee. A year later on 23 February 1943 it would become known as 1. italienische Armee.
**Became 90 leichte Division on 27 November 1941.

## Commanders of the Panzergruppe
15 Aug 1941–9 Mar 1942: Gen d. Pz. Tr. Erwin Rommel (promoted to Colonel General (Generaloberst) on 31 January 1942).
9–19 March 1942: while Rommel was on sick leave, Lieutenant-General Ludwig Crüwell was acting commander.

19 Mar–22 Sept 1942: Generaloberst Erwin Rommel (promoted to Field Marshal (Generalfeldmarschall) on 22 June 1942 after capturing Tobruk).

22 Sept–24 Oct 1942: Knight's Cross holder General der Kavallerie (then Gen d. Pz. Tr.) Georg Stumme who was acting commander while Rommel was at home on sick leave. Thus Stumme was commanding when the Allies under General Montgomery attacked at El Alamein. Stumme suffered from high blood pressure and died of a heart attack whilst visiting the front line on 24 October, after his staff car had been attacked by British anti-tank and machine-gun fire. 'We all deeply regretted the sudden death of Stumme,' wrote Rommel. 'He had spared no pains to command the army well and had been day and night at the front.'

24–25 Oct 1942: Lieutenant-General Wilhelm Ritter von Thoma was acting commander while Stumme was missing and Rommel was returning from Europe. He was captured as already explained.

25 Oct 1942– 23 Feb 1943: Field Marshal Erwin Rommel.

23 Feb–13 May 1943: Generale di Armata Messe, took command and, for the first time, German divisions came under Italian field command. Giovanni Messe was one of the most experienced and able of the senior Italian generals, having taken part in the invasion of Greece and then commanded the Italian Expeditionary Force in Russia. He was sent to Tunisia to become C-in-C of the Italian First Army (1 italienische Armee) making a good impression on Rommel and clearly being immensely proud to be taking over from him. Messe was promoted Field Marshal on the day of the surrender, 13 May 1943, and went into captivity with more than a quarter of a million Axis troops.

## Main staff officers

COS: Major-General Alfred Gause;[3] Colonel Fritz Bayerlein; Colonel Siegfried Westphal

Ia: Lieutenant-Colonel Siegfried Westphal (later became COS); Major F. W. von Mellenthin; Major Richard Feige

OQu: Major Otto; Major Schleusener

Ic: Major F. W. von Mellenthin (later became Ia); Major Josef Zolling; Major Liebl

IIa: Major Schräpler

IVb: SMO Staff Dr Asal

Signals Officer: Colonel Buchting

Engineer Officer: Colonel Hecker; Colonel Bulowis

Major-General Alfred Gause was a highly intelligent, easy-going East Prussian with a dry sense of humour. Born in Königsberg in February 1896, he joined the army in March 1914, fought throughout the Great War with 18th Engineer Bn, was wounded several times and rose to the rank of Oberleutenant. Post-war he served with the Reichswehr and was later taken into the new Wehrmacht. On 1 April 1939 he was promoted Colonel and during the defeat of France he served as Chief of Staff (COS) of X Army Corps. Later he joined XXXVIII Corps as von Manstein's COS, then became the German

liaison officer to the Italian High Command. On 1 June 1941 he was pro-
moted to Major-General and a month later named as COS of Panzergruppe
Afrika. He was sent with his small, but highly effective staff, to help Rommel command the new Panzer Group. Gause, brought with him just 20
other officers, but all were first-rate staff officers, like Westphal and von
Mellenthin. There was also a civilian representative of the German Foreign
Ministry, Constantin Freiherr von Neurath, who would become one of
Rommel's most trusted associates. Rommel thought very highly of Gause,
recommending him for the Knight's Cross (awarded on 13 December 1941.)
Wounded near Tobruk, Gause went back to North Africa during the winter
of 1942/3, served as COS of a special staff and was then named COS of Army
Group Africa. He held the post until 13 May 1943, being promoted to Lieutenant-General in April. Flown out of Tunisia immediately before the surrender, he would serve as COS to Rommel's Army Group B (see later). Later
he would be COS of Fifth and Sixth Panzer Armies, then took command of
II Army Corps which he commanded until the end of the war. Captured by
the Russians, he was not released until October 1955.

## ORGANISATION OF MAIN UNITS OF PANZERGRUPPE AFRIKA, NOVEMBER 1941
Rommel now had some 119,000 troops under his command, but only 400
tanks of which 150 were obsolete Italian models. The outline organisation
of the Axis forces prior to the next major bout of fighting has been given
already, and the detailed organisations of 15th and 21st Pz Divs of the DAK
were covered in the last chapter. Here, therefore, it is necessary only to cover
details of the 'Afrika Division z.b.V.' and the Savona Infantry Division of the
DAK, and to give more information about the other four Italian divisions
now under Rommel's command, together with Gambara's free-ranging XX
Corps, before dealing with the different weapons, vehicles and equipment
which the Italians brought to Rommel's command.

### Afrika Division z.b.V.
Later to be known as 90 leichte Division, it was organised in August 1941
from various independent units that were already serving in North Africa,
plus additional troops who had arrived by air. It also contained a proportion
of veterans from the French Foreign Legion. Its new title came into effect in
late November 1941. It would fight throughout all the campaigns thereafter,
suffering heavy casualties at El Alamein and during the retreat and finally
surrendering on 12 May 1943.

### *Divisional Commanders*
17 July–10 Dec 1941: Major-General Max Sümmermann, until he was killed
    when low-flying RAF aircraft attacked his command vehicle on 10
    December, during the withdrawal through Cyrenaica. Knight's Cross
    winner Colonel Johann Mickl then commanded until 28 December,
    when Veith took over.
28 Dec 1941–28 Apr 1942: Major-General Richard Veith, until he was wounded
    in the battle of the Gazala Line. He was later promoted to Lieutenant-

General in August 1942, while serving in Army Group North (Russia).

29 Apr–14 June 1942: Major-General Ulrich Kleemann, who went on to command Sturm (Assault) Div Rhodos and then IV Pz Korps. Born in Thuringen in 1892, he was awarded the Knight's Cross in October 1941, while commanding 3 Rifle Bde, then the Oakleaves in September 1943.

14–18 June 1942: Colonel Werner Marcks – Rommel speaks of him as being: 'the fine commander of 90 leichte'. He was to be promoted to Major-General in 1944 and Lieutenant-General in 1945, being awarded both the German Cross in Gold and the Knight's Cross with Oakleaves. He commanded 1st Pz Div then 21st Pz Div, and was taken prisoner in Russia, not being released for ten years.

18–19 June 1942: Colonel Erwin Menny, who was later to reach the rank of Lieutenant-General, command various infantry divisions, and win the Knight's Cross.

19–21 June 1942: Colonel Werner Marcks again.

21 June–8 Sept 1942: Major-General Ulrich Kleemann; he was wounded on 2 September when his car struck a mine near Alam el Halfa ridge and Major-General Ramcke took temporary command. Kleemann was promoted to Lieutenant-General in 1943 and Gen d. Pz. Tr. in 1944, and was awarded the Knight's Cross with Oakleaves.

8–17 Sept 1942: Major-General Bernhard Hermann Ramcke, described as being 'lithe and pugnacious', a veteran of the fighting in Crete, whose tough paratroops could always be depended upon in a fight. He was one of the Luftwaffe's most highly decorated officers, winning (like Rommel) the Knight's Cross with Oakleaves, Swords and Diamonds.

17–22 Sept 1942: Colonel Hermann Schulte-Heuthaus. He was later promoted to Major-General and awarded the Knight's Cross in January 1942.

22 Sept 1942–12 May 1943: Lieutenant-General Theodor Graf von Sponeck. Holder of the Knight's Cross, he handled the division brilliantly during its dogged withdrawal across North Africa. He was taken prisoner on 12 May 1943.

### Senior Divisional Staff

Ia: Major von Ziegler und Klipphausen; Major Schumann
Ib: Major Lippmann; Major Übigau; Captain Hayessen
Ic: Lieutenant Wiesse; Lieutenant Hiltmann; Captain Kircher
IIa: Major Kolbeck
IIb: Lieutenant Rauert
SMO: Dr Werlemann
Div Vet: Prof Dr Schmidt

### Divisional Orbat

Div Staff and Div Map-store 259 (mot) 259 (attached to Panzerarmee Afrika in January 1942)
Inf Regt 155 (mot)
Inf Regt 200 (mot) (not formed until 24 March 1942, by combining one battalion of Inf Regt 155 with III Bn Inf Regt 347)

Inf Regt Afrika 361 (mot) (unit contained many French Foreign Legion veterans)

Pz Gren Regt Afrika (mot) (previously known as Bde Gp 288)

Kolbeck Bn (not formed until 22 November 1942 and commanded by Major Kolbeck)

Heavy Infantry Gun Companies 707 and 708 (placed under command of 164 leichte Div on 14 Aug 1942)

Anti-Tank Bn 190 (mot)

Artillery Regt 190 (mot) (originally Artillery Regt 361)

Recce Bn 580 (mot) (originally Recce Company 580 )

Signals Bn 190 (mot)

Engineer Bn 900 (mot)

Reinforcement Bn 190

Ambulance Platoon 638 (mot)

MT Workshop Platoon 566

Ammunition Resupply Company 540 (mot)

Bakery Company 535 (mot)

Butchery Company 517 (mot)

Divisional Resupply Branch 190 (mot)

Military Police Troop 190 (mot)

Field Post Office 190 (mot)

Initially the Italian 2nd 'celere' Artillery Regiment was part of the division, and three Italian infantry battalions (2/255, 3/347 and 2/115 (mot)) were attached.

**55 Savona Infantry Division**
Outline organisation of this Italian division was:
Div HQ CG Generale Fedele de Giorgis
15 Inf Regt
16 Inf Regt
12 Arty Regt
MG Bn 155 (attached)
4 Bn Genoa Cavalry (armoured cars) (attached)
Coy Arditi (storm troops) (attached)
Oasis Bn 300 (German) major elements (attached)

**Other Italian Units**

**XXI Corps** (CG Generale di Corpo d'Armata Enea Navarrini)
Corps Artillery Task Forces (Raggruppamenti):
16th (three bns of 105/28 guns), 24th (two bns of 105/28 guns and one of 100/17 guns, of which one bn of 105/28 guns was detached to XX Armd Corps)
Army Artillery Task Forces (Raggruppamenti):
5th (four bns of 149/35 guns), 8th (by October 1942 this would consist of one bn 149/40 guns, one bn 152/37 guns and one bn 149/28 guns).

3rd 'celere' Artillery Regt (one bn 100/17 guns and two bns 75/27 guns)
304th Raggruppamento Guardia alla Frontiera (Frontier Guard)
340th Engineer Bn

**17th Pavia Infantry Division** (CG Generale Franceschini)
27th and 28th Infantry Regiments
26th Artillery Regiment (two bns 75/27 guns and one of 100/17 guns, of which one bn 75/27s was detached to XX Corps)
5th Light Tank Bn (attached)
6th Bn Lancieri Aosta (armd cars) (attached)

**25th Bologna Infantry Division** (CG Generale Gloria)
39th and 40th Infantry Regiments
205th Artillery Regiment (two bns 75/27 guns and one of 100/17 guns)

**27th Brescia Infantry Division** (CG Generale Zambon)
19th and 20th Infantry Regiments
27th MG Bn
1st 'celere' Artillery Regiment (two bns of 75/27 guns) (attached)

**102nd Trento Motorised Infantry Division** (CG Generale Stamponi)
61st and 62nd Motorised Infantry Regiments
7th Motorised Bersaglieri Regiment
55th Anti-tank Bn
46th Motorised Artillery Regiment (two bns 75/27 guns and one of 100/17 guns) (attached)

**Italian XX Armoured Corps**
(CG Generale Gastone Gambara) (as deployed on 17 November 1941)
Milizia Artiglieria Marittima (MILMART)[4] (three batteries of 102/35 guns) (attached)
One bn of motorised Engineers
1st Carabinieri Paratroop Bn

**132nd Ariete Armoured Division** (CG Generale Balotta)
132nd Medium Armoured Regiment
32nd Light Armoured Regiment
8th Motorised Bersaglieri Regiment
132nd Motorised Artillery Regiment (two bns of 75/27 guns) (attached)
one bn of 75/27 guns detached from the Pavia Division
one bn of 105/28 guns detached from 24th Raggruppamento corps artillery

**101st Trieste Motorised Infantry Division** (CG Generale Piazzoni)
65th and 66th Motorised Infantry Regiments
9th Motorised Bersaglieri Regiment
21st Motorised Artillery Regiment (attached)

508th Anti-tank Bn (mixed 47mm anti-tank and 20mm AA/anti-tank
  guns)

*Raggruppamento Esplorante* (RECAM)
52nd Medium Armoured Bn
3rd/32nd Light Armoured Bn
Experimental light tank and armd car company
MG Company
Two bns of Giovanni Fascisti Infantry
One bn of police units (one armd car company and two motorcycle coys)
Artillery
'Flying' Batteries including 1st and 3rd bns (65/17 guns); one indep bty
  65/17 guns; one bty 100/17 guns; one bty 20mm AA guns


## THE ITALIAN SOLDIER: EQUIPMENT, WEAPONRY AND UNIFORMS

It could well be argued that North Africa was primarily an Italian war,
with the Germans only providing support, and certainly if one looks
merely at the sheer numbers of troops involved, this is borne out, especially when one realises that the Italians were also mainly responsible for
manning a large amount of the base and rear areas in Tripolitania. Even
if one only considers those 'at the sharp end', the number of Italian divisions involved is greater. But the quality of weapons, vehicles, equipment
and, it must be said, fighting ability of the troops, is weighted heavily in
the German favour. The Italians had been in North Africa for nearly three
decades before the war; their obsolescent equipment had been adequate
against the badly armed, disorganised local tribesmen, but had shown
itself to be totally inadequate against the British. Nevertheless one should
not discount the considerable part played by the Italian forces in all of
Rommel's campaigns, so it is relevant to look briefly at the Italian fighting soldiers who were now, for the most part, under his direct command.

**The Italian soldier.** All Italian male citizens were liable for military service
between the ages of 18 and 55. Before being called-up they might well have
served between the ages of eight to 18, with the Young Fascists (there were
even similar organisations for Arab youngsters in the Italian colony in Libya).
Despite all Mussolini's efforts and their illustrious ancient past, however,
they were not naturally warlike, many recruits being basically hard-working,
unskilled farm labourers. Rommel is quoted by Marshal Ugo Cavallero as saying that the Italian soldier was: '... disciplined, sober, an excellent worker and
an example to the Germans in preparing dug-in positions. If attacked he
reacts well. He lacks, however, a spirit of attack and above all, proper training.'[5] The quotation goes on to affirm that the lack of transport, service and
supply, modern weapons, especially tanks, was a major cause of their poor
showing. This is substantiated by Bastico who is quoted as saying that '... the
prime reason for this attitude is not a lack of aggressive spirit on the part of

our men, but a deficiency – both in quality and quantity – in arms and logistics'. He goes on to cite the Trento Motorised Division which had 80 per cent of its vehicles out of action at one time!

## Armoured Fighting Vehicles

The Italians used armoured cars, tanks and carriers in North Africa, but they suffered from being mainly inferior to their British counterparts, and their armoured soldiers generally showed a lack of aggression, so the armour was often not used to its full potential. Tanks were quite well designed, but on the whole they lacked armour, had poor suspensions, were underpowered and inadequately armed, so they presented few problems to the heavier British tanks like the Matilda II for example. The armoured cars were a mix of out-dated Bianchi autoblindata of 1931 vintage and the more modern and useful AB 40 and 41. The Italians also adapted a number of light armoured personnel carriers for desert use, e.g., the Carro Protetto As 37, based on the MS 37 4-wheel drive desert truck, which could carry eleven men; additionally, various weapons were carried 'portee' on similar vehicles, the most successful being the Camionetta SPA 43 (also known as the Sahariana Ante Aera SPA), which was a long, low 4-tonner, mounting one or two 20mm AA guns, designed for mechanised cavalry use on long-range desert patrols.

**Tanks** (carro armato)

| Type | Weight (tons gross) | Crew | Armament | Remarks |
|---|---|---|---|---|
| Tankette CV 3/33 & 33/2 | 3.2 | 2 | one/two MG | to accompany infantry |
| L35/1f | 3.2 + trailer (500 litres) | 2 | flame-thrower | flame-thrower |
| L6/40 | 6.8 | 2 | 20mm gun + two MGs | light tank |
| M11/39 | 11 | 3 | 37mm gun + two MGs | medium tank |
| M13/40 | 14 | 4 | 47mm gun + two MGs | medium tank |

The main tank machine gun was the 8mm Mitragliace Breda modello 38 per carri armati, a version of the modello 37; it was produced from 1938 for tank use.

**Armoured Cars** (autoblindato)

| | | | | |
|---|---|---|---|---|
| Bianchi 1931 | | 2 | one MG | modernised version of WWI armd car designed for use in Libya |
| Fiat 611A | 7 | 5 | two MGs (611B had a 47mm gun) | heavy armd car |

| | | | | |
|---|---|---|---|---|
| Lancia IZM | 4.3 | 6 | three MGs | standard WW2 armd car |
| AB 40 | 6.85 | 4 | three MGs | entered service 1940 |
| AB 41 | 7.4 | 4 | 20mm gun+ MG | most widely used Italian armd car |

## Artillery

Of all the arms in the Italian Army, artillery was probably the best trained and most efficient. Many artillery units fought bravely throughout all the campaigns. In addition to the towed anti-aircraft and anti-tank, light and field, medium and heavy artillery, they also had a useful range of self-propelled (semovente) artillery pieces as the details below show.

## Examples of Italian Artillery

| | Date | Calibre (mm) | Shell weight (kilograms) | Max range (metres) |
|---|---|---|---|---|
| **AA** | | | | |
| 76/45 | 1912 | 76.2 | 6.3 | 6,400 ceiling |
| 90/53 | 1938 | 90.0 | 10.0 | 12,000 ceiling |
| **Light** | | | | |
| 65/17 | 1913 | 65.0 | 4.3 | 6,800 |
| 75/18 | 1935 | 75.0 | 6.3 | 9,400 |
| **Field** | | | | |
| 75/32 | 1937 | 75.0 | 6.3 | 12,500 |
| 100/17 | 1914 | 100.0 | 12.5 | 9,260 |
| **Medium** | | | | |
| 105/28 | 1914 | 105.0 | 15.5 | 13,200 |
| **Heavy** | | | | |
| 149/35 | 1910 | 149.0 | 41.0 | 6,600 |
| 149/40 | 1935 | 149.0 | 50.8 | 22,000 |
| 210/8 | 1908 | 210.0 | 100.6 | 8,000 (howitzer) |
| **Anti-tank** | | | | |
| 47/32 (MO35) | 1935 | 47.0 | 1.5 | 8,200 |

## Examples of Semovente

**75/18 series.** The most important series was the 75/18, 75/32 or 75/34 da M40, M41 and M42, which was based on the M13/40, M14/41 and M15/42 tank chassis, a box-like superstructure replacing the turret, and the main armament (a 75mm howitzer) protruding through the front armour. A total of 474 were built from 1941 to 1943 to provide close support to the armoured divisions, initially in North Africa. They could carry 40 rounds of howitzer ammunition, carried a crew of three, had a top speed of 22mph and a range of 125 miles. The largest (M42) weighed 15 tons.

**47/32 su L6/40.** Using the L6/40 light tank, this 6.5-ton semovente mounted a 47mm anti-tank gun. There was little space for the 3-man crew because 70 rounds of ammunition were carried. Nearly 300 were built from 1941 to 1942 for use in the Western Desert

Before leaving artillery, it is worth noting that the Italian 90/53 AA/anti-tank gun was a truck-mounted weapon which had a performance on a par with the German 88mm, but it was always in short supply, and not being mounted on a 4-wheel drive truck, its mobility was poor off main roads. The Germans had supplied a battalion's worth of their 88mm guns to the Italians, which they put to good use.

## Infantry weapons

The Italians had a large range of different types of small arms in service, including many obsolete weapons,[6] but the main standard issue were: one revolver and two automatic pistols (modello 89 a 10.35mm cal revolver, Glisenti modello 1910 and Beretta modello 1934 both 9mm automatics); two rifles (6.5mm Fucile 91 and the new 7.35mm Fucile 38); two carbines (6.5mm Moschetto 91 and 7.35mm Moschetto 38); two elderly 9mm sub-machine-guns (Moschetto automatico OVP and Beretta 1918/30) and one more modern Beretta, the 38A which became a favourite with the Allies whenever they could acquire them; large numbers of Fiat 14 and 14/35 6.5mm machine-guns were in service, also the 6.5mm Breda modello 30; finally, the 45mm Brexia light mortar. Heavier weapons included: the Breda RM modello 37 light 47mm anti-tank gun (could also be used as an infantry support gun); the Model 35 20mm AA/anti-tank gun (which was devastating against low-flying aircraft although its ceiling was only 2,300) metres; the obsolescent 65mm infantry gun of Great War vintage, which had a maximum range of 6,500 metres and could fire HE, AP and shrapnel; the modello 35 81mm mortar (cf. British 3in mortar). There were three models of hand-grenade: the OTO 35, SRCM M35 and Breda M35. All were very light and relied upon blast, smoke and noise, rather than on lethality. The official side-arm was of course the bayonet (various types), but there was also a combination bayonet/entrenching tool, and a combat dagger, the latter being the official side-arm of the Fascist Militia.

## Uniforms

Tropical uniforms had been designed originally for service in Ethiopia (1935-6), being of similar cut to the standard grey-green temperate climate woollen tunic but made of light khaki linen. Unlined, the jacket had dark brown plastic buttons, and shoulder-straps. NCOs wore their rank badges on the upper arm. There was another type of jacket which was very popular with officers (and soldiers when they could get them!) because it was very comfortable to wear, called the Sahariana which eventually became the official officer's tunic. It was a 4-pocket bush jacket, with a conventional collar and cloth waist belt. Other forms of dress included a dark khaki cordellino 4-pocket tunic and an unlined pullover khaki tunic which opened to the waist. Tropical shirts were also of khaki linen (officers usually wore tailor-made shirts of a similar pattern), and there was a mixture of trousers, breeches, shorts and pantaloons, mainly in khaki–olive green linen. Tan-coloured lace-up high boots were worn, but the most common ORs pattern was the same as the temperate climate boot but in tan leather. Officers favoured knee-high riding-boots, and puttees and leather leggings were also worn by all ranks. It is true to say that many variations in uniform were permitted, because of shortages (many ships were sunk en route for North Africa), including the mixing of tropical and temperate clothing. Headgear included steel helmets (M33 pattern), crash helmets (for tank crews), tropical peaked caps (for officers), tropical side caps and pith helmets; specialised units (e.g., the Alpini and Bersaglieri) wore their own traditional head-dress which included grey-green felt caps and a red felt fez with a long blue woollen tassel.

Much of the soldier's personal equipment was of Great War vintage, revolver holsters varying, for example, from grey-green or khaki canvas, to chemically dyed leather. Ammunition pouches, bandoliers, etc., were in leather or canvas, and knapsacks, rucksacks and haversacks were all made of light, waterproof canvas in a variety of colours. The inevitable gas mask (Model 33 carried in a square bag or Model 35 in a cylindrical bag) was standard, as were aluminium water-bottles and mess-tins. Shelter quarters (also worn as ponchos) were made in khaki although the European pattern were also issued, and first field dressings were wrapped in waterproof paper. Officers normally also had binoculars and compasses in leather cases, and brown leather covered map cases.

## Rations

The Commissariat Service was responsible for supplying and distributing rations, and their units/establishments included bakeries, depots, refrigerator plants (in the rear areas) and factories to produce the tinned food such as meats, soups, etc. These included the dreaded AM tinned beef. The Italian soldiers called it: 'Arabo Morto' (Dead Arab) so it was no more popular with them than with their allies! As most of the soldiers were Roman Catholics they needed – and were granted – Papal dispensation to eat meat on a Friday. Sometimes, especially on operations in the desert, soldiers received a ration of AM plus two hard corn 200gm 'hard tack' biscuits, but they also did from time to time receive such luxuries as chocolate, sweet cakes and tinned marmalade. Cigarettes were issued, as and when available, the most hated brand being MILIT. Rex Trye explains in his book *Mussolini's Soldiers* that the soldiers interpreted the initials as: M = Merda (shit), I = Italiano, L = lavotara (worked) I = in, T = tubetti (little tubes)! The daily water ration was laid down as being five litres per man, per day, with 20 litres being allocated to animals, but these were naturally dependent upon a regular supply being available.

## PANZERGRUPPE OPERATIONS

The first operation carried out by the new Panzergruppe was a limited attack in early September 1941, code-named 'Midsummer Night's Dream' (Sommernachtstraum), the objective being what Rommel mistakenly believed was a large British fuel and supplies dump in Egypt, at Bir Khireigat, fifteen miles in from the frontier. Rommel saw it as an essential preliminary to another assault on Tobruk, with the secondary somewhat hopeful aim of capturing information on British orders of battle which would be most helpful in the future. Two battlegroups (Kampfgruppen) 'Schuette' and 'Stephan' from 21st Panzer Division moved off in three columns:

| **Schuette** | **Stephan** |
|---|---|
| A/T Bn 605 (one coy) | Pz Regt 5 plus various attached |
| MG Bn 8 | artillery and AA btys |
| AA Bn 606 ( one coy) | |
| Engr Bn 200 (one coy) | |

The third column (working with Schuette) consisted of empty lorries. The idea was for the Schuette battlegroup to break in and grab the supplies, load them on to the lorries, while Stephan kept away unwelcome visitors. Also involved was 3 Recce Bn which provided lots of dust, movement and radio 'chat' in the area of the frontier. With Rommel in the lead, the columns advanced but found nothing, the enemy having withdrawn in front of them (probably pre-warned by radio intercept). The only definite plus was the capture of a vehicle belonging to the South African armoured car screen, which contained important documents and cipher material, but otherwise the raid was a failure. Furthermore the columns ran out of fuel and, while immobilised, were attacked by South African aircraft. The casualties included the driver of Rommel's Mammoth, when the vehicle was hit by a bomb. Rommel was forced to call off the raid and beat an undignified retreat. There is some evidence to suggest that the 'important documents' were planted and that the Germans were allowed to capture them. Certainly their contents, and the lack of any supply dumps near the frontier, convinced Rommel that no attacks were being planned and that he could get on, unhindered, with taking Tobruk, to which project he turned all his energies.

The Panzergruppe defences were now extended some twenty miles inland to Sidi Omar, to protect Rommel's rear while he assaulted Tobruk. Defences were thickened up, especially by the laying of extensive mine-fields. The layout was:

a. Around Tobruk. Italian XXI Corps (W to E: Brescia, Trento and Bologna Divisions, with Pavia Division slightly farther south of El Adem and El Duda). To their east were 15th Panzer Division and the new 90 leichte Afrika Division, charged with assaulting Tobruk from the SE and supported by the Panzer Group artillery under General Böttcher from gun positions between El Duda and Belhamed.

b. Between Tobruk and the frontier. With its HQ at Gambut, was the rest of the DAK, acting as Rommel's mobile reserve, with 21st Panzer Division on the Trigh Capuzzo, halfway to the frontier from Tobruk, and Recce Bns 3 and 33 covering the desert flank westwards from Sidi Omar along the Trigh el Abd. The15th Panzer Division was ready to rejoin the DAK if the enemy did attack.

c. The frontier defences were held by the Savona Division, the coastal sector being in German hands, and the Panzergruppe's Engineer HQ in overall command of the mixed German and Italian force (which included the Halfaya Pass garrison).

d. Rommel had also persuaded Marshal Bastico to deploy XX Mobile Corps farther south of Tobruk (Bir Hacheim–Bir El Gubi), to guard against any wide encircling movement.

### Operation 'Crusader'

Rommel now had an imposing force making up his Panzergruppe, but the enemy also had built up his forces since 'Battleaxe', forming the new Eighth Army. This was now very definitely a Commonwealth force, containing strong contingents from Australia, New Zealand, India and South Africa, as well as British – the official history records that of the 239,000 troops landed in Egypt between January and July 1941, 95,000 were from the Commonwealth. A new commander, General Sir Alan Cunningham, recent victor in East Africa, was chosen to command the new Army, which contained seven divisions with much new equipment, including 300 cruiser tanks, 170 Infantry tanks and 300 of the new American 'lend-lease' M3 lights – known by the British as 'Stuarts' and by the crews as 'Honeys',[7] together with 34,000 lorries, 600 field artillery guns, 240 AA guns, 200 anti-tank guns and 900 mortars. The British preparations for a massive offensive did not go unnoticed, reports from spies, air reconnaissance, etc., all confirming what had already become obvious to many senior commanders who did not have Rommel's fixation over Tobruk (even Hitler and Jodl had told Rommel to: 'leave Tobruk alone and get ready to meet Auchinleck's attack').[8] Rommel flew to Rome with von Ravenstein, determined to make the Italian High Command change their minds and to accept that it would be much harder to deal with any attack if Tobruk remained in enemy hands. After much heated argument he convinced them, having personally guaranteed that there would be no danger because 21st Panzer Division could hold off any enemy assault while Tobruk was being dealt with. The attack was scheduled for 23 November. Rommel and von Ravenstein, who had now been joined by their wives, decided to stay in Rome for Rommel's birthday (on the 15th), so he was away from North Africa when a daring attempt was made by British Commandos to kill him.

    **The Commando Raid that failed.** A party of Commandos led by Major Geoffrey Keyes was landed on the night of the 15th by two submarines not far from Beda Littoria, where the British mistakenly thought Rommel had his HQ. It had been prepared as the HQ for the Panzergruppe, but rejected by Rommel as being much too far behind the lines, and he had moved forward some months before to Cantoniera Gambut, between Tobruk and Bardia. The requisitioned buildings, which still had plates on the doors suggesting that the Panzergruppe HQ was in residence, were actually occupied by the Ib chief supply officer (Quartiermeister

(Qu)). But even the senior 'Qu' staff – Major Schleusner and Captain Otto – were absent, both being in hospital at Apollonia, the former with dysentery, the latter with inflammation of the lungs. Dogged by disaster, Keyes was killed during the raid and buried with full military honours together with four Germans also killed, while the entire Commando, less one sergeant and two men who evaded capture and made it back to British lines, were taken prisoner. The gallant Major Keyes was awarded a posthumous Victoria Cross.

Cunningham's main aim was to destroy as much enemy armour as possible, this becoming almost as much an obsession to the British general as the Desert Fox's fixation with Tobruk. But, as General Sir William Jackson points out in *The North African Campaign 1940–43*, while Rommel not only had a sound and balanced plan for the storming of Tobruk, he also had been training his troops all through the summer to fight a properly co-ordinated action against any relieving enemy forces. Cunningham, on the other hand, was far from clear as to how he would destroy the enemy armour, having no personal experience of armoured warfare and therefore being entirely in the hands of his so-called 'armoured advisers', whose expertise had been sadly depleted by the death in an air crash of Lieutenant-General Vyvyan Pope in October 1941 – he was to have commanded XXX Corps, the main armoured element of Eighth Army.

The basis of 'Crusader' was that Allied XIII Corps would contain Halfaya Pass while also outflanking it to strike towards Fort Capuzzo; XXX Corps would swing wide to the south between Bir Sherferzen and Fort Maddalena, then strike north-westwards towards Gabr Saleh, to take on the enemy armour, defeat it and move on NW to relieve Tobruk. The attack began well for the British on the 18th with 7th Armd Div reaching Gabr Saleh virtually undetected and thus unopposed, thanks not only to their strict observation of radio silence, but also to the fact that unexpected, very heavy rain had severely limited both air and ground recce.[9] Cunningham's forces did not meet any real resistance until they reached Sidi Rezegh on the 19th, although there was determined action on the flanks, especially from the Ariete Division around Bir el Gubi and elements of 21st Pz Div on the other flank. In the former location, the newly arrived 22nd Armd Bde was lured into making a head-on assault, without adequate artillery and infantry support, on to well-emplaced anti-tank guns, thereby losing a large proportion of its brand-new Crusader cruiser tanks. At first, Rommel thought the British assault was only limited, but once the extent of the operation was appreciated, 21st Pz Div retaliated, striking first eastwards towards Sidi Azeiz on the 19th, then turning SW the following day towards Gabr Saleh, inflicting heavy losses on 4th Armd Bde.

On the morning of the 21st, Rommel ordered the DAK to attack towards Sidi Rezegh, where 7th Armd Bde had overrun the airfield, destroying some nineteen Axis aircraft. 7th Armd Bde was now making towards Tobruk, where the garrison was getting ready to break out and link up with them, but had to turn to face Crüwell's DAK, losing some two-thirds of its tanks in the ensuing battle on the 22nd. Rommel invariably kept his panzers together, hurling them at the scattered enemy units, making the most of their superior mobility and firepower. On the left of XIII Corps, 2nd New Zealand Division had managed to get behind the German/Italian frontier positions and was moving up towards Sidi Azeiz. Bitter fighting continued around Sidi Rezegh, with both sides suffering heavily. That night, 15th Pz Div, which was going to the support of 21st Pz Div, ran into 4th Armd Bde and inflicted heavy casualties. On the 23rd, the 'Sunday of the Dead' (Totensonntag) – the day on which all Germans honoured their fallen countrymen of the Great War – the confused fighting continued, with both sides suffering heavily. But the panzers were again able to take on the scattered British forces piecemeal and destroy them: 'What does it matter if you have two tanks to my one,' Rommel later asked a captured British officer, 'when you spread them out and let me smash them in detail?' Unfortunately for the Panzergruppe, the considerable British losses wrongly convinced Rommel that he should now make a determined effort to get to the frontier quickly with the bulk of DAK, so as to cut off as much of the Eighth Army as possible. This manoeuvre has been rightly described by many historians as being one of Rommel's most controversial acts. Despite the serious misgivings of his senior staff officers (Mellenthin and Westphal) who did not think that he should move the bulk of his mobile forces so far from the area around Tobruk, Rommel was deaf to all such cautionary advice. He also ignored the strong New Zealand force which was moving on Tobruk from Bardia (and would achieve a short-lived link up with the besieged garrison at El Duda).

Leaving his staff to cope with the battle still raging around Sidi Rezegh, he shot off to complete the destruction of the 'remnants of the enemy' and to cut off their withdrawal into Egypt. At the head of the hastily gathered DAK, he was soon speeding eastwards along the Trigh el Abd, causing consternation everywhere and causing many of the enemy to flee in front of him – Cunningham himself was almost captured, the Blenheim bomber he had just boarded being shelled as it was taking off. Rommel also had his own narrow escape; his staff car's steering column snapped, leaving him, Gause and his ADC, Alfred Berndt, stranded and alone as their escort armoured car had been left far behind and the vehicles in front were fast disappearing. They managed a few more miles, and then the engine gave up. While they stood shivering in the rapidly cooling evening gloom, they were lucky enough to be spotted by General Crüwell and his Chief of Staff, Colonel Fritz Bayerlein, who were in their Mammoth ACV on their way back to their HQ at Gasr el Abid. They were of course inside Egypt and could not find their way back through 'The Wire', which marked the frontier. Even with Rommel driving, they were continually out of luck, so were forced to leaguer up for the night, constantly in fear of discovery by one of the many enemy vehicles which came close by, but they were never challenged. At dawn, Rommel again took the wheel, quickly found the gap in the wire, slipped through and reached Gasr el Abid a few hours later.[10]

Westphal, back at Panzergruppe HQ at El Adem, was by now extremely worried by what was going on at Sidi Rezegh and around Tobruk, and even more convinced that the 'Race to The Wire' was a mistake. He therefore started sending signals urging the return of the DAK. Neither Crüwell nor Rommel could be reached by radio – Rommel's normally accompanying radio truck had stuck fast in the desert sands – so a light aircraft was dispatched to find him, but this was shot down. Eventually Westphal decided to act on his own initiative and sent out recall orders to 21st Pz Div. Rommel was not pleased when he found out, initially considering that the orders must have been sent by the enemy. He was still furious when he at last reached El Adem, but sensibly took himself off to his tent before exploding. Next day, when he was able to determine how strong a threat the enemy still presented, he had the good grace to tell his Ia that he had taken the correct decision. In fact, although circumstances on the battlefield were against Rommel's daring advance, German overall successes during these early phases of 'Crusader' had convinced Cunningham that there was nothing for it but to order a full-scale withdrawal, in order to save his forces from annihilation. He was prevented from doing so by Auchinleck, who flew forward and forbade Cunningham to make any such withdrawal, ordering him to continue with the offensive. But although this partly restored the situation, 'The Auk' was now convinced that Cunningham had 'lost his bottle' and swiftly replaced him with General Sir Neil Ritchie, his deputy chief of staff, through whom he could exercise full control.

Increasing British pressure and the New Zealand link-up with the Tobruk garrison were visible signs that, although the Panzergruppe had won the battle 'on paper', they were so weakened that they could not continue the fight – DAK, for example, was down to just a handful of tanks by early December. Supplies of everything were running low and it was not long before Rommel came to the inevitable conclusion that he might well have to withdraw from Cyrenaica completely. If he had known just how close he had come during his frontier gallop to the two enormous British supply dumps that were supporting 'Crusader', things might have turned out very differently.[11] Only about one third of the 120,000 tons of Axis supplies sent to North Africa in recent weeks had actually arrived, thanks to the British stranglehold on their supply routes across the Mediterranean. In early December Rommel was told categorically by Rome that he could not expect to receive any further reinforcements until January 1942. It is true that he had inflicted considerable casualties on the enemy – an estimate at the end of November, quoted by Rommel in a proclamation to his troops calling for one last effort from them, gave Allied casualties as 814 tanks and armoured cars destroyed, 127 aircraft shot down, more than 9,000 prisoners taken and huge quantities of *matériel* captured. On the debit side both the Germans and Italians had each lost some 4,000 men which included of course the capture of General von Ravenstein (GOC 21st Pz Div), while DAK and the Ariete Division were down to 40 and 30 battleworthy tanks respectively.

On 1 December, despite these problems and against Crüwell's protests, Rommel decided to send out two mobile battlegroups (each based on an infantry battalion with anti-tank and artillery support), one down the coast road (Via Balbia) the other down the Trigh Capuzzo, to take the pressure off the frontier garrisons. The composition of these battlegroups was:

| Via Balbia | Trigh Capuzzo |
|---|---|
| Commander: | Commander: |
| Lieutenant-Colonel Geissler | Lieutenant-Colonel Knabe |
| HQ Inf Regt 200 | II Bn Inf Regt 104 |
| Motorcycle Bn 15 | 1 coy Anti-tank Bn 33 |
| 1½ btys Arty Bn 33 | three tanks |
| 1½ coys Anti-tank Bn 33 | |

The northern group was ambushed and almost totally destroyed near Bardia; the other clashed with 4th Indian Division and was heavily attacked from the air and forced to withdraw. To make matters worse, the British had managed to put together a sizeable force and lift the siege of Tobruk (after 242 days). The British force met the exhausted remnant of the DAK at Bir el Gubi on 5 December and for the next few days the battle raged. Rommel had expected Italian support from Gambara's mobile corps, but it never arrived and to make matters worse, 15 Pz Div commander (General Neumann-Silkow) was killed on 7 December. Marshal Bastico, the overall Axis commander, heard that Rommel was planning to withdraw and, after trying unsuccessfully to get Rommel to visit him, went up to the Front himself and told Rommel that he would not authorise a retreat. Rommel replied that it was entirely the Italians' fault because they had let him down. After a heated exchange, Rommel refused to amend his decision and, on 7/8 December, the westerly withdrawal began. 'We're pulling out,' Rommel wrote to his wife on 20 December. 'I hope we manage to get back to the line we've chosen.' He went on to tell her that he had at last managed to get a bath and a change of clothes, having slept in his coat for the last few weeks. A few supplies had arrived – the first since October – and in his next letter he tells her that they have little ammunition or petrol and no air support, but that he is hoping to get the bulk of his force through to Agedabia and make a stand.

Fortunately for Rommel the Allied advance was very hesitant and they made no effort to outflank the withdrawing Axis forces, who had completed the difficult withdrawal by Christmas Day. One of the casualties was General Max Sümmermann, commander of 90 leichte Division, who was killed on the 10th when his command vehicle was strafed. There was not much ground action because, to be fair, the British were by then far too stretched and had outrun their supply lines. The only Axis forces unable to withdraw were the frontier garrisons, which all held out bravely until January: Bardia falling on the 2nd, and Bach's heroic little garrison at Halfaya Pass sticking it out until the 17th. Rommel makes a special point of praising the bravery and skill of Italian Generale di Georgis who had commanded the mixed German/Italian garrisons. But the loss of these garrisions added to the overall losses, so that by mid-January 1941, the total number of prisoners taken since 'Crusader' began was in excess of 33,000. More importantly, although the British and Commonwealth forces had lost more tanks than Rommel, replacements for them would be much easier to obtain, thanks to generous American assistance. And besides, they had retaken the whole of Cyrenaica, driving Rommel and his Panzergruppe right back to where they had started the previous March – no wonder Churchill wrote that it was: 'a moment of relief and indeed of rejoicing about the Desert War'.

## PANZERARMEE AFRIKA OPERATIONS (JANUARY– JULY 1942)

On 5 January 1942 the Axis forces received their first sizeable reinforcement convoy, which landed 54 tanks, 20 armoured cars, numerous anti-aircraft and artillery guns, together with a significant quantity of fuel and ammunition. Most of the new panzers were allocated to Pz Regt 8 (15th Panzer Division), 'as good as a victory in battle' is how Rommel described their safe arrival. Indeed, with these reinforcements the 'Desert Fox' soon felt able to resume the offensive, advancing from his base at El Agheila on 21 January and quickly retaking Agedabia and Beda Fomm. Rommel had originally planned the advance merely as a spoiling action to dissuade the British from advancing, but after hearing via his radio intercept that the enemy were having severe logistical problems, he decided to turn it into a major assault. Clearly he felt that his 'star' was once again in the ascendant, Hitler having just awarded him the 'Swords to the Oakleaves' of the Knight's Cross for his brilliantly executed withdrawal from Cyrenaica, and his reputation with the enemy had increased to almost mystical proportions. Churchill was to say of him in the House of Commons later that: 'We have a very daring and skilful opponent against us, and, may I say across the havoc of war, a great General.' Auchinleck even had to go to the lengths of issuing a special directive to all Commanders and Chiefs of Staff which contained the words: 'There is a real danger that our friend Rommel is becoming a kind of magician or bogeyman to our troops, who are talking too much about him ... I wish you to dispel by all possible means the idea that Rommel represents something more than an ordinary German general ... it is a matter of the highest importance.'

For his part, Rommel was busy exhorting his troops – Hitler would raise the status of Rommel's command to that of a Panzerarmee on 30 January – to greater efforts in a Special Order of the Day (issued on 21 January 1942). 'German and Italian soldiers!' it read: 'You have fought hard battles against an enemy superior in numbers; however, your morale remains unbroken. At the moment we outnumber the enemy immediately in front of us. The Panzergruppe will therefore launch an attack today and defeat them. I expect every soldier to give of his best during these decisive days. Long live Italy! Long live the greater German Reich! Long live the Führer!'

Rommel's forces advanced in three columns: in the north (on or north of the Via Balbia) was a mixed group of mobile infantry and artillery from 21st Panzer and 90 leichte Divisions, under command of Colonel Marcks (Inf Regt 104) and with Rommel's *Gefechtsstaffel* in close attendance; in the centre was Generale Gambara's Italian XX Mobile Corps; to the south in the desert some twenty miles south of the Via Balbia, was the remainder of DAK under Crüwell. During the first day of the advance, they succeeded in pushing the British back through a number of pre-planned delaying positions and next day the Marcks column reached Agedabia. The advance continued to Antelat and then on to Msus, from where Rommel sent part of his force to cut off British 1st Armoured Division, but this only partly succeeded. The British had lost many of their tanks and other weapons, but DAK had also suffered heavy casualties. Taking Benghazi on the 29th, they continued to push forward for the next few days, until Eighth Army reached the Gazala Line (a series of brigade-sized defensive 'boxes', linked and protected by extensive minefields, running down from Gazala to Bir Hacheim in the desert, well to the south. The 'boxes' were surrounded with wire, mines, slit trenches and pillboxes, and inside them were enough supplies to withstand a siege of at least seven days.

There were continual command problems on the British side during this period, which led, for example, to Godwin-Austen (GOC XII Corps) resigning after being overruled by Ritchie about the evacuation of Benghazi. The 'Auk' thought long and hard about sacking Ritchie who by now had clearly lost the confidence of his corps commanders, but decided against it despite being prodded to do so by London. The command problems are best explained by a comment made by General Sir William Jackson in his *North African Campaign*, that at this time: 'the British High Command in Cairo and the Western Desert remained a well-meaning democracy in which senior commanders continued to treat orders as a basis for discussion.' This was no way to run a war against someone like Rommel!

## Operation 'Venezia'

Rommel returned to Africa on 29 March, after obtaining a qualified agreement from Hitler that he could attack again in May, break through the Gazala Line and take Tobruk, but should then go on to the defensive. He was optimistic and eager to attack before the British could launch any assault of their own, which Churchill was pressing Auchinleck to do. For the next few months, therefore, there was a lull in the fighting while both sides built up their strength again. Rommel's plan for the assault on the British line was both bold and optimistic. He planned to make a strong, feint attack on the centre of the Gazala Line, as though he was aiming to break through the minefields directly towards Tobruk, by the shortest – and most obvious – route. Having got the enemy looking in the wrong direction he would then lead his mobile forces around the southernmost 'box' at Bir Hacheim, then drive north-eastwards to Acroma and El Adem, take on and rout the enemy mobile forces in the open desert, before attacking the heart of the British positions from the east. He would then move on to assault Tobruk and deal with any enemy forces trying to withdraw into the fortress or escape into Egypt. For this operation, he divided his Panzerarmee into two groups:

**Northern force** (for feint attack)
(under command of Crüwell)[12]
Italian X Corps (Generale Gioda), comprising Brescia (Generale Lombardi) and Pavia (Generale Torriano) Divisions
Italian XXI Corps (Generale Navarrini), comprising 'Sabratha' (Generale Soldarelli) and Trento (Generale Scotti) Divisions
15th Inf Rifle Bde, comprising two regimental rifle groups from 90 leichte Division
Army Artillery

**Southern force** (for the southern sweep, code-named 'Venezia')
(under command of Rommel)
DAK (now commanded by General Nehring), comprising 15th Pz Div (General von Värst), 21st Pz Div (General von Bismarck) and 90th leichte (General Kleemann) less its infantry (with the northern force)
Ariete Armd Div (Generale de Stephanis)
Trieste Mot Div (Generale La Ferla)

**Weaponry.** Rommel always considered that the tanks of his panzer divisions and the 88mm Flak/anti-tank guns were the most important weapons in the desert battles. He had a total of some 560 tanks, which included many new arrivals. For example, between January and May 1942, a total of twenty PzKpfw II, two hundred and eleven PzKpfw III, forty-nine PzKpfw IV and four PzBefWeg had been shipped in as replacements. In addition ten PzKpfw II and thirty-four PzKpfw III were sent for 3 and 7 Companies of Pz Regt 5 (21st Pz Div). This gave the two panzer divisions the following tank strength:

| **15th Pz Div** | **21st Pz Div** |
| --- | --- |
| twenty-nine PzKpfw II | twenty-nine PzKpfw II |
| one hundred and thirty-four PzKpfw III* | one hundred and twenty-two PzKpfw III** |
| twenty-two PzKpfw IV | nineteen PzKpfw IV |
| four PzBefWeg | four PzBefWeg |

*only three, **only fifteen, had the new long-barrelled 50mm gun
(Source: Jentz)

The Italians were still equipped with their light cruiser M11/40s and M13/40s all of which were outgunned and had easily penetrable armour, but their SP guns (semoventi) were extremely useful.

Rommel also had forty-eight of the highly lethal 88mm FlaK/Anti-tank guns which were undoubtedly battle-winners, being able to penetrate a staggering 84mm of armour plate at 2,000 metres. The Germans had also pressed into service numerous captured artillery pieces, even including some from the Russian Front!

In the air, the Luftwaffe had both a slight numerical superiority in aircraft and probably the best fighter aircraft of the period – the single-seat Messerschmitt Bf–109F, which had a maximum speed in excess of 370mph, a normal range of 350 miles and was armed with a 15mm MG151 cannon and two MG17 machine-guns. It was followed towards the end of 1942 by the 109G (known as the 'Gustav') which accounted for 70 per cent of the total Bf-109 production.

Opposing the Panzerarmee was a wide mix of armour – some 850 tanks in total (nearly 300 more than Rommel had) – varying from thickly armoured 'Infantry' tanks, like the elderly Matilda Mk II and the more modern Valentine in the two army tank brigades, to the latest American lend-lease M3 Medium Grant, 167 of which had now entered service in the two armoured divisions. (This new tank was known to the Germans as MIII 'Pilot' – they had found a photograph thus marked and thought that 'Pilot' was the tank name). Its excellent 75mm gun and thick frontal armour (up to 50mm) came as something of a surprise to them, Rommel writing in his diary: 'The advent of the new American tank has torn great holes in our ranks. Our entire force now stands in heavy and destructive combat with a superior enemy.' Another witness was Heinz Werner Schmidt, Rommel's erstwhile ADC, who was now serving with an infantry company in 15th Pz Div and vividly recalled seeing his 50mm PaK anti-tank gun shells bouncing harmlessly off the Grants, whose return fire caused many casualties to his company.

Summary of numerical balance of tanks and aircraft:

| Tanks | German and Italian | | Allied | |
|---|---|---|---|---|
| Medium | PzKpfw II | 50 | Grants | 167 |
| | PzKpfw III | 242 | Stuarts | 149 |
| | (incl 19 'Specials') | | Crusaders | 257 |
| | PzKpfw IV | 40 | Valentines | 166 |
| | | | Matilda II | 110 |
| TOTALS | | 332 | | 849 |
| | | | | |
| Italian | M13/40 & M14/41 | 228 | | |
| | | | | |
| Reserves | PzKpfw II | 10 | Grants | 75 |
| | PzKpfw III | 38 | Stuarts | 70 |
| | PzKpfw III 'Specials' | 19 | | |
| | PzKpfw IV | 1 | | |
| | PzKpfw IV 'Specials' | 9 | | |
| TOTALS | | 77 | | 145 |
| GRAND TOTALS | | 637 | | 994 |
| | | | | |
| Serviceable aircraft in forward area | | 497 | | 190 |
| Elsewhere within reinforcing range | | 1,000 | | 749 |
| TOTALS | | 1,497 | | 939 |

(Source: *British Official History*, vol III, p. 220)

## A Tactical Advantage

Although Rommel knew that the odds were in the enemy's favour as far as both men and *matériel* were concerned, and that they had shorter lines of supply and were in strong defensive positions, he was entirely confident of victory because he considered, with some justification, that the higher level of combined arms training, the innate ability of the German commanders to make the best of any given situation, and, above all, his supreme confidence in his own proven abilities, made him absolutely sure of success.

### 'Rommel an der Spitze!' (Rommel leading!)

The British and Commonwealth forces on the Gazala Line had appreciated that Rommel would try the southern approach around Bir Hacheim, but were convinced that this would be a feint, and that the main attack would come through the minefields in the centre. So when their intercept picked up a message at dawn on 27 May to the effect that Rommel was leading a panzer column around the Free French-held Bir Hacheim, surprise was almost complete. The positions in the south of the Gazala Line (apart from Bir Hacheim) were all pushed back. But when the southern force turned north-eastwards and moved to cross the Sidra Ridge they were heavily attacked from both sides, lost many tanks and could not be resupplied. For two days they were held in an area south of Sidi Mufta, which came to be called 'the Cauldron' (*Hexenkessel*). The main Axis force was now concentrated in this area, with its back to the British minefield (through which their supply columns were still trying without success to reach them), preparing for the inevitable British counter-attack. This did not come until 5/6 June and was easily beaten off with heavy losses. On 10/11 June the gallant defenders of Bir Hacheim were finally forced to withdraw, but not until Rommel had expended considerable effort on them, especially from the air. Next day the panzers also burst out of 'the Cauldron' striking to both south and east. They beat off numerous unco-ordinated counter-attacks, and forced Eighth Army to evacuate the Gazala Line completely and fall back to Tobruk and further east. By 18 June the German forces had once again invested the fortress and began a blistering attack at dawn on the 20th. This time the garrison was unable to withstand the pressure, especially after heavy dive-bombing attacks, and by 1600 hours most of the main defences had been overrun and the airfield taken. Next day, at 0800 hours, Major-General Klopper, the South African garrison commander, formally surrendered. It was to be the highspot of Rommel's career in the Western Desert; Hitler promoted him to Field Marshal – the youngest in the German Army. But he had lost a major portion of his armour and numerous vital personnel – for example in Panzerarmee HQ, both Gause and Westphal had been wounded and two others killed. Gause was replaced by Bayerlein (from DAK HQ), and Mellenthin (Ic Intelligence) replaced Westphal as Ia. Total casualties had been less than 3,500.

This was not to be the end of Rommel's advance. Eighth Army, still in considerable disarray, was given permission to withdraw to Mersa

Matruh, having lost more than 50,000 men and much of its armour. Auchinleck at last relieved Ritchie and took personal command. He quickly appreciated that his forces were far too dispersed and decided that when the enemy attacked he would withdraw to the more easily defensible El Alamein positions. Rommel was not slow to oblige, even though he was down to fewer than 60 operational tanks. His forces attacked on 26 June astride the southern escarpment, and swiftly surrounded Matruh. Next day the garrison split up and broke out in small parties, while the British armour fell back eastwards in front of the panzer divisions, 21st Pz Div being heavily involved with 2nd New Zealand Division, while 1st Armd Division struggled to hold 15th Pz Div. The 90 leichte cut the coast road at Sidi Abd el Rahman on the 29th and the scattered units of Eighth Army fell back to El Alamein.

## Strike for the Delta!

Rommel did not give the opposing forces much of a breather and, despite being seriously short of everything was determined to continue to press ahead, now that the glittering prizes of Cairo, the Delta and the Suez Canal all seemed to be within his grasp.[13] He was assisted in this by having captured large stocks of enemy supplies (Rommel still used to recall the cornucopia of delights which they had found in Tobruk long afterwards, for example, to his ADCs, when he was in France in 1944), and swiftly sent DAK and the Italian Mobile Corps on towards the Egyptian frontier, after allowing them only one day to re-organise. 'I was determined at all costs', he wrote in his diary, 'to avoid giving the British any opportunity of creating another front and occupying it with fresh formations from the Near East.' After considerable argument with higher HQ, especially with Kesselring, who still wanted to mount a major offensive against Malta, Rommel gained the necessary sanction to pursue the enemy east of the frontier, his leading troops often mingling, unobserved with the retreating enemy – made all the easier as many of their wheeled vehicles were now captured British MT, and the mix of uniforms made them practically indistinguishable! By 1 July they had closed up on the line El Alamein–Ruweisat Ridge–Deir el Munassib, but this was to be the limit of their success. During 2–4 July, Rommel made a number of attacks, but they were all repulsed with considerable loss. On the night of 10/11 July, the newly arrived 9th Australian Div attacked Italian XXI Corps positions on Tell el Eisa (north-west of El Alamein) and routed the Sabratha Division, Rommel having to send one of his ever decreasing reserve German units to plug the gap. Next day Trieste Division was also routed and the situation only saved by units of 164 leichte Division (see below for details) who had just arrived by air from Crete. British counterattacks along the Ruweisat Ridge on 14/15 and 21/22 July, although they made only limited progress, finally convinced Rommel that a stalemate had been reached. This was true on the other side as well where, despite continuous pressure from Churchill, Auchinleck refused to consider any further attacks, but chose rather to build up his forces. This caused him to be replaced by General Sir Harold Alexander, and a new GOC-in-C was brought in for Eighth Army, namely Lieutenant General Bernard Montgomery. Here was an opponent who in some ways mirrored Rommel. He was a great showman who quickly realised that he must swiftly inject some pride and sense of purpose into the demoralised Eighth Army troops and give them a plan which they could understand and make work, namely, one based on holding ground and fighting doggedly, two things that the British and their Commonwealth Allies could do superlatively well – always provided that they believed in what they were doing. The new commander had the necessary charisma to make them believe – and made strenuous efforts to get his message across quickly, by visiting widely and talking informally to the soldiers. He was ideally supported by the charming, polite, suave Alexander, who was perfectly suited to the political and military intrigues of Cairo, yet no stranger to the battlefield.

**Loss of Radio Intercept.** One of the most grievous losses suffered at this time was the capture of 621 Radio Intercept Company and the death of its brilliant commander, Lieutenant Alfred Seebohm (see Chapter 4). This loss had a major impact on Rommel's intelligence gathering, leaving him as it were 'groping in the dark'.

## Casualties

The summer campaign had caused considerable casualties on both sides. Rommel himself quotes the following figures for the period 26 May–20 July 1942:

Allied Casualties: 60,000 British, South African, Indian, Australian, New Zealand and French taken prisoner, 2,000 tanks and armoured vehicles destroyed.

Axis Casualties: German 2,300 killed, 7,500 wounded 2,700 taken prisoner; Italian 1,000 killed, 10,000 wounded, 5,000 taken prisoner.

## Alam el Halfa

The British and Commonwealth forces now held the Ruweisat Ridge–Alam Nayil–Alam el Halfa features in considerable strength and were determined not to budge. There was to be no withdrawal, so Montgomery moved up everything he could prise out of GHQ Cairo so as to strengthen his positions. He sent the 'evacuation' transport to the rear and stocked all locations with as much ammunition, fuel, water and supplies as possible. He also got across his main tactical message, namely that there would be no more 'swanning' or 'cavalry-like charges', divisions would be fought as divisions, the overall plan being to wait for the enemy to come and then defeat him from strong defensive positions, using well-sited anti-tank guns and hull-down tanks. And, most importantly, he made it clear that orders were orders and not merely a basis for discussion!

Rommel's intention was to assault the British positions as soon as he had received sufficient resupply, so he had to wait for this to arrive. But he well knew that his enemies would soon be receiving a large replenishment of men and *matériel* which he could not hope to match, so he could not put off his attack too long. After much deliberation, he decided that 30/31 August was the optimum date. Rommel was not a well man at the time, having been out in the desert far longer than any of his younger commanders and soldiers. His personal physician, Professor Dr Horster of Würzburg University, had been extremely worried by his chronic gastric problems and his fainting fits, accompanied by inflamed eyes, a nose infection and a swollen liver. The normally robust 'Desert Fox' was a shadow of his former self and eventually admitted that he was a sick man. He even proposed that Guderian should come out to assist him, but this request was refused because, at that time, 'Schnelle Heinz' was in bad odour with the OKW and the Führer, so Rommel was forced to 'soldier on'.

**The Plan.** Rommel's basic plan recognised that the northern half of the enemy position was too strong to break through, so, while the newly arrived 164 leichte Division with Ramcke Para Bde attached and supported by Italian infantry divisions, mounted a limited attack on the coastal area to pin down the enemy, his mobile forces would assemble in the south towards the Qattara Depression, with 90 leichte in the north, then the Italian XX Mobile Corps, with Ariete and Littorio Armoured Divisions in the centre, and finally, on the southern flank, DAK, with their reconnaissance units on the extreme outer edge. They would force their way through the extensive minefields, then 'wheel' north-eastwards, past the main forward positions, aiming directly at the Alam el Halfa ridge, so as to cut the British off from their supply depots. Then, at leisure, they would turn westwards and annihilate them, leaving the way clear to march triumphantly on to the Delta. The main strike force comprised, as always, the 200 medium tanks of the DAK, of which just under half were 'Specials', recognised at that time as being the most powerful tanks in the Western Desert. They would be faced at Alam el Halfa by some 210 medium tanks in 8th and 22nd Armd Bdes, which included the majority of the new Grants, whose firepower was to have a decisive result on the outcome of the battle.

The attack was launched at 2300 hours on 30 August, the Panzerarmee having first to get through a series of minefields, which were covered by 7th Armd Div. This time Rommel had been unable to achieve any surprise despite trying hard; the Allies still had ULTRA, while he was now without his radio intercept. In addition, as soon as initial German troop movements had been detected ten days before the attack, the RAF had started bombing the panzers in their concentration area and had continued without any let-up. The initial attack was greatly hindered by the minefields and the accurate sustained fire of 7th Armd Div – Nehring was wounded, von Bismarck killed – and the persistent air attack continued unabated. Severe dust storms then sprang up which did not help visibility, although they did reduce air activity. On the Alam el Halfa position, 22nd Armd Bde were so well concealed that they had to show themselves deliberately in order to draw the German armour northwards. There were heavy casualties on both sides, but eventually Rommel had to withdraw and leaguer for the rest of the night, still well south of the main Alam el Halfa positions. Further assaults failed on the following day, and the night of 1/2 September was particularly bad, with continuous bombing and shelling wearing down even Rommel's iron will. By dawn on the 2nd it was clear that the attack had failed and all that was left was to plan an orderly withdrawal. The British put in a limited counter-attack and succeeded in driving the Panzerarmee back through the minefields, but they did not follow-up. After four days, the battle had ended, with heavy casualties on both sides, but particularly damaging to the Axis who had some 3,000 killed and wounded (roughly 2:1 German to Italian), and 50 tanks and 50 artillery and anti-tank guns knocked out. They also lost some 400 lorries. On the British side, the Eighth Army had just over 1,700 killed and wounded and lost nearly 70 tanks and 20 anti-tank guns. Most importantly, however, Eighth Army, under its new commander, had shown itself capable of beating the 'unbeatable' Afrika Korps, and even the wily 'Desert Fox' had failed this time. It was undoubtedly the major turning-point in the war in the Western Desert and marked the farthest east into Egypt that Rommel would ever achieve. Now it was time for Monty to 'knock the enemy for six'.

## Notes to Chapter 5

1. Within the DAK there were still two divisions: 15th Panzer and 5 leichte. The latter division was to be strengthened, renamed and reorganised as 21st Panzer Division on 1 October 1941.
2. As quoted in Green and Massignani.
3. Awarded the Knight's Cross in December 1941.
4. This had originally been Militia Dacos (coastal artillery), which changed its name to MILMART in 1939. A large organisation with some 33,000 all ranks, it employed some of its naval guns in North Africa, mounted on trucks and attached to Ariete Division as long-range anti-tank artillery from December 1941, one battery being responsible for inflicting heavy casualties on 22nd Armd Bde at Bir el Gobi.
5. Quoted in Trye, *op. cit.*
6. Shortly before the war, Italy had decided to change the calibre of its standard rifle, carbine and light machine-gun from 6.5mm to 7.35mm. A number of the new weapons were introduced, but the changeover was still under way and was further delayed when hostilities began, so a mix of small arms was to be found in units.
7. The first shipment of 84 M3s had arrived in July 1941 and had been used to re-equip 8th King's Royal Irish Hussars, subsequent shipments going to 1, 3 and 5 RTR of 4th Armd Bde, who first used their new tanks on 18 November 1941 at Gabr Saleh.
8. 'Desert Ups And Downs' in Young, *Rommel*.
9. The Germans had used the code-words for any enemy attack 'High Water' and 'Deluge', the former signifying a limited attack, the latter a major assault. So there was some confusion when the heavens opened and real 'deluges' were reported!
10. This was not the only close shave which Rommel had during his 'Race to The Wire'. The afternoon before he had visited a field hospital full of wounded British and German soldiers, only discovering that it was a

British hospital while on a tour of inspection – having been mistaken for a Polish general. He made a dignified exit and 'escaped' in his Mammoth!

11. The dumps were each some six square miles in area, only a few miles south of Gabr Saleh, with just one brigade available to guard them. DAK troops actually drove through a water point on the northern edge of the more easterly dump, without realising it was there.

12. Crüwell had just lost his wife who had died of scarlet fever, leaving four young children to be cared for by relatives.

13. The nearness of the Axis troops caused a major 'flap' in Cairo, with many people desperately trying to escape to Palestine, while masses of secret documents were being burnt in the British Embassy and GHQ. Sensible precautions such as the evacuation of non-essential personnel, women and children, or the drawing-up of demolition plans, all increased the panic which reached its height in the first week of July.

# 6
# Panzerarmee Afrika
## Alamein to Tunisia
## (September 1942 – January 1943)

**The Lull before the Storm**

Montgomery and his revitalised Eighth Army had undoubtedly inflicted a decisive defeat upon the hitherto unbeatable DAK. They were helped of course by the steady stream of information produced by ULTRA and by the fact that the 'Desert Fox' was feeling very ill after eighteen months' continuous command. He would be unable to take sick leave until the end of September, and, ill or not, there was still a great deal to be done. Rommel knew that Montgomery would attack once he had built up his forces, so it was essential to construct as strong a defensive line as possible. In this he was aided by the fact that, unlike the position at Gazala, the Qattara Depression prevented a wide sweep around the southern flank. This shortened his defensive line which was convenient given his numerical inferiority. He guessed that there would be 'hard pounding' of the type not seen since the end of the Great War, and accordingly built his defences in depth, holding the line with his infantry and keeping his armour uncommitted and ready to counter-attack.

The main static defensive line was based upon his 'Devil's Gardens', namely extensive minefields[1] adjoining 'no man's land', wherein were thousands of captured enemy bombs and shells (suitably wired) and all available anti-tank and anti-personnel mines. Captured Allied minefields were incorporated into the system, so there were British, Egyptian, French, German and Italian mines, some laid in tiers up to three deep. Although a careful sweep would find the first, and experienced sappers might discover the second layer, it is highly doubtful that anyone would anticipate yet a third below that! There was a preponderance of anti-vehicle mines; only some 3 per cent of the total half million mines laid were the highly lethal anti-personnel 'S (Schuh) mines, which scattered steel pellets at chest height, having 'jumped' into the air when set off by tripwire or by being trodden on. The minefields were covered by small outposts in which Rommel had dogs to give early warning of intruders. The main defensive positions, some 1–3,000 metres in depth, were located anything up to 2,000 metres behind the minefields. Farther back (but not too far) were the panzer divisions, positioned to bring fire to bear or to counter-attack swiftly.

Rommel estimated that the British had a two to one superiority in tanks, even when counting the 300 obsolescent Italian tanks. Furthermore, many of the British tanks were modern, newly acquired 'Lend-Lease' American mediums (Grants and Shermans), while only about one-sixth of the total

German tank force were the more powerful PzKpfw IV. The German historians Spielberger and Feist confirm this in their book *Armor in the Western Desert*, quoting the opposing tank forces as being:

| British | German |
|---|---|
| 170 Grants | 85 PzKpfw III L/42 |
| 252 Shermans | 88 PzKpfw III L/60 |
| 216 Crusaders Mks 1 & 2 | 8 PzKpfw IV L/24 |
| 119 Stuarts | 30 PzKpfw IV L/43 |
| 194 Valentines | |
| Total 1,029 | Total 211 |

They also do not of course include the smaller, now obsolescent, PzKpfw Is and IIs.

Infantry was more balanced of course, but the British also had more supporting arms such as artillery, engineers, etc. They also had the great advantage of short, well-protected lines of supply – a mere 40 miles of easy motoring back to the Delta, while Rommel's vulnerable umbilical cord stretched unendingly through the hostile desert over which the British had almost total air superiority.

Rommel was to adopt a principle which he had used before, namely of bolstering up his Italian units by inserting German formations between them. This made for difficult relationships and showed only too clearly that their Army Commander did not entirely trust the Italians to fight with the same tenacity and bravery which he could expect from his 'Afrikaners'. To be fair to the Italians, this was a consequence of their obsolescent weapons and outdated equipment rather than their fighting ability. In addition of course, Rommel was short of everything and had recently asked for the following as the minimum required to bring his army up to fighting trim:

a. Some 11,200 reinforcements (including 6,000 from Germany).
b. 3,200 vehicles (including 1,200 from Germany of which 120 were modern, medium tanks).
c. 70 field guns.
d. 30,000 tons of supplies in September and a further 35,000 tons in October.

From north to south the line comprised:

a. From the sea to the railway – two battalions of Ramcke's paratroops, and some Italian Bersaglieri.
b. From the railway to Kidney Ridge – 164th leichte Division.
c. Opposite Miteiriya Ridge and down to Ruweisat Ridge – Trento Division plus one of Ramcke's paratroop battalions; Bologna Division with two more paratroop battalions on their flank.
d. Down to Munassib – Brescia Division plus two more German paratroop battalions (these were German paratroops from Crete).
e. Munassib to Himeimat – Folgore Parachute Division.
f. South of the Himeimat in the no man's land down to just east of the Qattara Depression – Recce Bn 33 and Kiehl Combat Group.

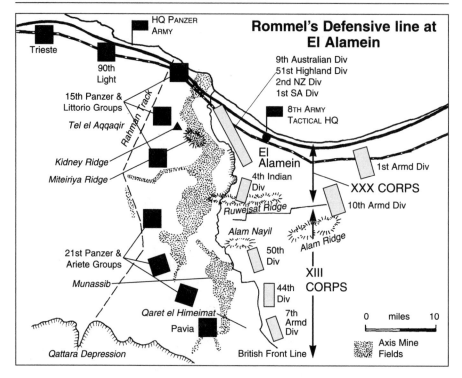

Behind the static defensive positions were the mobile troops, with 15th Pz Div and Littorio Armd Div 'paired' in the north in an area six miles SSW of Sidi Abd el Rahman; in the south were 21st Pz Div and Ariete Armd Div located to the NW of Gebel Kalakh. In both cases the divisions were grouped into three mixed battlegroups, with their divisional HQs located adjacently. Behind these were 90th leichte and Trieste Divs, Rommel's only reserve, grouped together and guarding the coast at El Daba against amphibious landings.

Rommel decided that, despite the proven superiority of the DAK when operating in the open desert, this time he could not risk putting the main weight of the defence upon such operations because of three factors:

a. First and foremost was the shortage of fuel for the AFVs and soft-skinned vehicles. Shortages had always been apparent and were never made up, despite all the promises from Adolf Hitler and the German and Italian staffs. In fact, when the battle began the situation was even worse than he had ever imagined. When Rommel was on his way back to North Africa, he discovered to his chagrin, on cross-questioning Rintelen in Rome on the 24th, that they had only enough fuel for three days' fighting.

b. The enemy now had air superiority, which put a severe strain not only on the tactical use of tanks and motorised columns in the desert, but also on the security of the tenuous lines of supply.

c. The balance between motorised and non-motorised elements of the opposing forces had also swung in the Allied favour. Such Panzerarmee reinforcements as had arrived were mainly non-motorised, so were of little use in mobile warfare.

## Orbat of the Panzerarmee

Before going into any details of the Second Battle at El Alamein, let us look at the detailed order of battle of Rommel's Panzerarmee, which now comprised some 104,000 men of whom less than 50 per cent were German.

## ORBAT OF PANZERARMEE AFRIKA as at 15 August 1942

### Army Headquarters (Armeeoberkommando)
### German formations

Deutsches Afrika Korps (15th and 21st Pz Divs) with 25,000 men, 371 tanks, 246 anti-tank guns, 72 artillery pieces, 5,600 other vehicles (including 600 tracked vehicles of various types)

90 Light (leichte) Div with 12,500 men, 220 anti-tank guns, 24 artillery pieces (the balance was not sent to Africa), 2,400 vehicles (including 250 tracked)

164th Inf Div with 11,500 men, 45 anti-tank guns, 36 artillery pieces, 300 other vehicles (including captured British vehicles)

Parachute (Fallschirmjäger) Brigade Ramcke

### Italian formations

X Corps (Brescia and Pavia Inf Divs)

XX Mobile Corps (Ariete and Littorio Armd Divs, Trieste Motorised Div and Folgore Parachute Div)

XXI Corps (Trento and Bologna Inf Divs)

### Army Troops and supporting units

Brigade Staff z.b.V (mot) 15 (z.b.V. = for special purposes)

Battle echelon (Kampfstaffel) (mot)

Army Map Store 575 (mot)

Air staff Libya (Kommandeur der Luftwaffe (Koluft))

Infantry Brigade Group 288 (mot) (an *ad hoc* formation Sonderverband)

Reconnaissance HQ 2 (Army)/14th Pz Div

Anti-tank Bn 605 (mot)

Artillery Staff 104 (Arko 104) (there were approx 3,300 men, 56 artillery pieces and 1,000 vehicles of which 100 were tracked, in the Army Artillery)

Staff Artillery Regt 221 (mot)

Staff Heavy Artillery Regt 408 (mot)
  2. and 3. Batteries/408
  5. /Artillery Regt 115
  Artillery Bn 364

Staff Heavy Artillery Bn 528
  2. and 3. Batteries/528

Artillery Battery 528

Artillery Battery 533
Artillery Battery 902
Staff 1. /Artillery Regt 115 (mot)
   4. /Artillery Regt 115 (mot)
   6. /Artillery Regt 115 (mot)
   4. /Army Coastal Artillery Battery 149
Artillery Survey and Mapping Troops 721 – 730 inclusive (mot)
Observation Bn 11 (mot)
  Staff Battery
  Sound Ranging Battery
  Flash Spotting Battery
AA Bns 606, 612, 617 (mot)
AA Regt 135 (mot) (Luftwaffe)
Army Construction Unit 73 (mot)
Construction Bn 85
1. /Local Defence Bn 278
Signals Regt 10 (mot)
Special Messenger Staff (Luftwaffe)
V, VI, XII and 'Tripolis' Army Radio Stations
Special Operations Radio Troop 'Afrika'
Signals platoon 937
Supply Regiment 585 (mot)
Staff Supply Bn 619 (mot)
Unloading Staff for special duties 681 (mot)
Staff Supply Bns for special duties 792 and 798 (mot)
Supply Bns 148 (Italian), 149 (Italian), 529, 532, 533, 902, 909 (mot)
Vehicle Repair Bn 548 (mot)
  Tank Recovery Platoon (mot)
  Tyre Section 13 (mot)
  Tyre and Spare Part Depot 548 (mot)
  Tyre Repair Section 573 (mot)
  Vehicle Workshop Platoon 534 (mot)
  Volkswagen Vehicle Workshop Platoon (mot)
  Bosch Vehicle Workshop Platoon (mot)
Ammunition Administration Platoons 542–547 inclusive
Petrol Analysis Troop 12 (mot)
Army Petrol Oil and Lubricants (POL) Administration Pl 5 (mot)
POL Platoons 979, 980 and 781
Technical Stores Administrative Service (mot)
Army MT Parks 560, 566 (mot)
Ordnance Stores Platoons 1, 2, 3 (mot)
1. /Bakery Company 554 (mot)
Butchery company 445 (mot)
Supply Depots 317, 445 and 'Afrika' (mot)
Staff Comdt Rations Office 556
2/Medical Company 592 (mot)
1/Hospital Transport Company 705 (mot)

'Tripolis' Base Hospital
5/ Base Hospital 542 (mot)
Base Hospital 667 (mot)
Light Base evacuation hospital (mot)
Medical Equipment Park 531 (mot)
Secret Field Police (mot)
Patrol Headquarters (mot)
Military Police Troop (mot)
Local Defence Guard Bn 'Afrika'
Garrison Commanders 'Misurata' 615, 'Barce' 619, 'Tripolis' 958, 'Benghazi'
    959 and 'Derna'
Tripoli Depot Commander (km 5)
Prisoner of War Transit Camp 782
13/Demonstration Regt 'Brandenburg' 800
SS Regiment 'Speer'
Field Post Offices 659, 762 (mot)
Field Post Office (mot) for Luftwaffe
Army Postal Service (mot) for special purposes.

### NEW FORMATIONS
We have already covered the outline orbat of most of the formations in the
Panzerarmee except for 164th leichte Division and the Ramcke Parachute
Brigade, which were both newly joined.

### 164th leichte Division
This was formed in November 1939 as 164th Lehr Infantry Division. It
fought in Greece and Crete, being flown from there, minus its vehicles, to
North Africa in July 1942, and was redesignated 164th leichte 'Afrika' Division shortly after relieving 90th leichte on operations. Its first battle was on
30 August 1942 and the Division took part in the rest of the campaign,
finally surrendering on 13 May 1943.

### Divisional Commanders
Aug–late Nov 1942: Colonel (later Major-General) Carl-Hans Lungershausen, except for a short period (31 Aug–18 Sept) when he temporarily
replaced Major-General von Bismarck as commander 21st Pz Div, and
Colonel Hermann-Hans Hecker took over 164th leichte. General Lungershausen was promoted to Lieutenant-General on 1 January 1943 and later
served in Sardinia and Italy, being awarded the German Cross in Gold.
6–30 Dec 1942: Colonel Siegfried Westphal (Rommel's Ia) in temporary
command.
1–16 Jan 1943: Major-General Kurt Freiherr von Liebenstein. He was made
acting commander of DAK on 16 January, then of 'Kampfgruppe DAK' on
10 February, holding both commands simultaneously until he was injured
in a car accident on 17 February.
16 Jan–17 Feb 1943: Colonel Becker of Artillery Regt 220 took over temporary command.

17 Feb–13 Mar 1943: Major-General Fritz Krause.
13 Mar–13 May 1943: Major-General von Liebenstein. Holder of both the German Cross in Gold and the Knight's Cross, he served as a Major-General in the Bundeswehr from 1956.

## Senior Divisional Staff

Ia: Colonel Markert

Ib: Captain Gerhardt

Ic: Lieutenant Leihner

IIa: Major Werner

SMO: Dr Ziegler

## Divisional Orbat

Div Staff

Pz Gren Regts 125, 382, 433 (mot)

Heavy Inf Gun Coys 707 and 708
  (both transferred from 90th
  leichte 14 Aug 1942)

Artillery Regt 220 (mot)

AA Bn 609 (mot)

Engineer Bn 220 (mot)

Reconnaissance Bn 220 (mot)

Signals Coy 220 (mot)

Medical Coy 220 (mot)

Ambulance Pl 220 (mot)

Workshop Coy 220 (mot)

Chief of Supply Services 220 (mot)

Bakery Coy 220 (mot)

Butchery Coy 220 (mot)

Supply Depot 220 (mot)

Military Police Troop 220 (mot)

Field Post Office 220 (mot)

## Parachute Brigade Ramcke

On arrival in North Africa in mid-July 1942, the first active elements of the Brigade (288 Special Parachute Brigade) on landing were assigned to 15th Pz Div. But as soon as the rifle battalions had arrived the Brigade, under Brigadier-General Hermann Ramcke, was placed directly under the control of Panzerarmee Afrika. The Brigade then consisted of four rifle battalions, an artillery battalion, one anti-tank company and one engineer company.[2] The battalion commanders were: Majors Kroh, von der Heydte, Kagerer and Huebner. Having been air transported to North Africa, the Brigade had few vehicles of its own, so AA Regt 135 was detailed to transport them to the front and to supply them thereafter. They were split up (see above) to bolster the Italian positions during the El Alamein battle. When the Italian positions were overrun, the paratroopers did not surrender, but began to withdraw on foot, having no transport. Near Fuka on 6 November, they audaciously hi-jacked a British transport column while it was bivouacked for the night. Now fully motorised, they quickly rejoined the retreating Panzerarmee and withdrew safely. Ramcke was awarded the Oakleaves to his Knight's Cross for this remarkable feat. He was later sent back to Europe to form 2nd Parachute Division, which served in Brittany during the Allied invasion, and commanded the very brave and lengthy defence of Brest for which he was awarded the Diamonds to his Knight's Cross.

## Sick leave

On 16 September, General Georg Stumme arrived to become Rommel's deputy, a post which had been vacant since Crüwell had been captured during the Gazala battles. A first-rate panzer commander, Knight's Cross holder Georg Stumme, who had handed over 7th Pz Div to Rommel in 1940, had gone on to command XXXX Pz Corps in the Balkans and Russia, where he had been arrested for a security violation, relieved of his command and court-martialled together with his Chief of Staff, Colonel Gustav Franz. Both men were given a five-year prison sentence, but Göring, who had been the president of the court-martial had been very impressed by Stumme, and Field Marshal von Bock made a personal appeal on his behalf to Hitler. The result was a commutation of sentence for both of them and a posting to North Africa. In contrast to Rommel, Stumme appeared robust and healthy, but as it turned out, looks can be deceptive.

Rommel 'handed over' to Stumme during the following week, and, with considerable misgivings, left to go to Rome. His misgivings were not directed personally at Stumme, but rather because of the fact he well knew that Montgomery would attack, probably with the new moon in October, and felt guilty about leaving his 'Afrikaners'. He flew to Derna on 23 September, then on to Rome on the 24th, where he went to visit Mussolini, taxing him with the importance of keeping his army properly supplied.[3] He then flew to Germany and on the 26th arrived at the Führer's HQ in East Prussia, to be presented with his Field Marshal's baton and to ask yet again for supplies and reinforcements for his army. Hitler gave Rommel many promises as to what would be supplied, including such new weapons as the Tiger heavy tank and the Multiple Rocket Launcher, plus new self-propelled artillery. It would be some months before either Tiger or Nebelwerfer arrived in North Africa, but here is as good a place as any to describe them briefly.

**PzKpfw VI.** The 56-ton Tiger I was probably the most feared tank of the war. It entered production in August 1942, the first glimpse of it by the Allies being a photograph in the National *Zeitung* newspaper on 11 December 1942, which showed a Tiger of 501 Heavy Tank Battalion driving through the streets of Tunis – so Hitler did keep his promise albeit a few months late! The tank mounted the highly lethal 8.8cm KwK 36 gun which could penetrate 90mm of homogeneous armour at 2,500m, for which 92 rounds were carried. Secondary armament were two MG34s. Its wide tracks (725mm), powerful 650bhp Maybach HL 210 engine and good suspension, gave the 5-man tank a good cross-country performance (although not anywhere near as good as, say, the Allied Sherman), together with a top speed of 38km/h and a range of some 140kms. A total of 1,354 were built; they could easily deal with any contemporary Allied AFVs. Small numbers of Tigers were sent to North Africa towards the end of 1942, but although on occasions they individually knocked out substantial numbers of Allied AFVs, there were never enough of them to make a real impact.

**Nebelwerfer.** The 15cm Nebelwerfer 41 was a 6-barrelled rocket-launcher system, mounted on the same carriage as the 3.7cm PaK anti-tank gun and fitted with a simple sighting system. The rockets had a range of just over 7,000 metres, contained some 5½ pounds of explosive and were known as

'Moaning Minnies' by the Allies because they made a distinctive droning sound in flight. With a 4-man crew, it first entered service in 1942 and in time became the standard launcher on all fronts. Its disadvantage was its obvious 'signature' – the clouds of dust when it fired and the conspicuous smoke trails left by the rockets. Many different types of towing vehicle were used although the preferred one was the SdKfz 11/1 half-track.

Rommel's sick leave cannot have been all that much of a rest, including as it did such 'PR Spectaculars' as the official opening of the 1942/3 War Winter Help Programme at the Berlin Sports Palace on 30 September, and the Press Conference at the Propaganda Ministry on 3 October, at both of which he was the focus of much media attention. Even when he 'escaped' to a mountain resort near Weiner Neustadt, his thoughts were constantly filled with worries about his 'Afrikaners' – and rightly so!

## Montgomery attacks!

Sick, frustrated and isolated, Rommel eventually received the news he had been expecting but dreading when on the afternoon of 24 October, Field Marshal Keitel rang to say that the British had been attacking at El Alamein with powerful artillery and bomber support since the previous evening. Worse still, Stumme was missing, so it was highly probable that the Axis forces were leaderless and was he well enough to return and take command? Rommel said that he was, and spent some anxious hours waiting for further news. That evening Hitler personally called him to say that Stumme was still missing – either dead or a prisoner – so could he prepare to leave for North Africa immediately? The 'Desert Fox' flew back next morning, and at 2325 hours on 25 October all units of the Panzerarmee received a brief signal containing the words: 'I have taken over the army again. Rommel.' All must have breathed a sigh of relief, but only Rommel knew that it was now a very different 'ball game', commenting in his papers that: '... there were no more laurels to be earned in Africa'. He had received reports from his staff as to how far short the promises of supplies had fallen, but even they did not give the whole sorry picture, which he had only discovered for himself when he returned.

Stumme had suffered a strange fate. After a sleepless night on the 23rd, listening to the British barrage, unparalleled in the Desert War, unable to reply because of (in his opinion) ammunition shortages, he had received only scattered reports on what was happening, so decided to drive up to the Front to see for himself. This proved to be fatal because he soon found himself surrounded by the enemy. Colonel Buechting, the only officer with him, was shot through the head, Stumme jumped out of the car, presumably to get to cover, but when the driver (Corporal Wolf) managed to turn the car around, he ran back and clung to the outside. But somewhere in the desert, while Wolf was concentrating on getting clear of the enemy, Stumme had a heart attack and fell off. He was later found dead at the side of the track. General von Thoma took over until Rommel arrived back. Rommel pays tribute to Stumme, saying how much they regretted his death and that he had spared no pains to command the army well, being at the Front day and night. Stumme had admitted his lack of

**Above:** Two Italian M13/40 medium tanks provide a back drop to this medal presentation in which Rommel is being decorated by General Gariboldi with the Italian 'Medal for Bravery'. (Rommel Museum, Herrlingen)

**Right:** General Rommel outside his spartan desert quarters, near Tobruk. He took a pride in living rough like his men and was far fitter than many much younger men. (IWM - RML 16)

**Top:** Looking tired and dispirited, Rommel stands in the front of his Horch staff car during the withdrawal to Sidi Omar, 25 November 1941. His Chief of Staff, Major General Alfred Gause, is just behind him. (National Archives)

**Above:** Rommel in his Panzerspähwagen (SdKfz 250/3), watching Italian motorised units passing along the Via Balbia near Tobruk in 1942. (Col Ted Bock)

**Left:** Rommel's aide Lieutenant (later Captain) Alfred Ingemar Berndt, who was a tough member of the SS and thus an avowed Nazi. He acted as a go-between to Hitler and looked after Rommel when he was ill. (National Archives via David Irving)

**Top:** Rommel was very 'PR' conscious and took the trouble to cultivate the media. In North Africa he had his own war correspondent, Lutz Koch, seen here interviewing him on 20 June 1942, when Tobruk fell. Rommel was awarded his 'Diamonds' and also promoted to field marshal – the youngest in the German Army. (National Archives)

**Above:** Taking part in this map briefing are, left to right, Colonel Fritz Bayerlin (then CoS), Colonel von Mellenthin (then 1a) and, on Rommel's right, General Walther Nehring who took over the DAK from him but was then wounded on 31 August 42. (IWM - HU 6510)

**Right:** Rommel, plus tartan scarf, with his brilliant Chief of Staff, Oberst (later General der Kavallerie) Siegfried Westphal, near Agedabia, January 1942. (Author's collection).

**Above:** General der Kavallerie Georg Stumme, who took over from Rommel when he went on sick leave in September 1942, but suffered a fatal heart attack while reconnoitering on 24 October 1942 at the start of the Battle of El Alamein. (Tank Museum).

**Below:** General Wilhelm von Thoma, who was acting commander after General Stumme suffered a heart attack while Rommel was on

sick leave. He was captured by the British on 4 November and dined with Montgomery, with whom he is seen here. (IWM - E 19129)

**Above:** General Ludwig Crüwell, who took over the DAK when Rommel was promoted to command the Panzergruppe. He was captured when shot down in his Storch on 29 May 1942. (Tank Museum)

**Above:** Major-General Johann von Ravenstein, commander of 5 leichte/21 Pz Div from 23 July until 29 November 41, when he was captured by the New Zealanders. He is seen here in captivity. (IWM - E 6956)

**Right:** General der Panzertruppe Hans Cramer, the last commander of the DAK, who surrendered in Tunisia and was a prisoner of war from 16 May 1943 until 15 May 1944, when he was repatriated because of his chronic asthma. (Tank Museum)

**Left:** At von Arnim's headquarters in Benane, Tunisia, during a visit by Field Marshal Kesselring and some of his staff. (Rolf Munninger)

**Left:** Major-General Neumann-Silkow, commander of 15 Pz Div, from July 1941 to 6 December 1941, when he was seriously wounded by shellfire; he died two days later in Benghazi hospital. (Brig P.A.L. Vaux)

**Left:** Marching into captivity. Colonel-General Jürgen von Arnim, – who took over Heeresgruppe Afrika from Rommel on 9 March 1943 and had to surrender just two months later at the end of the Tunisian campaign. (IWM - NA 2875)

**Right:** Rommel talking to the redoubtable paratrooper Major-General Bernard Hermann Ramcke (with binoculars). His audacious capture of an entire British truck convoy saved his 800 paratroopers during the withdrawal after El Alamein. (IWM - HU 17182)

**Below:** Rommel discusses Luftwaffe operations with Major-General Frölich, who commanded the Luftwaffe elements in direct support of the DAK. (Colonel T. Bock)

**Below:** Rommel in conversation with Field Marshal Albert Kesselring, who as C-in-C South (Italy), was nominally responsible for German forces in North Africa. An extremely able officer, he did not often see eye-to-eye with Rommel. (IWM - HU 5622)

**Right:** Field Marshal Kesselring at Castell Benito aerodrome, Tripoli, November 1941, talks with newly-arrived German troops. (Rolf Munninger)

**Above:** Field Marshal Gerd von Rundstedt, C-in-C West, was Rommel's immediate boss in north-west Europe. Initially he was contemptuous of the youngest field marshal (at 68, he was the oldest), but generally they worked reasonably well together as von Rundstedt was quite happy to let Rommel do all the work. Their major disagreement, however, concerned the command and location of the panzer forces. (IWM - MH 10132)

**Above:** The majority of the panzers were under the command of General Geyr von Schweppenburg's Panzergruppe West. The autocratic von Schweppenburg would not accept Rommel's opinion that if the panzers were held too far back they would never be able to get forward because of Allied air supremacy. Events would prove Rommel correct, as von Schweppenburg later admitted. (Tank Museum)

**Above:** Lieutenant-General Hans Speidel, Rommel's brilliant Chief of Staff, who was also heavily involved in the plot to assassinate Hitler, but managed to outwit the Gestapo despite losing his job. (National Archives)

**Above right:** Standing behind Rommel during one of his tours is his able ADC Major Helmut Lang, who would remain with him right to the

end. Lang was a highly decorated panzer officer. At Rommel's side (partly hidden) is Vice-Admiral Friedrich Ruge, Rommel's friend and confidant. (David Irving)

**Below:** Rommel inspects western Atlantic Wall defences. He kept up a punishing schedule, minutely inspecting all the defences. (IWM - HU 3060)

**Above:** German troops working on beach defences of the Atlantic Wall run for cover as an Allied photo reconnaissance aircraft flies low over them. (Tank Museum)

**Below:** One of the heavy guns that defended the Atlantic Wall, after its capture by the British. Their calibres ranged from 28cm up to a massive 40.6cm (Tank Museum)

**Top left:** A German machine-gunner (MG 34) in a somewhat exposed concrete position right down on the beach near Arromanches. (IWM - HU 20741)

**Centre left:** Infantrymen on a training exercise prior to the invasion, photographed at Arromanches, sheltering behind the low wall and picket fence on the promenade, which would hardly provide effective cover! (IWM - HU 20742)

**Bottom left:** An off-duty group from the garrison at Arromanches, pose for a snap to send home. They seem to want to go to Paris – I cannot imagine why! (IWM - HU 20738)

**Above:** A group of soldiers of the Arromanches garrison prior to the invasion. The soldier in the centre of the front row is wearing his Markmanship Lanyard. (IWM - HU 20737)

**Right:** A good close-up of three German paratroopers, wearing their special steel helmets. Two are wearing the camouflaged field jacket, and the one on the right appears to be wearing his jump smock (Fallschirmschützenbluse). (IWM - MH 6371)

**Left:** Waffen SS wearing their familiar camouflaged jackets and helmet covers, which were sometimes also worn by army units. (IWM - MH 226)

**Right:** The best-known self-propelled gun on the PzKpfw II chassis was the Wespe (Wasp), which mounted a 10.5cm howitzer. (Rudlof Wulff)

**Right:** These Panthers, photographed near Bayeux, were superior to all Allied tanks; had there been more of them close to the beaches it might have been a very different story. (Tank Museum)

**Below:** Two Sd Kfz 232 8-wheeled heavy armoured cars. The basic model was armed with a 2cm cannon; the 233 mounted a 7.5cm support gun. (Author's collection)

**Above:** 'For you the war is over.' Wounded German soldiers who have been taken prisoner leaving the battlefield under escort (the British soldier with them can just be seen on the left). (IWM - B 6008)

**Left:** Gruppenführer Sepp Dietrich made a dynamic impression on Rommel who respected him from their first meeting in Italy when he was commanding the crack SS division 'Liebstandarte Adolf Hitler'. Rommel visited him on 17 July when he was commanding I Panzer Corps. (Tank Museum).

'African experience' and had recommended that Rommel return. Rommel also comments that Stumme was known to suffer from high blood pressure, so should never have been selected as being fit for tropical service.

## The Battle

'The battle which began at El Alamein on 23 October 1942 turned the tide of war in Africa against us and, in fact, probably represented the turning-point of the whole vast struggle.' So wrote Rommel in his diary, undoubtedly putting the importance of the El Alamein battle into perspective. But this is not the place to recount the second battle of El Alamein in every detail. Nevertheless an outline is necessary in order to maintain the battle record of the Panzerarmee. Following a devastating artillery bombardment by some 1,000 guns, and supported by RAF bombers, which began at 2140 hours and lasted for about half an hour, the British infantry crossed their start lines under the light of a full moon, to advance along the coast road, against the Italian infantry who put up a strong and spirited resistance. There was also an armoured attack in the south, but this got bogged down in the minefields, so the main weight of the assault was in the north. The opening bombardment destroyed most of the Axis communications network, so reports from the front had virtually ceased (hence Stumme's need to get forward and find out what was happening). The northern thrust was then counter-attacked by 15th Panzer on both the 24th and 25th, which almost succeeded in stopping the British advance and certainly slowed it down, but in doing so the panzers suffered heavily from artillery fire and non-stop bombing attacks. By the evening of the 25th, only 31 one their 119 tanks remained serviceable. Furthermore the precious reserve stocks of fuel had all but been used up.

On 25 October, the Allied tanks of X Corps again endeavoured to force a breakthrough, but the Axis line held. Next day, the second phase of Operation 'Lightfoot' began, Montgomery revising his plans so as to get the assault moving again. Rommel wrote to his wife on 27 October: 'A very hard struggle. No one can conceive the burden that lies on me. Everything is at stake again and we're fighting under the greatest possible handicaps. However, I hope we'll pull through. You know I'll put all I've got into it.' For a week fierce fighting raged on and around the coast road, with both sides seeking to bring up uncommitted armour from the south. But whilst Montgomery had plenty in hand, Rommel was soon running out of both reinforcements and resupply, especially for his armoured formations. On 1 November he was forced to make a major withdrawal of his infantry in the north to prevent them being encircled, pulling them back some three miles, while the British launched another attack in the vicinity of Kidney Ridge, some ten miles from the coast. The 2nd New Zealand Division, with continuous artillery support, managed to clear a corridor through the 'Devil's Gardens' which allowed the British armour to get through the minefields and beat off a strong armoured counter-attack. Two days later, on 3 November, Hitler issued one of his stupid 'No Retreat' orders.[4] Rommel commented: 'Arms, petrol and aircraft could have helped us, but not orders.'

From then on Rommel was forced to circumvent orders from both Hitler and Mussolini, in order to save his army from destruction – something he would never have considered doing before. One immediate effect of this order was the loss of DAK's commander, the very experienced and highly respected General Wilhelm Ritter von Thoma, who was captured by the British in a forward area, as already explained in Chapter 4. The order was rescinded two days later, after Rommel had sent Lieutenant Berndt to the Führer's HQ to explain that if the order were complied with, the Panzerarmee would be destroyed in a matter of days. Nevertheless, the delay in withdrawing the Panzerarmee was to prove nearly fatal, although, acting on his own reading of the situation, Rommel had already pulled out much of the DAK, leaving behind the Italian infantry. By 9 November it was all over and the great withdrawal had begun.

In his review of the battle Rommel makes caustic comments about the fact that both German and Italian 'higher authorities' put the blame for the defeat, not upon their own inability to supply the wherewithal to enable Rommel's troops to carry on fighting, but rather in the actions of his command and of the troops themselves – saying for example, that Rommel was a defeatist and that his soldiers had thrown away their weapons. This type of accusation would later involve Rommel in many arguments and rows as he sought strenuously to vindicate his gallant troops. Indeed, the final point he makes is of the bravery of his soldiers, both German and Italian, at El Alamein, writing a '... glorious page in the annals of the German and Italian peoples'.

## The Great Withdrawal

There followed, from 4 November when the army retreated to Fuka until the fall of Tripoli on 23 January 1943, a long and expertly handled withdrawal. I have used the term 'withdrawal', despite the fact that even Rommel calls it 'The Great Retreat'. At no time during those endless weeks did the rearward movement become a rout. Fighting doggedly and with great skill, the Panzerarmee fell back through Cyrenaica from one position to the next as Eighth Army followed, initially in slow time, not reaching Mersa el Brega until 12 December, although Rommel's leading elements had arrived there on 12 November. Everywhere possible the Germans left cunningly placed mines and booby-traps, many being the brainwaves of the army's new engineer officer Major-General Karl Bülowius. Rommel rated the small, bespectacled, bustling pioneer as being one of the best engineers in the German Army. Bülowius went on to command the Division von Manteuffel in March 1943, was taken prisoner in Tunisia and committed suicide in an American POW camp on 31 March 1945 (see Chapter 7). Despite being desperately short of everything, especially fuel, under constant air attack and heavily outnumbered, the Panzerarmee continually eluded its pursuers, thanks in no small way to the iron hand with which Rommel controlled everything. Orderly withdrawal is probably the most difficult of all manoeuvres on the battlefield, yet Rommel, despite being sick in heart and body, handled it with consummate skill.

The line at Mersa el Brega was held by two 'Young Fascist' Divisions, Pistoia and Spezia, together with elements of Centauro Armoured Division as a mobile reserve. Rommel and his Panzerarmee now found themselves once more supposedly under command of Italian Marshal Ettore Bastico, ordered by both Hitler and Mussolini to hold the 100-mile-long Mersa el Brega line at all costs. The Italians were already busy strengthening it, but Rommel had other plans. Instead of defending there, he wished to withdraw all the way to Tunisia where the Gabes Gap – a 12-mile stretch of land that ran from the coast to a series of virtually impenetrable lakes and marshes – offered in his opinion, the best place to form a realistic defensive line. On 24 November Rommel and Kesselring were summoned to a conference with Italian Marshals Cavallero and Bastico at the Arco del Fileni (known as 'Marble Arch' to Eighth Army troops). Rommel was blunt, to the point and realistic. If the Mersa el Brega line was to be held he needed at least 50 new PzKpfw IV 'Specials', a similar number of 75mm PaK guns, plus some 80 of a larger calibre (100-150mm calibre), together with transporters and ample ammunition for them. He would also need a guaranteed 4,000 tons of ammunition and the same of fuel, plus confirmation of reinforcements for the Luftwaffe in North Africa. If these items were not delivered to the front lines within a week, he could not guarantee to hold a determined assault from the Eighth Army. Clearly he must have realised that these demands were impossible. The conference was a disaster, the others all accusing Rommel of being '... a prey to despair in defeat'. Indeed, instead of reaching a sensible compromise, he was told a few days later (via Bastico) that Mussolini wished him to attack the British advance guards and under no circumstances withdraw any further without permission from the Italian High Command. As always, Rommel took no notice of these 'orders', but instead told Generale Navarrini to prepare the army to withdraw to a defensive line through Buerat, some 250 miles westwards in Tripolitania, between Sirte and Misurata.

Having given this warning order Rommel decided that the only thing he could do was to go to the Führer, explain the situation and get his support, not only for the immediate future but also for the long-term policy which might well include the evacuation of North Africa. Rommel flew directly to Rastenburg on the 28th and asked to see Hitler. He noted, as he puts it '... a distinct chill in the air', but he bravely persisted with his detailed explanation of events, which were accepted and approved. However, when he mentioned long-term strategy it '... worked like a spark in a powder barrel'! Hitler was furious and most of his staff, as one might have expected, agreed with him. When, for example, Rommel told them that only 5,000 of the 15,000 fighting troops in the DAK and 90 leichte had weapons to fight with, he and his soldiers were accused of throwing their weapons away! Rommel strongly rebutted these allegations, explaining that the weapons had been 'battered to pieces' by the RAF and that his soldiers had performed miracles, maintaining a fighting withdrawal with hardly any fuel or ammunition. But there was no discussion because Hitler clearly had the reverses in Russia foremost on his mind. Rommel was told that it was vital to maintain a bridgehead in Africa, so the Mersa el Brega line had to be maintained at all costs. But Hitler promised that he would do everything possible to obtain supplies for the Panzerarmee and to facilitate this, Göring would accompany Rommel to Italy to negotiate with the Italians in view of his 'extraordinary powers'.

Rommel did not enjoy the journey, thoroughly disliking the antics of the Reichsmarschall which he was forced to witness. He also suspected that Göring was trying to manoeuvre the Luftwaffe into taking over control in North Africa where he could see greater glory for himself. This coloured all his thoughts and actions, Rommel commenting that Göring was 'during this period my bitterest enemy', vetoing every proposal which Rommel put forward and substituting his own 'absurd ideas'. The 'Desert Fox', therefore resorted to cunning, instructing his ADC, the staunch Nazi, Lieutenant Alfred Berndt, to make the 'Gabes Plan' (i.e., the withdrawal to Tunisia and the defence of the line through Gabes) 'palatable' to Göring. Berndt, who had a very persuasive tongue, managed to do just this, Göring '... beaming his approval', but their plan was scuppered by Kesselring when they reached Rome, who argued that it would drastically increase the air threat to Tunisia,[5] so Göring changed his mind. During the same conference the Reichsmarschall declared that Rommel had '... left the Italians in the lurch', but before he had a chance to reply, Mussolini interjected 'That's news to me; your retreat was a masterpiece, Marshal Rommel!' Indeed, Rommel says that on this occasion the Italians were far more amenable than the Germans and even supported his Gabes plan. But it was clear that nothing would be achieved, and indeed, at another conference on 2 December during which all the supply problems were discussed, Rommel stated that practically the entire shipping space was now being taken up with supplies for Fifth Panzer Army in Tunisia. Rommel gave examples of vital items (e.g., the latest type of 88mm guns) which had been diverted by Kesselring to Tunis, and as the discussions progressed he became more and more embittered. His final thoughts as he flew back to rejoin his 'Afrikaners' on 2 December, encapsulate his mood: 'I realised that we were now completely thrown back on our own resources and that to keep the army from being destroyed as the result of some crazy order or other would need all our skill.'

## Withdrawal from Mersa el Brega

Eighth Army had reached Agedabia on 23 November, but halted there to re-organise and did not close up to the Mersa el Brega positions until 11 December. Some days previously Rommel, appreciating that if he stood and fought there he would be encircled and overwhelmed, had begun to withdraw his Italian infantry – they are said to have left with blazing lights and blaring horns, but despite this their departure was not detected by the enemy. On the 11th the British barrage began, but by then all the Panzer-armee's infantry had departed and their remaining armour began to slip away, so that when the attack came in on the 12th, the lines were empty.

Rommel meanwhile had been strengthening the Buerat line, laying several tens of thousands of mines, this time mainly anti-personnel mines which were useless against tanks, but there was a reasonably formidable anti-tank ditch. The position had one major drawback, in that it could be outflanked at its southern end. This is what would happen, but not until 15 January so Rommel had time for some Christmas festivities, Christmas dinner arriving 'on the hoof' in the shape of a herd of gazelle – both Rommel and his interpreter, Wilfried Armbruster, each managed to shoot one from their moving staff car. The enemy did not arrive at the Buerat line for some days, by which time Rommel had once again moved his infantry back to the Tarhuna–Homs line, despite signals from Mussolini to hold the enemy on the new line. This was approved by the Italians, with the proviso that Rommel hold the enemy in front of Tripoli for at least six weeks. But Rommel knew the situation better than anyone else and was even more determined to save his men from such empty gestures. So by 19 January he was moving troops back across the Tripolitanian border to start to occupy the defensive position at Mareth, where a line of old French fortifications stood. Rommel was not entirely happy with the Mareth position; he had always wanted to withdraw even further, and when he talked about going back to 'Gabes', he had meant the Wadi Akarit area, some 40 miles west of Mareth.

Tripoli and its port facilities were evacuated during the night of 22/23 January. This was to be the start of the final phase of the conflict in North Africa, almost exactly two years after the arrival of Rommel and the first German troops in Tripoli. Rommel drove across the border in the early hours of 26 January, making for the Panzerarmee's new HQ location just to the west of Ben Gardane, where he would shortly receive a signal which relieved him of his command once the Mareth Line was reached.[6] His bad health was given as the reason for his dismissal, but it was clear that his enemies in higher command had had enough of his continued disobedience to their orders. But the actual date for the relief was being left up to Rommel to decide. What hurt him most of all was the fact that he would have to hand over to an Italian (Generale Giovanni Messe)[7] – 'That really was uncalled for,' he wrote, '... surely they could have found a German general to succeed me.' However, despite his immediate bitter comment that the handover should take place: '... the sooner the better', when he had had time to reflect, Rommel decided that he would not give up the reins that quickly and Messe, who arrived in North Africa at the beginning of February, would have to wait his turn. 'I am deeply sorry for my men. They are very dear to me,' wrote Rommel to Lucie on the 28th. But in the same letter he admitted to her that he was not feeling at all well and that Professor Horster was giving him sleeping-draughts. Nevertheless, despite everything, the 'Desert Fox' was far from finished.

## Notes to Chapter 6

1. Montgomery well appreciated that the defence would make the fullest use of minefields, and he had his engineers set up the 'Eighth Army School of Mine Clearance', to work out, then to teach the best and simplest way to gap them (e.g., the first 'Flail' tanks were used, based on the Matilda Mk II).

2. There were also other German parachute troops, who had arrived from Crete.
3. The lack of supplies was Rommel's major bone of contention with his allies. His demands for 30,000 tons in September and 35,000 tons in October were calculated on the minimum scales which he reckoned were needed for battle, i.e., eight daily issues of ammunition, 3,200kms-worth of fuel per vehicle and 30 days' issues of rations. In fact, by 23 October there were still short of everything. On his way back through Rome, Rommel demanded that all Italian warships (including submarines) should be immediately used to ferry ammunition and fuel to North Africa.
4. The shortened form which Rommel gives in his papers reads: 'To Field Marshal Rommel. In the situation in which you find yourself there can be no other thought but to stand fast and throw every gun and every man into the battle. The utmost efforts are being made to help you. Your enemy, despite his superiority, must also be at the end of his strength. It would not be the first time in history that a strong will has triumphed over the bigger battalions. As to your troops, you can show them no other road than that of victory or death. ADOLF HITLER.'
5. The 'Torch' landings had already taken place (8 November 1942), so the Axis was in effect now fighting on two fronts in North Africa.
6. This was not entirely news to Rommel as he had got wind of it some weeks earlier and had sent Berndt to see Hitler to find out the situation. The Führer had recovered from his anger with his favourite Field Marshal and told Berndt that he intended to give Rommel supreme command in Tunisia, provided that he was fit enough to take the reins and if a sensible command structure could be formalised. As will be seen in the next chapter, this was effected by the formation of the *Heeresgruppe 'Afrika'*, of which the Panzerarmee was but a part.
7. Messe had previously commanded the Italian Expeditionary Force in Russia.

# 7
# Tunisia and Army Group 'Afrika'
## (Heeresgruppe Afrika)

**Operation 'Torch'**

While the Panzerarmee was fighting for its life at El Alamein, the Allies landed far behind them in French North Africa on 8 November 1942. There was some immediate resistance from the Vichy French to the landings, but by 10 November a ceasefire had been agreed. Although the Allies progressed reasonably quickly thereafter, they still failed to make a sufficiently swift advance to capture Tunis and Bizerta before the Axis forces could react. With commendable speed, the Germans had seized El Aouina airfield just outside Tunis on the 9th and then flew in more troops with a view to establishing a perimeter to protect the rear of the German and Italian forces in Tripolitania. By mid-November the Axis had landed some 5,000 troops, mainly from Lieutenant-Colonel Koch's 5th Parachute Regiment. Kesselring, with Hitler's personal authority, was all set to deploy a reserve division from Sicily, but the niceties of obtaining permission from the Pétain government had still to be observed, so it was not until towards the end of the month when Pétain had given his approval, that the strength of the Axis forces was raised to some 15,000 with 130 tanks (including as already mentioned, some of the latest heavy Tiger I tanks) and a wing of fighter aircraft. This was still a relatively small force with which to combat the new threat, but sufficient to prevent the Allies from continuing their advance; a bridgehead was formed to protect the vital ports. The terrain was hilly, even mountainous in the west and north-west towards Algeria, while to the east and south the ground was flatter, but marshy in places. There were few decent roads, many of which were unusable in the extreme winter weather, and the civilian population was an unknown quantity for both sides – the Arab majority favouring whoever was winning at the time, while the French had divided loyalties, thus only the Italian settlers could be depended upon whole-heartedly to support the Axis.

**Outline of the campaign**

The campaign fell into three phases.

Phase 1: November–December 1942. Both sides scrambled for the important tactical and strategic ground. The Allies, mainly the British element of First Army, made a determined advance towards Tunis and Bizerta, but a German counter-attack drove them back. Rommel and his Panzerarmee played no part in this phase, apart from agreeing to release 21st Pz Div from DAK to the Tunisian Front in early January 1943.

167

Phase 2: January–April 1943. Once the weather permitted, the Germans renewed their attacks to enlarge the bridgehead area. Rommel's rearguard had arrived at the Mareth Line positions on 15 February, some eleven days after Eighth Army had held their victory parade in Tripoli, which was attended by Winston Churchill. In Tunisia American forces made a major assault on the right flank, endeavouring to drive back Rommel's panzer thrusts and join up with Eighth Army which had entered Tunisia from the south, thereby encircling the Axis forces. This was partly achieved but only after considerable losses to the inexperienced American troops at the hands of Rommel's veterans.

Phase 3: April–May 1943. 'Tightening the noose' around the Axis forces by both First and Eighth Armies, final assault through Medjez el Bab, leading to the surrender of Axis forces. Rommel had left North Africa before this final phase began.

### Organisation of Axis forces

The complex nature of the Axis forces in Tunisia necessitated the setting-up of various headquarters, the first being a headquarters to command the initial German arrivals, called *Stab Nehring*. This HQ was established on 14 November 1942. General der Panzer Truppe Walther Nehring, who had been wounded in the arm on 31 August 1942 while commanding DAK, and was convalescing in Germany, was sent back to North Africa to assume command of all German forces in Tunisia.[1] His HQ was established in Tunis, with a planning cell there under Colonel Harlinghausen, and a second cell under Colonel Lederer was established at Bizerta.

*Stab Nehring* changed its name to XC Korps on 19 November 1942 and was then absorbed by *Pz-AOK 5* (see below), so it was only in existence from 14 November until 9 December. Nehring did not carry on as commander; he was replaced by von Arnim, principally because he had let it be known that he doubted the wisdom of trying to hold on to Tunisia (as did Rommel).

### XC Korps Staff

COS: Colonel Pomtow                    IIa: Major von Saubert
Ia: Major Moll; Lieutenant Junker      SMO: Dr Herzberger
Ib: Captain Kirsten

### Tunis planning cell

11–18 Nov 1942: Colonel Harlinghausen
18 Nov–8 Dec 1942: Colonel Koch

### Bizerta planning cell

12–16 Nov 1942: Colonel Lederer
16–18 Nov 1942: Lieutenant-Colonel Stolz
18 Nov–8 Dec 1942: Col Freiherr von Broich

**Southern Sector**
late Nov–8 Dec 1942 – GOC of Imperiali Division
XC Korps Orbat
Corps Staff

| **Tunis bridgehead** | **Bizerta bridgehead** |
|---|---|
| 3/Tunis Field Bn 1 | 1/Tunis Field Bn 1 |
| Parachute Regt 5 (advanced | 4/Pz Bn 190 |
| det only) | 4/Artillery Regt 2 |
| one Parachute Coy | 5/Artillery Regt 190 |
| 14/Pz Gren Regt 104 | Assault gun Bn 557 (Italian) |
| one AA battery | Anti-tank Bn 136 (Italian) |

**Southern sector**
several Italian divisions

**Army Group 'Afrika'** (*Heeresgruppe Afrika*)
After Rommel's German–Italian Panzerarmee had arrived in Tunisia it was clear that the forces there were now too large and complex to be controlled by a single Army headquarters, so it was decided to form another major German headquarters – a Heeresgruppe – to deal with both German and Italian units. In line with the promises made by Hitler to Berndt, Rommel was given supreme command, Army Group 'Afrika' (Heeresgruppe Afrika) being formed under him on 23 February 1943 and consisting of the German–Italian Panzerarmee (1 italienische Armee) under Generale Messe and the Panzerarmeeoberkommando 5 (Pz-AOK 5) under Colonel General von Arnim.

**Heeresgruppe commanders**
23 February–9 March 1943: Field Marshal Rommel. His command came to an end with the recurrence of the ailments that had forced him to give up command of the Panzerarmee just before El Alamein. He left Tunisia on 9 March and did not return (see later).
9 March–13 May 1943: Colonel General Hans-Jürgen von Arnim, who handed over command of Pz AOK 5 to General Gustav von Värst.

**Heeresgruppe Staff**
Lieutenant-General Heinz Ziegler was the permanent deputy commander. He also took over as Chief of Staff from Oberst Fritz Bayerlin when he was transferred to become Chief of Staff of 1 italienische Armee. Other staff (from Pz AOK5) were:
Ia: Colonel Pomtow; Colonel Markert
Ic: Major Joseph Moll

**Heeresgruppe Orbat.** Its two major components were the Panzerarmee and the Pz AOK 5. The commanders, orbat, etc., of the Panzerarmee while it was in Tripolitania has already been covered in the previous chapter, but it had altered somewhat during the weeks following the withdrawal. Its outline organisation now that it was in Tunisia was:

### Deutsches Afrika Korps
(under Major-General Kurt Freiherr von Liebenstein)[2]
  15th Pz Div
  21st Pz Div (Transferred to the Tunis Front on 13 January 1943)
  Centauro Div (disbanded April 1943) under the command of Generale Count Carlo Calvi di Bergolo
  19th Flak Div
  (Also attached to DAK from 24 April 1943 was a very unusual division known as 999 leichte Afrika-Division. See page 176 for details).

### Italian XX Corps
(under Generale Orlando)
  Trieste Div (Generale Francisco La Ferla)        Young Fascist Div
  90 leichte Div

### Italian XXI Corps
(under Generale Berardi)
  Spezia Div                                        164 leichte Div
  Pistoia Div (Generale Guglielmo Falugi)

### SENIOR COMMANDERS AND OUTLINE ORGANISATION OF PANZERARMEEOBERKOMMANDO 5

### AOK Commanders
8–9 Dec 1942: Gen d. Pz. Tr. Walther Nehring
9 Dec 1942–9 Mar 1943: Colonel General Jürgen von Arnim
9 Mar–9 May 1943: Gen d. Pz. Tr. Gustav von Värst

Nehring and von Värst have already been mentioned. Hans-Jürgen von Arnim ('Dieter' to his friends) was born on 4 April 1889 in Ernsdorf, Silesia. He joined the army in 1908 and the following year became a Lieutenant in the 1st Guards Uhlan Foot Regiment. He served throughout the Great War as battalion adjutant and company commander, won both Iron Crosses and was wounded three times. At the end of the war he was on the staff of 4th Guards Infantry Division and became a member of the Reichswehr. By 1934 he was a Colonel and Ia of 22nd Inf Div in Bremen. When war began he was commanding 52nd Inf Div as a Lieutenant-General and led his division into France in 1940. He then took command of 17th Pz Div and distinguished himself as a tank commander on the Eastern front, winning the Knight's Cross on 4 September 1941 and being promoted Gen d. Pz. Tr. in Nov 1941. He then commanded XXXIX Panzer Corps in Russia until he was appointed commander of Pz AOK 5 in Tunisia. Rommel and he did not always agree on the conduct of operations in Tunisia. For example, when Rommel smashed through the Americans at Kasserine Pass on 18 February 1943,

Arnim did not make the anticipated supporting attack in the north until a week later, when Pz AOK 5 attacked British First Army, gaining ground but at considerable cost. When Rommel left Africa, von Arnim was made commander of the German forces, to command the now shrinking bridgehead which Hitler had ordered to fight to the last round. Short of supplies and air support, von Arnim was unable to resist Allied pressure and had to surrender, becoming a POW with some 275,000 Axis troops. He has been described by various historians as being 'energetic, prudent and enterprising', 'brave and fearless', 'a fully proven commanding general', and it has been said of him that 'in a continuous crisis situation he never rested and never lost his nerve'. But although undoubtedly an excellent tactician, he was perhaps too conservative strategically, especially in Tunisia. Nevertheless he was a brave and honourable soldier, being once described to historian Paul Carell as: 'one of the last knights of the Old School'. Obviously he did not see eye to eye with Rommel and on numerous occasions went above his head to deal directly with Kesselring, so there was no love lost between them. Von Arnim was taken prisoner on 12 May 1943 and remained in captivity until 1947.

## AOK Staff
COS: Lieutenant-General Heinz Ziegler (also deputy Army Commander);
Major-General von Quast
Ia: Colonel Pomtow; Colonel Markert
Ib: Major Josef Moll
Ic: Captain Kirsten
IIa: Major Max-Heinrich von Suebert
IIb: Major Hasler
IVb: Dr Wilhelm Schulz
Security Officer: Lieutenant Fiedler
Propaganda Officer: Lieutenant Haupt

General der Artillerie Heinz Ziegler was born in Darkhemen, East Prussia, in May 1894, joined the army in 1912 and in May 1914 was promoted to Lieutenant in the 15th Foot Artillery Regiment. During the Great War he commanded various artillery battalions, won both Iron Crosses and the Royal House Order of Hohenzollern (with Swords). Post-war he was in the Bomberg Frontier Guard, then joined 2nd Artillery Regt at Stettin. In 1938 he was promoted Colonel and was given command of 95th Artillery Regiment. Ziegler then went on to hold various staff appointments and was Chief of Staff XXXXII Army Corps in Russia, won the German Cross in Gold and was promoted to Lieutenant-General on the staff of the Chief of Army Equipment. He went with von Arnim to Tunisia as deputy C-in-C and on 20 February 1943 became acting commander of DAK. He was then decorated with the Knight's Cross. He left North Africa before the surrender to command 334 Inf Div on the Eastern Front on 24 May 1943. Thereafter he commanded III Pz Corps and finally Fourteenth Army which he left in November 1944, going then to the officer reserve.

## AOK Orbat (17 December 1942)

**Panzerarmee Staff**

### 10th Panzer Division

The division had been transferred from France to Tunisia in late November 1942. It then fought throughout the Tunisian campaign, finally surrendering on 9 May 1943, when only a handful of tanks remained. Its commanders were: on arrival, Lieutenant-General Wolfgang Fischer, who was killed when his staff car drove into an inadequately marked Italian minefield on 5 February 1943. Fischer was born in December 1888 in Carolath, Upper Silesia, and joined the army in 1911 as a lieutenant in the 154th Infantry Regiment. He fought throughout the Great War, winning both Iron Crosses. Post-war he served with the Reichswehr, was promoted to Colonel and took command of Rifle Regt 69 in March 1938, led them in Poland, and was awarded bars to both Iron Crosses. Next he commanded 10th Rifle Brigade in France where his exploits earned him the Knight's Cross on 3 June 1940.

He then took his brigade to Russia where he won the German Cross in Gold. Promoted to Major-General in August 1941, he became commander of 10th Panzer Division in Russia, continuing to lead his division which suffered such heavy losses that it had to be withdrawn and sent to France to rest and be rebuilt. It then went to North Africa, Fischer still commanding, being awarded his Oakleaves (9 December 1942), until his death on 5 February 1943. He was posthumously promoted General der Panzertruppe.

His place was taken by Major-General Fritz Freiherr von Broich, who had won both the Knight's Cross in August 1942 and the German Cross in Gold in November 1941. Born in Strassburg in 1896, he served during the Great War and was promoted Major-General in January 1943. He died in 1974.

### Main divisional staff

Ia: Lieutenant-Colonel Burker who was wounded and replaced by Lieutenant-Colonel Graf Claus von Stauffenberg, who was also wounded and evacuated. He was to become a leading figure in the plot to assassinate Hitler and when it failed he was summarily executed.

Ib: Lieutenant von Hagen; Captain Sinkel.

Ic: Captain Buchstein; Captain Dr Menges

IIa: Captain Mangels

### 10th Panzer Division Orbat as at 1 January 1943

Div Staff and Map store (mot)
  Pz Regt 7
  Anti-tank Bn 80 (mot)
  Inf Regts 69 and 86 (mot)
  Airborne Assault Regiment

'Hermann Göring' (mot) (Luftwaffe)
Inf Bn A4
Artillery Regt 90 (mot)
Butchery Coy (mot)

172

AA Group Böhmer (Luftwaffe)
Motorcycle Bn 10 (mot)
Panzer Signal Bn 90 (mot)
Engineer Bn 90 (mot)
Div Reinforcement Bn (mot)
Div Supply Depot

Bakery Coy (mot)
Medical Coy (mot)
Ambulance Pl (mot)
Workshop Pl (mot)
Military Police Troop (mot)
Field Post Office (mot)

**Division von Broich***
20 AA Division (Luftwaffe)
I/AA Regt 54 (Luftwaffe)

II/AA Regt 54 (Luftwaffe)

**Intelligence Group 210**

**Propaganda Platoon Tunis**

**Army Reserve**
Tank Battalion 190
Heavy Tank Battalion 501 (Tiger)

Reconnaissance Battalion 190

**Imperiali Division (Italian)**

NB. Additional troops were added to Pz-AOK 5, in particular 21st Panzer Division (from the Panzerarmee) and 334th Infantry Division. The full orbat as at 1 March 1943 is given in Annex 'A' attached.

**Panzerarmee Orbat (1 March 1943)**

**Panzerarmee Staff**

**10th Panzer Division**
Pz Gren Regts 69 and 86, each
with one battalion
Pz Regt 7 with one battalion
Anti-tank Bn 90

Motorcycle Bn 10
Mixed Artillery Regt 90
Engineer Bn 49

**21st Panzer Division**
Pz Gren Regt 104
Pz Regt 5
Artillery Regt 155
2/AA Bn 25 (Luftwaffe)

Signals Bn 200
Reconnaissance Bn 580
Engineer Bn 220

**334th Infantry Division**
Gren Regts 754 and 755
Mountain Regt 756

Artillery Regt 334
Mobile Bn 334

**Division von Manteuffel***
Parachute Regt Barenthin
Field Bn T3
Draft Conducting Bn A30

IV/Artillery Regt 2
Parachute Engineer Bn 11
Regt 10/Bersaglieri (Italian)

**19th/20th AA Divisions**
3 AA Regt                              3 AA Group

**Units under direct Army control**
Heavy Tank Bn 501 (Tiger)              Reconnaissance Bn 190
Signals Bn 190                         Survey and Mapping Unit

**Battlegroup Buhse** (formed before the German attacks on Sbeitla on 15–16 February 1943)
Gren Regt 47                           I/Artillery Regt 22

**Battlegroup Schmid**
Parachute Regt 5 (Koch)                II/Artillery Regt 190
Regts 69 and 86 (one bn from           Mixed Artillery Regt 90
   each)                               Draft Conducting Bns A24 and A33

**Sector Benigni (Italian)**
Inf Regt 91 (Italian)                  Artillery Bns 57 and 65
Draft Conducting Bn A28 (Italian)

**Sector Brandenburg**

**Sector German-Arab Troops**         **Sector Fullreide**
5 Bn                                   Gren Regt 165

**Sector North**
Regt Ballerstedt                       Regt San Marco (Italian Marines)

**Sector Tunis**                       Gren Regt 160

**Division Superga** (Italian) (Generale Dante Lorenzelli)
Inf Regt 92                            Artillery Regt 5
Field and Draft Conducting             Anti-tank Bns 1, 101, 136
   T5, A22, A25, A26

**Brigade Imperiali** (Italian) (Comandante di Brigata Generale Imperiali de Francavilla)
6 Bn                                   Artillery Bns 35, 58, 77
Pz Bn 15/M41                           Anti-tank Bn 557

*These are in essence the same division. All German units in Tunisia were known officially from 11 November 1942 as 'Stab Lederer', retitled 'Stab Stolz' on 16 November. Then, two days later, Colonel von Broich took command of 'Stab Stolz' and it was retitled 'Division von Broich'. Two days after von Broich was sent to take over 10th Pz Div on 5 February 1943 (Lieutenant-General Fischer having been killed in action), Major-General Hasso von Manteuffel took command and it was renamed

174

'Division von Manteuffel'. Born in January 1897, he was awarded the Knight's Cross in December 1941 while commanding Rifle Regt 6, then the Oakleaves (in 1943), Swords (in 1944) and Diamonds (in 1945). He later commanded the élite Gross Deutschland Division and also Fifth Panzer Army. Major-General Karl Bülowius took command on 31 March, but the name was not changed, remaining 'Division von Manteuffel' until it surrendered on 9 May 1943. Bülowius was born in Königsberg in 1890, served in the Great War, was promoted to Major-General in April 1942, awarded the German Cross in Silver. He died in a POW hospital in the USA on 27 March 1945.

### Orbat changes
There were a number of changes to the order of battle over the period, e.g.:
Division von Broich (as at 30 January 1943)
  Div Staff
  Parachute Regt Barenthin (mot) (Luftwaffe) comprising I and II Bns (infantry) and III Bn (Anti-tank)
  Inf Bn T3
  4 and 12/Arty Regt 2 (mot)
  4/Arty Regt 190 (mot)
  Recce Coy (mot)
  Para Pioneer Bn 11 (mot) (Luftwaffe)
  Panzer Signals Pl (mot)
  Bersaglieri Regt 10 (Italian) comprising: three inf bns, XVI, XXXIV, LXIII (containing an anti-tank platoon (mot)), a Flak coy, a Mortar coy and an MG coy); AA Pl (mot) (Luftwaffe); Dispatch Riders Pl (mot); Signals Pl (mot); Workshop Pl (mot)
  Workshop Pl 215 (mot)
Supply Depot (mot)

**Division von Manteuffel** (as at 18 March 1943)
  Div Staff
  Parachute Regt Barenthin (mot) (Luftwaffe)
  Panzergrenadier Regt 160 (mot) comprising: Pz Gren Bns A20, T3, T4 (mot)
  IV./'Afrika' Artillery Regt 2 (mot)
  AA battle troop (Luftwaffe)
  Parachute Engineer Bn 11 (mot) (Luftwaffe)
  Panzer Signals Pl 190 (mot)
  Bersaglieri Regt (mot) (Italian) comprising: three inf bns, XVI, XXXIV, LXIII; DR Pl (mot); Signals Pl; Workshop Pl (mot); Draft Conducting Bn
  Mechanised Supply Column 'Weber' (mot)
  Medical Coy 'Burgass' (mot)
  Workshop Coy 215
  Supply Depot (mot)
  Field Post Office (mot)
(Source: Bender and Law)

## WEAPONS, UNIFORMS AND EQUIPMENT

New items included:

**Rifle Grenade Device (Schiessbecher).** Rifle squads were issued with this simple piece of equipment, which, as its name implies, was cup-shaped and could be attached to any rifle to fire small HE (shrapnel effect) or AP grenades – there were also smoke and illumination grenades – so it could be used as a small mortar and as an anti-tank weapon. It consisted of a short, 30mm, barrel with rifling turning to the right and a bracket with two hooks that fastened to the normal rifle barrel behind the foresight. The rifled barrel had to be screwed into the front of the bracket using a special wrench. A grenade sight was mounted on the left side, marked from 50 to 250 metres. Grenades were inserted by hand into the front of the barrel and propelled by cartridges of varying strength. The accurate range for horizontal fire was 250 metres (although it supposedly had a maximum range of 400 metres); for steep angled fire the range was 25–75 metres. One man per rifle squad carried a Schiessbecher as well as his rifle, plus ten HE and five anti-tank grenades. He could fire it lying down, kneeling or standing. Other new infantry anti-tank weapons that were introduced in 1943, such as the Heavy Grenade Launcher 43 and the Panzerfaust, were not available in time to be used in North Africa.

**Maschinengewehr 42 (MG42).** This magnificent weapon first saw service in North Africa in 1942 and from then on it was one of the most effective machine-guns in the world. Like the MG34, it was a general-purpose weapon which had a wide variety of different mountings, but the main difference from its predecessor was its higher rate of fire – up to 1,500rpm as opposed to 800–900rpm. It weighed (with bipod) 25½ pounds, was fed by a 50-round belt and produced a highly lethal cone of fire. It had a new, simple locking system and easy barrel changing (needed because of the high rate of fire).

**Clothing.** It is worth noting that during the winter months, the climate in Tunisia, especially at night, was extremely cold, so the soldiers wore whatever items of temperate clothing they were fortunate enough to possess. For example, the woollen overcoat. In fact Rommel wore a soldier's greatcoat, embellished with red lapel facings, gold buttons and an 'AFRIKAKORPS' cuff title.

Some units that were sent to Tunisia later on (e.g., 334th Inf Div) could well have had the following items of equipment: a mix of web and leather equipment; 'tropical mountain issue' rucksacks of sand-coloured canvas and fawn leather; larger capacity water-bottles; Bergmanschue boots with cleated soles and 'elastic cloth' khaki-green puttees. Other units, for example the Waffen-SS in the Hermann Göring Division, would have worn camouflaged smocks and helmet covers in an oakleaf pattern.

### 999 leichte Afrikadivision

Formed in 1942 as 999 Afrikabrigade, this strange formation consisted of German soldiers who had mostly been court-martialled for such offences as black market activities, and who were considered as being suitable for 'rehabilitation' via combat duties! The formation was redesignated 999 leichte Afrika-division in March 1943. Its officers and NCOs were all carefully hand picked, the divisional commander being Lieutenant-General Kurt Thomas, who had served with Hitler's Headquarters Guard Battalion (cf. Rommel) until being promoted to Major-General to command 999 Brigade, then Lieutenant-General to command 999 Division. During the move of the division to North Africa, his plane was shot down and he was reported missing in the Mediterranean Sea on 5 May 1943. As a result the divisional headquarters was never fully organised. The division fought in Tunisia, first as individual regiments, then, from 24 April, the majority were attached to DAK and fought with them for the rest of the campaign until all were captured on 13 May 1943. An interesting feature of their uniform was that the rank and file were not allowed to wear national emblems, so there were no breast or cap eagles, no cockade or collar patches, and the belt buckle did not have the inscription 'GOTT MIT UNS' so presumably they were considered beyond redemption!

The units of the division that served in North Africa were:

HQ Division

| | |
|---|---|
| Rifle Regts 'Afrika' 961 and 962 (mot) | Astronomical Survey Section 999) (mot) |
| Artillery Regt 999 (mot) | Ambulance Pl 999 (mot) |
| Engineer Bn 999 (mot) | Military Police Troop 999 (mot) |

## Operations

Although Rommel was both ill and demoralised when he arrived in Tunisia, he rapidly regained much of his usual optimism and verve, especially when he was able to join in the action, which had a very positive effect upon his equally battle-weary troops. 'You should have seen their eyes light up when he suddenly appeared,' Rommel's aide wrote to Frau Rommel. 'It was just like the old days, among the foremost infantry and tanks, in the midst of their attack, he hit the dirt just like the riflemen when the enemy's artillery opened up! What other commander is there who can call on such respect!' He was faced with problems both at Mareth and to his rear. But the threat posed by Montgomery and his Eighth Army was not a pressing one, because it was clear that Monty would not attack until his overstretched army had 'got its act together'. So a determined assault upon the new enemy, First Army, was more pressing. The Allied positions now extended along the Eastern Dorsale and had been pushed back from their most forward positions by limited counter-attacks by von Arnim in January. Rommel's plan now was to strike towards Kasserine and Tebessa with a combined assault: *Frühlingswind*, being the code-name for von Arnim's attack and *Morgenluft* for Rommel's. But there was little co-ordination between the two attacks which began on 14 February. Von Arnim was more concerned with merely making limited improvements to his forward positions, while Rommel was determined to go 'all the way to Bône and Constantine'. The initial assaults went well, von Arnim's forces isolating the Americans in Lessouda and Ksaira and capturing Sidi Bou Zid.

That night the US forces managed to withdraw successfully from Djebel Lessouda, but the panzers advanced, taking Sbeitla on the 18th and pressing westwards towards Kasserine. Meanwhile Rommel had taken Gafsa (15 February) and Feriana (17 February) and was now also thrusting towards Kasserine, which was taken on the 18th, heavy casualties being inflicted on the 'green' American troops. From then on however, events went against the Axis. General Alexander, having taken over command of the Allied forces, ordered no further withdrawals and began sending units of British 6th Armoured Division to boost the Allied defences at Thala and Sbiba. They were able to prevent an Axis breakthrough and by the afternoon of the 22nd Rommel had decided to call off the attacks. Kasserine was retaken on 25 February. In sheer numbers of casualties it was a victory to the Axis – 10,000 Allied casualties against only 2,000 Axis, but, while the Allies could reinforce, the Axis were hard-pressed to do so.

Next followed the battle of the Mareth Line, Rommel seizing the initiative and attacking Eighth Army at Medinine (6–7 March), where they were held by Montgomery's batteries of anti-tank guns (estimated at more than 500 guns including some of the latest highly effective 17pdrs) and lost more than 50 tanks – one-third of their strength – being forced to pull back having achieved nothing. This would be Rommel's last battle in North Africa. After handing over command to von Arnim, he flew to Germany two days later to beg, unsuccessfully, for his army to be rescued, and, ostensibly, to complete his interrupted cure. He fully expected that he would be permitted to return to fight on, but he never did; Hitler refused to allow him to leave Germany.

On 20 March Montgomery put in a frontal attack on the Mareth Line, having sent part of his force (NZ Div, Free French forces and British 8th Armd Bde) on a 200-mile flanking attack, which turned the southern end of the line at El Hamma on 26 March. When the first frontal attack failed, Montgomery decided to reinforce his southern assault with an armoured division, supported by air. Threatened with encirclement, the Axis forces withdrew to Wadi Akarit. This position was assaulted on the night of 5/6 April.

By the middle of April, all the Axis forces had been 'squeezed' into a tight perimeter around Tunis and Bizerta, based on the last ring of hills before the coastal plain. They held First Army, but Eighth Army managed to advance just south of Enfidaville. The Axis forces were now heavily outnumbered, especially in tanks and guns (the nineteen Allied divisions were fielding 1,200 tanks and 1,500 guns; the thirteen Axis divisions had only 130 tanks and 500 guns). The end was inevitable, and at 1200 hours on 12 May 1943, Colonel General von Arnim, then Heeresgruppe commander, capitulated on behalf of both his Heeresgruppe Afrika staff and the DAK. General Cramer, commander of DAK, sent his last signal just before midnight that day: 'Ammunition shot off. Arms and equipment destroyed. In accordance with orders received the Afrika Korps has fought itself into the condition where it can fight no more. The German Afrika Korps must rise again. Heia Safari!'

ANNEX 'A' TO CHAPTER **7**

**Order of Battle of *Panzer-Armeeoberkommando 5 (Pz-A.O.K.5)***

HQ Staff Pz-AOK 5

**10th Panzer Division**

| | |
|---|---|
| Pz Grenadier Regt 69 (one bn) | SP Anti-tank Bn 90 |
| Pz Grenadier Regt 86 (one bn) | Artillery Regt 90 |
| Motorcycle Bn 10 | Engineer Bn 49 |
| Pz Regt 7 (one bn) | |

**21st Panzer Division**

| | |
|---|---|
| Pz Gren Regt 104 | Signal Bn 200 |
| Pz Regt 5 | Anti-tank Bn 580 |
| Artillery Regt 155 | Engineer Bn 220 |
| 2./AA Bn 25 | |

**334th Infantry Division**

| | |
|---|---|
| Grenadier Regts 754, 755, 756 | Mobile Bn 334 |
| Artillery Regt 334 | |

**Division von Manteuffel**

| | |
|---|---|
| Regt Barenthin | IV/Artillery Regt 2 |
| Field Bn T3 | Parachute Engineer Bn 11 |
| Draft Conducting Bn A30 | Regt 10/Bersaglieri (Italian) |

**19th/20th Flak Divisions**

| | |
|---|---|
| three AA Regts | three AA Groups |

**Under direct Army control**

| | |
|---|---|
| Heavy Tank Bn 501 (Tiger) | Recce Bn 190 |
| Sigs Bn 190 | Survey and Mapping Unit |

**Battlegroup Buhse**

| | |
|---|---|
| Gen Regt 47 | I./Artillery Regt 22 |

**Battlegroup Schmid**

| | |
|---|---|
| Para Regt 5 (Koch) | II./Artillery Regt 190 |
| Artillery Regt 90 | Draft Conducting Bns A24 and |
| A33 | |

**Sector Benigni** (all units Italian)

| | |
|---|---|
| Inf Regt 91 | Artillery Bns 57 and 65 |
| Draft Conducting Bn A28 | |

**Sector Brandenburg**

| | |
|---|---|
| **Sector German-Arab troops** | 5 Bn |
| **Sector Fullreide** | Gen Regt 165 |

**Sector North**
Regt Ballerstedt            Regt San Marco (Italian Marines)

**Sector Tunis**            Gren Regt 160

**Division Superga (Italian)**
Inf Regt 92            SP Anti-tank Bns 1, 101, 136
Field and Draft Conducting Bns        Artillery Regt 5
T5, A22, A25, A26

**Imperiali Brigade (Italian)**
six mixed inf bns            SP Anti-tank Bn 557
Tank Bn 15/M41 (Italian medium    Artillery Bns 35, 58, 77
    tanks)

## Notes to Chapter 7

1. Bender and Law quote George Howe as writing that the purpose of *Stab Nehring* was for planning the 'establishment of a bridgehead extending to the west at least as far as necessary for freedom of maneuver, and if possible as far as the Tunisia–Algeria border'.
2. Major-General von Liebenstein was wounded on 17 February 1943 and his place was taken temporarily by Lieutenant-General Heinz Ziegler. But General der Panzertruppe Hans Cramer took over on 5 March 1943 and remained in command for the remainder of DAK's existence.

# 8
# On to Italy

## Out of Africa

On or about 7 March Rommel finally made his mind up to visit Hitler again to try to get him to understand the true situation. Before doing so he had some good-byes to make, the first being at Beni Zelten, to General Heinz Zeigler, deputy commander of Pz AOK 5, and to Colonel Fritz Bayerlein, who had been appointed German Chief of Staff to Generale Messe. He then handed over command of the Army Group to von Arnim[1] and, at 0750 hours on the 9th, took off from Sfax airfield for Rome. On arrival he went immediately to the Italian Headquarters (Comando Supremo) and it was soon clear from the conversation he had with Generale Vittorio Ambrosio there, that the Italians had already decided that Rommel was not going to be allowed to return to Africa and that Hitler would order him to take sick leave. Rommel went on to see Mussolini. Although he had always admired the Duce, he still considered him to be: '... probably a great actor'! Mussolini was cordial, but it soon became clear that he too had little true idea of the actual situation in North Africa and Rommel left, '... heartily sick of all this everlasting false optimism'. He left too minus the *Medaglia d'Oro al Valor Militare* (Gold Medal for Military Valour) which Mussolini had been intending to present to him, but at the last moment had decided not to, because of Rommel's 'defeatist attitude'! Rommel then flew on to Hitler's Headquarters in Russia.[2] Hitler was away at the Front but returned that evening. Rommel thought the Führer was 'upset and depressed' and probably Hitler thought likewise about the 'Desert Fox': 'very low in spirit – his nerves shot to pieces'.[3] Rommel explained once again the problems confronting his 'Afrikaners', but Hitler was unreceptive and, as expected, ordered him to take some sick leave, so that he would be able to '... take command again for operations against Casablanca' – a remark which showed Rommel once more just how out of touch with the true situation Hitler was. Next day, somewhat unexpectedly, the Führer saw him for a second time and presented him with the *Brillanten* (Diamonds) to his Knight's Cross – Rommel was the sixth to receive this coveted award which was won by only 26 others. Then he was sent home, being met by Lucie and his 14-year-old son, Manfred, at Wiener Neustadt airfield.

Hitler had written to Mussolini, telling him that for the time being he had given Rommel leave, so as to restore his health. He also asked the Duce to keep the matter secret, in view of the harm it would do if the Allies discovered the change of command, because as he put it: 'Whatever posterity may judge of Field Marshal Rommel, to his troops and particularly to the

German soldiers he was beloved in every command he held. He was always dreaded as an opponent by his enemies and he still is.'[4]

## A New Command

By May, Hitler had earmarked Rommel for another high post, this time in Italy, namely to take overall command whenever it might prove necessary, should the Italians decide to opt for surrender. Rommel first found out that he was being considered for something new from his old SS aide, Alfred Ingemar Berndt, who was now back working in Goebbels' Propaganda Ministry. Berndt was somewhat hazy about the post, implying that Rommel's future sphere of influence would cover thousands of kilometres of European coastline – which is exactly what it eventually turned out to be, although first the Führer had more immediate needs for his abilities. Having heard from Berndt during the first week of May, on the 8th Rommel was ordered to report to Hitler in Berlin next day. 'I should have listened to you before,' Hitler told him, 'but I suppose it's too late now, it will soon be all over in Tunisia.'[5] It would appear that Hitler was determined to win back the adulation and support of his favourite Field Marshal and to some extent he succeeded, Rommel being in his company almost constantly for the next two months – 'under the sunray lamp' is how he succinctly put it, and clearly Hitler's magnetic personality did have this effect upon him.

Rommel's new appointment was to be kept secret from everyone – even from Kesselring, who, as C-in-C Southern Italy (*OB Süd*) was certainly going to be affected by the new HQ. So for May, June and most of July, Rommel did little overtly, spending his time recovering his health and forming an undercover headquarters, which received operational status in July, but whose true activities were still concealed. This HQ was first given the cover name of *Arbeitsstab Rommel* (Rommel's Planning Staff), then later called *OKW Auffrisschungsstab München* (OKW Refitting HQ Munich). He was also concerned in Operation 'Alarich', which was a plan to infiltrate large numbers of German troops into northern Italy, ready to defend against an Allied invasion, and a second plan, Operation 'Achse', which envisaged the need to disarm the Italian forces and, if necessary, to capture or destroy them. Rommel's staff was very small and came mainly from his 'Afrikaners', men such as Major-General Alfred Gause and Colonel von Bonin, both from the Panzerarmee, Captain Hermann Aldinger, his old adjutant, and the faithful Corporal Alfred Böttcher was still with him as private secretary. At the last minute, however, Hitler changed his mind and decided that Rommel would be C-in-C designate of the German forces in Greece, Crete and the Aegean Islands, able to '... jump over into Italy later on'. His HQ would be known as Army Group B, while Army Group E, (commanded by Colonel General Löhr) which was currently the highest German HQ in the Balkans, would merely control Serbia and Croatia instead of being *OB Südost*. No firm date was given for this change, but Rommel arrived in Greece on 23 July under orders from Hitler to survey the situation and report. Two days later he was told by the OKW that Mussolini had been overthrown and that he was to return immediately to see Hitler again.

On his return he was advised that his Italian assignment was now on once more and that his undercover HQ would 'emerge' in Munich as Army Group B. He was to be responsible for all German troops in northern Italy and also for Operation 'Alarich', the security of the necessary lines of communication being of vital concern once the troops had been infiltrated into northern Italy. Thus Rommel's army group was to be heavily involved in the protection of such vital areas as the Alpine passes, as well as with the actual details of the troop movements, which began on 30 July. The Italians did not like the movement of German troops into Italy and the Comando Supremo disputed every move, although it could do little to prevent the German build-up. Meanwhile, of course, there were still large numbers of German troops fighting in Sicily, most of whom would be successfully withdrawn to the mainland in mid-August, and the Allied invasion of Italy was still some weeks off. Field Marshal Kesselring, C-in-C South, also still had major forces with which to oppose the Allies and keep the Italians under control, so there was little the Italians could do. But, as Rommel noted in his diary, '... although they will obviously betray us, it's not politically possible to march in'.

The intention was that Army Group B would take command of all German formations in northern Italy, and that although Kesselring's *OB Süd* would keep command of those German formations in southern Italy plus those which might return from Sicily, he would be required to conform to any orders that Rommel might give him. Not unnaturally Kesselring objected to this arrangement, telling everyone that he could not serve under Rommel. Hitler vacillated until the middle of August, then decided on a compromise which left Italy divided by a line running through Pisa –Arezzo–Ancona. Rommel would command all troops north of this line (his western boundary was the Franco-Italian border, and eastern, the Italo–Croatian frontier). Three Corps HQ were earmarked for Army Group B, two of which were 'up and running' in Italy by mid-August: LXXXVII Corps from France and II SS Pz Corps from Russia. The third Headquarters, LI Mountain Corps, was still forming at Innsbruck. Eight German divisions had either crossed or were about to cross into Italy. Six of them were re-formed 'ex-Stalingrad' divisions from France and Denmark; one had been brought from Holland and the remaining one (SS Pz Div Adolf Hitler) had come from the Eastern Front.

On 17 August Rommel moved his HQ from Munich to Lake Garda, setting up with some difficulty as the Italians bitterly resented his presence in Italy and hindered his requests for permission to lay telephone lines back to Munich. It was also at this time that Rommel began to worry about his family and the ever-increasing danger they were in from Allied air raids, the Messerschmitt factories being close to Wiener Neustadt. This was alarmingly brought home to him by news that Gause had lost his house and all his possessions, although fortunately his family was not in residence at the time. It took Rommel some time to persuade Lucie to move, but eventually he managed it, although initially they had to occupy temporary accommodation until their new house at Herrlingen near Ulm in Swabia, could be got ready.

Lucie would generously offer the Gauses accommodation in the new house, but sadly this would lead to family arguments and eventually to Gause being replaced as Rommel's Chief of Staff (see next chapter).

By the end of August the situation had deteriorated to the point where the Axis had virtually ceased to exist. The Italians had moved troops to guard Rome against a German coup, also to protect Italian naval units at Spezia and towards the Brenner Pass, so that they were ready should the Germans try to take any 'collective hostility' against them. For their part, the Germans were ready to put Operation 'Achse' into action, ready to disarm all Italian troops except any who were prepared to go on fighting under German command. In the north, Army Group B was to increase the protection of the mountain passes and to occupy Genoa, Spezia, Livorno, Trieste, Fiume and Pola. The Order of Battle of Rommel's army was now as follows:

HQ (at Canossa, SW of Reggio nell'Emilia)

| Corps | Division | Area located |
|---|---|---|
| LI Mountain | 65th Inf | SW of Parma on loan from |
| (Feurstein) | | II SS Pz Corps |
| | 305th Inf | Carrara–Viareggio on loan from LXXXVII Corps |
| LXXXVII | 76th Inf | N & W of Gerona |
| (von Zangen) | 94th Inf | |
| II SS Pz Corps | 24th Pz | Parma–Modena |
| (Hausser) | 1st SS Pz Adolf Hitler | |
| | 44th Inf | Brenner Pass–Bolzano |
| | 71st Inf | Trieste–Gorizia |
| Controlled by | 3rd Pz Gren | Rome |
| Fliegerkorps XI | 2nd Para | Rome |

(Source: Table in Molony, et al.)

## Corps Commanders

**LI Mountain Corps.** General der Gebirgstruppen Valentin Feurstein. He was born in 1885 in Bregenz. He served in the Austrian Army, reaching the rank of Major-General in 1935, then transferred to the *Reichsheer* and commanded 2nd Mountain Division. After commanding LI Mountain Corps, he became Inspector-General of the Tyrol and commander of the Alpenfront in April 1945. He was the holder of the Knight's Cross. Manfred Rommel describes him as being: '... a stocky, black-moustached man, regarded as a first-class mountain specialist'.

**LXXXVII Corps.** General der Infanterie Gustav-Adolf von Zangen. Born in Darmstadt in 1892, he served in the army throughout the Great War, then with the police before transferring back to the army in 1935. He was promoted to Major-General in 1942 while commanding 17th Infantry Division. He went on to command Fifteenth Army in France, Belgium and Holland and distinguished himself in organising the successful evacuation of most of it across the Scheldt. In August 1944 he was sent back to Italy to prepare the last line of defences from the approaches to the Alps to the Adriatic coast, with large numbers of the Todt Organisation labour force units to carry out the work. He was the holder of the Knight's Cross with Oakleaves.

**II SS Pz Corps.** Colonel General Paul Hausser. He had commanded 'Das Reich' SS Infantry Division in Russia and went on to command II SS Pz Corps in NW Europe. An able commander, he had fallen slightly foul of Hitler by disobeying orders in Kharkov, but as the SS then did spectacularly well, he was forgiven. In early July 1944 he was appointed directly by Hitler to command Seventh Army – the first SS officer ever to command an army and to reach the rank of Colonel General. Despite his age – he was nearly 60 when war began – he had remarkable stamina and was very fit. Guderian called him 'one of the most outstanding wartime commanders', the Führer said that he 'looked like a fox ... with his crafty little eyes', and Kesselring said that he was '... the most popular and ablest of the SS generals'.

### Divisional Commanders
**44th Inf Div 'Hoch Und Deutchsmeister'.** General der Infanterie Dr Franz Beyer. He was a Lieutenant-General when he commanded the division (promoted Gen d. Inf. in 1944). Reformed in Austria in 1943 after virtually ceasing to exist at Stalingrad, his division was an excellent fighting unit and fought well in Italy. It was later posted to the Eastern Front.

**65th Inf Div.** Lieutenant-General Gustav Heistermann von Ziehlberg. A Knight's Cross winner, who was born in Hohensalza in 1898, he was promoted to Major-General in August 1943. His division was severely mauled by the British on the River Sangro Line in October 1943. He was badly wounded the following month and Lt Gen Dr Georg Pfeiffer took command. The division later formed part of I Para Corps' attack at Anzio, then was transferred to North Italy.

**71st Inf Div.** Lieutenant-General Wilhelm Raapke. Born in Marienwerder in 1896, he commanded the division from its formation in Denmark in April 1943, through Italy and then in Hungary and Austria. He was the holder of the German Cross in Gold.

**76th Inf Div.** General der Infanterie Erich Abraham. Born in Marienburg in 1895. He took over the division in April 1943 and went on to command LXIII Corps. He was awarded the Knight's Cross with Oakleaves and the German Cross in Gold. In the late autumn of 1943 his division was sent to the Eastern front.

**94th Inf Div.** Lieutenant-General Bernhard Steinmetz. Born in Neuenkirchen in1896. He commanded the division for most of the Italian campaign. After Stalingrad the division had been reformed in France and sent to Italy where it fought in many of the major battles.

**305th Inf Div.** Lieutenant-General Friedrich-Wilhelm Bruno Hauck. He was born in Breslau in 1897. Winner of the Knight's Cross and the German Cross in Silver, he had been promoted to Major-General in June 1943. His division also fought in southern Italy, suffering many casualties south of Rome.

**3rd Pz Gren Div.** Lieutenant-General (later Gen d. Pz. Tr.) Fritz-Hubert Gräser. He was born in Frankfurt in 1888. He was awarded the German Cross in Gold and the Knight's Cross with Oakleaves. He went on to command XXIV Panzer Corps and then Fourth Panzer Army. His division (reformed in SW France in early 1943) fought in Italy, later in the Saar, Ardennes and Germany.

**2nd Para Div.** Major-General Hermann Bernard Ramcke. He had famously commanded Ramcke Para Brigade in North Africa (see earlier chapters). His senior Regimental Commander (Colonel Hans Kroh) took over in 1944 when he became commander of the fortress of Brest. Hitler ordered that the Diamonds to his Knight's Cross be parachuted in (on 20 September 1944). Ramcke held on until the garrison ran out of supplies and was forced to surrender.

**24th Pz Div.** Lieutenant-General *Reichsfreiherr* (Reichsbaron) Maximilian von Edelsheim. Born in Berlin in 1897. He was awarded the Knight's Cross with Oakleaves and Swords. Virtually wiped out at Stalingrad, the division was reformed in Normandy where von Edelsheim took command in March 1943. It was sent to Italy in August, and later sent back to the Russian Front.

**1st SS Pz Div.** Colonel General Josef 'Sepp' Dietrich. He had fought in the Great War as a sergeant tank commander/tank troop leader, being awarded the Iron Cross 2nd and 1st Class, together with Bavarian, Austrian and Silesian bravery awards. A rough diamond – he was one of the original Nazi storm troopers – he was at one time Hitler's chauffeur and bodyguard. He rose very quickly through the ranks of the SS, commanding *Leibstandarte* (Life Guard) SS Adolf Hitler, which became 1st SS Pz Div and later I SS Pz Corps. He was awarded the Knight's Cross, with Oakleaves, Swords and Diamonds, becoming one of the 27 most highly decorated members of the German forces of the war. He eventually became disillusioned with his Führer, but this did not prevent his imprisonment at the end of the war. He was released in February 1958, and died in 1966, aged 74.

### Outline Organisation of Divisions
(showing major units within divisions only)

### 44th Inf Div
131, 132, 134 Inf Regts; 96 Art Regt; 44 Fus Bn (Recce); 46 Anti-Tk Bn; 80 Eng Bn; 64 Sigs Bn

**65th Inf Div**
145, 146, 147 Inf Regts; 165 Art Regt; 165th M/cycle Regt; 165 Recce/Anti-Tk Regt (combined); 165 Eng Bn; 165 Sigs Bn
**71st Inf Div**
191, 194, 211 Inf Regts; 171 Art Regt; 171 Recce Bn; 171 Anti-Tk Bn; 171 Eng Bn; 171 Sigs Bn
**76th Inf Div**
178, 203 Inf Regts; 230 Fus Gren Regt; 176 Art Regt; 176 Fus Bn (Recce); 176 Anti-Tk Bn; 176 Eng Bn; 176 Sigs Bn
**94th Inf Div**
267, 274, 276 Inf Regts; 194 Art Regt; 194 Recce Bn; 194 Anti-Tk Bn; 194 Eng Bn; 194 Sigs Bn
**305th Inf Div**
576, 577, 578 Inf Regts; 305 Art Regt; 305 Recce Coy; 305 Anti-Tk Bn; 305 Eng Bn; 305 Sigs Coy
**3rd Pz Gren Div**
8, 29 Pz Gren Bns; 103 Pz Bn; 3 Mot Art Regt; 103 Pz Recce Bn; 3 Anti-Tk Bn; 3 Mot Eng Bn; 3 Mot Sigs Bn
**2nd Para Div**
2, 6, 7 Para Regts; 2 Para Art Regt; 2 Para Anti-Tk Bn; 2 Para Eng Bn; 2 Para Sigs Bn; 2 Para AA Bn; 2 Para MG Bn
**24th Pz Div**
24 Pz Regt; 21, 26 Pz Gren Regts; 89 Pz Art Regt; 24 Pz Recce Bn; 40 Anti-Tk Bn; 40 Pz Eng Bn; 86 Pz Sigs Bn; 283 Army AA Bn
**1st SS Pz Div**
1 SS Pz Regt; 1, 2 SS Pz Gren Regts; 1 SS Pz Art Regt; 1 SS Pz Recce Bn; 1 SS Anti-Tk Bn; 1 SS Pz Eng Bn; 1 SS Pz Sigs Bn; 1 SS AA Bn; 1 SS Projector Bn
(Source: 'Hitler's Legions')

NB. At this time Field Marshal Kesselring's *OB Süd* had two Corps under command: XIV Panzer (15th Pz Gren Div, 16th Pz Div, Hermann Göring Pz Div) and LXXVI Panzer (29th Pz Gren Div, 26th Pz Div, 1st Para Div).

### 'What a shameful end for an army!'
The Allied landings in Italy on 3 and 9 September 1943, together with the Italian surrender, naturally led to Operation 'Achse' being put into effect, with Rommel's troops rounding up and disarming Italian forces. Rommel wrote to Lucie: '... In the south, Italian troops are already fighting alongside the British against us. Up north, Italian troops are being disarmed for the present and sent as prisoners to Germany. What a shameful end for an army!'[6] In addition to sending Italians to Germany, Allied POWs had to be removed from their camps and sent to Germany – one estimate reckoned that some 800,000 Italians had been disarmed and 268,000 packed off northwards as potential slave labour. In the midst of these machinations, Rommel was suddenly wracked with pain, rushed to hospital and operated on for appendicitis. All went well and he was soon well enough to confer with Hitler and the OKW as to what should be done in Italy, and squabble

with Kesselring over the nuts and bolts of how it should be achieved. Eventually, after much indecision, Hitler decided that Italy should be placed under one commander and as Kesselring was keen to start fighting the Allies as far south as possible, while Rommel wanted to give up most of the country and make a firm stand in the north, along the line of the Apennines, he opted finally for Kesselring.[7] Rommel and his Army Group B HQ, would be moved to France for a fresh task, his eight divisions being switched under a new command known as Army Group C.

On 21 November 1943, Rommel took off from Villafranca airfield, leaving Italy for ever, and bound for the close *bocage* hills of Normandy, which as his son Manfred put it, was where his father's '... road to fame had passed in 1940 and which were to be the scene of his last military defeat'.[8]

### Notes to Chapter 8

1. It was not a happy parting. When he had first asked von Arnim to come to his HQ to take over, he discovered that, without his knowledge, Kesselring had ordered von Arnim and von Värst (he would take over Pz AOK 5 from von Arnim) to fly to Rome to see him. Rommel was furious and made Kesselring cancel his conference!
2. This forward HQ was known as 'Wehrwolf' and was located in the Ukraine, near Vinnitsa, some 100 miles SW of Kiev.
3. This is how Hans Jeschonnek, chief of the air staff, said Hitler had described him afterwards. (Quoted in Irving, *Trail of the Fox*).
4. Irving, *op. cit.*
5. *The Rommel Papers.*
6. Ibid.
7. In mid-November Hitler had decided that Rommel should take over from Kesselring and then, while the orders were being transmitted, changed his mind and ordered Kesselring to take supreme command from 21 November 1943.
8. *The Rommel Papers.*

# 9
# North West Europe

## PREPARATIONS

### The Grand Tour

Following Hitler's decision to give Kesselring complete charge in Italy, the OKW were all for disbanding the staff of Army Group B. But as von Rundstedt's chief of Staff, General Günther Blumentritt explains, Hitler had other ideas: 'Against this Hitler ordered its revival. He knew that in 1944 something vital would occur in the west or on some other front, and on that account wished to hold this valuable Staff in reserve. But in order to keep Rommel and his Staff employed until a responsible position could be found for him somewhere, Hitler decided to entrust him with the inspection of western defences.'[1] He gave Rommel certain instructions (based on Führer Directive No 51), the details of which Blumentritt says OB West were never able to discover exactly, although OKW later confirmed the outline content. Basically Hitler's aims in appointing Rommel were threefold:

a. So that he would familiarise himself with that sector of the Western Front which would undoubtedly be the decisive one, namely the Channel coastal area.

b. To have him take all necessary steps to rectify any shortcomings in the Atlantic Wall defences, making full use of the Todt Organisation, etc.

c. To avail himself of Rommel's experience in fighting against the Allies, in particular the British.

'Special Inspector Rommel' (Blumentritt's words) had the authority to report direct to Hitler, which inevitably led to friction, not so much between the two field marshals and their headquarters (OB West and Army Group B), but rather in 'departmental circles' and in relations with the Luftwaffe's Third Air Fleet and the Kriegsmarine's Western Naval Group. Leaving the command and control problems aside for the present, let us first look at what Rommel did on the ground. He had in fact begun to assemble his inspection team while he was still in Italy, requesting (on Gause's advice) the assignment of Vice-Admiral Friedrich Ruge as Naval Liaison Officer (*Marineverbindungsoffizier*) whom David Irving describes as being: 'a jovial, cocky Swabian'. There was an immediate mutual liking and he quickly became a firm and trusted friend, ' ... a man in whose company the Field Marshal always took pleasure, to whom he could talk frankly and freely'.[2] Ruge had arrived on 30 November 1943, having travelled by train via the Brenner Pass, and was staying with Rommel's naval LO in San Vigilio on Lake Garda. 'I reported in this irregular attire,' he wrote later, referring to his warm and unmilitary muffler, ' ... but it seemed unimportant, since Rommel was apparently less interested in the uniform than in the man inside it. Rommel appeared smaller than I had imagined him, rather serious, full of energy and very natural.'[3] Soon after his arrival Rommel sent Ruge off to Berlin to see the Kriegsmarine staff and collect as much background material as possible to help them with their task – maps, tide tables, shipping details, etc. He would meet the rest of the team en route (he actually rejoined Rommel in northern Jutland on 2 December). It was very fortunate that Ruge had personal knowledge of most of the coastline because a great deal of the material he so painstakingly collected in Berlin was destroyed during an air raid there before he left.

A special train had been arranged for the team, with spacious compartments in a 'parlour car' which Ruge reckoned had been designed for a 'Balkan potentate'. There was a large briefing room and a dining-car. The team boarded the train at Munich on 1 December, bound for Copenhagen where the tour would begin with a visit to General Hermann von Hannecken, who was commanding all German forces in Denmark (he was C-in-C from 27 September 1942 until 27 January 1945). Rommel met von Hannecken on the evening of 3 December, and began the tour next morning at Esbjerg on the west coast of Jutland. They spent ten days in Denmark and by the end of the tour Rommel had realised that this part of the much publicised 'Atlantic Wall' was a hollow sham and that a vast amount of work would be necessary if a determined enemy assault was to be defeated. He would quickly discover that this applied to much of the rest of the supposedly impregnable defences. Rommel had already decided that any invasion must be defeated on the beaches before the enemy could gain a foothold – 'the main battle line will be the beach' was the message he propounded over and over again. In his logical way he reasoned that mobile warfare – of which he was a master – would be impossible against an enemy with total air superiority and a vast preponderance of mechanised weapons – tanks, guns, vehicles at their disposal. ' ... I therefore consider', he wrote, 'that an attempt must be made, using every possible expedient, to beat off the enemy landing on the coast and to fight the battle in the more or less strongly fortified coastal strip.' He was to hold this view throughout his period of command of Army Group B despite the attempts of others who wanted to fight the battle differently. It was fortunate for the Allies that Rommel's advice was not followed to the letter.

After concluding that Denmark showed (according to Ruge) '... how overtaxed the Wehrmacht was – a handful of modestly trained and equipped static divisions (coastal defence units) had to defend hundreds of kilometres of excellent landing beach', most of the team moved on to Rommel's new headquarters at Fontainebleau, while the 'Desert Fox' flew to southern Germany for a few days' leave; he rejoined them on 18 December. The new HQ was in a small, luxurious château which had once belonged to Madame de Pompadour. The following day Rommel visited Field Marshal von Rundstedt in Paris, writing to Lucie afterwards that: 'R is very charming and I think everything will go well.' Undoubtedly there was a certain amount of mutual respect between the two of them – von Rundstedt at 68 was Germany's most senior soldier, and Rommel, a mere 52, its youngest field marshal. Although von Rundstedt saw Rommel as a possible threat, he was happy to let the younger man do all the work, while, as General Hans Speidel succinctly puts it, Rundstedt's ' ... character, personality and mobility were failing, and at a time when supreme efforts were demanded, Rundstedt remained unknown to the soldier at the front, while Rommel ceaselessly exerted his remarkable powers of leadership on the soldiers personally, sparing himself not at all ...'[4]

While his main headquarters staff began to settle into 'Maison Pompadour' at Fontainebleau, Rommel and his inspection team continued their tour, beginning the inspection of the most important part of the 'Atlantic Wall' on 20 December. Rommel was extremely disturbed by what he saw: the lack of proper defences, the relatively poor quality of many of the troops charged with the task of meeting the coming invasion, and any coherent command structure sadly lacking. He did not break for Christmas, but continued his tours and reports: ' ... out on the move a lot,' he wrote to Manfred, 'and raising plenty of dust wherever I go.' He went everywhere and saw everything, including secret 'V' weapon sites, Luftwaffe and Kriegsmarine units and headquarters, and everywhere he went he imparted his own special 'Rommel Magic'. His staff were appalled at the pressure under which he worked – and drove them! – and the spartan regime under which he operated. The ordinary soldiers, who probably had never seen a field marshal in their lives, were naturally favourably impressed by his interest in their jobs, but anyone who had been 'living the soft life' – irrespective of rank – swiftly found himself on the receiving end of his wrath. A perfect example was Colonel General Hans von Salmuth, commander of Fifteenth Army, who protested when Rommel told him that he wanted his troops to lay more mines than ever before. Salmuth told him that he wanted: 'fresh, well-trained soldiers, not physical wrecks,' then patronisingly went on: 'Stick around a bit and you'll soon see that you can't do everything at once. ... If anybody tells you different, then he's either just trying to flatter you or he's a pig idiot.' Once Rommel's staff were out of earshot the furious Field Marshal gave Salmuth a tongue lashing that left him red-faced and speechless. 'He's quite a roughneck that one,' beamed Rommel to Ruge as they began their journey back to Fontainebleau. 'That's the only language he understands.'[5]

The team dined together at 'Maison Pompadour'. Ruge lists them as being: the Field Marshal, Major-General Gause (Chief of Staff), Major-General Meise (Engineers), Major-General Gerke (Signals), Colonel von Templehoff (Operations), Colonel Lattman (Artillery) and Colonel Krähe. Later they were joined by Lieutenant-Colonel Stubwasser (Intelligence), Colonel Freiberg (Personnel), Lieutenant-Colonel Olshausen (deputy transport officer) and various staff officers – Lieutenant Hammermann, Captain Lang and the Prince of Koburg. In addition of course there were the naval and air representatives: Vice-Admiral Ruge and the Luftwaffe Ia, Lieutenant-Colonel Wolfgang Queisner, who were usually known as Hilfsvolker (auxiliary tribes). Their ages, experience and interests were varied, but all joined in the conversations. Rommel did not try to dominate the dinner-table, but listened to others and displayed a good sense of humour. Ruge comments, however, that although Rommel was no prude, he frowned upon 'so-called humour'. He did not smoke, drank very little, insisted upon simple food and usually went to bed between 10 and 11 p.m. In short, Rommel was a man who, despite his fame: ' ... had remained a modest human being with an engaging personality'.

## Army Group B Assumes Command

Although the 'Desert Fox' would continue his duties as 'Special Inspector Rommel' for some months – he did not visit the western and southern coastlines until February – Army Group B officially took over responsibility for the Atlantic and Channel coasts, north of the River Loire, on 15 January 1944. This was the area in which Hitler was convinced that the Allies would land as this extract from a talk he gave to the C-in-C of the three Wehrmacht branches, and the army and fortress commanders on 20 March 1944 shows: ' ... It is obvious that the Anglo-Americans will and must land in the west ... The most suitable and hence most threatened areas are the two peninsulas in the west, Cherbourg and Brest, which are very tempting and offer the best possibilities for forming a beachhead.'[6] He went on to emphasise that it would be essential for the enemy to gain a port, so clearly the Germans knew nothing about the revolutionary Mulberry Harbours which the Allies were constructing. Rommel and his Army Group B were now locked into the overall German command structure in the west (see orbat opposite).

So, other than Adolf Hitler in Berlin, there was no overall supreme commander, Field Marshal von Rundstedt having no direct control over any sea or air forces. Admiral Theodor Krancke received his orders direct from the German Naval Staff, and General Hugo Sperrle got his from Göring. This would lead to many problems, as Hans Speidel wryly comments in *We Defended Normandy*: 'Operations at sea and in the air could thus be co-ordinated neither by the C-in-C in the West nor by the Army Group commander. The military commanders were only partially informed of the intentions of the other two services and usually too late.' Panzer Group West was created on 24 January 1944, with the aim of concentrating all armoured formations in the west under one command, but as Geyr von Schweppenburg held very different ideas from Rommel as to how they should be deployed and used in the coming battle, this proved a major disadvantage. LXXXVIII Army Corps was officially under the command of Luftwaffe General Friedrich Christiansen, the commander of all German forces in the Netherlands, but in practice orders from Army Group B went direct to General Hans Reinhard, the corps commander.

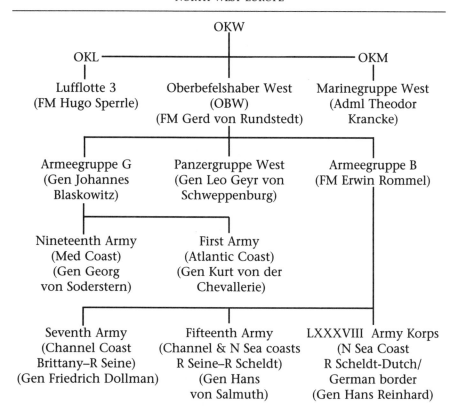

OKW

OKL

| Lufflotte 3 | Oberbefelshaber West | Marinegruppe West |
| (FM Hugo Sperrle) | (OBW) | (Adml Theodor |
| | (FM Gerd von Rundstedt) | Krancke) |

OKM

Armeegruppe G
(Gen Johannes
Blaskowitz)

Panzergruppe West
(Gen Leo Geyr von
Schweppenburg)

Armeegruppe B
(FM Erwin Rommel)

Nineteenth Army
(Med Coast)
(Gen Georg
von Soderstern)

First Army
(Atlantic Coast)
(Gen Kurt von der
Chevallerie)

Seventh Army
(Channel Coast
Brittany–R Seine)
(Gen Friedrich Dollman)

Fifteenth Army
(Channel & N Sea coasts
R Seine–R Scheldt)
(Gen Hans
von Salmuth)

LXXXVIII  Army Korps
(N Sea Coast
R Scheldt-Dutch/
German border
(Gen Hans Reinhard)

## OB West

Field Marshal Gerd von Rundstedt's *Oberbefelshaber West* (OB West) was thus the senior ground headquarters, where von Rundstedt, 'The Grand Old Man of the German Army', had been brought out of semi-retirement to be in nominal charge of Hitler's anti-invasion preparations. Born in Aschersleben on 12 December 1875, he had first joined the army in 1892, held high rank in the Reichsheer post-war (he was a Colonel General in 1938) and also held high field commands throughout the war from the invasion of Poland onwards, being promoted to Field Marshal on 1 July 1940. At the end of 1941 he had gone into voluntary retirement after falling out with Hitler, but was recalled in July 1942 to become C-in-C West. His command position was 'on paper only' because every major decision was made by Hitler or 'rubber-stamped' by him – von Rundstedt once caustically remarked that the only troop formation he was allowed to move was the guard at the gate of his headquarters! His overall strategy was based upon mobile defence, so he was to some degree diametrically opposed to Rommel's 'Fight them on the Beaches' policy. Neither strategy would work against the Allied assault and eventually von Rundstedt would be removed yet again. Holder of the Knight's Cross with both Oakleaves and Swords, he died in Hanover in 1953. Von  Rundstedt and Rommel maintained a cordial relationship, although the former secretly considered that the 'Desert Fox' was only capable of low-level operations and not fully qualified for high command – this was probably an instance of Prussian snobbishness! In practice, after January 1944, he was content to leave Rommel to assume the main burden of responsibility. As the US Army official history records: 'In any case the clear fact is that after January 1944, Rommel was the dominant personality in the west with an influence disproportionate to his formal command authority.'

Von Rundstedt's Chief of Staff was General Günther Blumentritt, a highly experienced staff officer and holder of both the Knight's Cross with Oakleaves and the German Cross in Gold. Born in Munich in 1892, he had served during the Great War and in the Reichswehr post-war, being promoted to Major-General in late 1941. He was von Rundstedt's Operations Officer under COS von Manstein in 1939, when the invasion of Poland was being planned. Later he replaced plotter General von Stülpnagel as military governor of France. As von Rundstedt's COS, he had written to the OKW, drawing Jodl's attention to the fact that the German divisions manning the Atlantic Wall were unfit for a war of movement, including in his letter a list of the 47 German divisions that had been removed from OB West in 1943. There was a considerable bond between Blumentritt and von Rundstedt, whom he describes as being: ' ... one of Germany's greatest generals', going on to say: 'In joy and sorrow, in good times and in bad, we have stood loyally by each other in the spirit of true soldiership.' (This quotation is taken from Blumentritt's biography of von Rundstedt). They also shared imprisonment in England so he probably knew him better than anyone else.

## A Move to a New Location

Rommel was always unhappy with the location of his headquarters at Fontainebleau, considering it to be too far to the rear, although the surrounding woodland did give him plenty of opportunity to hunt and shoot which he loved, but which adversely affected his lumbago, preventing him from yet more hunting, but never from his whirlwind tours of the strategic area. He asked OKW to be assigned the existing headquarters at Soissons, north-east of Paris, which had been designed to control the aborted invasion of England in 1940 (Operation 'Sealion'), because it was ideally centrally located. This was refused, but Rommel had already selected another – a château built and expanded between the 12th and 17th centuries at La Roche-Guyon, some 50 miles west of Paris, overlooking the Lower Seine and less than 80 miles from the coast. Behind the tiny château rose sheer chalk cliffs into which German engineers had blasted a series of tunnels. They were not the first to tunnel in this way; the original building on the site of the château had been joined to an ancient keep high on the cliff top. The pioneers had made use of the old workings as a basis for their new ones, hollowing out living and working quarters for the 100 plus staff officers and soldiers who manned the headquarters. Only the senior staff were accommodated in the château, including of course Rommel, who occupied a modest ground floor apartment adjoining the rose garden.

By early March all the necessary preparatory work had been completed and HQ Army Group B moved in, arriving on the evening of 9 March. The château was owned by the La Rochefoucald family, who were allowed to stay on and with whom all soon formed a pleasant and amicable association, Rommel often shooting with the old duke, while the younger staff officers flirted with the duke's attractive daughter. The war had never before touched the sleepy little village which was now one of the most closely guarded in France, although Ruge had met the owner and his family before in 1941–2. He comments that it was nice to return to the familiar house and is also at pains to point out that although there were inherent dangers to the inhabitants which gave food for thought, ' ... it can be reported that the castle and the inhabitants later survived the storm'.

### HQ Army Group B

Now is a good time to look at the detailed organisation of Rommel's Headquarters, i.e., the *Offizierstellenbesetzung des Oberkommandos der Heeresgruppe B*. Annex 'A' to this chapter gives details of the list of the members of the Headquarters, prepared by the HQ adjutant on 15 May 1944. There were changes after that date, one of the most major alterations being the dissolution of the Quartermaster Division (Oberquartiermeister Abteilung) under Colonel Heckel at the end of May 1944, just a few days before the invasion. But probably the most important happening among the staff was the arrival of General Hans Speidel, to take over from Alfred Gause as Chief of Staff on 15 April 1944. As has already been mentioned this was basically because of domestic problems which had occurred between Lucie Rommel and Gause and his wife who had been staying with her after their own house had been bombed. Matters came to a head when Gause gave the faithful old Captain Hermann Aldinger a dressing-down for arriving late for work in the garden – Rommel had given his adjutant the task of directing the landscaping of the new garden – while Frau Gause had got more and more on Frau Rommel's nerves. Eventually she could stand it no longer and wrote to Rommel demanding that he replace Gause. Uncharacteristically Rommel, to quote historian David Irving, who says in *Trail of the Fox* that he ' ... meekly complied, writing to her on 17 March: "Let's draw a line underneath it all ... I am going to ... Of course, it's a tough decision for me to have to change my chief at a time like this."'

**Chief of Staff.** The new Chief of Staff was in fact the perfect man for the job. A bespectacled academic, his aesthetic, almost professorial, exterior belied his undoubted ability as a fighting soldier of some experience, although, as we shall see, this was not a view held by everyone. General Dr Hans Speidel was born on 28 October 1897 in Metzingen, Württemberg, so he was a Swabian like Rommel which gave them an instant rapport. He had joined the army on 30 November 1914, seen active service during the Great War in the same brigade as Rommel and had been accepted into the Reichsheer post-war. In 1932 he had taken 'leave of absence' from soldiering to become a Doctor of Philosophy and then a teacher and professor at Göttingen University. In 1933 he was Assistant Military Attaché in Paris. In

September 1939 he had been the Ia of 33rd Infantry Division, then Ia of IX Army Corps. He then served on von Küchler's staff in Eighteenth Army during the invasion of the Low Countries. He became COS to Otto von Stülpnagel in Paris 1940–1, then served on Fifth Army's Staff in 1942 and was COS of Eighth Army in Russia in 1943 as a Major-General. It was while he was serving in Russia during Eighth Army's difficult and heroic withdrawal, that Hitler had personally presented him with the Knight's Cross. He became Rommel's Chief of Staff in April 1944 and the two men quickly established a harmonious working relationship – despite the fact that Jodl (at OKW) had warned Speidel prior to his joining Army Group B to beware of Rommel's pessimism which he described as his 'African sickness' (*Afrikanische Krankheit*)! Speidel was also one of the most hard-working German officers as far as trying to arrange an armistice with the West. He knew of, and was in touch with, many of the leaders of the conspiracy to overthrow Hitler, but was not actually involved in any of the murder plots. He also involved Rommel in a very minor way in the subterfuge. Arrested on 7 September 1944, after refusing to destroy Paris, and accused of being implicated in the plot against Hitler, he was brought before a Court of Honour on 4 October, but managed to baffle even the most searching Gestapo questioning despite the fact that he had actually been involved. Speidel not only successfully protested his innocence, but also managed not to betray anyone, so despite everything – including Keitel's saying that Hitler believed Speidel to be guilty – he was declared innocent and released after some seven months in custody. So after the war he was able to tell the Allies exactly what happened. Also a holder of the German Cross in Gold, Speidel was made a Lieutenant-General in the Bundeswehr in 1955 and promoted to full General two years later to become C-in-C NATO Ground Forces.

### Rommel's Staff

**Aides.** At the start of this period of Rommel's career, he had a new young personal aide, one Lieutenant Hammermann – David Irving describes him as being 'much-decorated and one-eyed', but he was soon replaced by Captain Helmuth Lang on Colonel Rudolf Schmundt's advice. Schmundt, who was Hitler's senior Wehrmacht Adjutant, is reported to have said that Rommel needed an ADC who was a major, a highly decorated panzer officer and a Swabian. Elderly, mild and bespectacled, Lang was all these (except that he was only a captain), having won a Knight's Cross on the Eastern Front as a tank commander. He would remain with Rommel to the bitter end, keeping the Field Marshal's personal diary in which Rommel entered his private thoughts, as well as the official record (*Tagesberichte des Oberbefelshabers*), which concerned not only Rommel's activities, but also the day to day work of the Headquarters, details of visitors, etc. Unlike Rommel's headquarters in North Africa or France 1940, there was no Nazi liaison officer at HQ Army Group B.

**Staff Officers.** The Ia was Colonel Hans-Georg von Tempelhoff, suave, handsome, fair-haired, with an English wife. In his mid-thirties, a veteran of the Eastern Front, he had known Rommel since before the war and was a trusted friend from their days in Italy, when he had often talked about peace. Von Tempelhoff usually accompanied the Field Marshal on his tours and was with him immediately before and after his visits to the Führer. In *Knight's Cross* David Fraser explains how von Tempelhoff witnessed Rommel's '... alternations of ebullience and depressed return to reality after his meetings with Hitler', and even the nationality of von Tempelhoff's wife (she was English) would count against Rommel in Hitler's suspicious mind. His deputy was Major Winrich 'Teddy' Behr, whom Ruge describes as being: 'an excellent type of younger officer of the general staff'. He had served in both Russia and North Africa, winning the Knight's Cross whilst commanding the 3rd Company of 3rd Reconnaissance Battalion of the DAK, on 15 May 1941. His company knocked out the very first enemy armoured car to be destroyed by German forces in North Africa. Later, von Tempelhoff would have both Major Eberhardt Wolfram and Major Neuhaus on his staff. Wolfram would accompany Rommel on some of his last car journeys, but it would be Neuhaus who would be with Rommel and the faithful Lang, on 17 July 1944, when their car was strafed. In addition, as far as personnel work was concerned, von Tempelhoff was assisted by a Colonel Freyberg.

The Ic was Colonel Anton Staubwasser, who had been serving in the 'Foreign Armies West' in OKH before joining Army Group B, being so assigned because he was an expert on the British forces. He had been a student of Rommel's at Dresden and David Irving describes him as being 'honest and mild-mannered'. He laboured under difficulties because, apart from a few clerks and two interpreters, he had to rely on OKH for data, who were of course being fed the 'Fortitude' deception plan.[7] He often accompanied Rommel on his walks with his dogs in the woods around La Roche-Guyon. Artillery. Colonel Hans Lattmann was another old family friend who had the greatest admiration for the 'Desert Fox'. Rommel would do his best to help him when his family later got into serious trouble with the Nazi authorities – his brother, Major-General Martin Lattmann, holder of the German Cross in Gold, had deserted to the Russians at Stalingrad. This family skeleton in the cupboard was also going to be held as another black mark against Rommel by the ever-suspicious Gestapo.

**Engineer.** 'Bushy-browed' Lieutenant-General Dr Wilhelm Meise, holder of the German Cross in Silver, was an extremely able engineer, who had a great admiration for Rommel's own abilities in the field of engineering. David Fraser describes him as being 'indefatigable'. Meise wrote about Rommel later saying that in his opinion Rommel was ' ... the greatest engineer of the Second World War. There was nothing I could teach him. He was my master.'[8] He also often went hunting with Rommel.

**Signals.** Chief Signals Officer was 54-year-old Lieutenant-General Ernst Gerke who had also served in North Africa as Chief Signals Officer of Panzerarmee Afrika in early 1943.

**Air.** Just as the Kriegsmarine was represented by Vice-Admiral Ruge, so there was a Luftwaffe Liaison Officer at La Roche-Guyon – Lieutenant-Colonel Wolfgang Queisner. Although Rommel often had harsh words for the Luftwaffe (reflecting his dislike of Göring), he approved of Queisner who fitted in well with the army officers.

**Rommel's staff car.** The Field Marshal spent a great deal of time in his staff car, touring his Army Group area. The car was normally the powerful Horch and it was while travelling in it that he was strafed. It was being driven by his personal driver *Oberfeldwebel* Daniel, with Feldwebel Holke as air sentry (known as the 'Observer'), riding in the back. Ruge comments that Rommel often drove the car himself and then Ruge's own driver (Leading Seaman Hatzinger) had trouble keeping up with him on the flat, straight roads and only managed to catch up on the hills!

**Rommel's dogs.** Rommel had always had a fondness for dogs – not just for hunting with, although he normally chose terriers – but also as companions. While in France he was given a year-old terrier named Ajax, by the Todt Organisation,[9] which he then took home to Herrlingen as it was a good watchdog and barked loudly. Sadly it was run over in May 1944. He also had another terrier called Elbo, which he kept at the château.

## ARMY GROUP B: COMPOSITION, SPRING 1944

Field Marshal Rommel's Army Group B consisted of: Fifteenth Army (four Army Corps: LXVII, LXXXI, LXXXII and LXXXIX); Seventh Army (initially three Army Corps: XXV, LXXIV, and LXXXIV, plus later II Parachute Corps); and LXXXVIII Army Corps in the Netherlands. Given below is the orbat of Army Group B as it was in the spring of 1944, as detailed by Rommel's Chief of Staff, Lieutenant-General Hans Speidel, in *We Defended Normandy*. Inevitably between then and D-Day changes were made, which have also been included, so that the final order of battle which faced the Allied onslaught on 6 June 1944 can be clearly seen. Most of these alterations are as given by Admiral Friedrich Ruge, in *Rommel in Normandy* and in the various official histories. Despite the continual *cris de coeur* for more men from both Eastern and Italian Fronts, von Rundstedt's OB West and Rommel's Army Group B were strengthened, especially between April and May 1944 as the following table shows:

**Composition of OB West**

| Type of Division | Nos as at 4 April | Nos as at 28 May |
| --- | --- | --- |
| Static coastal | 26 | 25 |
| Infantry & Parachute | 14 | 16 |
| Armoured & Mechanised | 5 | 10 |
| Reserve | 10 | 7 |
| TOTALS | 55 | 58 |

Although the actual number of divisions gives only a vague measurement of their increased fighting value, there clearly were more troops present in OB West and Army Group B as D-Day approached, than there had been before Rommel arrived. More importantly, many divisions had been refitted and regrouped, although other divisions (mainly the reserve ones) had not completed their training or were still in the course of formation. There was one other significant change, however, and that was a doubling in tank strength – from 752 at the beginning of January 1944 to 1,403 by the end of April. The panzer, mechanised and parachute divisions would clearly prove to be difficult opposition for the assaulting forces, although the other formations were like the 'curate's egg' – only good in parts – at least they would be able to fight from well-prepared positions, on ground which they had occupied for some time and thus knew quite well. However, while the forward defences along the coastline were quite strong (see below for details), there was little depth, so there appeared to be no proper second line of defence once a determined assault had broken through the coastal 'crust'.

## THE NETHERLANDS

Befelshaber Nederland

LXXXVIII Corps

347th Inf Div        719th Inf Div        16th Luftwaffe Field
                                                  Div

The Wehrmacht commander in the Netherlands was Luftwaffe General F. 'Krischan' Christiansen, a distinguished Luftwaffe officer, with a remarkable 'tri-service' background. In the Great War he had been the captain of an auxiliary cruiser, then commanded the naval base at Zeebrugge. He was a holder of the coveted *Pour le Mérite* for bravery. Post-war he had worked for Dornier at Friedrichshafen as a naval aviation expert. In 1933, he was recalled and appointed a Major-General in the Luftwaffe, one of his pre-war jobs being as head of the Aviation and Sports Department of the Air Ministry, and in 1939 he was appointed as a General of Airmen in charge of the National Socialist Air Corps. In Holland he was mainly responsible for administration and internal security. Speidel describes him as being 'a bluff simple seaman, but not with the experience, education and qualities of mind to lead an army; he knew very little of land warfare.'[10] Reichsmarschall Göring sought to make up for 'Krischan's' deficiencies by putting one of his trusted men, Lieutenant-General Reinhard von Wühlisch, into his HQ as Chief of Staff. Wühlisch was a trained General Staff Officer and had served in the cavalry.

## LXXXVIII Army Corps
The ground forces in the Netherlands consisted of the three divisions of LXXXVIII Army Corps, 347th Infantry, 719th Infantry and 16th Luftwaffe

Field. The corps was commanded by General of Infantry and Knight's Cross holder, Hans Wolfgang Reinhard. He was born in Hohenstein-Ernsttal in 1888. He joined the army in 1908, then the Reichsheer in 1934, being promoted to Major-General in October 1937. LXXXVIII Army Corps had been formed in Holland in the early summer of 1942, with its Headquarters at Antwerp.

**347th Infantry Division.** Originally this was a 3-regiment static unit, mobilised in October 1942 and sent to Holland soon afterwards. It was reduced to just two regiments in 1943, when 862nd Grenadier Regiment was transferred to 274th Inf Div. The rest occupied a sector of the Dutch coast near Amsterdam until the invasion, when it was sent into battle in Normandy where it suffered heavy losses. Its commander in June 1944 was Lieutenant-General Wolf Trierenberg. He was born in Bavaria in June 1891, joined the army in March 1910 (10th Dragoon Regiment) and later served in the Reichsheer. He had been COS of VI Army Corps, commander of 12 Schützen Bde and then 167th Inf Div, before taking over the 347th on 8 December 1943. He was a holder of the Knight's Cross and the German Cross in Gold.

Units in 347th Inf Div were: 860th and 861st Grenadier Regts, 347th Artillery Regt, 347th Fusilier Bn, 347th Anti-Tank Bn, 347th Engineer Bn, 347th Signals Bn.

**719th Infantry Division.** This was a static, understrength division, formed from older men in April 1941 and initially sent to garrison Brittany seven months later. It was transferred to the Dordrecht area of Holland in late 1942 and remained there until going into action against the British in the summer of 1944, when its troops fought well despite their age. Its commander in early 1944 was Lieutenant-General Erich Höcker, who retired in May 1944 aged 61. Major-General Sievers would take over in July (see below). Rommel visited them in March 1944 and made a special point of commending the division on the progress of their defence works.

Units included 723rd and 743rd Infantry Regts, 719th Artillery Bn,[11] 719th Engineer Bn, 719th Signals Bn.

**16th Luftwaffe Field Division.** Formed in 1942 as a 2-regiment division, it was stationed in the Hague–Haarlem area of Holland from 1942 to 1943. In June 1944 it became a 3-regiment division, when 45th Field Infantry Regt was formed by reducing the other two regiments to two battalions each. It then garrisoned Amsterdam until being sent to Normandy in June. The following month it replaced Panzer Lehr Division in the front line and was almost immediately overrun by the major British assault, losing more than 75 per cent of its strength. The divisional commander in June 1944 was Lieutenant-General Karl Sievers who was an army officer, holder of the Knight's Cross and the German Cross in Gold. He went on to command 719th Inf Div.

## FIFTEENTH ARMY

Within the four army corps was a total of fourteen infantry divisions and three Luftwaffe field divisions; six infantry and two Luftwaffe in the front line on the coast; eight infantry and one Luftwaffe in the hinterland. The Army was commanded by Colonel General Hans von Salmuth. He was born in Metz on 29 November 1888. A highly experienced officer, he had joined the army in 1907, served in the Reichsheer post-war and was Chief of Staff to Field Marshal von Bock in the campaign against France and the Low Countries in May 1940. He had commanded XXX Corps in the Crimea in 1941 and led Second Army at Kursk until he was unjustly relieved of his command. He tried to patronise Rommel at one of their first meetings, which, as has already been explained, prompted the Field Marshal to give him a monumental telling off. Thereafter they got on better and better, so that by mid-May Ruge recalls that von Salmuth spoke of the Field Marshal '... with genuine affection. It was gratifying that the two men had found each other.'[12] Holder of the Knight's Cross, von Salmuth remained in command until he was relieved by General Gustav-Adolf von Zangen on 25 August 1944. HQ Fifteenth Army was located at Tourcoing. The four army corps were:

**LXXXI Corps.** This was formed in October 1939 in Poland as XXXII Corps Command, then in April 1940 it was sent to Copenhagen and two years later to NW France where it was upgraded to LXXXI Army Corps. It fought on the Western Front in 1944–5 and was destroyed in the Ruhr Pocket in April 1945. Its commander was Knight's Cross holder, Gen d. Pz. Tr. Adolf Kuntzen, who was born in Magdeburg in 1889, entered the army in 1909 and served as a Lieutenant in the 1st Regiment of Hussars during the Great War, then joined the Reichswehr. He commanded 3rd leichte Division from November 1938 as a Major-General, then 8th Pz Div, followed by LVII Pz Corps and XXXII Army Corps, before taking over LXXXI Corps on 1 April 1942.

**LXXXII Corps.** Formed in 1939 as XXXVII Corps Command and posted to France in 1940 where it remained, being upgraded in 1942 to LXXXII Army Corps. In 1944–5 it fought on the Western Front, then in the Saar, surrendering in May 1945, NE of Munich. It was commanded by Gen d. Art. Johann Sinnhuber, holder of the Knight's Cross and the German Cross in Gold. He was born in Wilkoschen, West Prussia, in 1887. He joined the army in 1907, and the Reichsheer in 1921. He was promoted to Major-General in April 1939 and commanded 28th Jäger Division. He became a General of Artillery on 1 October 1943, having taken over LXXXII Corps three months previously. After LXXXII Corps he was responsible for the defence of Hamburg–Bremen from 1 April 1945.

**LXXXIX Corps.** Formed in Belgium during the summer of 1942 as Korps 'Scheldt', it was upgraded to LXXXIX Army Corps in the winter of 1942/3 and fought on the Western Front 1944–5 until it was destroyed. The commander in 1944 was Gen d. Pz. Tr. Dr Alfred Ritter von Hubicki, who was born in Friedrichsdorf in February 1887. He joined the army in 1905 and was later commissioned into the artillery. He served in the Austrian Bundesheer and was promoted to Major-General in late 1935. In 1938 the Austrian army was taken over by the Reichsheer and later Hubicki became the commander of 9th Pz Div (1938–41), then of Korps Scheldt. He was discharged in March 1945, having been the head of the army mission in Slovakia from July 1944.

**LXVII Reserve Corps.** Formed in 1940 as LXVII Corps Command and converted to LXVII Reserve Corps in France during the summer of 1944 and transferred to the Somme area. It took part in the withdrawal from France and was in action again in the Aachen area in late 1944. It was destroyed in the Eifel and at Remagen in early 1945.

## The Front-Line Divisions

**47th Infantry Division.** (Under command of LXXXII Corps). Formed in the Calais area in February 1944, from 156th Reserve Division, it fought in Normandy, managed to escape being encircled at Falaise, but then suffered heavy losses and had to be reformed in Denmark. Thereafter it was redesignated as a 'Volksgrenadier'[13] division. Major-General Karl Wahle commanded until 4 September 1944 when he was taken prisoner. In *Rommel in Normandy* Ruge recalls meeting Wahle during one of Rommel's tours in March 1944, to present him with the Knight's Cross of the War Merit Cross, describing Wahle, who had been born in Dresden in 1892, as a '... friendly Saxonian'.

Main units included: 103rd, 104th, 115th Grenadier Regts, 147th Artillery Regt, 147th Fusilier Bn, 147th Anti-Tank Bn, 147th Engineer Bn, 147th Signals Bn.

**49th Infantry Division.** (Under command of LXVII Corps). Formed in the Boulogne area in February 1944 from 191st Reserve Division, it first fought in northern France in August 1944, took part in the withdrawal into the Low Countries and was heavily engaged near the Albert Canal and virtually destroyed. Reformed at regimental strength only, they went back into action near Aachen but were soon disbanded. The commander was Lieutenant-General Siegfried Macholz, winner of the Knight's Cross and the German Cross in Gold.

Main units included: 148th, 149th, 150th Grenadier Regts, 149th Artillery Regt, 149th Fusilier Bn, 149th Anti-Tank Bn, 149th Engineer Bn, 149th Signals Bn.

**70th Infantry Division.** Formed on Walcheren Island in 1944, it was given the nickname 'The White Bread Division', because many of its soldiers had stomach problems and so required special rations. In fact they fought extremely bravely when the island was attacked by the British and

Canadians in November 1944 and it took Montgomery's troops nine days of hard fighting to defeat them. It was commanded by Lieutenant-General Wilhelm Daser, who was born in Germersheim in 1884, so he was over 60 when he was captured on 7 November 1944. This division does not feature in Admiral Ruge's Orbat of Army Group B, as it presumably was considered to be too far away from the initial action in France to be mentioned.

Main units were: 1018th, 1019th, 1020th Grenadier Regts, 170th Artillery Regt, 170th Fusilier Bn, 170th Anti-Tank Bn, 170th Engineer Bn, 170th Signals Bn.

**344th Infantry Division.** (Under command of LXVII Corps). First formed in October 1942, it was initially assigned to occupation duties near Bordeaux in 1943, but later was ordered to defend a sector of the Bay of Biscay coastal area. Its first action was in the summer of 1944 and it suffered heavy casualties, then again in late August while covering Fifth Panzer Army's retreat, when it was all but wiped out by US First Army. Its commander was Knight's Cross holder Lieutenant-General Eugen-Felix Schwalbe, who went on to command LXXXVIII Corps, to direct the evacuation of Fifteenth Army across the Scheldt and to be promoted General of Infantry.

Main units were: 854th, 855th Grenadier Regts, 344th Artillery Regt, 344th Fusilier Bn, 344th Anti-Tank Bn, 344th Engineer Bn, 344th Signals Bn.

**348th Infantry Division.** (Under command of LXXXI Corps). Formed in October 1942 and sent to the Dieppe area, it lost one of its original three regiments in 1943, when 865th Grenadier Regt was combined with 347th Inf Div's 862nd Grenadier Regt to form 274th Inf Div. Their first action was in the autumn of 1944, when the Allies broke out of Normandy, crossed the Seine and attacked the rear of Fifteenth Army. They suffered heavy losses. Lieutenant-General Paul Seyffardt, holder of the Knight's Cross and the German Cross in Gold, was in command until he was captured in September 1944 during the retreat towards the Fatherland.

Main units were: 863rd, 864th Grenadier Regts, 348th Artillery Regt, 348th Fusilier Bn, 348th Anti-Tank Bn, 348th Engineer Bn, 348th Signals Bn.

**711th Infantry Division.** (Under command of LXXXI Corps). Formed in April 1941 and made up of older troops, it was sent to NE France in the summer of 1941, then to Rouen at the end of the year. It moved to the Deauville area, south of the Seine, in the spring of 1944, with its HQ at Pont-l'Evêque. Rommel's comments on the division when he inspected it in March 1944, included the fact that various Army Group orders did not seem to have percolated down to them so they were: ' ... in ignorance of the concept of a land front. The foreshore had not yet been closed off with barriers.' Fighting in Normandy, it suffered heavy casualties and had to be withdrawn to the Netherlands to be rebuilt. Commander of the division was Lieutenant-

General Josef Reichert, born in 1891. A Knight's Cross winner, he led the 711th throughout its battle history including being transferred to the Eastern Front, where it was surrounded and surrendered to the Russians east of Prague in May 1945.

Main units were: 731st, 744th Infantry Regts, 711th Artillery Bn, 711th Engineer Bn, 711th Signals Bn.

**17th Luftwaffe Field Division.** (Under command of LXXXI Corps). Formed and trained in Pomerania, it was posted to France for static duties, and in the spring of 1944 was located east of Le Havre, near the River Seine. It helped defend Paris after the Normandy front collapsed, but was almost completely destroyed by American forces in late August. Its survivors were absorbed into 167th Infantry Division. Its commander was Lieutenant-General Hans Kurt Höcker, born in 1894 and holder of the Knight's Cross and German Cross in Gold.

Main units were: 33rd, 34th Field Infantry Regts, 17th Field Artillery Regt, 17th Anti-Aircraft Bn, 17th Field Anti-Tank Bn, 17th Field Engineer Bn, 17th Field Signals Bn, 17th Field Fusilier Bn.

**18th Luftwaffe Field Division.** (Under command of LXXXII Corps). Formed in France, it was stationed in Northern France and Belgium throughout its operational service. Its third regiment was formed in early 1944, from the third battalions of 35th and 36th and called the 47th Infantry. It first saw action in August 1944 as part of Fifth Panzer Army in the defence of Paris, then in September was trapped in the Mons area of Belgium and almost obliterated, only some three hundred men escaping. Its commander was Lieutenant-General Joachim von Tresckow, a Pomeranian, who had been brought up in the old Prussian style and was sickened by the Nazis even as early as the Polish campaign. Holder of the Knight's Cross and German Cross in Gold, he had been von Kluge's Chief of Staff and was, according to Speidel: 'one of the most passionate and upright fighters against Hitler, a man of superlative character and high spirit'. He committed suicide on 21 July 1944, in order to escape the hangman. His last words were: 'God once promised Abraham to spare Sodom should there be found ten just men in the city. He will, I trust, spare Germany because of what we have done and not destroy her.'[14]  When Rommel inspected the division during one of his early tours he found that they had only 9,000 men, poorly trained with few NCOs and lacking in young officers. Von Tresckow told him that the division would never become a fighting unit until more young officers and NCOs were supplied.

Main units were: 35th, 36th, 47th Field Infantry Regts, 18th Field Artillery Regt, 18th Field Anti-Tank Bn, 18th Field Anti-Aircraft Bn, 18th Field Engineer Bn, 18th Field Signals Bn, 18th Field Fusilier Bn.

**In-Depth Divisions**
**64th Infantry Division.** Formed near Cologne on the Wahne Manoeuvre Area, mainly of men from the Eastern Front. They first went into action at Abbeville in August 1944, fought in the battle at the Albert Canal and were

left isolated when the rest of Fifteenth Army withdrew behind the Schelde. They fought bravely but were eventually totally destroyed and their commander captured on 2 November 1944. The division was commanded by Major-General Knut Eberding, holder of the German Cross in Gold. He was born in Schloss Reppline in 1895, and joined the army in 1914 as a Lieutenant in the Fusiliers. After the war he served with the Reichswehr and was a battalion commander in 1939. The division is not shown as under command of any of the four corps in Fifteenth Army.

Main units were: 1037th, 1038th, 1039th Grenadier Regts, 164th Artillery Regt, 164th Fusilier Bn, 164th Anti-Tank Bn, 164th Engineer Bn, 164th Signals Bn.

**85th Infantry Division.** (Under command of LXVII Corps). Formed in February 1944, from the men of several disbanded units, it was encamped in Northern France, in the rear area of Fifteenth Army, and was sent to Normandy in early August where it suffered heavy casualties, particularly in the Falaise Pocket. It was commanded by Knight's Cross holder, Lieutenant-General Kurt Chill, who was born in Thorn in March 1895. He joined 21st Jäger Regt in 1913, and after the Great War served in the police before rejoining the army. In 1942–3 he had commanded 122nd Jäger Division in Russia where he had been badly wounded.

Main units were: 1053rd, 1054th Grenadier Regts, 185th Artillery Regt, 185th Fusilier Bn, 185th Anti-Tank Bn, 185th Engineer Bn, 185th Signals Bn.

**89th Infantry Division.** Formed in 1944 from personnel in the reinforced infantry regiments of the Replacement Army, the division trained in Norway from March to June 1944, then returned to France and was first located in Normandy in the area Rouen–Le Havre. It suffered heavy casualties almost immediately, then was hit again in the Falaise area and had to be withdrawn after heavy British pressure. The 'Horseshoe Division' as it was called (from its divisional sign) was reformed but again suffered heavily in the battles on the Siegfried Line and by the middle of September it was once again a complete wreck. The divisional commander Colonel Rösler was replaced in September by Major-General Walter Bruns. The division is not shown as under command of any of the Corps.

Major units were: 1055th, 1056th Grenadier Regts, 189th Artillery Regt, 189th Fusilier Bn, 189th Anti-Tank Bn, 189th Engineer Bn, 189th Signals Bn.

**182nd Infantry Division.** (Under command of LXXXII Corps). Formed as a mobilisation division in 1939, it spent the period from November 1939 to September 1940 in Poland, then moved to Nancy. In 1942 its replacement units went back to Germany and the division was switched to a training role. After re-organisation it was moved to the Channel Coast, with its HQ at Cassel, although it was still being used as a training unit. It was not committed immediately because of its poor state of readiness and poor equipment (e.g., its four infantry gun companies had just four guns; its infantry had only one issue of ammunition and its artillery only two). Its commander, Lieutenant General Richard Baltzer, was the holder of the German Cross in Gold, who was born in Danzig in 1886. The division was sent to the Eastern Front in late 1944.

Major units were: 79th, 112th, 342nd Reserve Grenadier Regts, 34th Reserve Artillery Regt.

**326th Infantry Division.** (Under command of LXVII Corps). Formed in late 1942, it took part in the occupation of Vichy France, then was stationed in the neighbourhood of Narbonne from April 1943 to January 1944 when it was sent to northern France. Committed to the front line on 22 July, it was rapidly overrun at Caumont and later trapped in the Falaise Pocket. Remnants broke out and were later sent to Hungary to reform as a Volksgrenadier division. Its commander (1 June 1943–2 August 1944) was Lieutenant-General Viktor von Drabbich-Wächter, who was born in Strassburg in 1889. He was killed on the Eastern Front in 1944.

Main units were: 751st, 752nd, 753rd Grenadier Regts, 326th Artillery Regt, 326th Fusilier Bn, 326th Anti-Tank Bn, 326th Engineer Bn, 326th Signals Bn.

**331st Infantry Division.** (Under command of LXXXII Corps). Formed in Austria in late 1941, it was sent to the Eastern Front and fought there for two years, suffering heavy losses. In 1943/4 it was reformed in Germany and transferred to the Calais area. It saw action during the withdrawal through France and the defence of Paris, being almost annihilated by US First Army. Its survivors regrouped and later fought in Holland. It was commanded in 1944, by Knight's Cross winner, Major-General Heinz Furbach, who was born in Karlshof in 1895.

Major units were: 557th, 558th, 559th Infantry Regts, 331st Artillery Regt, 331st Anti-Tank Bn, 331st Engineer Bn, 331st Recce Bn, 331st Signals Bn.

**346th Infantry Division.** (Under command of LXXXI Corps). Formed in late 1942 and sent to France to the St-Malo sector until the spring of 1944 when it was transferred to Le Havre. Heavily involved in the Battle of Caen, it was soon decimated – for example, *Hitler's Legions* quotes its strength on 13 June as being down to fewer than sixty men per company. A month later only six of its anti-tank weapons were still operational. The remnants of the division were caught in the Falaise Pocket, but managed to break out, suffering further heavy casualties. From its formation the commander was Lieutenant-General Erich Diestel, holder of both the Knight's Cross and the German Cross in Gold.

Main units were: 857th, 858th Grenadier Regts, 346th Artillery Regt, 346th Fusilier Bn, 346th Anti-Tank Bn, 346th Engineer Bn, 346th Signals Bn.

**712th Infantry Division.** (Under command of LXXIX Corps). Created in April 1941 as a static division for the defence of NE France, it went to Normandy in January 1942, then to a sector of the Low Countries coast around Zeebrugge, where it remained until D-Day. Ruge reports on an inspection of the division by Rommel in late March without warning as the result of a mix-up. Rommel found that his orders to put in extra beach defences, following an earlier inspection in January, had not be acted upon, so he gave the 'responsible officer' a good dressing-down; he demanded that mined stakes be planted and would not accept the excuse that wood was in short supply! It was commanded by Lieutenant General Friedrich Wilhelm Neumann, who later commanded LXXXIX Corps.

Main units were: 732nd, 745th Infantry Regts, 652nd Artillery Bn, 712th Engineer Bn, 712th Signals Bn.

**19th Luftwaffe Field Division.** (Under command of LXXIX Corps). Formed in the neighbourhood of Munich in early 1943, it moved to France, but from June to December was sent to garrison Walcheren. In January 1944 it moved to the Ghent–Bruges area and while in Belgium was re-organised. Later it moved to the Thielt area and in June 1944, when the Italian Front was in crisis, it was moved to Italy, where it first saw action, suffered heavy casualties and was eventually sent to Denmark to be assimilated into the 19th Volksgrenadier Division. The commander while the division was in 15th Army Group was Army Lieutenant-General Erich Bässler, who later commanded 191st Reserve Division in France, from December 1944.

Main units were: 37th, 38th, 46th Field Infantry Regts, 19th Field Artillery Regt, 19th Anti-Tank Bn, 19th Field Engineer Bn, 19th Field Anti-Aircraft Bn, 19th Field Fusilier Bn, 19th Field Signals Bn.

**Divisional Changes Prior to D-Day**
By the time that the Allies landed, Fifteenth Army had lost 70th Division for reasons already explained, and neither 64th nor 89th feature any longer, presumably for similar reasons. But 48th, 84th, 165th and 245th Divisions had been added.

**48th Infantry Division.** (Under command of LXXXIX Corps). Formed from 171st Reserve Division in the Flanders area of Belgium in 1944, it contained many non-Germans, including a fair number of Poles. Rommel inspected this division (after having visited the 712th (see above) and was suitably impressed by its preparedness. Initially located on the Belgian coast, it was transferred to France once the Normandy front collapsed and first saw action in the area of Chartres in August. Not well trained, or loyal to Germany, it did not fight well and suffered badly under General Patton's rampaging US Third Army. Its commander, Knight's Cross holder, Lieutenant-General Karl Casper, was born in Rehden in 1893, served in the Great War, then joined the police, and returned to the army in 1935.

Main units were: 126th, 127th Grenadier Regts, 148th Artillery Regt, 148th Anti-Tank Bn, 148th Engineer Bn, 148th Signals Bn, 148th Fusilier Bn.

**84th Infantry Division.** (Under command LXXXI Corps). Formed in Poland in early 1944 from the remnants of various units, initially as a 2-regiment division. In May it moved to the Rouen area and in August was committed to the battle around Mortain and Vire, before being caught in the Falaise Pocket. Only about one regiment's worth of men escaped, the divisional commander being among those taken prisoner. It was then sent to the Somme area to reform. The commander, Lieutenant-General Erwin Menny, was born in Saarburg in 1893, joined the army in 1912 and served as a Lieutenant in the 22nd Light Dragoons. Post-war he was in the Reichswehr and was serving in Schützen Regt 81 in 1939. Holder of the Knight's Cross, he took over the division on 10 February 1944 and was taken prisoner on 28 August.

Main units were: 1051st, 1052nd, 1062nd Grenadier Regts, 184th Artillery Regt, 184th Anti-Tank Bn, 184th Engineer Bn, 184th Signals Bn, 184th Fusilier Bn.

**165th Infantry Division.** (Under command of LXXXIX Corps). Formed just after the invasion of Poland in 1939 in the Württemberg–Baden area, it was first stationed in Czechoslovakia until late 1940 when it returned to Germany. In 1942 it was transferred to France, then briefly went to Holland, before being part of the occupation forces in Vichy France in November 1942. Returning to Holland, it was initially positioned to defend the southern sector of the Dutch coastline, but was virtually disbanded between July and September 1944 and its personnel sent to reinforce other divisions on the Western Front. Its commander in early 1944 was Lieutenant General Baron von Schacky auf Schönfeld.

Major units were: 205th, 215th, 260th Reserve Grenadier Regts, 5th Reserve Artillery Regt, 9th Reserve Engineer Bn.

**245th Infantry Division.** (Under command of LXXXI Corps). It came into being in Germany in the summer of 1943 as a static division, and was then moved to northern France in the area of Fécamp. It escaped the initial Normandy campaign but was heavily engaged as the Allies thrust towards the Low Countries. It was involved in the Allied airborne assault to capture Arnhem, then in the Battle of the Scheldt in October–November 1944 as part of LXVII Corps. Withdrawn to refit, it was soon back in action again and was heavily engaged by US Third Army. Its commander was Knight's Cross holder, Lieutenant-General Erwin Sander, born in 1892, who entered the army in 1908, fought in the Great War, then served in the police before rejoining the army. An artilleryman, he was promoted to Major-General in November 1941 when he was commanding 170th Infantry Division.

Major units were: 935th, 936th, 937th Grenadier Regts, 245th Artillery Regt, 245th Fusilier Bn, 245th Anti-Tank Bn, 245th Engineer Bn, 245th Signals Bn.

## D-DAY ORGANISATION
The outline organisation of Fifteenth Army as at 6 June 1944 was:

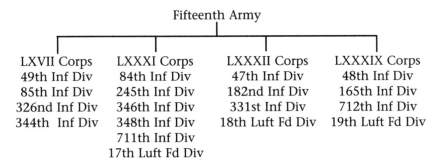

Fifteenth Army

| LXVII Corps | LXXXI Corps | LXXXII Corps | LXXXIX Corps |
|---|---|---|---|
| 49th Inf Div | 84th Inf Div | 47th Inf Div | 48th Inf Div |
| 85th Inf Div | 245th Inf Div | 182nd Inf Div | 165th Inf Div |
| 326nd Inf Div | 346th Inf Div | 331st Inf Div | 712th Inf Div |
| 344th Inf Div | 348th Inf Div | 18th Luft Fd Div | 19th Luft Fd Div |
| | 711th Inf Div | | |
| | 17th Luft Fd Div | | |

## SEVENTH ARMY
Rommel's other Army was Seventh, commanded by an artilleryman, Colonel General Friedrich Dollman. Born on 2 February 1882 in Würzburg, he had first entered the army in 1899 and after the Great War he served in the Reichswehr. He was an expert in long-range artillery and was appointed Inspector of Artillery in 1933, having been promoted to Major-General in 1932, was a General of Artillery in 1936 and a Colonel General in 1940. In October 1939 he had been appointed C-in-C Seventh Army at the age of 57 – the eighth most senior officer in the German Army. Although a very experienced gunner officer, his most recent combat experience had been the command of Seventh Army in 1940, crossing the Upper Rhine, attacking the Maginot Line and breaking through north of Belfort (even Speidel refers to this as being: ' ... not in itself a memorable operation'). For the next four years he would have a quiet existence commanding Seventh Army in France. Basically he did not approve of Hitler's methods, although in the early days they had got on quite well and he had been responsible for promoting good relations between the Army and the Nazi Party. Also, he was not very fit, being a large, corpulent man suffering from a bad heart. He would die after a heart attack at his battle headquarters in France on 29 June 1944, a few days after Hitler had demanded his dismissal for the loss of Cherbourg; both von Rundstedt and Rommel had refused to sack him. Speidel encapsulated Dollmann's views when he wrote: 'The methods of Hitler had wounded him deeply, both as a soldier and a man.'

Dollmann's HQ was at Le Mans and it would be his Army which would face the initial onslaught from the Allied invasion on D-Day, which struck the forward units of LXXXIV Corps (352nd, 709th and 716th Infantry Divisions).

### Army Corps
Seventh Army contained three (later four) Army Corps.

**XXV Army Corps.** Formed at Baden-Baden in 1938 as the Upper Rhine Frontier Corps, then redesignated XXV Corps in 1939. In 1940 it became part of the occupation forces in France, was isolated in Brittany in 1944 and surrendered in May 1945. The commander was General of Artillery Wilhelm Fahrmbacher, who had previously commanded VII Infantry Corps in the assault on Moscow. Born in Zweibrücken in 1888, Knight's Cross holder Fahrmbacker joined the army in 1907, served in the Great War, and in the post-war Reichswehr, was a Lieutenant-General in June 1939 and promoted to General of Artillery on 1 October 1940.

**LXXIV Army Corps.** Formed in Brittany in early 1944, deployed on the Western Front in 1944–5, destroyed in the Ruhr Pocket in April 1945. It commanded 77th, 266th and 353rd Infantry Divisions.

**LXXXIV Army Corps.** Formed as LX Corps Command, then upgraded to LXXXIV Corps in NW France in 1942. Bore the brunt of the D-Day landings and was later destroyed in the Falaise Pocket. The Corps Commander was Knight's Cross holder (with Oakleaves), General of Artillery Erich Marcks, who was born in Berlin on 6 June (a portentous date!) 1891. He joined the army in 1910, served in the Reichswehr post-war and was promoted to Major-General in April 1939. He was COS VIII Army Corps in September 1939, went on to command various corps before taking over LXXXIV Corps on 1 August 1943.

Despite having a wooden leg, Marcks was an energetic, capable and well liked commander. He considered that the invasion would come in Normandy, probably coupled with an assault on Cherbourg. He shared his birthday (6 June) with Lucie Rommel and got on well with Rommel – after they had dined together he wrote: 'We get on well together, although we're two very different sorts.'[15] Marcks was killed at Carentan on 12 June.

**II Para Corps.** The Corps comprised 3rd and 5th Parachute Divisions. Commanded by Lieutenant-General Eugen Meindl who rose to be a General of Paratroops, the Corps lost heavily in the Falaise Pocket, but Meindl managed to extricate 3rd Para Div (taking over personally when the Div Commander was badly wounded), 12th SS Div and HQ Seventh Army from the trap.

**The Divisions were:**

**84th Infantry Division.** Although this division was originally in Seventh Army, it was redeployed to Fifteenth Army, q.v.

**243rd Infantry Division.** (Under command of LXXXIV Corps). Created in NE Austria in the summer of 1943, it was posted to Brittany in October of that year, but was still not up to strength by June 1944. Furthermore it was short of mechanical equipment, e.g., only one of its three regiments was motorised, one had bicycles and the other horse-drawn vehicles. The Division would be in action on D-Day, covering the western sector of the Cotentin peninsula. It was commanded by the brave and efficient Knight's Cross holder, Lieutenant-General Heinz Hellmich. He was born in Karlsruhe in 1890, joined the army in 1910 and served post-war in the Reichswehr, being promoted to Major-General on 1 October 1939, his first command being 23rd Infantry Division. He took over 243rd Inf Div in early January 1944 from Major-General Hermann von Witzblen who had commanded from its formation. Hellmich was killed in a fighter-bomber attack on 16 June. His Division was under constant heavy attack from sea, land and air, and was almost totally destroyed in the battle for Cherbourg although some troops did escape. It was finally disbanded in August.

Major units were: 920th, 921st, 922nd Grenadier Regts, 243rd Artillery Regt, 243rd Fusilier Bn, 243rd Anti-Tank Bn, 243rd Engineer Bn, 243rd Signals Bn.

**265th Infantry Division.** (Under command of XXV Corps). Formed in the summer of 1943 at the Bergen–Hohne Training Area, from troops who had served on the Eastern Front. Sent to Brittany, they exchanged some personnel with 65th Infantry Division, then late in 1943 two battalions were sent to Russia. Post-D-Day part of the division fought in Normandy and was destroyed, other elements fought in the siege of Brest where they also were destroyed when the port was captured. The remainder of the division was surrounded at Lorient by US Third Army's thrust to Brest and was held in total isolation until the end of the war. The Commander was Knight's Cross holder Lieutenant-General Walther Düvert. He was born in Görlitz in 1893, first joined the army in 1911 and was a Lieutenant in Fusilier Regt 8 in 1913. Post-war he served in the Reichswehr and was promoted to Major-General in 1941.

Main units were: 894th, 895th, 896th Grenadier Regts, 265th Artillery Regt, 265th Fusilier Bn, 265th Engineer Bn, 265th Anti-Tank Bn, 265th Signals Bn.

**266th Infantry Division.** (Under command of LXXIV Corps). Formed in the summer if 1943 in the Müsingen Training Area, mainly from Eastern Front veterans and other recruits from the East, who were, to quote Ruge ' ... of very little combat value'. The Division moved to France in 1943 for coastal watch duties, but, lacking mechanised vehicles, was unable to escape from armoured thrusts as the US forces swept through the Brittany peninsula and most of the division were captured. The commander was Lieutenant-General Karl Spang. He was born in Mergentheim in 1886 and joined the army in 1905. An artilleryman, he served in the Reichsheer post-war and was promoted to Major-General in April 1938. He took over 266th Inf Div in June 1943 and was taken prisoner with his division on 8 August 1944.

Major units were: 897th, 898th, 899th Grenadier Regts, 266th Artillery Regt, 266th Fusilier Bn, 266th Anti-Tank Bn, 266th Engineer Bn, 266th Signals Bn.

**319th Infantry Division.** (Under command of LXXXIV Corps). Organised in late 1940, they took over the defence of the Channel Islands (Jersey, Guernsey, Alderney, Sark, Herm and Jethou) in 1941. They were also responsible for St-Malo and the adjacent coastline. Hitler was so convinced that the Allies would invade the islands that he reinforced the 319th until its strength was some 40,000 men – the strongest German division of the war! Bypassed by the Allied invasion, some of its troops were transferred to the Normandy front and fought in the battles in the Cotentin peninsula. The main body hardly fired a shot in anger and surrendered on 9 May 1945. The commander was Lieutenant-General Graf Rudolf von Schmettow, who took over in September 1943 from Lieutenant-General Erich Müller who went on to be the commandant of Danzig. German Cross in Gold holder, von Schmettow, was born in Berlin in 1891, joined the army in 1909, served with the Reichsheer post-war and was commanding 164th Inf Regt when war began.

Main units were: 582nd, 583rd, 564th Infantry Regts, 319th Artillery Regt, 319th Anti-Tank Bn, 319th Engineer Bn, 319th Signals Bn, 319th Recce Bn.

**343rd Infantry Division.** (Under command of XXV Corps). Formed in October 1942 at the Grafenwöhr Training Area in SW Germany, it was a static defence division so had little organic transport and was short of many other types of equipment. Sent to France in early 1943, it was stationed in the Brest area and took part in the siege, the survivors surrendering on 19 September 1944. Its commander was Major-General Erwin Rauch, holder of both the Knight's Cross and the German Cross in Gold. Born in Berlin in 1889, he joined the army in 1908 (35th Fusilier Regt) and was serving with Inf Regt 2 in 1939. He took over 343rd Div in February 1944 and was captured when his Division surrendered.

Major units were: 851st, 852nd Grenadier Regts, 343rd Artillery Regt, 343rd Fusilier Bn, 343rd Anti-Tank Bn, 343rd Engineer Bn, 343rd Signals Bn.

**352nd Infantry Division.** (Under command of LXXXIV Corps). Formed from elements of two other divisions (268th and 321st) in late 1943, it was allocated to a sector on the eastern side of the Cotentin peninisula, so it faced the full force of the D-Day landings, being pounded from sea, land and air. When Rommel had inspected them they had only four battalions and four batteries ready for combat; nevertheless they fought well. By 7 June it was down to battlegroup strength, but despite everything continued to fight bravely. Its survivors were eventually absorbed into 2nd Panzer Division. Reconstituted as a Volksgrenadier division, it went on to fight in the Ardennes and the Rhineland. Its commander at the time of D-Day was Lieutenant-General Dietrich Kraiss, who was killed at St-Lô on 2 August 1944. Holder of the Knight's Cross with Oakleaves and the German Cross in Gold, he was born in Stuttgart in 1889, joined the army in 1909 and served post-war with the Reichswehr. Promoted to

Major-General in June 1942, he took command of the 352nd on 6 November 1943.

Major units were: 914th, 915th, 916th Grenadier Regts, 352nd Artillery Regt, 352nd Fusilier Bn, 352nd Anti-Tank Bn, 352nd Engineer Bn, 352nd Signals Bn.

**716th Infantry Division.** (Under command of LXXXIV Corps). Formed in April 1941 from mainly older personnel, it was sent to the Caen area the following month. When Rommel inspected them they were occupying a 90-kilometre front with two regiments forward. On its right sector its coastal strongpoints were a satisfactory 600–1,000 metres apart, but on the left the gaps were between 3–3½ kilometres and, although some of the cliffs were very steep, this was far too far apart. Equally worrying, in view of its important location, Ruge reported on a lack of ' ... a clear understanding of the dangerous situation and of the determined will to prevent the enemy from reaching land'. The Division was still there on D-Day when it was assaulted by British Second Army whose progress they held up by stubborn fighting, although sustaining heavy losses. Withdrawn to Perpignan to refit, it was caught up in the battle for southern France instead, and again suffered heavy losses. Remnants escaped and were still fighting at the end of the war. The Division was commanded by an artilleryman, Lieutenant-General Wilhelm Richter from 1 April 1943 until September 1944. He was born in Hirschberg in 1892 and joined the army in 1913. Post-war he served in the Reichsheer and was commanding 30th Artillery Regiment in 1939.

Main units were: 726th, 736th Infantry Regts, 716th Artillery Bn, 716th Engineer Bn, 716th Recce Bn, 716th Signals Bn.

**91st Air Landing Division.** (Under command of II Para Corps). Formed in the Baumholder and Bitsch Training areas, mainly from replacement centre personnel, it was sent to the Cotentin peninsula, to fight as infantry, despite being equipped for air landing. From D-Day it was engaged against the American 82nd and 101st Airborne Divisions, suffering tremendous casualties in the first few days, so that by the end of the first week it was down to below battlegroup strength. It was later rebuilt and made a gallant stand at Rennes. Its commander was Knight's Cross and German Cross in Gold holder, Lieutenant-General Wilhelm Falley, the first German general to be killed during the invasion, when his HQ was attacked by American paratroopers before dawn on 6 June and he was hit by machine-gun fire. Born in Metz in 1897, he joined the army in 1915, served with the Reichswehr post-war and was commanding 1st Bn of Inf Regt 433 in 1939. He took over the 91st on 25 April 1944. NB. It had 6 Para Regt attached from 2nd Para Div in Normandy.

Major units were: 1057th, 1058th Grenadier Regts, 191st Anti-Tank Bn, 191st Engineer Bn, 191st Signals Bn, 191st Fusilier Bn.

**2nd Parachute Division.** (Under command of II Para Corps). The original 2 Para Bde had fought in North Africa and been evacuated before the final end there. Initially, the newly formed division was stationed in Brittany, then transferred to the Russian Front in 1943, where its 6th Para Regt was almost wiped out in that year. Finally withdrawn from combat in May 1944 and sent to Germany to refit, it was returned to Brittany, minus 6th Para Regt which was attached to 91st Air Landing Division in Normandy. The division was commanded by the famous General Hermann Ramcke (see earlier description in the North Africa chapters), but when he became commander of the fortress of Brest, the division was taken over by Colonel Hans Kroh. It put up fierce resistance in Brest but was eventually destroyed. A second 2nd Para Div was formed later in Germany and Holland, but it was destroyed in the Ruhr Pocket.

Main units were: 2nd, 6th, 7th Para Regts, 2nd Artillery Regt, 2nd Para Anti-Tank Bn, 2nd Para Engineer Bn, 2nd Anti-Aircraft Bn, 2nd Para MG Bn, 2nd Para Signals Bn.

**3rd Parachute Division.** (Under command of II Para Corps). Formed in the Rheims area in late 1943, with a cadre from 1st Para Div; when at full strength it contained more than 17,000 men. It never took part in airborne operations but fought as infantry when it was committed to the Normandy battle from the Brittany area. It suffered heavy casualties and by 11 July was down to about one-third of its original strength, then it was surrounded in the Falaise Pocket and most of its survivors were captured. Its commander was Major-General (later Lieutenant-General) Richard Schimpf, who was badly wounded at Falaise and, as has already been mentioned, the Corps Commander, Lieutenant-General Eugen Meindl, took personal command and managed to break out. Rebuilt in Holland, mainly using support unit personnel, the Division fought well once again during the Ardennes offensive, but was eventually surrounded in the Ruhr Pocket.

Main units were: 5th, 8th, 9th Para Regts, 3rd Para Artillery Regt, 3rd Para Anti-Tank Bn, 3rd Para Engineer Bn, 3rd Para Signal Bn, 3rd Para Heavy Mortar Unit.

**5th Parachute Division.** (Under command of II Para Corps). Also formed in the Rheims area (cf. 3rd Para), but in March 1943, and from the Demonstration Bn of XI Air Corps. Posted to Normandy, it was heavily engaged in the battle, trapped in the Falaise Pocket and later almost completely destroyed. It was rebuilt but not with trained paratroop personnel and, although it fought in later battles, was almost totally destroyed in the Ruhr Pocket. Its commander was Major-General Gustav Wilke.

Main units were: 13th, 14th, 15th Para Regts, 5th Para Artillery Regt, 5th Para AA Regt, 5th Para Anti-Tank Bn, 5th Para Engineer Bn, 5th Para Signals Bn, 5th Para Heavy Mortar Unit.

### Divisional Changes Before D-Day

As explained, 84th Infantry Division was transferred from Seventh Army to Fifteenth Army, but Seventh Army gained four more divisions: 77th, 275th, 353rd and 709th Infantry Divisions.

**77th Infantry Division.** (Under command of LXXIV Corps). Formed in Poland during the winter of 1943/4, some of its troops coming from the defunct 364th Inf Div, it was posted to Normandy between January and February 1944, being located on the coast between the Cotentin peninsula and Brittany, and was soon engaged by US forces endeavouring to cut off the German forces in the peninsula. Isolated in the northern sector and ordered to withdraw towards Cherbourg, the commander, Major-General Rudolf Stegmann, decided to disobey orders in a breakout which saved some 50 per cent of his men. Knight's Cross and German Cross in Gold holder, Stegmann was killed in a US air attack on 18 June 1944. He was born in West Prussia in 1894, joined the army in 1912 and post-war served in the Reichsheer. He was a Lieutenant-Colonel in 1939, commanding II Bn, 14 Schützen Regt. He took over the division on 1 May 1944 and his death in action probably saved him from execution by the Nazis. The senior regimental commander, Colonel Rudolf Bacherer, took over and completed the breakout. The decimated division went on fighting, repulsing several American attacks, but was eventually almost totally destroyed in the Dinard area.

Major units were: 1049th, 1050th Grenadier Regts, 177th Artillery Regt, 177th Fusilier Bn, 177th Anti-Tank Bn, 177th Engineer Bn, 177th Signals Bn.

**275th Infantry Division.** (Under command of XXV Corps). Formed in late 1943 from the disbanded 223rd Div which had been virtually destroyed at Kiev, it was sent to Brittany in early 1944 before it was completely formed. Samuel Mitcham in *Hitler's Legions* describes the division as consisting of: ' ... the divisional staff, one regimental staff, one artillery unit, two battalions of "old men" and little else'. So the sector had to be provided with another regimental staff and one battalion from 343rd Infantry Division together with two battalions from the previously withdrawn 243rd Infantry Division. It also contained 27 companies of fortress cadre troops, seven eastern battalions, one Russian bicycle detachment and one Russian company of engineers. One Russian cavalry regiment was also on loan to the Normandy sector for installing mines. The Division entered the fighting in Normandy to replace the exhausted Panzer Lehr Division, but was practically annihilated by the American breakout operation 'Cobra' then further reduced in the Falaise Pocket, after which it was listed as destroyed by the commander of Seventh Army and taken out of the line to be rebuilt. It went on fighting both in the battle of the Hürtigen Forest and later in Czechoslovakia.

Main units were: 983rd, 984th, 985th Grenadier Regts, 275th Artillery Regt, 275th Fusilier Bn, 275th Anti-Tank Bn, 275th Engineer Bn, 275th Signals Bn.

**353rd Infantry Division.** (Under command of LXXIV Corps). Formed in October 1943 with cadres from 328th Inf Div and sent to Brittany, it was engaged in the Normandy battle almost immediately, and constantly in action throughout June and July. It broke out of the Falaise Pocket with II Para Corps, about 50 per cent managing to escape. The division was back in action by September, boosted with men of five local security battalions. It fought in the Siegfried Line battles, after which most of its personnel were absorbed into another division. Div HQ, however, was used to build another 353rd Division, which fought until the end of the war. The Commander from 20 November 1943 was Lieutenant-General Paul Mahlmann. He was born in Gispersleben in 1892, joined the army in 1914 and post-war served in the Reichswehr, being a Colonel commanding 181st Inf Regt in 1939. He was a holder of the German Cross in Gold.

Major units were: 941st, 942nd, 943rd Grenadier Regts, 353rd Artillery Regt, 353rd Fusilier Bn, 353rd Anti-Tank Bn, 353rd Engineer Bn, 353rd Signals Bn.

**709th Infantry Division.** (Under command of LXXXIV Corps). This was another understrength static division, made up of older men (average age in 1944 was 36) and formed in April 1941. It was sent to Brittany towards the end of the year and occupied a 220-km front line to the west of 716th Inf Div, between the Orne and the Vire. The Division was later transferred to Cherbourg, which it continued to garrison, fighting well in the siege. It was reinforced by 919th Grenadier Regiment (from 242nd Inf Div). It was commanded by Lieutenant-General Karl-Wilhelm von Schlieben. Born in Eisenach in 1894, he joined the army in 1914 and served post-war with the Reichsheer. Holder of the Knight's Cross and the German Cross in Gold, he surrendered the city on 30 June 1944.

Major units were: 729th, 739th Infantry Regts, 709th Artillery Bn, 709th Engineer Bn, 709th Signals Bn.

### D-DAY ORGANISATION
The outline organisation of Seventh Army as at 6 June 1944 was:

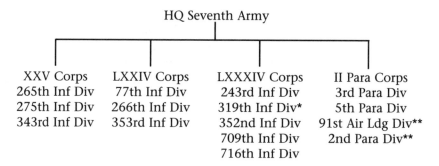

HQ Seventh Army

| XXV Corps | LXXIV Corps | LXXXIV Corps | II Para Corps |
|---|---|---|---|
| 265th Inf Div | 77th Inf Div | 243rd Inf Div | 3rd Para Div |
| 275th Inf Div | 266th Inf Div | 319th Inf Div* | 5th Para Div |
| 343rd Inf Div | 353rd Inf Div | 352nd Inf Div | 91st Air Ldg Div** |
| | | 709th Inf Div | 2nd Para Div** |
| | | 716th Inf Div | |

\* in the Channel Islands
\*\* still forming (as far as 2nd Para was concerned, 6th Para Regt was with 91st Air Landing Div, 2nd and 7th Para Regts were in Brittany.)

### The Panzers
As has already been mentioned, although there was universal agreement among the senior officers from OKW downwards that the panzer divisions

would play a major role – indeed, possibly the most decisive role – against any invasion, there were major disagreements as to how they should be deployed. Rommel, who had experienced at first hand the problems of trying to operate with tanks in an unfriendly air situation, wanted to deploy them 'in the shop window' down in support of the beachhead troops, so that they did not have to be moved, while Guderian and Geyr von Schweppenburg were all for keeping the armour far enough inland as to be easily switched to the main invasion front once that had been determined. Hitler went along with the latter scenario, but then vacillated, being unable to decide on the most likely area for the Allied landings. The upshot was that, as Rommel had warned, they had nothing where it mattered when the time for action arose.

In total there were ten panzer divisions and one panzergrenadier division supporting the forces in the west, with a tank strength of more than 1,500 – nearly 30 per cent of the Panzerwaffe's strength on paper. But some of these were refitting or recuperating from the horrors of the Eastern Front, and three of them had had no combat experience at all. The average strength in tanks per panzer division was only 75 (compared with 263 in a US armoured division of that period, of which 168 were medium tanks). Of these eleven vital divisions only six were located within Army Group B's area, and one of these was refitting:

| | |
|---|---|
| 1st SS Pz Div (refitting) | Pz Lehr Div |
| 2nd Pz Div | 21st Pz Div |
| 12th SS Pz Div | 116th Pz Div |

In addition, 17th SS Pz Gren Div, although located just inside Army Group G's area, was assigned to Army Group B's sector. They were in fact divided under two Corps HQ: I SS Pz Corps, with 1st SS Pz, 12th SS Pz and the crack Pz Lehr Divisions, plus 17th SS Pz Gren Div; XLVII Pz Corps with 2nd Pz Div, 21st Pz Div and 116th Pz Div. To complicate matters, the former was under von Schweppenburg's Pz Group West HQ, which was then directly under OKW as OKW Reserve, while the newly arrived XLVII Pz Corps was initially the armoured reserve for OB West. Although none were thus directly under Rommel, their importance does merit a few words of explanation about their organisation and commanders.

**Panzer Group West.** Gen der Pz. Tr. Freiherr Geyr von Schweppenburg's HQ was initially formed in November 1943, to take over the formation and training of all armoured units in the West and to advise von Rundstedt on their employment. Geyr was ordered to co-operate with and respect the wishes of the army group commanders.[16] Rommel had objected to this arrangement soon after he arrived and Hitler vacillated for some time before compromising, ruling that the three panzer divisions of XLVII Pz Corps (2nd, 21st, 116th) be assigned to Army Group B as their reserve, while the other four divisions (1st SS, 12th SS, Pz Lehr and 17th SS Pz Gren) be set aside as a central mobile reserve under the direct command of OKW. Geyr still retained responsibility for all training and organisation. It was a compromise that pleased no-one.

General Leo Freiherr Geyr von Schweppenburg was born in Potsdam in 1886, and had been a page to Wilhelm II of Württemberg. He joined the army in 1904, was a Lieutenant in the 26th Regt of Light Dragoons the following year and served in the Reichswehr post-war. An educated and cultivated man, from 1933 to 1937 he was Military Attaché in London, then Brussels and the Hague, was promoted to Major-General in 1935, Lieutenant-General in 1937 and Gen der Pz. Tr. on 1 April 1940. A Knight's Cross holder, this brave and highly experienced panzer officer had led XXIV, XL and LVIIII Panzer Corps before being selected as Inspector General of Armoured Troops in 1943. Despite his wide experience of armour, especially on the Eastern Front, he had not had to work under the dominance of total enemy air superiority, and tried to brush aside Rommel's criticisms by saying that even if Allied air power prevented daylight movement the panzers would still be able to move quickly by night. Not only did he fundamentally disagree with Rommel, but he also thoroughly disliked Rommel's Chief of Staff, commenting on one occasion that Speidel had never commanded anything larger than an infantry company. He was to have a narrow escape on 9 June, when his HQ was wiped out by the RAF. He was dismissed by Hitler in early July, survived the war and became an accomplished military commentator and historian.

**I SS Panzer Corps.** Formed in Germany in 1942, it operated in Russia in 1943, then in the West and finally, in January 1945, fought in Hungary and Austria. The commander in the West was the rough, tough, brave SS *Gruppenführer* (equivalent to a Lieutenant-General) Josef 'Sepp' Dietrich (see Chapter 8 for description). He made a considerable impression on Rommel and would go on to command Sixth SS Panzer Army, be promoted to *Oberstgruppenführer* (Colonel General) and be awarded the Diamonds to his Knight's Cross on 6 August 1944.

**XLVII Panzer Corps.** Formed in Danzig as an infantry corps in 1940, it reformed as a panzer corps later that year. It served on the Eastern Front from 1941 to 1944, then transferred to France where it fought in Normandy (Falaise) and later in the Ardennes. It was finally destroyed in the Ruhr Pocket. In France its commander was Gen der Pz Tr. Hans Freiherr von Funck. He was born in Aachen in 1891, had joined the 2nd Light Dragoon Regt in 1914 and post-war served with the Reichswehr. He was the Military Attaché in Lisbon in January 1939 and was promoted to Major-General in January 1941. He was a holder of the Knight's Cross with Oakleaves. When Dr Ley of the Labour Front made a 'ranting speech' on the radio describing the military conspirators who tried to murder Hitler as 'blue-blooded swine', he joined Baron von Lüttwitz and Count von Schwerin, both divisional commanders in Army Group B, in submitting protests against the speech. In fact 'Sepp' Dietrich made himself their spokesman!

**1st SS Panzer Division.** (Already described in Chapter 8). The *Leibstandarte Adolf Hitler* (Personal Standard of Adolf Hitler) was rebuilt and reinforced to a strength of some 21,400 men. By the time they had been heavily engaged in the Caen sector and escaped from the Falaise Pocket, they were down to 30 tanks. Later, in Hungary, when Hitler became displeased with their performance and ordered them to remove their 'ADOLF HITLER' cuff titles, the survivors of the battered division sent him a latrine bucket full of Iron Crosses and Knight's Crosses. Their commander in the West was SS Major-General Theodor Wisch, who had taken over from 'Sepp' Dietrich. Aged only 36 when he took command, he was badly wounded on 20 August in Normandy and had to hand over to Wilhelm Mohnke. A holder of the Knight's Cross, he was awarded the Oakleaves on 28 August, and Swords on 12 December 1944.

**12th SS Panzer Division.** The *Hitler Jugend* (Hitler Youth) Division was, as its name implies, recruited from Hitler Youth members in 1943, when the average age of its soldiers was only seventeen. Initially a training unit, it was sent to Belgium in 1943 and to France in April 1944. It was rushed to Normandy where it fought with fanatical bravery, coupled with considerable professional skill, but suffered heavy casualties. Their initial orders were simply to: ' ... attack the disembarked enemy and throw him back into the sea'. They played a major part in enabling German forces to escape at Falaise, although themselves down to fewer than 300 men and a handful of tanks when they eventually broke out. They were commanded in Normandy by SS General Fritz Witt who was killed by Allied naval gun fire on 16 June, his place being taken by one of the Third Reich's most colourful young panzer soldiers – Kurt 'Panzer' Meyer who became the youngest German divisional commander serving, and holder of the Knight's Cross with Oakleaves and Swords.

Main units were: 12th SS Pz Regt, 25th, 26th SS Pz Gren Regts, 12th SS Pz Artillery Regt, 12th SS Pz Recce Bn, 12th SS Pz. Engineer Bn, 12th SS Pz Signals Bn, 12th SS Anti-Tank Bn, 12th SS Projector Bn.

***Panzer Lehr* Division.** Also known as 130th Pz Div, the Division was formed from the demonstration (lehr) units of the Potsdam training school and the Bergen training area, specifically to assist in repelling any Allied invasion in the West. Sent to France in early 1944, it was then moved and spent some months in Budapest before returning to the Le Mans area in late May–early June. It was one of the strongest, best equipped and superbly manned of all the panzer divisions, having more than 100 tanks, 40 assault guns and 600 half-tracks. It helped to halt the British–Canadian advance at Caen, but suffered badly, losing more than 40 per cent of its strength. It was then practically annihilated by the US air assault on St-Lô, where it had been rushed to meet the US armoured threat there. The Division was later rebuilt and went on fighting until surrendering in the Ruhr Pocket. Its commander was Lieutenant-General Fritz Bayerlein, one of Rommel's protégés, who had been his Chief of Staff in North Africa before commanding 3rd Pz

Div in Russia. He was a holder of the Knight's Cross with Oakleaves and Swords, and the German Cross in Gold.

Main units were: 130th Pz Regt, 901st, 902nd Pz Gren Regts, 130th Pz Artillery Regt, 130th Pz Recce Bn, 130th Anti-Tank Bn, 130th Pz Engineer Bn, 130th Pz Signals Bn, 311th Army AA Bn.

**2nd Panzer Division.** Formed in 1935 (one of the first panzer divisions), it was transferred to Austria after the 'Anschluss' (Connection) and by September 1939 consisted mainly of Austrians. It fought in Poland and France, the Balkans, and Russia where it remained until sustaining heavy losses at Kursk. Withdrawn to refit, it was moved to France and took part in the Normandy battle in June 1944, eventually breaking out from Falaise, again after suffering heavy losses. It fought later in the Ardennes and by 1945 was down to just 200 men and a handful of AFVs. Its commander in France was Lieutenant-General Heinrich Freiherr von Lüttwitz, holder of the Knight's Cross and the German Cross in Gold, who went on to command XLVII Pz Corps. Born in Krumpach in 1896, he entered the army in 1914 as a Lieutenant in the 1st Uhlan Regiment, served in the Reichswehr post-war and was commanding 59th Motorcycle Bn in September 1939. He was wounded at Falaise.

Major units were: 3rd Pz Regt, 2nd, 304th Pz Gren Regts, 74th Pz Artillery Regt, 2nd Motorcycle Bn, 5th Pz Recce Bn, 38th Anti-Tank Bn, 38th Pz Engineer Bn, 38th Pz Signals Bn.

**21st Panzer Division.** (NB. The original 5 leichte/21st Pz Div was destroyed in Tunisia in May 1943). The reformed 21st Pz Div came into existence in Normandy in mid-1943, and was the only panzer division over which Rommel had been allowed to exercise any control prior to the invasion. He had practised them when they were stationed just south of Caen, in various manoeuvres to exploit any momentary weaknesses of the enemy just after landing. Although the Division contained some DAK veterans, it was equipped with poorly armoured light tanks and had been rated as unfit for service on the Eastern Front. After the withdrawal through France it was assigned to Army Group G. It was commanded throughout its second existence by Lieutenant-General Edgar Feuchtinger, holder of the German Cross in Gold, an artilleryman born in Metz in 1894.

Main units included: 22nd Pz Regt, 125th, 192nd Pz Gren Regts, 21st Recce Bn, 220th Pz Engineer Regt, 200th Pz Signals Bn, 305th Army AA Bn.

**116th Panzer Division.** Formed by combining the remnant of 16th Pz Gren Div with 179th Reserve Pz Div in France, after the former had suffered very heavy losses in Russia. Known as the 'Greyhound' Division' from its tactical sign, it was stationed on the north bank of the Seine and was not committed until late July. It managed to break out from the Falaise Pocket but suffered heavy casualties, being down to just over 500 men and 40 tanks. Its commander, Lieutenant-General Graf Gerhard von Schwerin, was relieved by Hitler in mid-September while the Division was fighting in the Aachen area. A Knight's Cross holder, with both Oak-leaves and Swords, the count was born in Hanover in 1899, entered the army in 1914 and eventually would be promoted to Gen der Pz. Tr. on 1 April 1945.

**17th SS Panzer Grenadier Division 'Götz von Berlichingen'** (named after a robber baron of the Middle Ages, or rather his notorious remark to the king – his name being a German euphemism for 'Kiss my Arse!'), was another SS élite formation. Formed in France in 1943 and drawn from German, Belgian, Romanian and Volksdeutsche troops, it was stationed just north of Poitiers in Army Group G's area as part of OKW reserve, but was quickly rushed to Normandy and by 11 June was heavily involved against American paratroops in the Carentan area. It next defended the St-Lô sector and was almost annihilated, was then absorbed into 2nd SS Pz Div and then withdrawn and rebuilt, to reappear in the Battle for Metz. Its commander was SS *Brigadeführer* (equivalent to Major-General) Werner Ostendorf, the former COS of II SS Pz Corps. He was badly wounded later and his place was taken by SS Colonel Eduard Deisenhofer.

Major units were: 37th, 38th SS Pz Gren Regts, 17th SS Pz Artillery Regt, 17th SS Pz Bn, 17th SS Recce Bn, 17th SS Anti-tank Bn, 17th SS Engineer Bn, 17th SS Signals Bn and 17th SS AA Bn.

## ORGANISATION AND EQUIPMENT

**Infantry.** As we have seen, the strength, ability, weapons and equipment, of the 58 divisions in von Rundstedt's OB West, varied tremendously, as did the age, fitness and battle experience of the troops, so it is more difficult to represent all the German opposition by one example. Furthermore, in early 1944 there had been an attempt to trim excess manpower off divisions, by reducing supply and support personnel without supposedly affecting fighting ability. This had reduced the numerical strength of infantry divisions from 13,656 to 12,769.[17] The new-style division comprised three regiments of two battalions each, a loss of three battalions, partly alleviated by the substitution of a fusilier battalion for the reconnaissance unit. It still had the same duties but was organised like a rifle battalion, except that one company had bicycles, and it had more transport (both mechanised and horsed). In practice it was soon thought of as an extra rifle battalion. At the same time as the regiment had lost one battalion, each company and rifle squad was reduced in manpower but their firepower was improved by the introduction of more automatic weapons. There were now, for example, only two officers and 140 men per company (compared with six and 187 in a US infantry company), but they had more firepower in some areas. However, this was by no means standard, because the static (*Bodenständige*) divisions were not re-organised, but retained their nine battalions, albeit weaker and less well-armed than those of the standard infantry division. There was also the need for the static units to reflect the nature of their coastal assignments and this led to many strange anomalies; for example, in LXXXIV Corps of Seventh Army, 716th Division had six battalions and only one Regimental HQ under its control on D-Day, while the 709th, which had two and a half times as much coastline to cover, had eleven battalions and three RHQs.

**Paratroops.** The 'cream' in every respect were the parachute divisions, which were administratively under the Luftwaffe, but tactically under army command. An élite arm, they were put on a par with the SS as far as recruiting, training and equipment were concerned. In Normandy they fought like infantry divisions, being invariably well-equipped, first-rate fighting units, although they did lack some heavy weapons such as heavy artillery. They also suffered from a chronic shortage of transport – 6th Para Regt had only 70 trucks which comprised no fewer than 50 different models! But their soldiers being young, well-motivated volunteers, with aggressive, able leadership, were able to give an excellent account of themselves.

**Panzer Troops.** We have already examined the panzer divisions in some detail and, although their tank strength was nowhere on a par with that of the Allies, the actual AFVs (tank v tank) were undoubtedly superior, notwithstanding that much of the heavier, more powerful equipment – such as the much feared Tiger tank – was sent to the Eastern Front rather than to OB West. Nevertheless tanks like the Panther were widely used in Normandy and proved highly effective. When Tigers did appear, truly remarkable achievements were possible – witness the entire British 7th Armoured Division being held up in Villers-Bocage by Michael Wittmann's single platoon of Tigers, reinforced with one PzKpfw IV. This small force practically annihilated the entire advance guard before they were themselves knocked out. But, as Rommel had foreseen, movement in a hostile air situation put all armoured units under great strain.

**Panther.** Much has been written about the excellence of the PzKpfw VI Tiger heavy tank, but I consider that the more commonly used PzKpfw V, Panther, was the best medium-heavy tank of its era. It had an unfortunate start to its career, being rushed into action in Russia before all mechanical faults had been eliminated, but once these had been eradicated it had a superlative battlefield record. In all, some 6,000 plus were built and it quickly became the most important tank on the assembly lines because it took only half the time to build as a Tiger. The effectiveness of its long 7.5cm gun was legendary; for example, during its first testing period in Russia, if the claims are to be believed, it knocked out a T-34 at a range of 7,224 metres (more than 4½ miles) with its first round![18]

The most important variant of the Panther to be produced was the Jagdpanther, one of the best tank destroyers ever built. Its 8.8cm PaK 43 L/71 gun, for which 57 rounds were carried , was put into full production in January 1944, but only 382 were built from then until March 1945.

222

## PzKpfw V Panther – Ausf D (SdKfz 171)

| Weight | 43 tonnes | Armour (mm): | |
|---|---|---|---|
| Dimensions | | Max: | 100 |
| (metres) | | Min: | 16 |
| Length: | 8.86 | Engine: Maybach HL 230P30 | |
| Height: | 2.97 | 700bhp | |
| Width: | 3.43 | Crew: | 5 |
| Armament/Ammunition | | Max Speed (km/h) 46 | |
| Main: | 1 x 7.5cm KwK | Range (km) | 200 |
| | 42 L/70 | | |
| | 79 rounds | | |
| Secondary: | 2 x 7.92mm | | |
| | MG34/MG42 | | |

**Jagdtiger and Royal Tiger** (Tiger II or Königstiger)

Having described Tiger in a previous chapter, it is worth also mentioning two other variants of the family, which came into service later in 1944 and were met in small numbers (fortunately!) as the fighting in NW Europe progressed. Both could deal with any tank opposition they encountered on the battlefield with ease, as one can imagine from their 'vital statistics':

| | Jagdtiger | Royal Tiger |
|---|---|---|
| Weight (tonnes) | 70 | 68 |
| Armament (main) | 128mm PaK 44 L/55 | 8.8cm KwK43 L/71 |
| Armour Thickness: | 250mm | 180mm |

Fortunately for the Allies, only 77 Jagdtigers and 489 Royal Tigers were built. But it must be said that the enormous production effort which this required would have been far better employed turning out more Panthers. The Royal Tiger first appeared in combat units in June 1944, although they had been issued to training units from February 1944 onwards. The Jagdtiger was not employed on the Western Front until the Ardennes offensive in late November 1944. Despite the fact that these AFVs were undoubtedly individually superior to Allied tanks, they were never available in sufficient quantity and all panzer units were constantly short of tanks. For example, even the best prepared of all the panzer divisions – 2nd Panzer – was short of Panthers, and the SS panzer divisions were also under subscribed. They were also constantly short of spare parts, and as German tanks tended to be more complicated than, for example, the relatively straightforward Sherman or T-34, they not only needed more effort to produce but also to keep them running. The limited industrial capacity in Germany, reduced as it was by 1944 thanks to constant Allied bombing, could not produce sufficient tanks and spare parts simultaneously. The situation was further exacerbated by the fact that some armament production officials put a far lower priority on producing spares than they did on new tank production. For these reasons panzer units suffered from a constant shortage of spare parts.

**Panzergrenadiers.** There was only one Pz Gren Div in the West during the invasion period (17th SS Pz Gren Div). Like all SS divisions it was stronger than an army pz gren div, but its combat strength was considerably below par. Its six rifle battalions were organised into two regiments, one of which was supposed to be motorised with one battalion armoured. In fact, four battalions had improvised MT (including even some old Italian trucks), while the other two only had bicycles. The tank battalion had 37 assault guns instead of 42 and no tanks. Its personnel strength should have been 18,354, but it was 17,321 on 1 June 1944. The anti-tank battalion had only one company (9x75mm and 3x76.2mm guns) instead of three and its AA battalion's manpower was short by one-fifth.

### The Coastal Defences

Rommel had considerable knowledge of obstacles, having both constructed and fought his way through, a wide variety of types in North Africa, especially minefields. He was fascinated by mines which he thought were the 'ideal weapon'. During an early inspection tour, one of his party had remarked upon the beauty of the spring flowers in the fields all around them. 'Make a note,' Rommel had replied, 'this area will take at least a thousand mines!' On yet another occasion, when asked if he would like to visit the famous porcelain works at Sèvres, he had quickly agreed because he wanted to see if the factory could turn out waterproof casings for his sea mines!

By the end of April 1944 Rommel had organised the construction of some half a million beach obstacles, such as iron stakes and similar barriers, right down to the low tide mark and into the shallows, so as to impede landings on the most probable beaches. Many had mines attached or, where there was a shortage, *ad hoc* but highly effective 'mines', made from fused shells, with their fuses pointing seawards. Then there was 'Rommel Asparagus' designed to impede paratroops and aircraft landings, which were erected in all the surrounding fields. Concrete blockhouses were built for the heavy coastal artillery batteries and some four million land mines laboriously dug in and charted. But it was an uphill task, 'the job is being very frustrating,' wrote Rommel to Lucie in late January 1944. 'Time and again one comes up against bureaucratic and ossified individuals who resist everything new and progressive. But we will manage it all the same.'

Although it was clearly vital to install as many beach obstacles as possible, in the event many were rendered totally useless because the Allied landing took place at low tide, so that the obstacles were clearly visible and could be made safe or avoided.

Ruge lists the following major points that emerged from Rommel's constant inspection tours:

a. No unified basic concept existed for the defence. Some commanders in some areas were doing their best to build defences in their immediate area, but nothing was co-ordinated.

b. Defence of the few major ports had been taken according to clear plans, although not all were yet completed. Useful information had been gained from British raids in France (e.g., at Dieppe, where harbour protection batteries had been located outside the defensive zone and had thus been easily eliminated by the enemy).

c. Despite the fact there were apparently good personal relations between the different service branch commanders, co-operation at the highest command level was inadequate, the three branches of the Wehrmacht (land, sea and air) following different directives. This resulted in such anomalies as placing naval batteries and Luftwaffe radars in front of the infantry positions which were actually there to defend them!

d. No agreement had ever been reached about the basic principles of siting coastal artillery. Fortunately for the Allies, this was never satisfactorily resolved in France, so coastal artillery lacked sophisticated fire control systems. Despite Rommel's observation as early as 5 December 1943 that: 'Antipathy against the artillery's indirect firing methods seems to be universal in the navy,' it was never rectified.

e. Rommel considered that sea mines were one of the best ways of stopping and damaging an assaulting enemy, so he advocated having strings of moored mines farther out and ground mines (acoustic or magnetic) in the shallower water (10–30m depth). The need for the latter was something that had not been considered before, and the Mine Research Command were still in the process of perfecting one.[19]

f. There was a lack of striking power and flexibility among the troops stationed in Denmark, as a consequence of the major differences between what was supposed to be there 'on paper' and what was actually there 'on the ground'. As we have already seen, Rommel would find this situation repeated throughout his new command; he was particularly worried about the fact that the horse and the bicycle were more in evidence that the aircraft and the tank!

## OPERATIONS

### 5–6 June 1944

Prior to D-Day, Rommel had been trying hard to get Hitler to visit the Western Front, so that he could explain the up-to-date situation, make him realise how short Army Group B was of both manpower and *matériel*, and impress upon him the vital necessity of being able to control the deployment of the vital panzer divisions. Rommel also wanted to acquire two more panzer divisions, an AA corps and a Nebelwerfer brigade for Normandy. When it became clear that Hitler would not come, Rommel decided to go to see him instead, so he spoke to von Rundstedt and then to Schmundt (Hitler's adjutant) and arranged a personal interview for 6 June. It had been decided that the period 5–8 June was an unlikely time for the Allies to contemplate any invasion because the tides were unfavourable and none of the Luftwaffe's reconnaissance reports showed any obvious indication of preinvasion activity. So it was agreed that Rommel would go to Berchtesgarten, via his home in Herrlingen, a visit which coincided with Lucie's birthday which was also on 6 June. Air travel had been banned for senior officers because of the threat of Allied air interference, so Rommel set off by car on the 5th and was at home on the fateful night of 5/6 June.

**HQ Fifteenth Army.** During the evening of 5 June, the headquarters radio intercept had, as always, been carefully monitoring the BBC's coded broadcasts to the French Resistance and had come to the conclusion that the invasion would take place within the next 48 hours. Although General von Salmuth was somewhat sceptical, he put his army on full alert and authorised the sending of the following message to his Corps HQs and other relevant outstations by teleprinter: 'Broadcast from BBC 2115, June 5 has been processed. According to our available records it means: "Expect invasion within 48 hours, starting 0600 June 6."'[20] The message was also sent to OB West, who passed it on to OKW.

**HQ Seventh Army.** Fifteenth Army did not send the teleprinter message to HQ Seventh Army. Further down the line in their sector, General Erich Marcks was in the command post of his LXXXIV Corps at St-Lô. The staff had planned a small celebration in honour of his 54th birthday, but the party

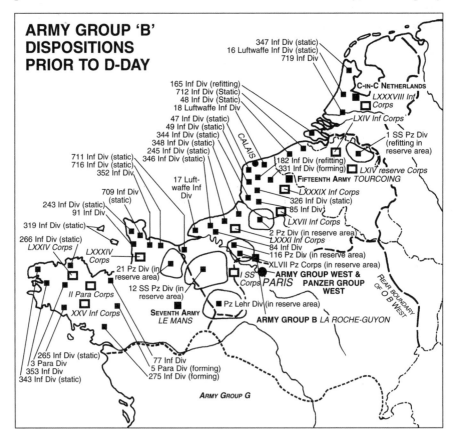

**ARMY GROUP 'B' DISPOSITIONS PRIOR TO D-DAY**

347 Inf Div (static)
16 Luftwaffe Inf Div (static)
719 Inf Div

165 Inf Div (refitting)
712 Inf Div (Static)
48 Inf Div (Static)
18 Luftwaffe Inf Div

47 Inf Div (static)
49 Inf Div (static)
344 Inf Div (static)
348 Inf Div (static)
245 Inf Div (static)
346 Inf Div (static)

711 Inf Div (static)
716 Inf Div (static)
352 Inf Div

709 Inf Div (static)

243 Inf Div (static)
91 Inf Div

319 Inf Div (static)

266 Inf Div (static)
LXXIV Corps

LXXXIV Corps

21 Pz Div (in reserve area)

12 SS Pz Div (in reserve area)

II Para Corps

XXV Inf Corps

265 Inf Div (static)
3 Para Div
353 Inf Div
343 Inf Div (static)

77 Inf Div
5 Para Div (forming)
275 Inf Div (forming)

CALAIS

17 Luftwaffe Inf Div

C-IN-C NETHERLANDS
LXXXVIII Inf Corps
LXIV Inf Corps

1 SS Pz Div (refitting in reserve area)

182 Inf Div (refitting)
331 Inf Div (forming)  LXIV reserve Corps
FIFTEENTH ARMY  TOURCOING

LXXXIX Inf Corps
326 Inf Div (static)
85 Inf Div
LXVII Inf Corps

2 Pz Div (in reserve area)
LXXXI Inf Corps
84 Inf Div
116 Pz Div (in reserve area)
XLVII Pz Corps (in reserve area)

I SS
Corps PARIS

ARMY GROUP WEST & PANZER GROUP WEST

Pz Lehr Div (in reserve area)

SEVENTH ARMY
LE MANS

ARMY GROUP B LA ROCHE-GUYON

REAR BOUNDARY OF O B WEST

ARMY GROUP G

was cut short because Marcks was very disturbed by enemy activity in his area and was not really in the mood for celebrating. He was still there at 0111 hours when the commander of 716th Infantry Division, Major-General Wilhelm Richter, reported by field telephone that enemy paratroops had landed east of the River Orne. A few minutes later Marcks' chief of staff telephoned HQ Seventh Army and spoke to the army chief of staff, Major-General Max Pemsel, who passed on the information to Speidel. He then placed Seventh Army on full alert. Pemsel made further calls to Army Group B later in the early morning, to report seaborne landings.

**HQ Army Group B.** At Rommel's HQ, the chief of staff, Hans Speidel, was alone when he received these first reports of enemy paratroop landings near Caen and in the south-east of the Cotentin peninsula, in the early hours of 6 June. Their strength and purpose was not clear, but HQ Army Group B ordered all units to battle stations. Further reports of paratroop landings and the bombing of coastal defences followed between 0300 and 0400 hours. Speidel remained sceptical about the paratroop landings, especially after reports of dummy paratroops being found, which reinforced his personal conviction that the Normandy assault was merely a feint to disguise the real landings which would come in the Pas-de-Calais. Waves of Allied aircraft were detected approaching the area, and at 0530 hours a heavy sea bombardment began. Coastal defences put their automatic defence measures into operation and the code-word 'Operation Normandy' was flashed out from La Roche-Guyon, and subsequent orders were issued. But the complete Allied air superiority over the battlefield and its approaches made it impossible to get any visual confirmation of what was happening. Speidel rang Rommel between 0600 and 0630 hours, told him the situation and what action he had taken and his C-in-C approved all the measures he had put into operation. Cancelling his visit to Hitler, Rommel returned to France post-haste, leaving Herrlingen at about 1030 hours, with his aide Captain Hellmuth Lang and his driver Corporal Daniel. They were back at La Roche-Guyon by 2000 hours on the 6th, despite having on occasions to use side roads for fear of Allied aircraft.

**HQ OB West.** As the reports built up of more and more landings by sea and air, von Rundstedt's HQ gradually came around to the opinion that this was a major Allied assault. Von Rundstedt, despite his own standing orders, began to release panzer elements and to move them forward. He even asked OKW to release more panzer divisions, but at OKW Jodl was asleep and his staff were loath to wake him or the Führer. Even when the reports became more serious no one would wake Hitler, much to von Rundstedt's growing annoyance. At 0900 hours Schmundt woke his Führer who summoned Jodl and Keitel to give him a briefing at about midday. It is said that Hitler was quite upbeat about the invasion news, appearing eager to get to grips with the enemy. Unfortunately for those who were actually doing the fighting, every decision took an age to make as they constantly had to be viewed against the backdrop of: 'was it or was it not the real invasion?'

This was to be the pattern that would continue throughout D-Day. Commanders 'at the sharp end' were taking appropriate action, committing their forward troops to battle, sending out reconnaissance forces to discover the extent of enemy operations, then requesting the necessary armoured support to deal with them. Their requests mainly went unheeded, red tape at each level preventing swift deployment. Even when permission was given the panzers had great difficulty in advancing, being harried at every point by Allied aircraft.

## THE ALLIED LANDINGS

The Allied seaborne landings had all taken place in Seventh Army's sector, British and Canadian troops of British Second Army landing at Sword, Juno and Gold beaches, all of which were located within 716th Infantry Division's sector, roughly between Ouistreham in the east (just to the south of the area in which British 6th Airborne Division had landed) and Arromanches in the west; the Americans of US First Army had landed at Omaha beach in 352nd Infantry Division's sector between Vierville and Colleville, and some fifteen miles further west at Utah beach around la Madeleine, in 709th Infantry Division's area, not far from the US 82nd and 101st Airborne landings north of Carentan around St-Côme-du-Mont and Ste-Mère-Eglise. The British and Canadians had met stiff resistance, but with the help of specialised armour were able to push forward towards Caen and to capture the Bayeux–Creully road, repelling a counter-attack by 21st Panzer Division. In the west, Utah beach was swiftly taken and a link-up achieved with the airborne forces inland. On Omaha, however, things went seriously wrong. Here, lacking amphibious tank support, which had been badly affected by rough seas, troops of US V Corps were pinned down by 352nd Infantry Division and were unable to make much headway until that evening. By midnight on the 6th, the British had gained a bridgehead some 20 miles wide by 3–6 miles deep, and the Americans had gained two smaller footholds. More than 130,000 Allied troops were defending their hard-won coastal areas, and a further 23,000 airborne troops were scattered over a wide area, causing all sorts of problems for the harassed defenders. All Army Group B's immediate reserves had been committed and the commanders of the coastal units now waited impatiently for the arrival of the panzers which would throw the enemy back into the sea. But of course nothing came. All the higher headquarters were still vacillating as to whether this was the main Allied landing or whether another would come (as they expected) in the Pas-de-Calais, so they refused to release the armour, despite the fact that von Rundstedt's HQ had alerted both *Panzer Lehr* and SS *Hitler Jugend* Divisions. When armoured units did begin to move towards the coast they were severely hampered by almost continual Allied air attacks. It was all coming to pass exactly as Rommel had foretold. Instead of hitting the enemy on the beaches and driving him back into the water before he had got even a toe-hold, he had been allowed to gain a foothold, so the battle would be a far more difficult one to win.

## 7–9 June 1944

While the Allies sought to build up their ground forces in the Normandy bridgehead, Army Group B tried hard to prevent them from doing so and endeavoured, without success, to drive those who had landed back into the sea. As on D-Day, they had to suffer continual heavy naval shelling and air attacks. Dietrich's I SS Panzer Corps was the force selected to carry out the first major counter-stroke against the enemy beachhead on 7 June, but his troops had been severely harassed and delayed by air attacks on their way forward and were badly disorganised. Rommel made a formal complaint to OKW about the total lack of Luftwaffe support. The counter-attack was first postponed from 0800 to 1200 hours and then put off again until the following day. It did not actually take place until 9 June, by which time the enemy had built up his forces – the estimate was that by now British Second Army had ten motorised/armoured divisions ashore, so although there were some local successes, the German advance to the coast was halted. In addition, as always, saturation bombing and continuous naval gunfire caused

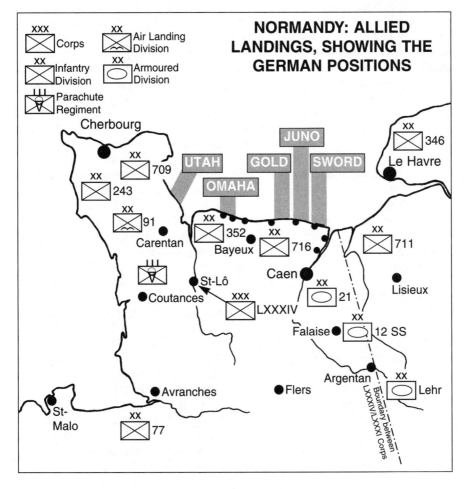

heavy losses to both men and *matériel* (Speidel emphasises considerable destruction of vital signals equipment). To the west, in the Cotentin peninsula, US First Army had some nine divisions ashore, so were able to begin to threaten the major deep water port of Cherbourg, although it would not be finally captured until 27 June after a spirited siege.

### 10–16 June 1944

Rommel summarised the position a few days after the invasion: 'The course of the battle in Normandy to date gives a clear indication of the enemy's intentions:

a. to gain a deep bridgehead between the Orne and Vire, as a springboard for a powerful attack into the interior of France, probably towards Paris.
b. to cut off the Cotentin peninsula and gain possession of Cherbourg as soon as possible, in order to provide himself with a major port of large landing capacity.'[21]

He went on to explain that the enemy had been considerably slowed up by the stubborn defence of the coastal units and therefore had had to employ far more troops than expected, but that now he was building up his forces under the complete protection of superior air and naval cover, to which: '... neither our air force nor our navy is in a position, especially by day, to offer him any resistance.' Enemy air superiority had also prevented reinforcements from moving up fast enough so that proper counter-attacks could be launched. All that the Army Group could do now was to form a continuous line between the Orne and the Vire, strengthen it with such forces as did manage to arrive and endeavour to build up an armoured reserve. Once this had been achieved, he intended to shift the 'centre of gravity' of operations to the Carentan–Montebourg area, destroy the enemy in that area and thus divert the growing danger to Cherbourg. But all such operations were tremendously hampered by the following major factors:

a. The immensely powerful – at times overwhelming – enemy air superiority, which extended anything up to 60 miles behind the front lines, completely paralysing German movement, while giving the Allies a free rein everywhere. He quotes the Allies as being able to send out 27,000 sorties on one day, and although this is definitely a major over-estimate, the effects of Allied air power were clearly disastrous.
b. The role of the heavy naval guns; more than 640 were being used against his ground forces with considerable effect, but the German navy and air force were unable to do anything to silence them.
c. The superiority of all types of American equipment, together with the vast quantities of artillery ammunition and air support the enemy were using, enabling them to start actions at ranges in excess of 2,500 yards, where German forces could not touch them.
d. The quantity and flexibility of use of airborne forces and paratroops.

Rommel asked for Hitler to be informed that, despite all the problems, his troops were fighting with ' ... the greatest doggedness and the utmost pugnacity'. Hitler's response was to veto Rommel's proposed shift of emphasis against the American bridgehead and to order him to attack at Caen instead. Nothing ever came of this, however, because the British were able to reinforce their troops in the area far more quickly and thus to seize the initiative. The main rules for engagement emanating from OKW and Hitler were to prohibit Rommel from taking any kind of offensive action, but rather ordering him to fight a static battle, holding on to as much ground as possible. Such tactics, inhibiting as they did any manoeuvre whatsoever, would prove no more successful in the close *bocage* country of Normandy than they had done in the open steppes of Russia.

General Geyr von Schweppenburg's Western Panzer Group had been brought up on 7 June, but it was not until the night of 10/11 June that its commander felt able to take any positive action. His orders were to throw the enemy out of Normandy, using all the armour at his disposal, but after the failure of I SS Pz Corps, he was very wary indeed. Then disaster struck. The Panzer Group's Headquarters was hit by saturation bombing, knocking out all their signals communications facilities, killing General Ritter und Edler von Dawans (Chief of Staff) and his Ia, together with various other staff officers; even the C-in-C was slightly wounded. He would be unable to reorganise his HQ until the last week of June, so there would be no determined counter-offensive and quite soon the panzers would be forced on to the defensive by the advancing Allied armour. In the west in the American sector some reinforcements would arrive, but only in dribs and drabs so that a properly co-ordinated counter-attack force could never be organised. Speidel lists the following troops as being 'thrown in' against the American bridgehead: parts of 243rd, 91st and 77th Infantry Divisions, 3rd Parachute Division, part of 17th SS Panzer Grenadiers and 30th Brigade. The reinforcements 'straggling in' from 8–9 June onwards were: *Panzer Lehr* Division, 346th and 77th Infantry Divisions, then 2nd Panzer Division on the 13th and 1st SS Panzer Division on the 18th. The destruction of the railways by Allied bombing and the continual harassment by the French resistance fighters (Maquis) made all troop and supply movements extremely difficult. Occasionally the weather would reduce Allied air activity (e.g. on 9–10 June), but it was still difficult for the defence to react quickly and move reinforcements forward while they were relatively safe from air attack.

There were limited successes however; the troops of both Seventh and Fifteenth Armies fought back savagely, yielded ground stubbornly and inflicted heavy casualties on both Allied divisions – witness the already mentioned destruction of the entire advance guard of the famous British 'Desert Rats', the 7th Armoured Division at Villers-Bocage on 13 June by Michael Wittmann's Tigers; and on the less experienced American troops, facing combat for the first time, who suffered grievous casualties – the war diary of Heeresgruppe B stating that in one particular section of the front 1,000 dead GIs were counted in a 'complete defensive success'. 'Very heavy fighting,' Rommel wrote to Lucie. 'The enemy's great superiority in aircraft, naval artillery, men and *matériel* is beginning to tell. Whether the gravity of the situation is realised up above, and the proper conclusions drawn, seems to me doubtful.'[22]

## 17–30 June 1944

The weather did come to the assistance of the harassed defenders on 19 June, when a terrible storm in the Channel almost completely destroyed the Mulberry artificial harbour opposite the American beaches and badly damaged the one opposite the British and Canadian beaches. But by combining what was left at Arromanches disaster was averted, so that by the 22nd supplies were once again rolling steadily ashore, although the need to capture Cherbourg became more pressing. This was achieved on 26 June, but the harbour remained unusable until late August. Elsewhere Allied progress was slow, especially around Caen, where British Second Army sought to draw off as much of the opposition as possible, so as to take the pressure off the American sector and allow them the chance to build up for a major breakout.

### Conferences with Hitler

Two conferences took place during the invasion battles, between Hitler, von Rundstedt and Rommel. The first was on 17 June near Soissons and the second at Berchtesgarten on the 29th. During the first of these Rommel asked Hitler to come to visit the troops, in order to get an accurate picture of what was happening, emphasising that Churchill had already visited the British bridgehead. He also put forward a plan to engage the enemy in a mobile battle rather than continuing the rigid 'holding the line' doctrine. Although privately he reckoned that it would have only a one in four chance of success, he considered that was preferable to the rigid warfare which was inevitably going to lead to the slower but more certain destruction of his Army Group. At the meeting he was cautioned against changing his tactics, and Hitler never did visit the front, so the first conference came to naught. The second meeting was even worse. It was very clear that both Hitler and the OKW had a very confused and totally incorrect impression of the actual state of affairs in Normandy. The OKW was far too confident in the ability of the German forces to deal with the Allied invasion, while Hitler seemed obsessed with fanciful ideas about new weapons – such as the supposed imminent arrival of 1,000 new jet fighters, which would turn the tables on the enemy's air superiority, together with special bombs to use against battleships. Having given his views on the situation, Hitler asked them for theirs and both Rommel and von Rundstedt gave him their answers without pulling any punches. Rommel even concluded by asking Hitler how he imagined the war could still be won! This produced a furious argument which the two field marshals expected would result in their both being sacked. In fact only von Rundstedt was recalled, being replaced by Field Marshal von Kluge.

Günther von Kluge had begun his Second World War career as C-in-C of Fourth Army for the invasion of Poland. An artilleryman, born in Posen in 1882, he had served during the Great War, then with the Reichswehr, receiving steady promotion so that by 1935 he was a Lieutenant-General, commanding VI Corps at Münster. He did well in Poland and again in France, being highly spoken of as being both an active and energetic commander, who liked to be up among his fighting troops. His ability not only led to the award of a Knight's Cross (later he would earn both the Oak-leaves and Swords) but also to his promotion to Field Marshal. He then went to the Eastern Front where, despite mixed success and failure, found himself replacing von Bock as C-in-C Army Group Centre. It was at this time (July 1943) that he developed an intense personal hatred of the armoured expert Heinz Guderian, even challenging him to a duel and asking Hitler to be his second! Hitler dealt surprisingly sensibly with the affair, ordering them to settle their differences peacefully. He also never lost his regard for von Kluge, giving him a large personal financial gift on his 60th birthday and continuing, despite his far from brilliant showing in Russia, to have trust in his abilities, remaining fully convinced that von Kluge was 'his man'. In fact, many historians consider von Kluge to have been the 'eternal fence-sit-ter', neither pro- nor anti-Nazi. but always prepared to compromise and change with the wind. And this is exactly what he did when Hitler appointed him to relieve von Rundstedt. Until now he had been very anti-Rommel, prepared to believe what those in Hitler's HQ had said – namely that Rommel was 'independent, defeatist and disobedient'. He therefore gave Rommel a severe dressing-down on their first meeting. As one might expect, the 'Desert Fox' was not prepared to accept such a rebuke, writing to von Kluge on 5 July, when sending him his comments on the military situation in Normandy, that he demanded to know why, in the presence of his Chief of Staff and Ia, von Kluge had said that he (Rommel) must: 'now have to get accustomed to carrying out orders'.

To be fair to von Kluge, as soon as he had had a chance to inspect the Front and fully appreciate the true situation which Rommel had to no avail so often described to Hitler and his lackeys, he 'changed with the wind' and came to the conclusion that Rommel was entirely correct. There-after he fully supported Rommel, but by then of course it was too late. In any case, fate would soon take a hand and cut short their working relation-ship. Von Kluge himself was not destined to last much longer either. Just a month after Rommel had been strafed, von Kluge would, on 18 August, while on his way back to Germany to answer accusations that he was impli-cated in the bomb plot to kill Hitler, take poison and end his life. He wrote a suicide letter to Hitler, which contained the words: 'Both Rommel and I, and probably all the commanders here in the west with experience of bat-tle against the Anglo–Americans with their preponderance of *matériel*, fore-saw the present development. We were not listened to. Our appreciations were not dictated by pessimism but from the sole knowledge of the facts.'[23] He closed by begging the Führer to make peace and put an end to 'this frightfulness'. According to Jodl's evidence at Nuremberg, Hitler read the letter without comment, then passed it to Jodl. Hitler also denied von Kluge any military honours at his funeral.

## 1–16 July 1944

Towards the end of June, the Allied beachhead had been made fully secure and the Allied forces were sufficiently powerful to begin the next stage, the battle for Normandy. Although the thick *bocage* country, with its high hedgerows and sunken roads favoured the defence, the might of the Allied war machine pushed inexorably forward on all fronts, albeit very slowly. Nowhere was this more apparent than around Caen, the outskirts of the city not being reached until 13 July. It would be another week before the city would fall, and even then its ruined streets merely provided yet another obstacle. The first major assault around Caen (Operation 'Epsom') was contained by the defenders, while in the west at St-Lô, the Americans were also halted by determined resistance. The successful breakout battles – Operations 'Goodwood' in the east and 'Cobra' in the west would not be possible until later in the month, when the Allies had built up even greater strength.

## 17 July 1944

Before these Allied assaults, a dramatic turn of events would personally affect Rommel. As always the 'Desert Fox' was rushing about in the front line, constantly visiting his forward troops. On the 17th he had first gone to the forward positions of 277th Infantry Division in I SS Panzer Corps' sector, then to 276th Infantry Division in XLVII Panzer Corps' sector. Finally he went to see the commander of I SS Panzer Corps, 'Sepp' Dietrich, in St-Pierre-sur-Dives. When Rommel was preparing for the long journey back to La Roche-Guyon, Dietrich suggested that, in view of the continual danger from Allied aircraft, he should travel in a more manoeuvrable, less obvious, Volkswagen, rather than in his more powerful Horch staff car. Rommel decided to stick with his own staff car. The other occupants were: Major Neuhaus, Captain Lang, Daniel his personal driver and Feldwebel Holke (aircraft lookout). It was to be a traumatic journey.

## ANNEX 'A' to Chapter 9
## Main staff members of Army Group 'B' (Heeresgruppe B) as at May 1944

| | |
|---|---|
| Commander: | Field Marshal Erwin Rommel |
| Chief of Staff: | Lt Gen Hans Speidel |
| ADC | Capt Helmuth Lang |
| ADC | Lt Max Scheer |
| ADC (at Herrlingen) 03 | Capt Hermann Aldinger |

**General Staff**

| | |
|---|---|
| 1a | Lt Col Hans-Georg von Tempelhoff |
| 1d | Maj Winrich 'Teddy' Behr |
| Staff officer 01 | Lt Maisch |
| 04 | Lt Dummler |
| 1a (Survey and Mapping) | Maj Karl Wagner |
| 1c | Lt Col Anton Staubwasser |
| Staff Officer 05 | Lt Kurt Utermann |
| Interpreter | Lt Gustav Etter |
| Interpreter | Lt Gerhard Mackenroth |

**Artillery Staff**

| | |
|---|---|
| Artillery commander | Col Hans Lattmann |
| Adjutant | Capt Hugo Kracht |

**Engineer Staff**

| | |
|---|---|
| Gen of Engineers | Lt Gen Wilhelm Meise |
| Engineer Officer | Maj Johanns |
| Adjutant | Lt Borzikowsky |

**Signals Staff**

| | |
|---|---|
| Gen of Signals | Lt Gen Ernst Gerke |
| Adjutant | Capt Walter Kaboth |
| Telephone Officer | Maj Baumann |
| Wireless Officer | Maj Osterroth |

**A & Q Branch**

| | |
|---|---|
| IIa | Col Freyberg |
| Asst IIa | Lt Cristoph Weinert |
| HQ Commandant | Maj Alfred Jamin |
| Head of Medical Services | Dr Friedrich Scheunig |
| Rations Officer | Capt Egon Schumacher |
| Vehicles Officer | Lt Heinz Schon |

**Quartermaster Division** (Dissolved at the end of May 1944)

| | |
|---|---|
| Chief of Supply & Administrative services | Col Heckel |
| Staff Officer Qu1 | Maj von Ekesparre |
| Ord Officer | Capt Wilhelm Fleiner |
| Paymaster | Lt Johann Furtner |
| Purchasing Officer | Capt Georg Wels |
| POL Officer | Maj Johannes Heynold |
| Ammunition Officer | Maj Rohner |
| Field Medical Officer | Dr Merkle |
| Assistant MO | Dr Breitfeld |
| Veterinary Officer | Dr Hofmann |
| Vehicles Officer | Lt Gehrels |
| Instruments & Spares | Capt Karl Simon |
| War Artist | Maj Geschwendter |
| Interpreter | Lt Leopold Priebisch |

**Naval Branch**

| | |
|---|---|
| Admiral | Vice Admiral Friedrich Ruge |
| Assistant | Capt Werner Peters |
| Adjutant | Lt Frauendorff |

**Air Branch**

| | |
|---|---|
| 1a/Luftwaffe | Lt Col Wolfgang Queisner |

1c/Luftwaffe                                    Lt Col Hans Stehnken

**Camp Staff**
Commander                                       Lt Anton Faiss
Grenadier Platoon Comd                          Lt Josef John
Recce Platoon Comd                              Lt Edgar Wehlau

**Notes to Chapter 9**
1. Blumentritt, *Von Rundstedt.*
2. Fraser, *Knight's Cross.*
3. Ruge, *Rommel in Normandy.*
4. Speidel, *We Defended Normandy.*
5. Irving, *Trail of the Fox.*
6. Ruge, *op. cit.*
7. The Allied deception plan was ingenious and complex, aiming to highlight the Pas-de-Calais as being the location for the coming invasion which was due, according to 'Fortitude', in May 1944.
8. Irving, *op. cit.*
9. The Organisation Todt (OT) was a semi-military governmental unit set up in 1938 for the purpose of constructing (with slave labour) military installations and special highways for AFVs. It was run by Dr Fritz Todt until his death in 1942, then by Albert Speer.
10. Speidel, *op. cit.*
11. After the division had been badly mauled, it was reformed at Dordrecht and sent to the Saarbrucken area where its artillery was known as 'The Artillery Museum of Europe' because its guns were so old and diverse! (See Mitcham, *Hitler's Legions*).
12. Ruge, *op. cit.*
13. From September 1944, Himmler's Reserve Army formed new divisional units from two main sources: remnants of units that had suffered heavy casualties in action; 'recruits' combed out of industry. There were some fifty such divisions formed, all roughly half the strength of a normal infantry division, but with increased automatic weapons and *Panzerfaust* (hand-held light anti-tank weapons). They were mainly used in the defence of the Fatherland.
14. Quoted in Brett-Smith, *Hitler's Generals.*
15. Quoted in Irving, *op. cit.*
16. OB West Order of 19 November 1943
17. See Harrison, *European Theater*, p. 237.
18. This was quoted in the US Army in WWII 'The Ordnance Department Planning Munitions for War', but it really does tax credibility – even on the Russian steppes could one see that distance to engage?
19. Ruge describes the proposed coastal mine as being cheap and easy to manufacture, consisting of a concrete block filled with a 50kg explosive charge, with a 2m high 'Rommel-32' light steel frame on top which carried on its point a lead horn, the normal firing mechanism of a moored mine. A 25m rope could be fastened to the horn and if the vessel

touched the rope, the pull would bend it and detonate the mine. Rommel asked for its manufacture to be speeded up.

20. Teleprinter message 2117/26 as quoted in Ryan, *Longest Day*.
21. *The Rommel Papers*.
22. Quoted in Law and Luther, *Rommel*.
23. Quoted in Brett-Smith, *op. cit.*

# 10
# The End

**Wounded**

On Monday, 17 July 1944, after leaving 'Sepp' Dietrich at St-Pierre-sur-Dives, Rommel was keen to get back to Headquarters at La Roche-Guyon as quickly as possible, having been informed of a new Allied breakthrough. This is probably why he had declined Dietrich's offer of an inconspicuous Volkswagen 'Beetle' and was travelling in his Horch staff car. Nevertheless he appreciated the need to be on the lookout for enemy aircraft, which were invariably attracted by dust or vehicular movement on the roads. Afterwards, Lang recalled passing a number of wheeled vehicles in flames and being forced to make detours by second class roads to avoid enemy aircraft. At about 1800 hours, when they had reached the small town of Livarot, they saw a swarm of enemy fighter-bombers circling above the town and learned that they had been attacking traffic for at least two hours. The aircraft – British Spitfires – did not at first appear to have noticed their car as it continued along the N179 main road out of Livarot, heading for Vimoutiers. Then, all at once, the air observer shouted that two enemy aircraft were approaching fast and Rommel, who was studying the road map, shouted to Daniel to speed up and to be ready to turn off at a small tree-lined side road some 300 yards ahead.

They didn't quite make it. A few yards before the corner the first aircraft attacked, flying at high speed only a few feet above the tree-tops, strafing the car with bursts of well-aimed cannon-fire and also with its machine-guns.[1] The left side of the car was hit by the first burst, one cannon-shell striking the driver, completely shattering his left shoulder and arm, causing him to lose control; the car careered wildly all over the road. Rommel was also wounded, both by flying glass and by hitting his left temple and cheekbone on the Horch's heavy superstructure, causing a multiple fracture of the skull which knocked him out. Major Neuhaus suffered a fractured pelvis. The car struck the stump of a tree on the verge, skidded out of control across to the left side of the road then back again to the right where it turned upside down in the drainage ditch. Rommel, who had been holding the door handle at the beginning of the attack, was thrown out as the door swung open when the car turned over and now lay unconscious on the road, some 20 yards to the rear.

Lang and Holke, both uninjured, scrambled out and took shelter in the ditch as the second aircraft made its attack and tried to bomb them. Once this danger had passed they rushed to rescue the Field Marshal and to carry him, still unconscious, into shelter. He was bleeding profusely from many wounds on his face, particularly from his left eye and mouth. It took about forty-five minutes to get medical assistance, which ferried them initially back to Livarot where they received first aid from a French doctor in a local pharmacy, then to a Luftwaffe hospital in Bernay about 25 miles away. Daniel was given a blood transfusion, but died during the night. Rommel was diagnosed as having severe skull injuries which included: a fracture at the base of the skull, two fractures of the temple and the cheek-bone destroyed, a wound to the left eye, plus numerous other wounds caused by glass fragments and finally, severe concussion. It was clear that his chances of recovery were not good. It was some three hours before the news percolated back to Army Group B, where General Speidel immediately telephoned von Kluge who decided to take direct control of Army Group B, while remaining C-in-C West. As David Irving comments, 'Now he, Kluge, would have complete tactical control in Normandy after all, without interference from a headstrong Rommel. Kluge moved his desk to the château, leaving Blumentritt to mind shop in Paris.'

Rommel was in the competent hands of Professor Esch, the Luftwaffe's senior neurosurgical consultant. It is reported that he was amazed that his patient had survived in the first instance and now with his rapid progress. Rommel, as one might have expected, was a difficult patient, despite his injuries, which included an inability to open or move his left eye, plus complete deafness in his left ear. On 23 July he was moved to a large 1,000-bed hospital at Le Vesinet just outside Paris. From there he sent his first letter to Lucie on 24 July (he dictated, but could not sign it) in which he said that he was being very well looked after, but that he would probably not be moved again for at least two weeks. He expressed his grief at the death of Daniel ' ... an excellent driver and a loyal soldier', and also says how shattered he was to hear about the attempt on Hitler's life. His Führer sent him a telegram on that same day saying: 'Accept, Herr Feldmarschall, my best wishes for your continued speedy recovery.' But all was not well between them and, while Rommel was anxious to get back to his family in Germany and recuperate in their care – and thereby removing himself from the possibility of capture by the Allies – he was, as Liddell Hart puts it, unwittingly sealing his own fate ' ... for Hitler had probably by that time already decided on his death'.

It has never been entirely clear as to how much Rommel actually knew about the plot to assassinate Hitler. This is clearly not the book in which to go into all the details of how the finger of suspicion fell upon Rommel, but obviously he felt very strongly that the OKW had lost its grip on the war and that the best thing Germany could do was to make peace with the Western Allies in order to prevent the Russians from reaching Berlin first. Indeed that is basically what he had written to von Kluge just before the accident, intending for Kluge to add his support and then to send it on up the line to Hitler. While he was prepared to do this in his usual open-handed manner, Rommel was no conspirator, nor would he have treated the solemn oath he had sworn to his Führer so lightly, as to break it in such an underhand and secretive way. Speidel was of course implicated but initially anyway avoided direct suspicion. Rommel on the other hand was supposedly named by General von Stülpnagel, a co-conspirator with Colonel Klaus von Stauffenberg who had planted the bomb at Hitler's Headquarters on 20 July. General von Stülpnagel had been summoned to Berlin the following day and had attempted suicide en route, realising what was in store. But instead of a quick death all he succeeded in doing was wounding and blinding himself. During the operation on his wounds – performed so that he would be better able to give evidence against his fellow conspirators, rather than for any humanitarian reasons – he was alleged to have muttered Rommel's name. The listening Gestapo noted this down and passed it on to Keitel, who naturally told Hitler. Speidel, who had been dismissed as Chief of Staff Army Group B, was ordered to report to Berlin for questioning on 8 September. He visited Rommel two days before this and, according to Speidel in *We Defended Normandy*, Rommel called Hitler a pathological liar and said that he had gone completely mad. But this is still not direct evidence that Rommel had been implicated in the plot at any stage.

Unhappily tied to a sickbed, fretting about his injuries and thirsting to get up and back to the Front, Rommel must have by now begun to realise that he was far too badly injured ever to get a field command again and that he was going to need a long, slow recuperation just to restore himself to full health. He had arrived in Herrlingen in mid-August and his son Manfred was posted to his staff from his gun site on the outskirts of Ulm, in order to help look after him. The news that von Kluge had committed suicide and that Speidel had been arrested by the Gestapo must have filled Rommel and his family with dread; these were direct indications of approaching disaster. Clearly they were being closely watched, so both Rommel and his son took to carrying a pistol whenever they went out, and Rommel managed to get an armed sentry from the local garrison to stand guard on the house. But it was only a matter of time before the Gestapo would strike.

Characteristically Rommel wrote a frank and open letter to Hitler on 1 October, praising his erstwhile Chief of Staff Hans Speidel and including the words: 'I cannot imagine what can have led to Lieutenant-General Speidel's removal and arrest.' Clearly he was implying that he thought that the arrest was because of failure in the battle for Normandy, rather than anything to do with the assassination attempt. But he was enough of a realist to appreciate that if Hitler believed that Rommel's friends and subordinates were implicated it stood to reason that he must similarly be under suspicion.

### Suicide or Disgrace

Then, on 7 October, Rommel received a telephone call from General Wilhelm Burgdorf of the Army Personnel Branch, asking Rommel to go to Berlin on the 9th for an important conference with the Führer on the 10th. He would be fetched by a special train. Rommel was suspicious. 'I'm not that much of a fool,' he is reported to have said, to his old friend Admiral Friedrich Ruge, when he visited on 11 October. 'We know these people now. I'd never get to Berlin alive.' He also told the brain specialist, Professor

Albrecht, who was treating him, and he immediately certified him unfit for travel, but this action would only give the 'Desert Fox' a short respite. On 13 October, Rommel received a message to say that two general officers were coming to see him the following day. That morning he told his son that two senior officers were coming to discuss his future employment, whether it was to be, as he put it, 'a People's Court or a new command in the East'. Scores of Gestapo personnel were known to be surrounding the house. When the generals arrived at about midday the only men in the house with Rommel were his elderly ADC Captain Hermann Aldinger, a badly wounded veteran NCO and Manfred, so it is difficult to imagine them being able to defend him for long, though this must have been uppermost in their minds.

The two generals were Wilhelm Burgdorf and Ernst Maisel, the former powerful and florid, the latter small and slender. They were polite and courteous, but they brought a terrible message – he was being charged with high treason by Hitler. There was no possibility of escape, but he had the choice of taking poison or of facing a public trial. The 'carrot' was that if he chose the former his name and reputation would be protected, he would be given a state funeral and, most importantly, his family would be safe, whereas if he chose the latter anything might happen to them. For Rommel there was really no choice; he would naturally give his own life to safeguard his beloved wife and son.

Having said his good-byes to them, and elicited from them a promise to observe ' ... the strictest silence' so that Hitler would have to keep his word, Rommel left quietly with the two generals and twenty minutes later the telephone rang to report his death. Afterwards it turned out that the car had stopped just a few hundred yards up the hill away from the house, at the edge of a wood. Maisel and the driver got out, leaving Rommel with Burgdorf. When they returned Rommel was dead. His body was later taken to the hospital at Ulm. In what was described by Manfred Rommel as being 'the most despicable part of the whole story', the Rommel family received a series of bland letters of sympathy from members of the Government including Hitler, Göring and Goebbels. Rommel was buried after a state funeral on 18 October 1944.

## The Legend Lives On

Rommel had chosen to wear the uniform of his beloved Deutsches Afrika Korps on the day when he was forced to commit suicide, and it is probably as the 'Desert Fox' that he will be best remembered. But the DAK was just one of the 'armies' that he had commanded – from platoon right up to Army Group he had exerted his genius upon the battlefield in two world wars. A careful and methodical planner when required, he was undoubtedly at his best as a dashing field commander, ideally suited to making instant decisions in the heat of battle. In addition, of course, like so many great military men, there were many sides to Rommel as well as his almost uncanny knack of being in the right place at the right time on the battlefield – 'the Front is where Rommel is' is how his troops put it. But there was also Rommel the thinker, Rommel the author, Rommel the athlete, Rommel the engineer, Rommel the spartan, Rommel the devoted family man and at the same time there was Rommel the autocrat, Rommel the 'blinkered' soldier who could see no wrong in the Führer and his Nazi Party until it was too late – so that suspicion and a trumped-up charge would cost him his life. Nevertheless, the period he spent in North Africa and the remarkable success he had there in 1941 and 1942, gave him a reputation with both friend and foe alike, which has placed him at the top or very near the top of tactical military genius in war. He had risen from Lieutenant-Colonel to Field Marshal in four years, become a hero to friend and foe alike, yet his fate was to be murdered by those he had served so faithfully. Perhaps Speidel captured the true essence of Rommel when he wrote: 'Erwin Rommel, a *miles fati*, and so he remains, the model of the good German soldier. His life, work and death are a legacy of manly and human endeavour that his country can treasure for evermore.'[2]

## Notes to Chapter 10

1. The official RAF *History* credits the pilots of No 602 Squadron (City of Glasgow) with the attack, but another reliable source names Squadron Leader J. J. Le Roux, DFC, the South African OC 602 Squadron, as the Spitfire pilot who actually strafed Rommel's car.
2. Speidel, *We Defended Normandy*.

# Select Bibliography

Barker, A. J. *Afrika Korps*. AP Publishing, 1978

Baynes, John. *The Forgotten Victor*. Brassey's (UK), 1950

Bender, Roger James, and Law, Richard D. *Uniforms, Organization and History of the Afrikakorps*. R. James Bender Publishing, 1973

Blumentritt, General Günther. *Von Rundstedt, the Soldier and the Man*. Odhams Press, 1952

Brett-Smith, Richard. *Hitler's Generals*. Osprey, 1976

Buffetaut, Yves. *Rommel: France 1940*. Editions Heimdal, 1985

Carell, Paul. *Foxes of the Desert*, repubd Schiffer Military History, 1994

Douglas-Home, Charles. *Rommel*. Weidenfeld and Nicholson, 1973

Forty, George. *Afrika Korps at War*. vols 1 & 2, Ian Allan Ltd, 1978

– *Tank Commanders, Knights of the Modern Age*. Firebird Books, 1993

Fraser, David. *Knight's Cross*. Harper/Collins, 1993

Greene, Constance McLaughlin, Thomson, Harry C., and Roots, Peter C. *US Army in WWII: The Ordnance department, planning munitions in war*. Office of Chief of Military History, US Army, 1955

Greene, Jack, and Massignani, Alessandro. *Rommel's North Africa Campaign: September 1940 – November 1942*. Combined Books Inc, 1994

Harrison, Gordon A. *The European Theater of Operations: Cross-Channel Attack*. Office of the Chief of Military History, US Army, 1951

Hogg I. V. (introduction only). *German Order of Battle 1944*. Greenhill Books, 1994

Howe, George. *US Army in WWII. Northwest Africa: Seizing the Initiative in the West*. Office of Chief of Military History, US Army, 1957

Irving, David. *The Trail of the Fox*. Weidenfeld and Nicholson, 1977

Jackson, W. G. F. *The North African Campaign 1940–43*. B. T. Batsford Ltd, 1975

Jentz, Thomas L. (ed.). *Panzer Truppen*. Schiffer Military History, 1996

Keilig, Wolf. *Die Generale des Heeres*. Podzun Pallas-Verlag GmbH, 1983

Kennedy, Major Robert M. *The German Campaign in Poland (1939)*. Department of the Army pamphlet 20-255, 1956

Kurowski, Franz. *Knight's Cross Holders of the Afrikakorps*. Schiffer Military History, 1996.

Law, Richard D., and Luther, Craig W. H. *Rommel, a Narrative and Pictorial History*. R. James Bender Publishing, 1980

Liddell Hart, B. H. *The Other Side of the Hill*. Cassell, 1948

McGuirk, Dal. *Rommel's Army in Africa*. Century Hutchinson, 1987

Mitcham, Samuel W. *Hitler's Legions*. Leo Cooper, 1985

Molony, Brigadier C. J. C., *et al. History of the Second World War: the Mediterranean and Middle East.* vol. V, HMSO, 1973

Nash, D. B. *Imperial German Army Handbook, 1914–1918.* Ian Allan Ltd, 1980

Rommel, Erwin. *Infantry Attacks!* Greenhill Books, 1990 (English trans of *Infanterie Greift An,* written by Rommel in the 1930s)

– *The Rommel Papers,* ed. B. H. Liddell Hart, Collins, 1953

Ruge, Friedrich. *Rommel in Normandy.* Presidio Press, 1979

Ryan, Cornelius. *The Longest Day,* New York, 1960

Schmidt, Heinz Werner. *With Rommel in the Desert.* Harrap, 1951

Snyder, Dr Louis L. *Encyclopedia of the Third Reich.* Blandford, 1989

Speidel, Lieutenant-General Hans. *We Defended Normandy.* Herbert Jenkins, 1951

Spielberger,Walter J., and Feist. U. *Armor in the Western Desert.* Arco Publishing Inc, 1968

Trye, Rex. *Mussolini's Soldiers.* Airlife Publishing Ltd. 1995

Whalley, Barton. *Covert German Rearmament 1919–1939.* University Publications of America Inc, 1984

Young, Desmond. *Rommel.* Collins, 1950

**Other Sources**

*After The Battle Magazine,* No 19. Battle of Britain Prints,1977

*Vocabulary of German Military Terms and Abbreviations,* Revised to 1942, HMSO, 1943

# Index

Höcker, Gen Hans, 204
Holker, LCpl, 198, 234, 236
Holz, Karl, 47, 53
Homs, 165
Horster, Professor Dr, 96, 149, 165
Hoth, Gen Hermann, 38, 53, 54, 55, 60,
   63, 66
Hulsen, Gen van, 98

**I**
Italian Navy, 112
Italian rations, 76
Italian request for German tanks, 75
Italian soldier, the, 131 *et seq*
Italian surrender, 187

**J**
Jerrycan, the, 77
'Jock columns', 109, 123
Jodl, Gen Alfred, 33, 74, 137, 194, 196,
   227, 233
Jutland, 190

**K**
Kasserine, 177, 178
Keitel, Gen Wilhelm, 33, 118, 160, 196,
   227
Kesselring, Field Marshal Albert, 94, 163,
   164, 167, 171, 182, 183, 185, 187, 188,
   189
Keyes, Maj Geoffrey, 137
Khamsin, 113
Kidney Ridge, 153, 161
Kircheim, Gen Heinrich, 98
Kleeman, Gen Ulrich, 98, 127, 128, 144
Kleist, Gen von, 53
Klopper, Gen, 146
Kluge, Field Marshal Gunther von, 53, 55,
   60, 232, 239
Krause, Gen Fritz, 157
Kriegschule, the, 12
Kriegsmarine, 111, 112, 189, 190, 191,
   192, 198
Koch, Col H., 214
Koch, Lutz, 96
Koenig, LCpl, 47
Krais, Gen Dietrich, 212
Krancke, Admiral Theodore, 192
Kuntzen, Gen Adolf, 201

**L**
La Ferla, Gen, 144
La Roche-Guyon, 194 *et seq*, 197, 227,
   234, 238

La Rochefoucauld family, 195
Lake Garda, 183, 189
Landings, Allied D-Day, 28 *et seq*, 229
   (map)
Landrecies, 61, 62
Lang, Capt Hellmuth, 192, 196, 227, 236
Lattmann, Col Hans, 197
Lattmann, Gen Martin, 197
Le Cateau, 62, 64, 65
Le Vesinet hospital, 239
Lederer, Col, 168
Libya, 73 *et seq*, 75, 134
Ley, Dr, 218
Liebenstein, Gen Kurt von, 81, 87, 98,
   157, 170, 180 (note)
Liège, 52
Lille, 40, 64, 65
List, Gen, 53, 54
Livarot, 238
Loehr, Gen, 182
Lombardi, Gen, 144
Lörzer, Gen Bruno, 112
Loyalty Oath, 30
Luftwaffe, 84, 91, 100, 111, 145, 164,
   189, 191, 192, 198, 199, 200, 204, 207,
   225, 229, 239
Lungerhausen, Gen Carl-Hans, 157
Lüttwitz, Gen Heinrich von, 218, 220

**M**
Machine-guns, 20, 176
Macholz, Gen Siegfried, 202
Maginot Line, 52, 57, 60, 61, 64
Mahlmann, Gen Paul, 216
Maisel, Gen Ernst, 241
'Mammoths' (Mammuten), 96, 136, 139
Manstein, Field Marshal von, 52, 53, 75,
   126, 194
Manteuffel, Gen Hasso von, 162, 173,
   174, 175
'Marble Arch', see Arco del Fileni
Marcks, Gen Erich, 210, 226
Marcks, Gen Werner, 128, 143
Mareth, 165, 168, 177, 178
Mechili, 98, 118, 121
Medinine, 178
Medjez el Bab, 168
Meindel, Gen Eugen, 210, 214
*Mein Kampf*, 29, 34
Meise, Gen Dr Wilhelm, 191, 197
Mellenthin, Maj F. W. von, 126, 127, 139,
   146
Menny, Gen Erwin, 89, 128, 208
Mersa el Brega, 116, 162, 163, 164